THE SECRET WAR

The shape of things to come: Ju52s land German airborne forces in Czechoslovakia in 1938.

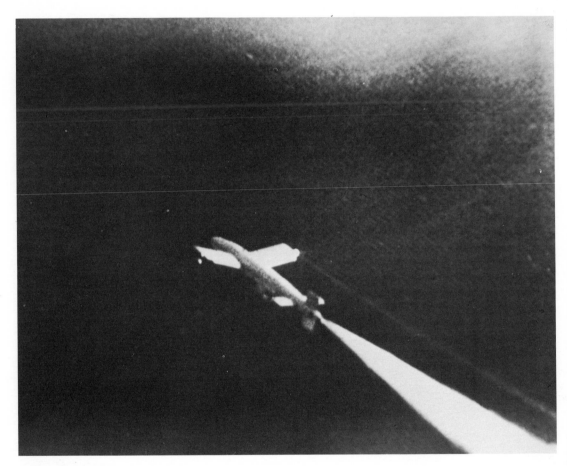

The Blohm und
Voss 143. One of
many guided
missiles developed
by the Germans
during the war, the
BV 143 was tested
in 1941 as a guided
aerial torpedo for
use against
shipping, but did
not enter
operational service.

BRIAN JOHNSON

THE SECRET WAR

METHUEN
NEW YORK TORONTO LONDON SYDNEY

First published 1978 by the
British Broadcasting Corporation

This edition published in the United States by
Methuen Inc, 777 Third Avenue,
New York, NY 10017

ISBN 0-458-93340-6

LCCCN 77-18632

© Brian Johnson 1978

Printed in England

CONTENTS

Introduction – A Letter from Oslo   9

1. The Battle of the Beams   11

2. Radar   63

3. Terror Weapons   123

4. The Battle of the Atlantic   189

5. Misfortunes of War   239

6. Enigma   305

Notes   350

Picture Credits   352

For all who worked in the small back rooms

ACKNOWLEDGEMENTS

This book is based on the BBC Television Series *The Secret War*, and I am indebted to the researchers who gathered the material for the original six programmes upon which I have drawn heavily. Charmian Campbell researched 'The Battle of the Beams' and 'Radar', interviewing many of the participants in Britain and Germany. Susan Bennett tracked down witnesses in Germany, Poland and France to uncover much of the Enigma story. Kate Haste combed the Public Records Office for information on the V1 and V2, in addition to interviewing many of the men and women involved.

My colleague Fisher Dilke, who wrote the television Enigma programme, greatly assisted with additional research in the preparation of the final chapter of the book.

I am indebted also to the Public Record Office for allowing Archive material to be quoted.

Finally I wish to place on record my indebtedness to Tony Kingsford and Paul McAlinden of BBC Publications for their sympathetic editing and presentation of the manuscript.

The British
Consulate
in Oslo.

INTRODUCTION:
A LETTER FROM OSLO

On 19 September 1939 in a speech in Danzig Hitler boasted of fearsome secret weapons against which Germany's enemies would be defenceless. Confirmation of the development of at least some of that arsenal was soon to come from a most unexpected source – Germany – in what must rate as one of the most incredible windfalls even in the long history of espionage. In the small hours of 5 November 1939 a parcel was left on a window-ledge of the British Consulate in Oslo, in what was still neutral Norway. Addressed to the Naval Attaché, it contained several pages of German typescript and a small electronic device which, when examined in London by Dr R. V. Jones, of Air Ministry Scientific Intelligence, proved to be an early proximity fuse for an anti-aircraft shell and was clearly included to authenticate the much more important typescript. Subsequently known as the *Oslo Report*, this set out the scope of German military scientific research, including such highly classified information as the identity of Peenemunde as an important research centre.

The Junkers 88, the Luftwaffe's new secret wonder plane, the correspondent stated, was to be used as a high-speed dive bomber – a fact unknown in Britain. He detailed German radar developments and confirmed that radar had been instrumental in directing fighters to a squadron of Wellington bombers that had been decimated on a raid on Wilhelmshaven. He explained the working of a German night-bomber radio aid, which later became known as the *Y-Geräte* and which was to figure in the soon-to-be-fought *Battle of the Beams*. The report also significantly outlined German rocket development.

The letter was simply signed 'A German scientist who wishes you well'. His identity has never been established, but he must have been highly placed. In London many sceptics rejected the authenticity of the document, and others claimed it to be a plant – a propaganda exercise to undermine moral. Jones did not subscribe to these views, considering the document to be genuine; indeed, he later said that 'during the few quiet moments of the war I used to turn up the Oslo Report to see what was coming next'.

The Oslo Report was a clear warning that the war was to be a struggle as much between scientists as fighting men – a war which Britain, uncharacteristically, was well placed to fight. This was due in no small measure to the decision taken in 1938 to compile a register of some 5000 scientists. Thus highly capable men from universities and industry were ready to form the nucleus of a formidable army that was to wage a strange electronic war of secrets.

Above: This
He111, forced
down early in the
war comparatively
undamaged, was
repaired and test-
flown by the RAF.
Although it carries
RAF markings, it
still retains the
unit emblem of its
late owners –
Kampfgeschwader
26. It was possibly
from this machine
that RAF
Intelligence Officers
salvaged the scrap
of paper which gave
the first clue to
'Knickebein' whose
aerials can be seen
underneath the
fuselage just to the
left of the roundel.

1. THE BATTLE OF THE BEAMS

In the early months of 1940, the German Air Force, the Luftwaffe, began to fly night bombers over the blacked-out towns and countryside of Britain: not the massed formations that had been feared but single aircraft which appeared to be probing night defences – which incidentally were at that time practically non-existent. However, one night in March 1940 one of these nocturnal wanderers, plotted by ground radar, was intercepted by a night fighter which made a lucky visual contact and shot it down.

The crashed aircraft, a Heinkel 111, bore the marking '1H+AC' which identified its unit as Kampfgeschwader (Bomber Group) 26. It was, as a matter of routine, examined by RAF Technical Intelligence Officers; the examination must have been thorough, for salvaged from the wreckage was a scrap of paper which seemed to have been an aide-mémoire for the navigator. In translation it read:

'*Navigational aid:* Radio Beacons working on Beacon Plan A. Additionally from 0600 hours Beacon Dühnen. Light Beacon after dark. Radio Beacon Knickebein from 0600 hours on 315°.'[1]†

The importance of the fragment was the reference to 'Radio Beacon Knickebein' – it was the first time that this code-name had been mentioned and the fact that it was given a bearing indicated some sort of directional beam.

By coincidence, soon after that another Heinkel 111 was shot down with the identical markings 1H+AC – it must have been a replacement aircraft for KG26's earlier loss. This too carried compromising literature – a diary kept by one of the aircrew, which had an entry:

'5.3.40. Two thirds of the Staffel [Squadron] on leave. In afternoon studied about Knickebein, collapsible boats, etc.'[1]

'Knickebein' literally means 'crooked leg', although it is also the name of a magic raven in a German fairy story. Clearly it was necessary to find out more about this secret device. An obvious and time-honoured method of discovering one's enemy's secrets is in the interrogation of prisoners.

Many German aircrew prisoners of war were to some extent victims of their own propaganda; they had been led to believe that if they were captured they would be either shot out of hand or, at the very least, tortured. They were not therefore prepared for the highly skilled and civilised in-

Opposite: A fighter pilot's view of an He111. Like most German bombers in 1940, the Heinkel's defensive armament was inadequate against Spitfires and Hurricanes. Although still handicapped then by lack of airborne radar, RAF night fighters nevertheless shot down several bombers on visual interception.

†The footnote figures refer to the notes on p. 350.

terrogation which they received from Squadron Leader Felkin of Air Intelligence 1(k) at Trent Park, Cockfosters, north of London. During the course of one interrogation, Squadron Leader Felkin questioned a prisoner

Trent Park, the main interrogation centre for captured Luftwaffe aircrew. Today it is a Teachers' Training College.

about Knickebein: the man hedged, then conceded that 'it was like "X-Geräte"', adding that a shortwave beam was used, 'which would not be more than a kilometre wide over London'.[1]

This was not the first time that prisoners had made reference to 'X-Geräte' although it was the first time it had been coupled with Knickebein. An earlier Intelligence report dated 4 March 1940 stated:

'The X-Geräte is a bombing apparatus involving an application of pulse radio technique [with] . . . a system of intersecting radio beams from German transmitters, so that a small area of intersection occurs in which the characteristic signals of two stations combine and give a signal which might even be made to operate the bomb release gear automatically.'[1]

The evidence had been passed to Dr (now Professor) R. V. Jones, of Air Scientific Intelligence, who after considering the available information felt that, although far from conclusive, there was a strong enough case for him to include it in his report, 'Indications of New German Weapons to be used against England':

'It is possible that they have developed a system of intersecting beams, so that they can locate a target such as London with sufficient accuracy for . . . indiscriminate bombing. No information is available concerning the wavelength to be employed, but the accuracy of location expected by the Germans is something like a half metre† over London from the Western

---

†The figure of half a metre was typed in error; Jones had dictated 'half a mile'.

frontier of Germany. Efforts are still being made to determine the probable wavelengths so that counter measures can be employed.'[2]

The report had been written on 23 May. The German Air Force had already begun to raid Britain at night and it was thought by Air Intelligence that the bombers might well be using a beam system such as had been outlined in Jones's report, but it was at that time very difficult to obtain further information about Knickebein. The Germans had by now occupied the Low Countries and most of France; Dunkirk was only days away. It was hardly the ideal time for the recruitment of agents. However, the next vital clue in the Knickebein puzzle was to come from the Germans themselves.

The speed of the German advance had meant that the forward units of the Luftwaffe, already using bases in Northern France in preparation for the expected invasion of Britain, could only keep in touch with their headquarters by radio. Orders were transmitted in the supposedly unbreakable Enigma Code: one such message was sent on 5 June to the Chief Signals Officer of Fliegerkorps IV and, as the five-letter groups were being decoded by the Luftwaffe cipher clerks, the intercepted signal was also being processed at Bletchley Park, England.

The story of the penetrating of the Enigma code forms the subject of chapter 6; sufficient for the moment to say it *was* broken and the message to Fliegerkorps IV, one of the earliest decodes, was sent to Group Captain Blandy of the RAF 'Y' Service, the department of Air Intelligence responsible for the monitoring of Luftwaffe radio traffic.

A German field radio station. The Luftwaffe relied heavily on radio communications, especially in occupied countries where telephone lines were unreliable or non-existent. Enigma was used to encode the signals.

The decoded message read:

'Knickebein, Kleve, is established [or confirmed: the German is ambiguous here] at a point 53°24' North and 1° West.' ('Knickebein, Kleve, ist auf punkt 53 grad 24 minuten Nord und ein grad West eingerichtet.')[1]

This meant nothing to anyone else in the Air Ministry, but Group Captain Blandy luckily passed it to Dr Jones. It was the vital clue for which he had been waiting. 'Knickebein' he already knew as the codename of a suspected beam system; Kleve is the German spelling of Cleves (the town from which Anne of Cleves came), which was significantly the westernmost point in Germany, and therefore a likely site for a beam transmitter intended to cover England. 53°24' North 1° West is in England; it is a point in open country near Retford, roughly where the Great North Road, the old A1, crosses the 1° West Meridian.

Jones concluded that the simplest interpretation was that a navigational aircraft had been out and located where the beam was on that particular occasion. The beam position may well have been intended for Sheffield and a reconnaissance aircraft had established that it was off target, hence the reason for sending the message in the first place. By way of confirmation, it had been established that Fliegerkorps IV's bomber units were KG4 and KG27, equipped with Heinkel 111s, and their aircraft were known to have been over England on the night of 5 June, the date of the original Enigma message. (Before Jones had seen the decode, incidentally, others at the Air Ministry had taken it to mean that an illicit radio beacon was being operated near the Great North Road: a search party found nothing there or in the surrounding farms, which were also searched, much to the disappointment of the local police who had hoped to catch a German spy red-handed.)

In a report, Jones summarised this new Intelligence:

'. . . that the Germans possessed some method of establishing intersections over England, known as Knickebein; and that such intersections could be observed by means of equipment carried in Heinkel 111s. Moreover the accuracy of intersection was 1 minute, or roughly 1 mile square. . . . It is impossible [he concluded] to rate this independent contribution too highly.'[1]

The meeting with Group Captain Blandy had been in the morning of 12 June 1940. That afternoon, Jones had another appointment: this one with Professor F. A. Lindemann, his old Oxford tutor, now Scientific Adviser to the Prime Minister, Winston Churchill.

Lindemann had not seen the Enigma intercept so it was something of a coincidence when, after asking Jones some questions about German radar, he then enquired if there had been any developments about X-Geräte, which he knew had been mentioned by prisoners. Lindemann was in a position of considerable influence and Jones, concerned about the German beams, needed all the backing he could get for further investigation. He therefore showed him a copy of the decoded message but Lindemann was not to be convinced, pointing out that, at the high frequencies necessary for an ac-

curate beam from Cleves to England – 260 miles – the curvature of the earth would prevent its being received over Britain.

Fortunately Jones was familiar with this argument: he had put up a similar proposal for a navigation aid for the RAF before the war, only to have it turned down on this very ground. However T. L. Eckersley, a radio propagation expert from the Marconi Company and now a consultant to the Air Ministry 'Y' Service, had written a paper in which he had computed the range of a hypothetical VHF transmitter on the Brocken – a mountain in central Germany. The paper had indicated that it could be expected that a VHF signal from Cleves should be detectable over most of England. Jones decided to use Eckersley's paper to try to convince Lindemann the next day of the feasibility of the German beams; but in the next twenty-four hours a great deal more happened.

Firstly, Jones got in touch with Squadron Leader Felkin and told him of the positive evidence he now had from the intercepted German message and asked if any of the men he had interrogated from KG4 and KG27 had given anything away about Knickebein. Felkin replied that they had not during the questioning but, he added, on returning to their room, which was bugged, they had talked among themselves. On comparing notes on their interrogation one man had said that his questioner had asked about Knickebein; another said that he too had been asked. They both laughed and one said, 'They'll never find it; they'll never find it!' To Jones this was an irresistible challenge: the Knickebein receiver *must* be in the aircraft.

The first German aircraft to be shot down over Britain was a Heinkel 111 of 1/KG26 which had been attacked by Spitfires of 602 Squadron and crash-landed near Edinburgh on the 28 October 1939. Its radio equipment was undamaged and had been sent to the Royal Aircraft Establishment at Farnborough for examination. A written report had been issued which had described the complete radio installation: it was the standard Luftwaffe equipment of that time, comprising excellent receivers and transmitters of

From left to right, R. V. Jones, Professor F. A. Lindemann and T. L. Eckersley (postwar photographs).

the FuG10 type for long- and short-wave telephony and telegraphy; the aircraft had also carried a direction-finding set and a Lorenz Blind Landing set: the EBL2. Nothing unusual, the report concluded: everything was appropriate to a night bomber. However, on reading the report, Jones wondered about the Lorenz set, the EBL2: this, after all, was a beam receiver, of a sort, although it normally operated only at short range, thirty miles or so, and was designed to guide an aircraft to its airfield in bad visibility. He wondered, nevertheless, whether there was anything unusual about the captured set. He telephoned the author of the report, Squadron Leader Cox-Walker, at Farnborough and asked if there had been anything odd about the EBL Lorenz receiver. Cox-Walker thought for a moment and said 'No'. Then he said, 'Wait a minute – yes, you know we were surprised that it seems so much more sensitive than they would need for blind landing.'[3]

That was it. The laughing prisoners at Trent Park had assumed that the British would fail to see the wood for the trees; that they would think, as had indeed been the case, that the EBL was just an ordinary Lorenz Blind Landing set.

The RAF knew a good deal about the Lorenz system: there was a Blind Landing Development Unit at Boscombe Down and a handbook had been published – Air Publication 1751, 'Blind Approach Pilot's Handbook' – which described the technique. There was nothing secret about it: the Lorenz system had been in use in military and civil aircraft in several countries since the mid-1930s to enable pilots to land at airfields at night and in bad weather. How did it work?

It was essentially a system whereby two directional-beam aerials were placed so that they radiated two wide beams of a radio signal which overlapped along the centre line of the airfield runway. The aerials were automatically alternately switched to the transmitter so that one radiated only morse dots and the other dashes. The spacing of the dots and dashes was such that where the beams overlapped, the dots and dashes joined to give a continuous note; this area of the continuous note, known as the equi-signal, was very narrow indeed and quite accurate enough for a pilot with a suitable receiver to land on the exact centre line of the runway. The frequencies used internationally for this purpose were between 28 and 35 mHz. The Lorenz technique was simple but it called for a high standard of flying on the part of the pilot, who had to be very proficient in the difficult art of instrument-flying, that is flying without reference to a visual horizon. Initially, while about fifteen to twenty miles away, the aircraft Lorenz receiver would be tuned to the appropriate frequency; then the pilot, if his aircraft was to the left of the airfield runway, would hear morse dots in his earphones; he would then steer his aircraft to the right until the dots became a steady note – the equi-signal. At that point he would have to turn left; if he did not turn far enough, the steady note would turn into dashes; too much, and he would be flying into the dot zone again. Thus by making small alterations left or right of his course, as indicated by the dots or dashes, he would be able to keep in the equi-signal

A typical radio installation in a night bomber (Ju88) c. 1940. A signals mechanic is plugging in a replacement transmitter. This FuG10 equipment was modular and extremely advanced, all the connections being made automatically, thus avoiding vulnerable plugs and cables.

Below left: A still from a Luftwaffe instructional film on the radio installation in a Ju88.

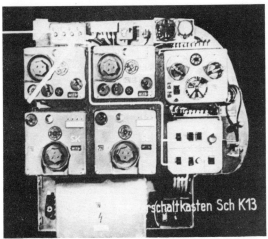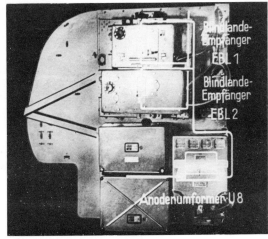

Above: On the reverse side, the Lorenz sets, EBL1 and EBL2.

Left: A captured EBL2 receiver. The five high-gain pentode valves gave the set unusual sensitivity. This was the clue to its true function – the reception of the Knickebein beams.

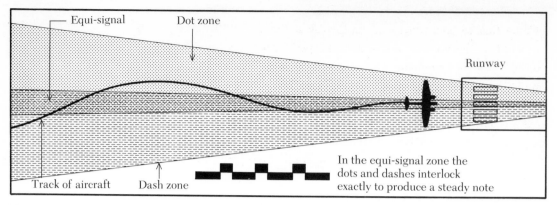

Equi-signal

Dot zone

Runway

Track of aircraft

Dash zone

In the equi-signal zone the dots and dashes interlock exactly to produce a steady note

The Lorenz Beam for Blind Landing.

and thus be aligned with the unseen runway. As he got nearer, the beam got narrower and more accurate until, at touchdown, it was less than the width of the runway. The accuracy of the system was such that a skilled beam pilot could detect a shift of a hundredth of the equi-signal width.

In practice it was not quite as straightforward as outlined above; the pilot had crosswinds and turbulence to contend with and the need to adjust his rate of descent, all on his instruments. Nevertheless, it was a practical aid (although it has long since been superseded by much more sophisticated modern Instrument Landing Systems – ILS). But the important point about Lorenz was the range. Under normal conditions it was considered to have a maximum of thirty miles.

In view of the abnormal sensitivity of the captured EBL2 receiver, Jones was convinced that Knickebein was a long-range version of the Lorenz system, used to detect the equi-signal not for thirty miles but nearer 300. It would, of course, be used in the reverse sense because the bomber would be flying away from the transmitter, not towards it, and this would mean it would get less accurate with increasing range. However, if a second intersecting beam were used, it would still be accurate enough to mark a target.

If the Germans were using these beams, then it meant that their radio technique was far ahead of Britain's at that time. There was, for example, the difficulty of the frequencies: the captured Lorenz set had preset tuning of several frequencies around 30 mHz. If Jones's theory was correct, then these higher frequencies would *have* to bend round the earth to be detectable over England. Yet this was not considered feasible at that time and had been the basis of Lindemann's objection. But Jones was concerned that if he was right then the threat was grave indeed: all German bombers carried the Lorenz equipment as standard, therefore all German bombers were potential beam flyers. He decided that he must convince the Professor: so on 13 June, the day after the previous meeting with him, he went to see him, this time taking the paper by Eckersley which appeared to support his theory. Lindemann was then sufficiently convinced to write a minute to Churchill that same day:

'There seems to be some reason to suppose that the Germans have some type of radio device with which they hope to find their targets. Whether this is some form of RDF [Radar] or some other invention, it is vital to investigate and especially to seek to discover what the wavelength is. If we know this, we could devise means to mislead them. . . With your approval, I will take this up with the Air Ministry and try to stimulate action.'[4]

At the bottom of Lindemann's letter, Churchill jotted a note before passing it on to Sir Archibald Sinclair, his Secretary of State for Air: 'This seems most intriguing and I hope you will have it thoroughly examined.'

It was now 14 June: the German Army was marching into Paris and it could only be a matter of days before the French would sue for peace. The Luftwaffe would then be able to concentrate their bomber force, operating from bases in France, against Britain: they would also then have new and nearer sites for beam transmitters.

Meanwhile, Squadron Leader Felkin was endeavouring to obtain further evidence from prisoners:[5] on 14 June he had received a new batch, including one man from KG26. As KG26 was known to be concerned with Knickebein, there was some hope that this airman, identified as A231, might know about it. Subsequent interrogation showed that A231 was anti-war and was to prove very helpful. He drew a sketch of a transmitting tower he had seen at Rechlin – the Luftwaffe research establishment. The drawing agreed with a mysterious tower photographed by Bomber Command on Hornum, which had been puzzling Intelligence for some time.

A231 volunteered a number of supplementary details, including the fact that the dots and dashes were on opposite sides of the main beam as compared with normal Lorenz practice, adding:

'As soon as the aircraft picks up the beam, the pilot flies a level course, seeing that the Turn and Bank Indicators, the Altimeter and the Artificial Horizon all read zero. He then flies along the Beam.'

A231 must have been mistaken when he stated that the altimeter should read zero when flying the beam (although it could explain how he came to be captured).

As the evidence for the existence of the beams strengthened, Air Marshal Philip Joubert was appointed by the Secretary of State to take charge of the investigation. Most of the evidence was available for a meeting in his room at the Air Ministry on 15 June, with both Lindemann and Jones present, when it was agreed that immediate action should be taken.

Before any countermeasures could be undertaken, the beams had to be found, for no one in Britain had as yet heard the transmissions. The exact frequencies were unknown, as were the note and the keying characteristics of the dots and dashes. Several suggestions were put forward, including sending men up 350-ft coastal radar masts with VHF receivers; there was even a suggestion that balloons might be employed; but the obvious method of search was to equip an aircraft with a VHF set and endeavour to intercept the beam transmissions which, it was thought, would be found between 28 and 35 mHz. An RAF Signals Officer, Squadron Leader Scott-Farnie, predicted that the transmissions would be heard on 30, 31.5 or 33.3 mHz, since these were the three frequencies to which the Lorenz sets from crashed Heinkels were always found to be tuned. By 18 June, Wing Commander Blucke, from the Blind Landing Development Flight at Boscombe Down, had been briefed to prepare one of his aircraft, an Avro Anson, for an investigation flight. Skilled VHF operators of the 'Y' Service – mostly prewar radio amateurs – were posted to Boscombe Down where the special receivers were to be fitted to the aircraft.

As these preparations were being put in hand, the indefatigable Squadron Leader Felkin had collected yet more valuable and, as things turned out, timely evidence: on 18 June he received a miscellany of papers salvaged from German aircraft shot down over France (presumably before the Dunkirk evacuation). On one paper was written:

> 'Fernfunkfeuer – U.K.W.
> 1. Knickebein (G. Bredstedt n.ö Husum)
>   54° 39′
>   8° 57′
> 2. Knickebein
>   51° 47′ 5″
>   6° 6′
>   (b. Cleve)'[5]

This valuable find not only confirmed the earlier information about Cleves, but the reference to Bredstedt, in Schleswig-Holstein, gave the site of a second Knickebein transmitter, and also cleared up the obscurity of the very first mention of Knickebein, which it will be remembered was on a piece of paper salvaged from the Heinkel of KG26, and had referred to 'Radio Beacon Knickebein on 315°': a 315° bearing from Bredstedt passes through Scapa – where KG26 had been active.

During the next vital days Air Intelligence was to surpass itself. On 19 June a radio operator's log was found in a Heinkel, 5J+AH of KG4, shot down the previous night. The log included a list of normal German non-directional radio beacons, but the significant entry was the first: 'Knickebein Kleve 31.5'. This was most valuable, for it gave Jones a definite frequency, one that was almost certainly in use the night the bomber had been shot down – 31.5 mHz was, incidentally, one of the three frequencies that had been predicted by Squadron Leader Scott-Farnie.

On 20 June Squadron Leader Felkin produced another report,[5] the result of the interrogation of a new prisoner – A212. This man had stated that 'the X-Geräte is the codename for a directional apparatus for blind bomb-sighting, based on the intersection of two radio beams'. Felkin's report concluded: '. . . the evidence tends to show that the X-Geräte and Knickebein are exactly the same thing; but it must be remembered that there are other statements which indicate that they are not the same but similar.'

On 21 June yet more intelligence was forthcoming from Trent Park. From another German bomber, shot down during the night of 19/20 June, the radio operator had baled out; after making a safe landing he realised that he still had his notebook with him so, in a belated attempt at security, he tore it up into fragments (a figure of 3000 was given) and, while commendably attempting to bury the pieces, he was arrested. The pieces were recovered and Squadron Leader Felkin sat up until 3 am the following morning assembling the impromptu jigsaw, with the following result:

U.K.W.	54	38	7′ N	} Stollberg
Knicke.	8	56	8′ O	
	51		N	
	1	30′	O q m s) 30 Mh	
GLEVE	51°	47′	4	
	6°	6	2′	
	55°		N	
	2°		E q m s) 31.5	

This latest evidence confirmed the location of the second Knickebein transmitter, located near Bredstedt, which had first been seen on the paper from the KG4 aircraft (Stollberg and Bredstedt seem to have been alternative names for the transmitter in Schleswig-Holstein). Knicke was obviously Knickebein; 'Gleve' was a misspelling for Kleve; and, most important, a second frequency was quoted: 30 mHz. UKW is simply an abbreviation for Ultra Kurtz Wellen – or ultra-short wave – and 'QMS' was the international 'Q' code for a requested magnetic bearing. The other bearings given were something of a mystery as they were over the sea.

Jones now had a clear theory as to how the system probably worked. The two beams would be rotatable; they could therefore be made to intersect over any target in Britain and since they were of considerable distance apart – 400 kilometres – they would give a good angle of 'cut' – essential for accuracy. If the target were a midland town, for example, the pilot would intercept (say) the Cleves beam on 31.5 while over the North Sea, and establish himself in the equi-signal; he would then be able to adjust his heading to compensate for wind drift by maintaining the steady note in his earphones, any variation in his course being indicated by dots or dashes. This first beam would give him direction. When nearing the target, the radio operator would retune the special Lorenz receiver to 31.5 mHz, the frequency of the second beam transmitter at Bredstedt. This intersecting beam would indicate the range; dots would then be heard growing stronger as the intersection got nearer until they began to merge into a steady note. When they merged, the pilot would be in the equi-signal of the second beam and, depending on its width, exactly over the chosen target. If the width was known to the pilot, then it would be a simple matter of when to drop the bombs – accurately and without ever seeing the ground. If Jones was right, and all the evidence pointed in that direction, then the feeble night defences could very quickly be overwhelmed. The most pessimistic estimates of the accuracy of Knickebein beams would still enable a large factory complex to be effectively attacked.

The remarkable thing was that Knickebein's secret had apparently been penetrated purely by Intelligence. By 21 June a great deal seemed to be

Right: The aerials of the Knickebein transmitter at Cleves. About 100 feet high, the structure was rotated round a circular track.

Far right: A small later Knickebein transmitter in northern France, photographed by a British agent.

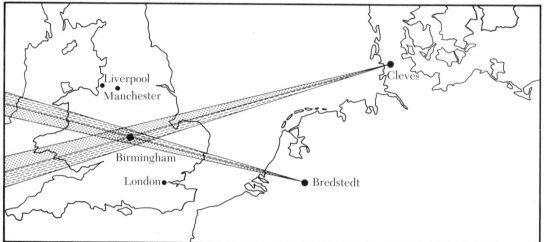

The Application of Lorenz to Knickebein.

known about the system, yet it had still not been heard. It was a considerable achievement and, in a report written at the time, Jones paid tribute to Squadron Leader Felkin:

> 'We therefore had by 21.6.40 two sites and two frequencies definitely fixed. The contribution of Air Intelligence 1(k) to the solving of the Knickebein mystery, which they themselves had discovered, must be rated very high indeed.'[5]

Jones's own contribution, one might add, was far from inconsiderable. Neither was that of the night-fighter pilots. In retrospect, they had been very lucky in shooting down the aircraft which carried much of the evidence that was to prove vital to the Knickebein investigation.

In early 1940 British night defences were, to say the least, inadequate; anti-aircraft guns were practically useless and the night fighters – Bristol Blenheims – were converted obsolescent twin-engined bombers, which lacked speed and, until later in 1940, any Airborne Interception Radar (AI). Without it the night fighter could only be vectored or steered into the general area of an intruder by ground radar and then hope to make an interception visually, and on most nights the chances of that were practically nil.

C. F. Rawnsley, who was a Blenheim airgunner with 604 Squadron, has written of the frustration and dangers of those night patrols in early 1940:

'Night after night we chased around after rumours and found nothing, and then had to grope our way back through weather which, that winter, was horrible. It was with sighs of relief that we bumped down on those small grass airfields dimly lit with paraffin flares. . . . We had no homing beacons and there was no system of blind approach, no way we could be talked down to a safe landing. Our radio was feeble and short-ranged and the blind flying instruments were astonishingly temperamental.'[6]

Paradoxically, the very lack of success made the task marginally easier. German bomber crews flying at night over England were so rarely attacked that they became careless; at least one aircraft was shot down with its navigation lights on. Others flew straight and level, even on bright moonlight nights, and the gunners of many bombers did not keep up a sufficiently vigilant watch; but until efficient airborne interception radar, fitted to high-performance fighters, became general, a German night bomber had to be very unlucky indeed to be shot down in the summer of 1940.

In view of the state of British night defences at that time, it is small wonder that the threat of the Knickebein beams was taken so seriously. Seriously enough for a meeting to be called on 21 June at 10 Downing Street, presided over by the Prime Minister. It was an august gathering: Sir Archibald Sinclair, the Secretary of State for Air, Lord Beaverbrook, Sir Henry Tizard, Watson Watt, Lindemann and most of the Air Staff. The meeting was convened for 10 o'clock – but the man they had come to hear was not among those present.

That day Dr R. V. Jones got to his office at his usual time to find a note on his desk requiring him to attend a meeting in the Cabinet Room at No. 10. He thought it was a practical joke: a not unlikely eventuality as he was (and still is) a noted practical joker. By the time he had made the necessary in-vestigation into the authenticity or otherwise of the summons, it was nearly half past ten; he hurried over to Downing Street to find that in his absence the meeting had been going on for some time. He took a seat at the end of the long table and, as the meeting continued, Jones realised that no one really knew enough of the detail; so, after ten minutes or so, when the Prime Minister addressed a question to him, he said: 'Well, Sir, would it help if I told you the story from the beginning?' 'Yes,' said Churchill, 'that's a good idea.' So Jones told him the story right from the first references to Knickebein, the mention of X-Geräte made by the prisoners, up to the latest evidence. He could see that he was making an impression and the Prime Minister asked him what could be done. Jones explained the various possibilities: putting in a false beam, interfering with the dots and dashes, or just straightforward jamming.

Winston Churchill's account of that same conference is contained in his book *Their Finest Hour*:

'Being master and not having to argue too much, once I was convinced about the principles of this queer and deadly game I gave all the necessary orders that very day in June, for the existence of the beams to be assumed and for all counter-measures to receive absolute priority. The slightest reluctance or deviation in carrying out this policy was to be reported to me.'

With this powerful backing, Jones could now intensify the investigation. The first thing was to be absolutely certain that the beams actually existed and that they were not a gigantic hoax put up to conceal some other weapon: he did not think so for a moment, but the fact remained that, up to the time of the Downing Street meeting, no signals that could be ascribed to the Knickebein beam had yet been detected.

The next step, therefore, was to try to intercept the beams using an airborne receiver. On the afternoon of 21 June, Wing Commander Blucke reported that the Anson aircraft were standing by. They had been fitted with American Hallicrafters S27 VHF receivers which had been designed for radio amateurs but were the only sets available which covered the predicted frequencies. (It has been said that an RAF Signals Officer bought the entire stock from Webbs Radio in Soho – on credit.) The installation of the sets had not been altogether straightforward as they had never been designed to operate in an aircraft and had to be modified to run from 28 volts DC instead of the normal 250 volts AC. The aircraft had to have VHF aerials fitted and mountings made for the sets. All this work was undertaken practically single-handed by Flight Lt Alway, an ex-BBC Engineer who was to lose his life later in the war.

A test flight made on the morning of 19 June had been unsuccessful, due to a fault in the radio's high-tension generator: this was corrected and a second flight was made during the night of 20 June, but nothing was heard. However, there was little enemy air activity that night, which could have explained the lack of beam signals. All was now ready for a third flight on the night of 21 June, the date of the Prime Minister's meeting; but before that there was to be yet another meeting. All in all it was to be quite a day for meetings. In France, Hitler was dictating the Armistice terms to the French delegation in the Forest of Compiègne, near Paris.

In London that same afternoon there was a smaller, though for those concerned no less dramatic, conference at the Air Ministry in Whitehall. Jones, some senior RAF Signals Officers and a scientist from Air Ministry Research Establishment (AMRE) had met to discuss the course that the listening flight should take that night. They were joined by T. L. Eckersley, whose paper on propagation had been used by Jones to convince Professor Lindemann that the beams were feasible. Eckersley, unknown to Jones, had been given all the facts about Knickebein and now dropped a bombshell. He rejected Jones's now accepted explanation of Knickebein, adding that he had made calculations which showed the reception of the beams was impossible on the frequencies apparently used by the Germans. Arnold Wilkins, the scientist from AMRE who was present at the meeting, remembers Eckersley saying that 'in his opinion the reception at any distance on this wavelength [9 metres] was quite impossible and that he'd stake his reputation on the statement'; which meant, of course, that any beam bombing system was not possible. The effect of this on Jones can well be imagined:

'It was an absolute blow from my point of view because if that really were

A Hallicrafters S27 VHF receiver. These sets were ideal for intercepting German air-to-ground signals, since they covered all frequencies from 10 metres (28 mHz) to 2 metres (142 mHz). This included Knickebein transmissions and both X- and Y-Geräte. In addition, these sets were used by 'Y' Service to monitor German aircrew radio traffic (which led to Operation Corona, see p. 114).

true, all the fuss that I had been the cause of would now be exploded, and what would happen to me for the rest of my life was problematic. . . . I pointed out to Eckersley that I'd used one of his own papers to convince Lindemann; that this showed quite clearly the beams would go that far. "Oh", he said, "well you don't want to believe that, I was showing how far they might go, but I don't really think they would go as far as that".'[3]

At that point, Group Captain Lywood, Principal Deputy Director of Signals, said: 'Here we have the world's expert on propagation, he says the beams are impossible, we ought not to waste any more time. I think we ought to cancel the flight.' Faced with this, Jones did the only thing possible: he said, 'Look, I was at a meeting in the Cabinet Room this morning and I heard the Prime Minister give orders for that flight to take place, and if it doesn't take place I shall see that he gets to know who it was who cancelled it.' Lywood then gave in and agreed to the flight, though making it quite clear that some of those present at that meeting did not expect that anything would be found. A course was agreed for the aircraft to fly and Jones went home to spend, as he later put it, 'the most wretched night of my life'.

The aircraft from Boscombe Down had been flown to Wyton, in Huntingdonshire, to be nearer to the East Coast over which any beams from Germany to the Midlands would have to pass. The machines – it is thought that three were prepared – were Mk 1 Avro Ansons and were old aircraft; at least one, so the archives at Boscombe Down show, had been recommended for write-off. They were slow (maximum speed 188 mph), fabric-covered, noisy, cold, but they were all that could be spared; it was only five days after Dunkirk and at that time bomb racks were being fitted to Tiger Moth trainers to enable them to attack the expected German invasion force. Seen in that light, the provision of three aircraft, however dilapidated, was remarkable.

The pilot who was to fly that night was Flight Lt Bufton, an experienced beam-approach pilot from the Blind Flying Development Unit at Boscombe Down; the radio operator for the Hallicrafters receiver was a Corporal

A Mk I Anson being manhandled from its hangar. Two 350-hp Armstrong Siddeley Cheetah IX radial engines gave it a maximum speed of 188 mph at 7000 feet. 'Faithful Annie' first appeared in 1935 and later versions were still in service with the RAF in the 1950s.

Mackie of the 'Y' Service, skilled in VHF techniques. Flight Lt Alway, who had installed the sets and flown on the two previous unsuccessful flights, was simply too exhausted to fly on this one.

In gathering darkness on the night of that incident-filled 21 June, the Anson lifted off the grass airfield at Wyton. The crew had not been told the Knickebein story; they had simply been briefed to search for radio signals with Lorenz characteristics on the two frequencies known to Air Intelligence: 30 and 31.5 mHz. If any signal were found they were to try to locate the equi-signal and establish its bearing.

The aircraft slowly climbed away from Wyton on a northerly heading; it was soon flying in heavy cloud and total darkness. Corporal Mackie, sitting in front of his American radio, with only the soft glow of its dial lights to relieve the gloom, was deafened by the crash of static in his headphones as he tuned the set continuously between the two given frequencies. For a time no signal was heard; then, as he tuned once more to 31.5 mHz, faintly at first through the noise, but rapidly growing louder, a series of morse dots. Calling over the intercom to the pilot that he'd located the signal, he switched the output of the receiver to Bufton and, as they listened, the dots grew very strong and clear and then merged into a steady note: they were flying in the equi-signal. A few seconds later, as they continued on their northerly heading, the equi-signal slowly turned into morse dashes. There could be no doubt about it: there was a Lorenz beam on exactly 31.5 mHz.

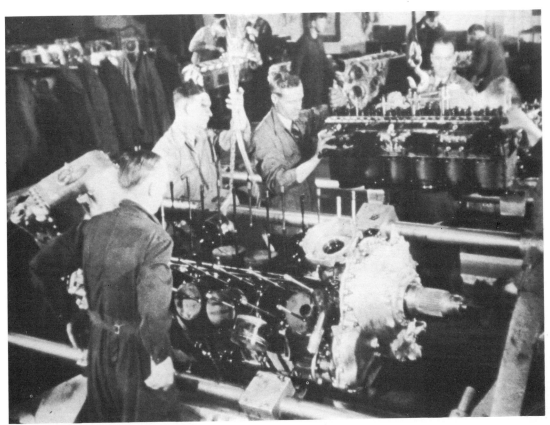

Rolls-Royce Merlin engines being produced at Derby.

The position was one mile south of Spalding as Flight Lt Bufton turned the aircraft and centred it in the equi-signal. From his compass he worked out the bearing: 284° True. The equi-signal was just 400 yards wide. When the bearing of the beam was transferred to a chart in the aircraft it passed over the Rolls-Royce aero-engine factory at Derby, the only factory in the country that was making the Merlin engine which was to power the Spitfires and Hurricanes in the Battle of Britain.

Later that night, Bufton and his observer, Corporal Mackie, discovered a second beam with Lorenz characteristics: it was synchronised with the first but had the dots and dashes reversed. This beam from the transmitter at Bredstedt was discovered over a point near Beeston. The secret of Knickebein was secret no longer. The achievement of the investigation flight, undertaken as it was in darkness and in heavy cloud, with both the pilot and observer unaware of the existence of the two beams, was remarkable.

The confirmation of the characteristics of the beams, even down to the second one having its dots and dashes reversed, just as one of the German prisoners had stated, had vindicated Jones.

'It is fitting [he wrote in his report] to close the account as far as scientific intelligence is concerned. In the course of ten days the matter has developed from conjecture to certainty. . . . Several technical points remain to be cleared up, but their elucidation is only a matter of time. . . . If our good fortunes hold we may yet pull the crooked leg!'[1]

The first priority was to set up some form of jamming, even if it was just crude radio noise. A new unit was quickly formed: 80 Wing. It was initially based in a disused garage in Garston, North Watford, and was commanded by an RAF Signals Officer, Group Captain E. B. Addison. From this modest beginning,

there was to develop a most telling weapon of the Secret War: RCM – Radio Counter Measures – soon to embrace far more than just the German beams, which were coded 'Headache'.

For the moment the problem facing 80 Wing was the provision of suitable jammers. This was by no means easy as most service transmitters at that time were half the known frequency of the Knickebein signals. Then someone remembered that Diathermy sets, which were used in hospitals for cauterising purposes, generated radio energy on a frequency around 30 mHz; they were not designed as radio transmitters, but it was thought they could be modified. A Harley Street specialist who was an expert in Diathermy agreed to help. 'Then,' said Group Captain Addison, 'go to Moss Bros and hire a Flight Lieutenant's uniform, then go round all the hospitals where you know there are Diathermy sets, pinch them, and bring them to us here and we will modify them.'[7]

The sets were duly commandeered by the bogus officer and were converted into 150-watt transmitters to be used as radio-noise jammers operating on the German beam frequencies. Several were placed in country police stations – one was at Glastonbury, another at Wimborne Minster, and one village bobby had the set installed in his bedroom and instructed his wife to operate it, should he be away on his beat when the call came to switch on.[8] It is doubtful if these low-powered sets were very effective but they did at least indicate to the German bomber crews that the British knew about their beams and therefore also knew their course and probable targets.

Meanwhile, much more powerful transmitters were being prepared at the Telecommunications Research Establishment at Worth Matravers, near Swanage. These, coded 'Aspirin', were much more sophisticated; they did not simply radiate crude noise, but continuous morse dashes, which had the identical tone and keying characteristics of the genuine beam signals, but without their directional properties. These signals were superimposed on the beam: to achieve this several were mobile and could be driven to sites under the beams; others were placed on high ground around the country. Eventually there would be twenty-eight 'Aspirins' available.[8]

To locate the bearing of the German beams, a complex organisation was set up, coordinated by Wing Commander Blucke at Headquarters Fighter Command at Bentley Priory, near Stanmore. The three Ansons were later to be joined by Armstrong Whitworth Whitleys – a rather unloved bomber but a much larger aircraft than the Anson. The small flight eventually became a very secret Special Counter Measures unit: 109 Squadron.

Each night the aircraft would take off and search for the beams, reporting the bearings of any found to Bentley Priory. To supplement the aircraft, several coastal radar towers were equipped with VHF receivers. As early as 26 June, only five days after the beams were first heard, the minutes of a conference held on that date in Air Marshal Joubert's room state:

'The RDF [radar] towers which have been equipped with [Hallicrafters] receivers are: Ottercops, Bawdsey, West Beckham, Staxton Wold and Dover. Of these stations, West Beckham and Bawdsey have been success-ful in receiving signals. Wing Commander Blucke states that they now act as guard stations to the extent that they can advise him as soon as the beams come on and he orders an aircraft to investigate immediately.'[9]

One can imagine how difficult it must have been to lug these heavy radio sets up the 350-ft radar towers, to say nothing of trying to receive a signal high above a coastal site in a howling gale. Arnold Wilkins, the scientist who had been present at the meeting when Eckersley had stated that the beams were impossible, remembers being involved in an early investigation into the possible use of the radar towers for intercepting the beams:

'I got to Dover and told the CO what I was proposing to do. I asked him whether there was a VHF receiver on the station; there was. I then proceeded to climb the tower. . . . When I was about 100 feet high, I heard somebody shouting to me from below: it was a very excited airman and he wanted me to come down. When I got down I was taken into the transmit-ter building, where a high-powered radar transmitter was working, to find that this man had got a receiver installed, connected to an indoor aerial an inch or two below the ceiling of the partly buried building, and in spite of the mass of wet shingle placed on top of the roof for bomb protection, the receiver was getting a quite strong signal from the Knickebein station at Cleves. I then went and phoned the Air Ministry and told them I didn't think there was any need to do this job on top of the tower. . . .'[10]

The implacable Mr Eckersley was still of the opinion that the Cleves beams 'did not extend to any great distance within our coastline' and that beams signals received on the ground in this country were 'in the nature of freaks'.

The task of intercepting the beams was made very much less difficult than it might otherwise have been by the almost incredible carelessness of the Germans. During the early part of that July, the beams were left on for very long periods – at times all day, probably to train their operators. This German lack of security was astonishing: they could easily have turned the beams round and tested them and trained the aircrews over Germany or one of the occupied countries, for most of Europe from the Arctic Circle to the Pyrénées was now under German control. The fact remains that they did not.

Throughout July the Luftwaffe was building up its strength in northern France: air bases were taken over from the French and new ones were being constructed. Intelligence reports indicated that preparations for a big air offensive against Britain, the prelude to an invasion, were going ahead. Enigma, the German code, was now being deciphered daily at Bletchley Park and, on 27 July 1940, this 'Ultra-Secret' source was almost certainly the one which gave Dr Jones vital information that a new development could be expected in the Battle of the Beams.

The message was to the effect that KG54, a bomber unit based in northern France, had requested that specialist technical squads from Fliegerkorps V should spend the week beginning 5 August 1940 with the unit, to tune the 'special Blind Landing receivers' (EBL2). Since KG54 operational area was not covered by either the Cleves or Bredstedt beams, it was obvious that new Knickebein stations were in the process of being set up; Cherbourg was a possibility. Soon more information from a 'source' (Enigma) stated that a Knickebein installation was being erected near Beaumont, on the Hague peninsula, north-west of Cherbourg at 1°51′W 49°40.5′N. This was confirmed by photographic reconnaissance aircraft by mid-August. It was the first photograph of a Knickebein installation: Bredstedt was beyond the range of PRU Spitfires and Cleves had been clouded over when attempts to photograph it were made.

This second-generation Knickebein was (though no one in Air Intelligence knew it at the time) much smaller than the gigantic array at Cleves; being nearer to Britain, the aerials were much more compact. The Hague station was joined by another near Dieppe, then several more along the coast.

On 1 August 1940, Hitler issued his 'Directive No. 17 for the conduct of Air and Naval Warfare against England', which stated in part: 'The German Air Force is to overcome the British Air Force with all means at its disposal and as soon as possible. . . . The intensified air war may commence on or after 6 August.' The Battle of Britain was about to begin.

But as well as the massive daylight attacks from the middle of August, the Luftwaffe began to intensify its night bombing. Aided by the Chain Home defensive radar with its intricate network of fighter control, RAF day fighters were to prove more than a match for the German bombers. At night, however, it was a very different story. Airborne Interception radar was still in its infancy and night fighters had to intercept largely by visual contact. The only defence against the destruction of key targets – power stations, gas works, aircraft factories – was to deny the enemy the use of his highly accurate navigation beams. Night after night the 'Aspirins' were operational and, gradually at first, then unmistakably, the German bombers were seen to be having difficulty in locating their targets.

The effect of the radio countermeasures was reviewed in a 'Most Secret' Report issued by 80 Wing.[11] In the section covering the Knickebein countermeasures for June/August 1940, it recorded that:

'The efficiency of Aspirins has been judged from three sources, namely:– Intelligence and Prisoners' Reports, Enemy Aircraft Track analyses, and direct observation by our own investigating aircraft [109 Squadron]; from the outset these sources showed that the method employed was having the desired effect.

'Prior to taking countermeasures, analysis of [Radar] tracks had shown that enemy aircraft were approaching their targets over a very narrow front, but shortly after commencing RCM [Radio Counter Measures] operations against these beams, there was considerable evidence of a tendency for tracks to wander, whilst broadening of the front of approach became obvious.

'Track analysis does not provide absolute proof of the efficiency of countermeasures of this sort, but it is of considerable value in showing whether or not a large number of aircraft are able to follow a beam. Later, although a few tracks appeared to follow the line of the beam settings, it was evident that little use was being made of the beams, and very soon prisoners' reports made it clear that it was becoming increasingly difficult for aircraft to follow the beam as our countermeasures became progressively more offensive in scope.

'Intelligence Reports provide further evidence of successful interference. As, for example, on one occasion during an approach to London, enemy aircraft control stations were heard to inform their aircraft that Knickebein was unserviceable. Later it was learned that many of the aircraft returned to their base without having reached their objective.

'At about this time the Enemy Air Staff asked for special reports on results obtained in the use of Knickebein, thus suggesting some anxiety as to its effectiveness. The enemy was undoubtedly aware of our interference and frequently, for a time, interchanged the frequencies of his beams, particularly those from Cherbourg and Dieppe.

'There have also been many cases of enemy aircraft endeavouring to reach their targets by means of the beams and getting lost. Prisoners of War from these aircraft described their experiences which clearly showed interference with the beams. Usually they were able to distinguish the presence of a beam but they failed to pick up the equi-signal zone. . . . On one occasion the crew of an aircraft . . . when they found their radio was useless, baled out.

'Knickebein continues to be used by the enemy but . . . from recent reports and from our own air tests, there can be little doubt that Knickebein . . . is of but scant use to German aircraft over this country.'

To try to control the countermeasures, the Germans now only switched on their beam transmitters at the last possible moment, and at times would align them on a 'spoof' target, hoping that the defences would be caught on the wrong foot when the beams were moved to the real target, but this stratagem turned out to be a double-edged sword, as an ex-Luftwaffe pilot of KG1 recalled:

'The Knickebein beams would be directed for an hour to a certain target. The bombers would set course, but not using the beam, then at a given time the beams would be turned on to the actual target – the idea was to confuse the defenders, only it also confused us, being very difficult for us to locate it [the beam] and then when we found it the countermeasures would make its use very limited.'[12]

Another German bomber pilot, Günther Unger, who flew Dornier 17s with KG76, conceded that:

'Knickebein was often interfered with by the English defence, but I do not think that I was personally misled by it. I had a good feel for it but I know that one of my observers, for example, found it impossible to pick out the right sound when the English interference transmitter was used to jam the Knickebein beam. I suppose it needed a special feel to detect the right sound in this medley of sounds, and many of us were distracted away from our targets.'[13]

Just how did the 'Aspirin' countermeasure transmitters achieve this? The technique of the German bombers using Knickebein was to navigate by normal methods, that is by compass, and at some point, usually over the Channel, to intercept the beam and then fly in the equi-signal, the steady-

Günther Unger (second from left) and his crew in front of their Dornier 17 after a raid over England. The aircraft has been hit by flak and has a flat tyre. This was the aircraft Unger flew in the attack on Coventry.

note area, until near the target. The Knickebein receiver would then be tuned to the second or crossbeam which would indicate the precise point at which to drop the bombs.

There would be little difficulty getting 'on the beam' over the Channel since, being near the transmitter, the beam signals would be very strong and the Aspirins would, to a large extent, be masked at this point. As the aircraft flew over the English coast, however, the Aspirin transmitters would become dominant: the once loud and clear steady equi-signal would now have the spurious dashes of the countermeasures transmitter superimposed. An inexperienced pilot hearing the dashes would assume that he had veered to the right of his intended course; he would have to correct this by turning the aircraft left, but instead of the equi-signal reappearing, he would still only receive dashes, for by now the Aspirins would be far stronger than the distant Knickebein transmitters. By the time the pilot had flown out of the area of an Aspirin, he would almost certainly be a long way from the true beam, and he would be far more likely to encounter the bogus dashes from another Aspirin transmitter than to regain the very narrow (400 yards) original equi-signal of the real beam.

The success of these countermeasures was to some extent made possible by the very character of the Lorenz signals. The transition from dots to steady equi-signal and from steady signal to dashes was not clear-cut: the dots would slowly merge with the steady note, the steady note would slowly resolve into dashes. A skilled pilot, one who had considerable experience of Lorenz flying, could turn this effect into a counter-countermeasure; such a pilot, for example the KG1 man quoted above, who had been a Blind Flying instructor, would never fly in the equi-signal, but on intercepting the beam would place his aircraft to one side, on the threshold of the dot zone where they were just perceptible. By doing this, the smallest deviation in aircraft heading would

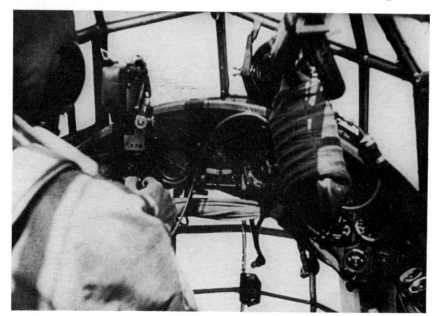

The pilot's cockpit of a 1940 Junkers 88. The MG15 7.9-mm gun was operated by the observer against head-on attacks.

immediately be revealed, since the dots would disappear or get stronger, and in this way a far more accurate course could be flown. Within the equi-signal a pilot could wander from left to right, making continuous corrections and always listening for dots or dashes. He was therefore fair game for the countermeasure dashes when they appeared. The experienced pilot would set up his bomber in the beam while over the Channel and, correcting for wind-drift, would then engage the autopilot which would maintain the aircraft on its precise course, flying through and ignoring the interference. Even without the autopilot, by listening to the just perceptible dots, it was possible to remain in the beam, for the pilot was maintaining a given situation, not anticipating a change. The counterfeit dashes, when they appeared would not 'feel right'; they were far stronger and better defined than the originals, with which they were not exactly synchronised. It was therefore possible to distinguish the true signal under them until it was obliterated. This would happen when the bomber was very near the masking transmitter and the experienced pilot would then simply maintain course on his instruments until clear of the Aspirin zone and then regain the true beam. Fortunately, not many Luftwaffe pilots had the very high blind-flying skill required to use the beams in this way.

The majority of German bomber pilots were trained to fly in daylight. The Luftwaffe was primarily conceived not as a strategic but as a tactical air force, to be used as long-range artillery for the army on the ground. That is the way it had been used to brilliant effect in Poland; night bombing was, to an increasing extent, forced upon them (as it was to be on the RAF) by the quality of the opposing fighters. Many crews were hastily retrained for night operations: specialist navigators as the RAF understood the term, using skills that had evolved through centuries of marine practice and trained in the use of sextant, star tables and astro-compass, were not part of the normal German bomber crew.

In the prewar Luftwaffe, the observer (Beobachter) was generally an experienced ex-pilot who was also the commander of the aircraft. This practice continued into the early days of the war, but as losses among bomber crews rose, the shortage of trained pilots was such that these highly skilled men were required either as instructors or to fly once more as operational pilots. Indeed, losses during the Battle of Britain were such that an order was issued to all bomber units to the effect that no aircraft was to carry more than one officer on operations. In this changed situation the pilot therefore became the commander, and hastily trained airmen replaced the experienced observers.

Thus the pilot became responsible for his own navigation. His observer's primary function became bomb-aimer, although he was also expected to map-read, use the D/F (Radio Direction Finding), look out for landfalls and generally assist with the navigation. He was also usually the front airgunner. In the three main bomber types used over Britain during the early war years, the Heinkel 111, Dornier 17 and Junkers 88, there was no special navigator's

Pilot and observer side by side in a Ju88 A-1. The lack of any dual controls is obvious.

The glazed nose of a Heinkel 111, the standard German medium bomber. First flown in 1935 as a commercial airliner, it was quickly developed as a bomber and, tested with the Legion Condor in Spain, it became the backbone of the Luftwaffe bomber groups, remaining in service until the end of the war, when the Spanish Air Force built it under licence (with Rolls-Royce Merlin engines) until the 1960s. The extensive glazing produced a 'hall of mirrors' effect in certain lights, which made landing difficult.

position with chart table and necessary instruments – compass, airspeed indicator, altimeter – as in RAF aircraft. The German observer sat next to his pilot (no co-pilots were carried in the Luftwaffe, none of the three bombers mentioned above had dual control); his training was brief and he relied on the beams and other radio aids as primary navigation instruments. Denied their aid, many bombers simply got lost. When that happened, the crews were prey to the natural fears of operational flying over hostile territory. The crew compartments, particularly in the Heinkel 111, were extensively glazed; this was excellent for daylight operation when escorted by a strong fighter formation, but at night it instilled a profound feeling of vulnerability. By September 1940, German bomber crews knew only too well how many of their fellow airmen had been lost in the costly daylight raids; the Luftwaffe was gaining a healthy respect for the RAF who, although British night defences were still very primitive, did to some extent enjoy a degree of psychological advantage. The days of easy German victories were fast receding.

Many captured Luftwaffe night-bomber aircrew when interrogated said that they knew the RAF had night fighters patrolling the beams, or concentrations of anti-aircraft guns ranged and waiting: they had not. Another belief widely held by captured crews was that 'the English are very good at radio' and that the beams were being diverted or bent. In addition there were the problems of long flights at night – the numbing cold, the continuous deafening noise and vibration of a piston-engined war plane (unbelievable to those whose experience of flying is confined to a holiday jet), the ever-present danger of airframe icing, failure of the oxygen supply, the strain for the pilot of flying for long periods on instruments in darkness, the worry that his home airfield could close due to bad weather. With the addition of eerie sounds of strange radio signals, soon the crews would believe that every cloud concealed a night fighter, that each searchlight was seeking them, and them alone, for the gunners below.

Here is part of a contemporary report of the fate of a Heinkel 111 G1+LK (KG55), reconstructed from the interrogation of the surviving aircrew after the aircraft crashed near Coventry. It illustrates perfectly the effect of the countering of Knickebein. The aircraft was one of a force taking part in a night raid on Birmingham, the Dieppe Knickebein was set on that city, and

'this particular aircraft had as an individual target, an aircraft factory to the north of Birmingham. . . . They picked up the beam (at 13,000 feet) over the Channel and started to fly along it. After a time the equi-signal became variable and then disappeared altogether, and no matter how they tried they could not pick it up again. Panic then seems to have overtaken the crew of the aircraft. They complained that the electrical apparatus of the aircraft had gone wrong and that neither the compass nor the artificial horizon were functioning properly and that the night was so dark the pilot could not keep the aircraft on a level course. . . . The W/T (radio) Operator, however, insists that his apparatus continued to function, which tends to disprove the notion that the electrical apparatus had gone out of order. Eventually the observer jettisoned the bombs and then he and the W/T Operator baled out. The pilot and a gunner were killed when the aircraft crashed.'[14]

That unfortunate aircraft was not shot down, or even shot at, the account contains all the classic symptoms of a pilot losing control through disorientation while blind-flying on instruments – a state of affairs precipitated initially by interference with the Knickebein beam. That Heinkel had been brought down by morse dashes radiated from a transmitter 13,000 feet below, as surely as if they had been bullets.

In this review of the undoubted success of RAF countermeasures against the Knickebein beams, one must, with regret, explode a popular misconception: the myth that the British 'bent' the beams. This was the ambition of Dr (now Sir) Robert Cockburn, one of the very able young scientists from TRE (Telecommunications Research Establishment) at Worth Matravers, who was very much concerned with the countermeasures to the beams:

'It was a very simple idea really; in the early Autumn of 1940 I had devised a scheme where a receiver on the coast near Swanage [Worth Matravers] picked up the [German] dots and then had them sent by land line to Beacon Hill, near Salisbury, where I was going to reradiate them.'[15]

Since these dots were picked up from the enemy transmission they would of course have been perfectly synchronised with the German dashes, enabling Dr Cockburn to create a false equi-signal and so truly bending the beams – even, if required, by a controlled amount – but it never happened.

'Such is the rough and tumble of war, I got all this set up and on the very night I was going to start, the telephone line [that was to relay the dots from the receiver at Swanage], for operational reasons, was pinched.'

The Aspirin asynchronous signals were by now proving effective and the 'bending' never took place.

The fact that the beams were not actually bent, however, did not prevent 80 Wing CO, Group Captain Addison, from being blamed whenever a lost German bomber jettisoned its bomb load:

'. . . these bombs were scattered all over the country and they fell in some very awkward places. I remember on one occasion some fell in the grounds of Windsor Castle. Next morning I was rung up by the very irate Comptroller of the King's Household to ask why I had dared to bend the beams over the grounds of Windsor Castle.'[7]

(Edward Addison must have been forgiven, for he retired as an Air Vice Marshal.)

The RAF was blamed by the Irish Government, too, when, as they put it, a large number of German bombers were 'diverted' to Dublin, which it was claimed was heavily bombed. Subsequent investigation revealed that one aircraft had dropped four bombs near Phoenix Park, killing twenty-eight people and injuring many more. It is likely that the lone bomber over Dublin was lost due to another British countermeasure, of which little is known even today.

In addition to the Knickebein beams, which were, strictly speaking, a bombing aid for a specific target and not a general navigational aid, the Luftwaffe had a network of Medium Frequency non-directional radio beacons (between 200–500 kHz). Some eighty of these were operational, scattered throughout German Occupied Europe. These beacons were low-powered transmitters, each of which radiated a continuous radio signal, each on its allotted frequency and identified by a call sign, usually a group of figures or letters sent automatically in slow morse every few minutes. The beacons were non-directional, in the sense that the signals they radiated had no special directional properties other than the geographical location of the transmitter; they were really radio lighthouses. The position of each of these beacons was of course marked on the German maps and known to the bomber

Above: Most German aircraft were fitted with D/F. In the Ju88 it had a remote control, enabling the pilot to rotate the loop aerial from the cockpit.

Above right: The 'Funker' (radio operator) was responsible for tuning in the correct Knickebein transmitter. The success of the 'Aspirin' jammers caused many to lose the beam.

Right: Meaconing.

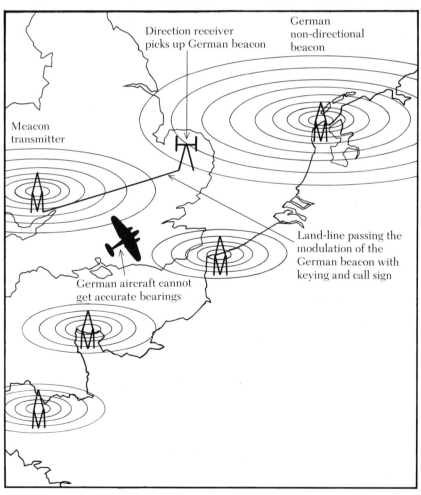

Direction receiver picks up German beacon

German non-directional beacon

Meacon transmitter

Land-line passing the modulation of the German beacon with keying and call sign

German aircraft cannot get accurate bearings

crews who, by using the direction-finding equipment in their aircraft could take bearings from them – a simple technique that was as old as radio and was in use in the First World War. By taking bearings from two or three different beacons, an aircraft could get a very reasonable 'fix' or position. The British knew this, of course (the RAF used the same technique); that is why from the outset of the war all BBC medium-wave transmitters were synchronised into groups on common frequencies. This denied the Germans the use of these powerful stations as beacons, since if several in different geographical locations were on the same frequency, it would be impossible to know which one was which. If an enemy aircraft got to within fifty miles of a BBC transmitter, then it shut down, because at that short range the ambiguities caused by the other, more distant, transmitters on the same frequency would not be very great, and unless the aircraft was hopelessly lost, the D/F operator would know which the nearest transmitter must be. The point of all this is simply that the night bomber got very little, if any, assistance from domestic medium-wave transmitters and had to rely on their own beacons.

The German beacons were countered in a very elegant way. Around the south and east coast of Britain, receivers with directional aerials were tuned to a number of enemy beacons; the received signals were then sent over GPO land-lines to counterfeit beacon transmitters in Britain which reradiated them on the same frequency and with the genuine call signs of the original beacons. It did not matter how often the enemy changed the call signs; the distant British masking beacon would change automatically since it was modulated by the output of the receivers tuned to the German transmitters. This masking of the beacons, which began in August 1940, was called 'Meaconing' and it was to be very successful.[16] A later development was to intercept radio messages from German aircrews asking a base station to take a bearing from the aircraft transmission, then 'Meacon' the aircraft transmitter, which resulted in the aircrew being given wildly incorrect positions with errors of up to 100 miles, or in some cases the confused ground stations declining to give any bearings at all.

To return to the Battle of the Beams: the situation by the beginning of September 1940 was that the Knickebein beams were proving to be of very limited use to the night-bomber force; most crews only used them at the start of their flight to assess wind drift, then flew by normal navigation, which in bad weather or on very dark nights was often inaccurate. The Aspirin countermeasures had been successful.

However, the German night bombers had not been stopped; large numbers had not been shot down; there had been very heavy raids and many people were killed. What had been achieved, nevertheless, was very important; the enemy had not been able to hit precise targets – the vital factories, airfields, railway junctions – which they could have done if the beams had not been countered.

Then, late in the afternoon of Saturday 7 September 1940, at the height of the Battle of Britain, the great air attack on London – the 'blitz' – began.

The London skyline during the blitz.

The River Thames – the unjammable beam – photographed during a raid. There was a serious proposal to camouflage rivers with coal dust: it worked well provided they were not tidal. The barrage balloons were to prevent dive-bomber attacks.

Escorted by a similar number of fighters, 625 bombers switched their attacks from airfields and bombed the docks and East End. That night the attacks continued: an endless stream of bombers – some 250 – dropped 330 tons of high explosive and thousands of incendiaries, causing nine huge fires in the East End, which were out of control. To add to the chaos, the code word 'Cromwell' was issued through a misunderstanding, causing church bells – the signal for invasion – to be rung up and down the country.

For the next fifty-seven consecutive nights, the capital was bombed from dusk to dawn: the German aircrews were following a beam which no one could jam – the River Thames. By New Year's Day 1941, some 13,000 people had been killed and 16,000 severely injured in London alone. Coastal towns –

A photograph taken at the height of the London blitz. Between 7 September and 13 November 1940 German bombers attacked the city every night except one.

Bristol, Southampton, Plymouth, Liverpool – were also heavily bombed – all targets that were relatively easy to find without the use of the beams.

In spite of these very serious raids, there was some consolation in that the vital factories in the industrial Midlands were relatively safe, due almost entirely to the defeat of the beams. But Dr Jones was worried that, although it seemed that the beams had been countered and that Knickebein and X-Geräte were one and the same thing, this had not been proved. He was on the lookout for a possible second beam system. He did not have long to wait. In the small hours of a night early in September 1940, his telephone rang. It was a colleague, Frederick Norman, a professor of German and one of the intelligence men at Bletchley Park. An Enigma intercept had been decoded, and as soon as Norman had seen it he rang Jones: 'We've got something,' he shouted into the telephone. 'God knows what it is, but I'm sure it's for you. Can you come down in the morning?'[3]

At Bletchley Park next day the translated intercept was waiting. It was the lead to the second system, the mysterious X-Geräte.

On 11 September, after his visit to Bletchley, Jones wrote an interim report based on the 'Ultra Secret' evidence which, even in that 'Most Secret' document, was guardedly ascribed to 'a completely reliable source'. The conclusion was that 'the enemy was putting the finishing touches to a group of "at least five" high-powered beam transmitters near Calais'.[17]

The beams from these new transmitters had apparently been tested over England on two or three occasions between 23 August and 6 September. They were also connected with a bomber unit based at Vannes, in northern France, and the report continued: 'The personnel concerned with these transmitters

An X-Geräte clock
from a captured
He111 of KGr100.

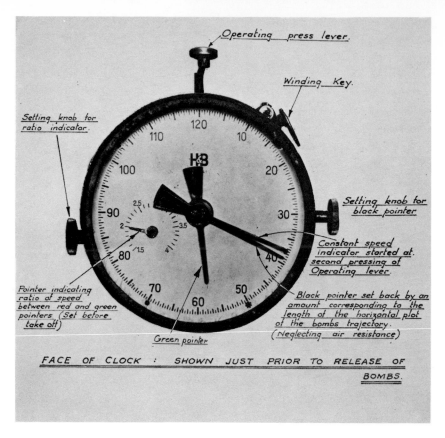

FACE OF CLOCK : SHOWN JUST PRIOR TO RELEASE OF
BOMBS.

is also concerned with the fitting of an "X-Geräte" into an aircraft [a Heinkel
111] 6N+LK.'

6N was known to be the aircraft unit code of KGr100, a unit that specialised
in blind flying. The inference Jones drew was inescapable:

'. . . the X-Geräte and KG100 are closely associated. It will be recalled that
there has already been some doubt concerning the identity of Knickebein
and the X-Geräte; it is now certain that they are not the same, although
they employ similar principles. . . . It is suggested that the X-Geräte may be a
fully automatic system of blind bombing.'

The 'Y' Service, in the course of their routine electronic surveillance, had
picked up new enemy radio transmissions on 74 mHz (4 metres) a week or so
earlier. The signals were clearly not for communication, being similar to
Knickebein and having a Lorenz characteristic, although with a different
modulation note and rate of keying of dots and dashes; they were, too, on a
much higher frequency. The 'Y' Service had reported that the signals appeared to originate from two sources, the Calais region and Le Havre, and
had concluded that they might be intended for the navigation of minelayers or
MTBs (Motor Torpedo Boats).

The discovery of these new beam signals was a disquieting one. The
Germans appeared now to be exploiting their geographical gains. They held
the whole of the coastline from Brest, on the Bay of Biscay, to Den Helder in
northern Holland: from this great arc they could set up the new beams

stations, which would not only give good intersection but, being much nearer to England than the original Knickebein beam transmitters, could employ higher frequencies, giving greater accuracy.

Before September was out, Jones had confirmation that the new beams, the X-Geräte, were beyond doubt the successors to the earlier, and now largely defeated, Knickebein. Once again Enigma was the source.

The cryptanalysts at Bletchley Park had made further decodes which formed the basis for another Air Scientific Intelligence Report from Jones.[18] This one, dated 25 September 1940 and entitled 'The X-Geräte', although classified, like the earlier report, 'Most Secret', has on the cover the clue to its Enigma-Ultra Secret origin:

'The information contained in this report comes from an extremely secret source. No further circulation of this information should therefore be made without reference to S.R.3. (Dr R. V. Jones).'

The introduction stated:

'Since the date of the first Interim Report (11.9.40) considerably more evidence has become available concerning X-Geräte. It is opportune to summarise . . . the new evidence and to give an appreciation of the present position.'

A great deal of information was apparently obtained from that Enigma intercept, for the report contained precise information about the transmitters:

'Several transmitters have been identified as being concerned in the X-Geräte operations of KGr100. In the main, they are known by the names of German rivers: Weser, Elbe, Rhein, Isar, Oder and Spree. Of these, the positions of two are known exactly:

Weser: 49°42′ 19.28″ N   1°51′24.87″ W
Spree: 49°41′ 43.13″ N   1°55′37.10″ W

They are therefore only 5.5 Kms apart, on the Hague Peninsula. Isar, Rhein and Elbe are in the Calais-Boulogne region.'

The Enigma intercept gave details of transmissions, probably testing, which had taken place on the night of 19/20 September and from these details Jones came to the conclusion that there were two types of beam, 'fine and coarse'. The coarse was thought to be the one transmitted between 65–75 mHz. The astonishing thing, however, was the degree of accuracy specified: the beams were to be directed to the nearest five seconds of arc, or 12.5 feet at 100 miles.

The coordinates of the Weser and Spree transmitters tended to support the possible accuracy. They were, Jones argued,

'given to the nearest 0.01 second, or 1 foot. . . . To measure positions to this accuracy is a tedious process; astronomical methods are known to have been employed.

'The Germans . . . will not have wasted time in unnecessary over-determination of site positions, unless their bombing method merited this accuracy. . . .

'However incredible it may seem, it must be accepted that the Germans have a method of blind bombing which they expect to be at least accurate to the nearest 10 seconds of arc, or 25 feet at 100 miles. . . .

'The accuracy of the X-Geräte system over London is expected to be of the order of 10–20 yards. A tentative method of operation is advanced involving a coarse and fine beam directed over the target, with one coarse and two fine cross beams. It is shown that this eliminates major bombing errors. The coarse beams are thought to be in the 65–75 mc/sec (mHz) band, and the fine beams on 10–50 cms.'

After considering the method of operation, which turned out to be substantially correct, Jones in his report turned to the question of countermeasures:

'If the ["fine"] transmissions are really on 10 cms we have little hope of countering them, but they may be somewhat longer. There is some hope that if the coarse beams were jammed the fine beams would be too sharp to be usable alone, so it is imperative that immediate counter action be taken against the 65–75 mc/s transmissions. A search for the fine beams could profitably be made in the equi-signal region of the coarse beams.

'At least some of the transmissions can be jammed, because it is known that there was on one occasion a complaint of jamming of the Rhein transmissions by some other German Air Signals Unit.'

The X-Geräte beams were given the code name 'River' by 80 Wing (they were also coded 'Ruffian' for a time), and they were to be used only by a specialist unit, KGr100; for, unlike the Knickebein beams which could be received by any Luftwaffe bomber on its Blind Landing set, these 'River' beams required very special equipment in the aircraft.

There were four main beams. A Directional Beam, known as the Pilot's Approach Beam, was laid exactly over the centre-line of the target from the transmitter site near Cherbourg; this bore the code name 'Weser'. Three cross-beams, coded Rhein, Oder and Elbe, were arranged to cross the main beam at certain intervals short of the target. The bombers, Heinkel 111s of KGr100, would take off from their base at Vannes in Brittany and fly the 150 miles towards Cherbourg: there the pilot's approach beam would be intercepted. This beam was very complex, since it was in reality two beams superimposed – a 'coarse' and a 'fine'. The coarse beam was, as its name implies, wide and therefore easy to locate. Once the pilot was flying in it, he would gradually align his aircraft with the fine beam; this was very narrow, with an equi-signal zone only 20–30 feet wide. These beams had the same Lorenz characteristics as Knickebeins but were not monitored aurally; the pilot and the observer had visual 'Kicking' meters which showed if the aircraft was straying from the centre of the fine beam to either left or right. The pilot was only concerned at this stage with keeping the aircraft accurately aligned with the Approach Beam, correcting for wind drift, and maintaining a given altitude.

The observer had a separate receiver; this was tuned to the cross-beams

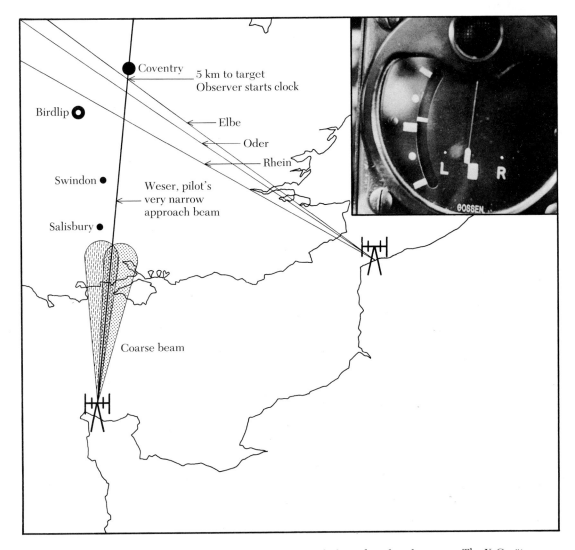

The map shows:
- Coventry — 5 km to target — Observer starts clock
- Birdlip
- Elbe
- Oder
- Rhein
- Swindon
- Weser, pilot's very narrow approach beam
- Salisbury
- Coarse beam

GOSSEN

L links R

from the Calais area. He too had a visual indicator and also a bomb-release computer, which looked like a large clock with three hands – one green, one black and one red – and was in fact clockwork. These hands were preset with the aid of charts to take into account altitude and wind speed.

Some distance from the target, the first crossbeam which intersected the approach beam was encountered; this was a coarse warning beam, coded Rhein. The pilot now had to fly very accurately along the exact centre of the directional beam. The observer was alerted for the intersecting of the second fine cross-beam, Oder (only 20–30 yards wide), thirty kilometres from the target. On intercepting this signal, he started the clock: the green and black hands now began to move together. Fifteen kilometres from the bomb release point the third beam, Elbe, was intercepted. The observer now pressed the control lever on the clock again, stopping the green and black hands (which gave the ground speed) and starting the red hand moving towards the now stationary black hand. In less than a minute, when the red and black pointers coincided, an electrical circuit was completed and the bombs were dropped.

The X-Geräte beams as they would have been set for the raid on Coventry.
Inset: An X-Geräte kicking meter. It shows the aircraft slightly left (*links*) of the beam.

The practical accuracy of this bombing system was about 100 yards at 200 miles, slightly less than that theoretically predicted by Dr Jones, but near enough, taking into account the ballistics of individual bombs and the possibility of different wind gradients during the actual drop. It was certainly the most precise method of blind bombing yet devised by any air force up to that time, and good enough to hit a large individual factory. There was some evidence that KGr100 had used X-Geräte on a small scale during an attack on Birmingham on 26 October 1940.

KGr100 was to develop a new concept of bombing, using not only the new beams but another original technique that was to have a profound effect on night bombing and one which was, ironically, to be instrumental eventually in destroying many German cities. The concept was simple. A small force of KGr100 bombers would fly the accurate X-Geräte beams and use them to drop flares and incendiary bombs to mark the target with large fires. The de-Knickebeined main force would then fly to the burning city, drawn like moths to a candle.

The use of the technique operationally on a small scale gave Jones the clue to the fire-raising activities of this specialist unit. Some senior RAF officers would not believe it, claiming that the countermeasures (to Knickebein) were so successful that the German pilots were dropping flares to see where they were! This was not, fortunately, a widely held view, for as early as 27 September, just two days after Jones's second report on the X-Geräte, a high-level conference was held

'. . . on an instruction by the Chiefs of Staff Committee to discuss the steps to be taken to counter certain German VHF Navigational Beams which it is anticipated the enemy intend to use for accurate bombing purposes over the London area.' [19]

The conference had available the views of two eminent scientists: Professor Lindemann and Professor (later Sir) Edward Appleton. At this early stage there was the possibility that the 'fine' beams might be transmitted on centimetric wavelengths around 10 cms. If that had been the case it would have been very difficult to jam them successfully (even to hear them could present difficulties; special receivers would have had to be constructed). In the meantime, the 'coarse' beams which had been intercepted in the 70–74 mHz band were to be countered by modifying a number of army gunlaying radars to operate in the same way as the successful Aspirin jammers had against Knickebein. This too was not easy, because the radar sets were designed as pulse transmitters and their efficiency was to be much reduced in their new role. These new jammers against the 'River' beams were called 'Bromide': an appropriately stronger analgesic than Aspirin.

There remained the problem of the 'fine' beams and the possibility that they could have been transmitted on centimetric wavelengths. This turned out not to be the case: the 'fine' beams were also transmitted in the 70–74 mHz band, the 'fineness' being the result of two signals superimposed in a very complex way. The ambiguity about the centimetric beams was quickly cleared up, but it was a considerable worry at the time for two reasons. Firstly, British scientists had only just managed, as we shall later learn, to generate high power on 10 cms with the newly devised and highly secret cavity magnetron. Secondly, a jammer on 10 cms would also require magnetrons, which at that time were still hardly out of the laboratory.

The magnetron was the only device that could generate high power on these extremely short wavelengths, and it was to revolutionise radar. If, as at first seemed possible, the Germans were about to transmit beams on wavelengths as short as 10 cms, then it would seem probable that they too now had a practical magnetron. The serious threat which the new beams posed, however, was such that the conference decided to release 'at least seven magnetrons immediately, six from Air Ministry Research Establishment at Worth Matravers and one from GEC'. Had this been done, it would probably have interfered with vital research into the new airborne 10-cm radars. Fortunately they were not required. (We now know that the Germans did not possess any magnetrons, nor would they until, much later in the war, RAF bombers were shot down over Germany and their magnetron-equipped H2S radars captured.)

One very interesting point emerges from a study of the minutes of this meeting: Professor Lindemann proposed a passive counter to the possible 10-cm beam, which was prophetic. He postulated that a large number of dipoles (half-wavelength aerials) cut to the frequency of the enemy beams and suspended from either balloons or the coastal radar masts 'would deviate the beams'. This proposal was in essentials anticipating 'Window' ('Chaff' in the US) – strips of aluminium foil dropped from RAF aircraft later in the war, which were an extremely effective counter to enemy radar.

The first three or four Bromide 4-metre jammers, converted from the Army radar sets, were ready in early November; just in time, for intelligence reports, mostly from Enigma intercepts, were giving indications that the X-Geräte beams and KGr100 were to be involved in a very big raid on England.

On Sunday 11 November 1940, Jones was in his office where he received an unusual signal.[3] It was an instruction to the X-Geräte beam stations to prepare for operation against three targets: Nos. 51, 52 and 53. These numbers referred to some target list the Luftwaffe had drawn up for the beam stations. There was also an order to the German Air Force as a whole about a major operation coded 'Moonlight Sonata'. Intelligence reports from prisoner of war interrogations also indicated very large-scale raids planned on the Midlands between 15 and 20 November, the period of the full moon.

At about 5.30 on 14 November, Group Captain Addison of 80 Wing rang Jones to tell him that his listening aircraft had been up and that the 'Rivers' beams seemed to be set for a town in the Midlands: could Jones let him know the Germans' target? As Jones stated in the 1977 BBC television programme *The Secret War*,

'I did not know. The Enigma had not [been] broken that night in time, although it had by the following morning . . . but that was too late. So I couldn't tell him where the target was.'

One can imagine Group Captain Addison's concern. He had only six operational Bromide jammers available that night and wanted to be sure they were used to the best effect. Apart from the lack of numbers, there was an additional problem – that of the frequency of the jammers. It was far more difficult to measure the frequency of the X-Geräte beams than those of the earlier Knickebein, due to the much shorter wavelength. To measure these very high frequencies accurately required precise wavemeters on the ground. The beam frequencies were known to be either whole or half numbers, e.g. 70 or 70.5. There were therefore some twenty possible channels.

The 80 Wing search aircraft had landed and, due to calibration errors on their receivers, which had never been designed for frequency measurement, the operators had brought back figures like 69.5 and 73.7 mHz. 69.5 should probably have been 70, but 73.7 could have been either 73.5 or 74.0. When Group Captain Addison rang and asked what frequency the jammer should be set to, Jones was presented with a dilemma:

'It was a most diabolical bit of gambling, as you can imagine, because if one's wrong then perhaps there would be 500 people dead in the morning. I did my best [and gave Addison likely frequencies] and went home, still wondering where the target was.'[3]

At that moment the aircrews of KGr100 and other Luftwaffe bomber units were climbing into their aircraft. In all, some 500 planes were bombed up and ready. The pilots and observers carried precisely-marked maps: each bomber had its individual target marked in red. The maps were all for Target 53 – the city of Coventry.

At the Luftwaffe airfield at Vannes in Brittany, on the Bay of Biscay, Horst Götz, an experienced pilot of KGr100, taxied his Heinkel 111 over the grass field. It rode easily, for it was lightly loaded, bombed up only with incendiaries and flares, as were all the bombers at Vannes that night. They all had a Viking ship painted on the aircraft side and the unit marking, '6N': the pathfinders of KGr100. These Heinkels also had three radio masts on the top of the fuselage instead of the normal one – the aerials for the X-Geräte.

Thirty-six years later Flugkapitän Horst Götz recalled that November night in 1940:

'The Coventry raid had at that time no special significance for us in KGr100. All we knew was that night various bomber squadrons would be following us and that our planes were loaded only with incendiaries.

'I see from my log book that at 1828 I was amongst the first planes to take off on this raid. However, shortly before the English coast my Heinkel developed engine trouble and I had to turn back. The weather was good and I got back all right.'[20]

The Heinkels of KGr100 would have slowly climbed over Brittany to about 16,000 feet and then set a cruising speed of around 230 mph, faster than the Heinkels of the normal bomber units, being lightly loaded. The aircraft flew

A Heinkel 111 KGr100, probably photographed in Norway where the unit was stationed before their attacks on England. The Viking ship emblem of KGr100 can be seen on the side of the cockpit. The aircraft is equipped with X-Geräte and the additional aerial mast is clearly visible.

An observer in an He111 map-reading by moonlight. Although it is not possible to say that this photograph was taken on the actual Coventry raid, conditions were perfect that night and the full moon was bright enough for map-reading.

The cockpit of an He111. Surprisingly, not one of the 499 bombers in the raid on Coventry was attacked by night fighters.

in a long loose stream, each about ten miles apart. Over the Channel the 'coarse' Weser beam from the transmitter near Cherbourg would be picked up, although the bombers would fly well to one side or the other, crossing the Dorset coast between Swanage and the Isle of Wight. (Just before this point Horst Götz was forced to turn back.)

The remaining twelve Pathfinders flew on. That brilliant moonlit night the crews were expecting heavy attacks from night fighters but, in spite of this exceptional visibility, no attacks were made. This was surprising, since the night was so light that the observers, prone in the glazed noses of the Heinkels, were able to map-read the moonlit countryside 16,000 feet below as if by day.

The bombers would have had their engines desynchronised over England. This was done to counter the sound locaters that were thought by the German Air Force to be used to detect their aircraft (some detectors were still in use in 1940, but probably as a cover for radar; they were useless as an anti-aircraft ranging system). This desynchronising was very unpopular with the aircrews since it caused the whole bomber to vibrate in sympathy with the pulsing of the engines. Far below, the deep rhythmic throb of the out-of-phase engines was a characteristic of German bombers, well remembered by those who heard it; it was frequently used to differentiate, rather unreliably, between 'ours' and 'theirs'.

The track of the 'fine' Weser approach beam on the night of 14/15 November 1940 was 006° True, passing a mile or two to the east of Salisbury over the White Horse Hills, near Lambourn, then over the Cotswolds to Coventry. The bombers must have crossed the Thames about ten miles to the east of Witney and the observers would then be watching the visual indicator for the first of the crossbeams, 'Rhein' from Calais; the interception point was somewhere over Chipping Norton. That night the X-Geräte in the twelve Heinkels of KGr100 worked well; the first of the flares and incendiaries fell on their targets in the city at about 7.10 BST.

Fires quickly started – beacons for the main-force bombers that were following the pathfinders. This new technique of using specialist units with highly accurate navigation aids to locate and mark individual targets was to alter the whole concept of night bombing. Innovated by KGr100 over Coventry, it was later to be perfected with terrible consequences for the Germans by the RAF Pathfinders over the Reich.

For ten hours through the night of 14/15 November, 499 Luftwaffe bombers kept up the attack; their targets included five major factories producing aircraft engines and components. Günther Unger, an Unteroffizier who piloted a Dornier 17 of KG76 that night, had taken off at about one o'clock and remembers that

'the raid took place in exceptionally good weather – we started at Abbeville directly on the coast and as we were flying over the Channel we could clearly see Coventry burning. We had no need of radio aids.

'I attacked at around two-thirty and by then there was no defence. The

A Dornier 17 of the type which Günther Unger flew on the Coventry raid. The Do17 was already obsolescent and was being withdrawn from front-line bomber squadrons operating over Britain by the end of 1940, to be replaced by the Ju88.

flight had been routine, there was very little flak and no night fighters and when we reached the target there was a huge sea of flames. I have never seen such a concentration of fire during a raid, not even on London. Usually in our target cities the area of fires was dispersed, but not this time. There was no chance of missing the target.'[20]

Official reports published after the war put the weight of the attack at 503 tons of high explosive – some 1500 bombs, 50 landmines of 2000 lbs each, and probably up to 30,000 incendiaries:

'. . . At a very rough estimate one third of the factories in the city [were] either completely demolished or so damaged as to be out of commission . . .'.[21]

In addition, over 500 people were killed and more than 1200 injured. The damage to private property was heavy: 60,000 buildings, which included three-quarters of the city's private houses and the Cathedral.

The KGr100 stream passed very close to two of the six Bromide jammers that night: one on Birdlip Hill, near Gloucester, had only been in operation since 3 November: it was about twenty-five miles from the Weser beam. Even nearer was the Kenilworth jammer; it was only three miles from the centre of the beam; this transmitter had been in operation for just a week on the night of the raid. There was a third Bromide at Hagley, midway between Coventry and Birmingham. This was the first to go into operation (on 1 November). The remaining jammers, at Kidsgrove, near Crewe, and Windlesham, Surrey (this one had only become operational that night), were not really in range.

Near or far, none of these jammers caused the needles of the X-Geräte indicators in the Heinkels so much as to flicker; nor did the pilots and observers hear any interference in their headsets. It is fair to ask why the countermeasures had failed, enabling this very heavy attack on Coventry to be made.

The reaction of Dr Jones, who, it will be remembered, had had to make the very difficult decision about the frequencies to which the Bromides had been set, was that he had been wrong. In fact this was not the case. The 'Y' Service had monitored the beams in use during the raid and could confirm that the jammers were on the right channels as predicted by Jones, but – and this is a very large but – the frequency of the modulation, that is the note of the Bromides' false dashes, was incorrect. They had been set up very quickly (one that night) and someone had set the modulation to 1500 Hz. The new X-Geräte beam note was higher: 2000 Hz.

So the Bromides were ineffective. If the three near the beams, Birdlip Hill, Kenilworth and Hagley, had been transmitting the correct note, the X-Geräte beams could have been rendered ineffective, or at least less effective. It was, it is true, an exceptionally bright night; even so there could have been a chance that some at least of the KGr100 pathfinders could have gone astray and dropped incendiaries on the wrong target. As it was, the whole force had unerringly found their correct targets.

The failure of the countermeasures was due to a most unfortunate mistake – and an inexcusable one, for to measure the audio frequency of the beams only required a VHF receiver, a variable frequency audio-oscillator, and a reasonable ear. The local signal produced by the oscillator is made to 'beat' with the unknown frequency from the receiver until it is in 'tune'; the calibration of the oscillator will then give the frequency of the received signal. Anyone not totally tone deaf could achieve this in under a minute.

The difference between 2000 and 1500 Hz is not very great, and it could be argued that, listening in a piston-engined bomber, the difference would pass unnoticed, but, as we have seen, the beams' signals were not being monitored by human ears alone; the meter was the main indication and the jammers had not had any effect on this because of certain safeguards in the receivers. At the time of the Coventry raid, 80 Wing knew nothing of these safeguards; they could have done but for a very unfortunate series of events.

Eight days before the Coventry raid, in the small hours of 6 November, a Heinkel 111, lost and out of fuel, was force-landed by its crew in shallow water at West Bay, near Bridport. One member of the crew was killed in the crash, but the other three waded ashore and gave themselves up. The men were surprised to find their captors English: they had thought that they had been flying over Spain when they had run out of fuel. This minor success of RAF 'meaconing' of the German beacon at St Malo was to have unforeseen effects.

The wrecked bomber was stranded between the high- and low-water marks. An Army unit stationed nearby waited for the tide to recede, mounted an armed guard and began recovery work. At this point, the Navy showed up with an inshore vessel and claimed the Heinkel as a Navy prize, the Captain pointing out that the wreckage was below the high-tide mark.

The Army officer in charge seems to have been outranked, for he released the mooring ropes and the Navy began to heave the Heinkel towards the ship, with the object presumably of securing it alongside. The rope parted and the aircraft, not surprisingly, sank into West Bay for the second time. At this the

Opposite: The versatile Ju88 night bomber was one of the most successful German designs. The 1940 variant, powered by two Junkers Jumo 211 J-1 12-cylinder, liquid-cooled engines of 1340 hp', had a top speed of nearly 300 mph at 17,000 feet – very fast for a bomber – enabling it to evade RAF Blenheim night fighters with ease. Note the external bomb racks.

Navy seem to have lost interest; at all events the Army eventually got the, by now, very bent bomber on to the beach above the high-tide mark.

When an officer from the Air Force Technical Intelligence got to it, he quickly realised that this was no ordinary Heinkel. It carried the code 6N+BH and on its nose was painted a Viking ship in sail. Most important of all, on the top of its battered fuselage were three vertical aerials: it was from KGr100 and it was equipped with the highly secret X-Geräte.

Left: Bristol Blenheims, powered by two 840-hp Bristol Mercury VIII engines, had a maximum speed of 260 mph. 200 of these bombers were converted into night fighters with kits supplied by the Southern Railway.

80 Wing Periodical Report No. 12, written on 27 November, twenty-one days after the bomber had crashed, noted:[22]

'During the week some very valuable finds have been made amongst the jetsom on the Bridport Beach. These are the two beam receivers . . . the 'clock' from the KGr100 He111 aircraft that came down in the sea on 6 November. Fortunately their robust structure had very well withstood the battering they have received and investigation of the apparatus is now proceeding. . . . One of the receivers . . . has now been sent to RAE [Farnborough] for careful examination of the components, from which it will be possible to gauge the sensitivity and selectivity of the instrument – knowledge which will more readily enable us to determine the extent of the interference that our 'Bromides' are likely to produce. . . .'

The answer was to be depressingly little, for it was revealed that the sets had a very narrow band-pass filter in the audio output, which was centred on 2000 Hz with a tolerance of $\pm$ 50 Hz. Therefore the Bromide jammers with the dashes modulated at 1500 Hz might just as well not have been switched on; their signals would have had no effect at all. Since the visual indicators and the crews' headsets were *after* the filter, none of the bogus dashes would be either seen or heard.

Sir Robert Cockburn was at that time with the Counter Measures Unit at the TRE (Telecommunication Research Establishment) at Worth Matravers and he was

'really quite appalled to hear that such a gross boob had been made. It must have been a failure of communication; somebody rung up and given the wrong frequency.

'Now the question arises, would the Coventry raid have been as destructive as it was if we had jammed [the beams] with the correct modulation. It was a bright moonlight night, I remember it very well because I was returning from London and the moon was shining all over the New Forest. The bombers were going over . . . it was a very, very clear bombing night. So I'm not so certain that they would not have got away with it perfectly well even if the beams had been jammed. On the other hand I'm not certain they would have got the accuracy; they were extremely accurate on Coventry, and that was a direct result of having uninhibited use of X-Geräte.'[23]

The Germans were to enjoy the use of X-Geräte for some time. The question of the modulation having been solved, the next problem was to get sufficient Bromide transmitters for effective jamming. There were eventually seventeen of them, but it was not until early December that the last one, at Loughborough, was operational. Heavy attacks on Bristol, Portsmouth, Birmingham and Liverpool and a very heavy 300-bomber raid on Sheffield were to follow. 'It seems', 80 Wing reported on 3 January, 'that KGr100 continue to reach their target under all but the very worst conditions. . . .'

Gradually, as RAF techniques improved, it seemed that some success was being achieved in the Radio War. It was, in any event, being claimed. In a secret review, 'Radio Counter Measures, June 1940 to April 1941',[24] the anonymous author stated (somewhat paradoxically) that:

> 'the success of radio counter measures had, to some extent, been nullified by reason of the large fires started by the fire raisers of the German Air Force, and which acted as an excellent guide to the target for the remainder of the raiding aircraft.'

The fact that only KGr100 were using X-Geräte, and its sole purpose was to enable them to start fires, would seem to make the claimed success of the countermeasures a distinctly qualified one.

To be fair, Knickebein was by that time very well jammed and the main force bombers were denied its use other than in the early stages of their flight – doubtless the sole reason for the continuance of the system. If, however, the Bromide jammers were claimed as successful, how were KGr100 finding the targets in 'all but the worst conditions'?

It should be borne in mind that the concept of pathfinding was based on a very small number (just over 2% at Coventry) of highly-skilled pilots and navigators, *aided* by X-Geräte beams to find and mark the target. Horst Götz stated in an interview (in 1976) that the pathfinding duties of KGr100 were in addition to other duties;[25] he mentioned, for example, flying over the Atlantic on anti-shipping sorties which called for the highest navigational skills. He went on:

> '. . . the crews . . . were all old experienced sergeants, sergeant majors or officers, who had trained before the war. They had relatively few casualties: experienced crews were lost every now and again but not through navigation or flying difficulties. It was our new replacement crews who had the high casualties.'

Götz himself seems to bear this out: he had well over 1200 hours of combat time in his log book before attacking Britain in 1940, and went on to become a jet test pilot and was flying an operational Arado 234 Jet over England in late 1944.

Pilots of that calibre would squeeze the last operational ounce out of the beams and the jamming could never, with the resources available in 1940, be 100 per cent efficient. Even had they been, then many of the KGr100 crews, as the RAF Pathfinders did later in the war, would have reached the targets by conventional navigation. The normal Luftwaffe bomber units, many of which had suffered heavy losses of experienced crews during the daylight battles, were now using hastily trained replacements. With the Knickebein countered, these young pilots and observers to a large extent relied on the KGr100 fire-raising to mark their targets.

This was realised by the countermeasures staff and a new phase of this war of move and countermove was entered: Operation Starfish. Since the enemy airmen were being guided by fires, the obvious counter was another fire. Big fires were lit in open spaces around possible target areas to confuse the bomber crews. These fires were known as 'Starfish'. They were used quite successfully for, in those early days of mass-bombing attacks, the raids were spread over as much as ten hours, each aircraft making its own way to the target. Thus, even if the skilled sergeants of KGr100 marked the correct target, there was always the chance that following aircraft with less experienced crews, human nature being what it is, would bomb the first likely fire they saw and this is just what happened.[26] 80 Wing, who controlled the decoys, reported:

'Starfish have attracted the attention of the enemy on numerous occasions, drawing a considerable number of bombs. On the other hand, there have been some occasions, particularly when visibility conditions were good, when Starfish were ignored. Outstanding successes were achieved at Cardiff on 4 March [1941], at Bristol on 16 March and at Portsmouth on 17 April. On the first occasion Home Security Specialists reported that no less than 102 high explosive bombs had been aimed at the Starfish. The total weight of bombs being 25 tons. . . . 300 bombs were dropped on the Downside Starfish, Bristol. . . . The largest number of bombs ever [up to April 1941] collected by a decoy fire fell on the Sinah Common Starfish near Portsmouth. No less than 170 bombs, 26 landmines, 20 oil bombs and innumerable incendiary bombs were dropped, representing 95% of the enemy effort against Portsmouth.'

The decoy sites, designed by an Army officer, Colonel Turner, started operating in January 1941. He had arranged a network of perforated pipes, laid out to resemble an industrial target; oil was pumped through the pipes and then ignited to give the appearance of a typical fire raid. To make the decoy more convincing, jets of water played at intervals on the fires to simulate roofs collapsing and minor explosions. This was achieved by using municipal automatic lavatory cisterns, flushing at intervals.

These sites were often manned by RAF corporals, who sat in a dug-out and controlled the oil fires by remote electrical igniters. It must have been a most unpopular posting but, according to the recollection of Air Vice Marshal Addison in 1976, they had no casualties: 'We used to ring up to ask how they were getting on. I won't repeat what they said.'[7]

As a postscript to Starfish, Colonel Turner was also responsible for the 'Q' Sites. These were decoy airfields with flare-paths and dummy wooden aircraft, which were built at £50 a time in film studios' scenery workshops (including the Gaumont British Studio in Lime Grove). The sites seem to have been successful and were attacked: they were even realistic enough for some RAF aircraft to attempt to land on them. The Germans, however, discovered the location of some of the sites, and there is a delightful story that a Ju88 dived out of cloud one day and dropped a bomb on a 'Q' site among the dummy wooden aircraft. The bomb did not go off; it too was made of wood. One hopes that story is true.

In addition to what could be described as these defensive countermeasures, there were also offensive actions against the beam transmitters themselves. Between the beginning of December and Christmas Day 1940, ten sorties were flown by Whitley bombers of 109 Squadron against the

Cherbourg 'River' stations. The raids were flown in appalling weather and the results were inconclusive. Only once did the stations go off the air, but due to the very bad visibility it was uncertain if this was because of the bombing or the transmitters being switched off to deny the attacking aircraft the use of the beams as a bombing aid in reverse.

As the Germans had found during the early stages of the Battle of Britain, radio or radar transmitters were very unrewarding targets, being hard to hit and, even when they were, they were soon either repaired or duplicate equipment quickly placed in service.

By the New Year of 1941 the night-bomber force of the Luftwaffe was still formidable: they had 550 front-line aircraft serviceable and, although the counters to X-Geräte were now showing signs of success at last, the night bombers were still not defeated. The 'Y' Service 'watchers', as they were called, had found new beam-like signals transmitted on a new frequency band – 40–60 mHz. The Battle of the Beams was about to enter its third and final phase.

As early as July 1940, an Enigma message was intercepted to the effect that 'it is proposed to set up Knickebein and "Wotan" anlagen [installations] near Cherbourg and Brest'. On learning this, Dr R. V. Jones sought out his colleague Professor Norman in Enigma Intelligence at Bletchley Park, and asked him if there was anything odd about 'Wotan':

'He said, "Well, he was head of the German Gods." Then he said, "Wait a minute, one eye! One beam!" He shouted down the telephone. "One beam! Can you make a system work with one beam?" And I said I could use a beam in the ordinary way and then for example we could use the ranging system mentioned in the Oslo Report. He said "That will be it!" and so we started to look. . . .'[3]

Then in November another Enigma message was deciphered. The message was addressed to a known beam station site and simply said: 'Target No. 1 for Y', followed by a set of coordinates. Now it was known to Intelligence that Target No. 1 was the Royal Armoured Corps Bovingdon depot in Dorset, but what Jones considered significant was the fact that the message had been sent to just one station and gave only a single set of coordinates for the target location, which meant that whatever this unknown system was it only required a single station and therefore it was possibly a single beam. Confirmation which pointed to a new beam came on the night of 21/22 December. RAF Radio Surveillance at Kingsdown in Kent intercepted a message to a German aircraft over Southend. Its ground station had signalled, 'Turn round and make a new approach'; then 'measurement impossible, carry out task on your own'. The Kingsdown station then received rapid dashes on 43 mHz; a D/F bearing was taken, which passed through Poix, near Amiens. That night another 'Y' Service listening post at Hawkinge in Kent received the dots on the same frequency.

Next night a Whitley of 109 Squadron took off from Wyton and found beam signals on 43 mHz coming from Poix; the pilot reported difficulty in distinguishing dots from dashes owing to the high keying rate.

From other ground listening and further Enigma intercepts it was becoming clear that these signals were yet a third beam system: the 'Y'-Geräte or 'Wotan'. It was coded 'Benito' by 80 Wing and immediately the RCM group at the Telecommunication Research Establishment at Worth Matravers led by Dr Robert Cockburn got to work to devise a counter. The signals were very complex; so complex that it was obvious from the start that they could only be interpreted by some form of visual indicator. By the end of January 1941, the scientists at TRE had been able to analyse the wave-form of the Benito signal on a cathode-ray tube, to assess its method of operation and to devise a counter.

'Benito' was by far the most ingenious of the three beams, yet paradoxically it would be the easiest to jam. In essence it was much as the Bomber Guidance System described in the Oslo Report: that too had been a single-beam system. A ground station in northern France transmitted a double signal – one for range and the other for direction. All the signals in the Y-Geräte system were transmitted on frequencies between 42.1 and 47.9 mHz, around 7 metres. (This choice of wavelength was, as we shall see, unfortunate.) The range station transmitted a steady signal of 3 kHz (a fairly high whistle): this signal was also keyed to pass instructions to the aircraft by morse code. When the aircraft required a range report, that is how far it was away from the ground station, the steady note was changed for a much lower one of only 300 Hz.

The signal was picked up by the aircraft's receiver and then reradiated on a slightly different frequency, about 3 mHz away, back to the ground station. The ground station displayed the waveform of the original audio signal and the retransmitted one on a cathode-ray tube and compared the phase difference, which gave the transit time of the signal from ground to aircraft and back. This enabled the operators to measure very accurately how far the aircraft was away. The order of accuracy was 100 yards at 250 miles.

That is only part of the story: there was another station which transmitted the directional beam in the form of a highly complex signal. In essence it was a Lorenz type of beam but the keying was of the order of 180 a minute. The Left/Right impulses were distinguished by the relationship of the dots to a synchronising pulse which could only be interpreted by an automatic device which decoded the signals. This device not only gave a visual indication on a Left/Right meter, but could also steer the aircraft via the autopilot, which could maintain it on the beam far more accurately than any pilot. Over the target the bombs would be dropped by ground-station command.

The system, ingenious though it undoubtedly was, had three basic flaws:
1. It was a transponder; that is, it required the aircraft to radiate a radio signal, which could be used by a night fighter to 'home' on to.
2. It was automatic, and automatic systems are often easier to deceive than those with a human observer.

3. Being ground-controlled, any one station could only handle one bomber at a time and the communication channel would be potentially easy to jam.

Within two months of the first Y-Geräte signals being identified, the system was countered. It was very simply done, and done so subtly that at first the Germans did not realise that it was being interfered with at all.

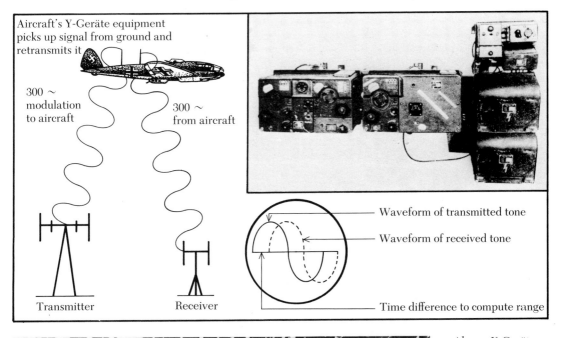

Aircraft's Y-Geräte equipment picks up signal from ground and retransmits it

300 ~ modulation to aircraft

300 ~ from aircraft

Transmitter

Receiver

Waveform of transmitted tone

Waveform of received tone

Time difference to compute range

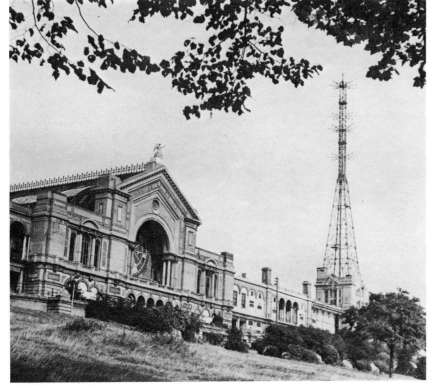

Above: Y-Geräte.

Inset: Airborne Y-Geräte equipment. Unlike earlier beam systems it was automatic, and therefore fairly easy to jam without the operators being aware.

Left: The prewar BBC Television transmitter at Alexandra Palace in North London which was used to jam Y-Geräte.

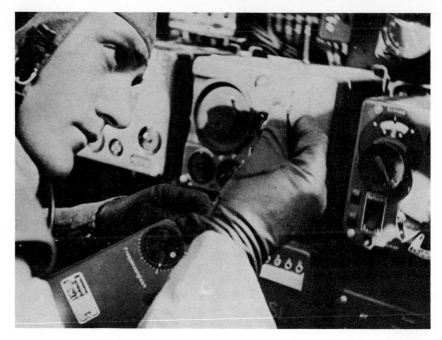

Y-Geräte was countered so subtly that German aircrews thought that their own equipment was faulty.

A receiving station at a BBC site in Swains Lane, Hampstead, picked up the ranging signal from the aircraft: it was sent by an existing land-line to the powerful, but until then dormant BBC television transmitter at Alexandra Palace a mile or so away. This powerful transmitter was designed to work on 45 mHz and that was soon converted to the Y-Geräte ground-station frequencies and reradiated the ranging signal from the aircraft. This unscheduled BBC transmission caused severe ambiguities to arise and, since this subtle counter was not obvious to the enemy, there soon arose a good deal of mistrust between the ground stations and the aircraft, each accusing the other of having faulty equipment.

A second 'Domino' station, as the counters to the 'Y' beams were coded, was constructed on Beacon Hill, near Salisbury, with Alexandra Palace giving complete coverage over Southern England.

As it happened, the countermeasure to these beams was put into operation the very night that KG26, who had been issued with brand-new Heinkels installed with the 'Y' beam equipment, tried to use it operationally as pathfinders. They very quickly gave up. Later, when a captured 'Y' beam aircraft installation was examined, it was found that it could have been jammed another way. This was due to a lapse on the part of the designers of the directional part of the device, with the result that a very small radio signal, only one tenth of the strength of the beam, could jam the vital synchronising pulse, thus rendering the beam useless. This could have been avoided by the Germans by the inclusion of two small components.

By March 1941 the German night blitz was virtually over; the three beam systems had been countered and by then the RAF night fighters were beginning to get into their stride. A new aircraft – the Bristol Beaufighter – with an efficient new Airborne Interception Radar, AI Mark IV, together with improved Ground Controlled Interception Radar, were shooting down night bombers in significant numbers.

Just when the scientists were wondering what would happen next, the unbelievable occurred. In May the German night bombers left their bases all over Western Europe to fly East – to Russia. The bombers would return in the later years of the war but by that time RAF air superiority was such that they were never again the force or the threat they had been in 1940. The Battle of the Beams was over.

It had been a decisive battle, the first of its kind to be fought. It has been said that the First World War was fought by chemists and the Second by physicists. The scientists of TRE and the men and women of 80 Wing won this first round. They were, of course, helped by Intelligence, particularly Enigma, and, if mistakes were made, it should be remembered that this vital struggle was fought at a time of great hardship. Britain was facing almost certain defeat in the winter of 1940–1: invasion was expected at any time up to the end of September and the country stood alone against the most efficient war machine the world had yet seen. Germany had long been actively preparing for war; their beams were set up, tested and refined as early as 1938. All the counters were conceived and put into operation in weeks, sometimes in days, so that it is not surprising that mistakes were made; indeed the wonder is that they succeeded at all – but they did.

Just how important had this silent, secret, second Battle of Britain been? Professor R. V. Jones, who fought this battle from the first, puts it this way:

'This had been our only defence; night fighters, until airborne radar was good enough, were powerless, anti-aircraft guns were inaccurate, therefore we could not stop the bombers. Our only hope was to throw them off. Well, we didn't always succeed but we did certainly on a fair number of occasions, with the result that a good many people were alive at the end of the war who otherwise wouldn't have been and a good deal less vital damage was done. . . . If one thinks of what could have happened if with Knickebein all the German Air Force could have bombed accurately. Well, we saw what happened when things went wrong as at Coventry. . . . That could have happened every night.'[3]

The giant German airship 'Graf Zeppelin', which made two flights off the east coast of England in the summer of 1939 to try to intercept and analyse the pulses of the RAF's early warning radar.

2. RADAR

In the spring of 1939 reports were reaching General Wolfgang Martini, the Luftwaffe head of signals, that a number of tall masts were being erected on British coastal sites between the Isle of Wight and the Firth of Forth. The masts were usually in groups of three; they were 350 feet high and the stations below them were known to be manned by the RAF. Clearly their purpose was connected with some form of military radio, radar being considered a likely possibility.

German radar was at that time showing very promising results and, not unnaturally, it was a matter of some importance to the Luftwaffe to try to discover if the British had an operational radar network comparable with their own.

The task was not that simple. All radar work in Britain, as elsewhere, was a closely guarded state secret and, although the German civil airline DLH (Deutsche Lufthansa) had been in the habit of making their landfalls en route to Croydon over the first of these strange stations at Bawdsey, near Felixstowe, little was discerned that was of any use to the German scientists. The tall masts seemed all wrong for radar. The German equipment operated on very short wavelengths – around 50 centimetres – and their aerials were in the form of parabolas; it was assumed therefore that the British were a very long way behind, for no parabolas were seen. Nevertheless, the tall and numerous masts were supporting aerials for some reason and it was decided, at a high-level meeting in Berlin, to try to discover their purpose by flying along the British coast on what must have been the first scientific intelligence flight.

The ideal vehicles for this electronic interrogation, General Martini pointed out, were to hand: the recently retired 776-foot Zeppelins, LZ127 and LZ130. LZ130, 'Graf Zeppelin', was overhauled and fitted with ultra-high-frequency radio receivers, cathode-ray tubes and aerials. Skilled signals personnel led by the General himself were on board when, at the end of May 1939, the giant airship slipped from its mooring mast at Frankfurt and headed west for the Suffolk coast and the Bawdsey Research Station.

Off the British coast, the signallers tuned their sets across the ultra-high-frequency bands that would, it was thought, be the most likely to yield the tell-tale pulses of British radar. Bawdsey was a disappointment, however, producing nothing but static. The Graf Zeppelin then slowly flew north, parallel to the East Coast and just far enough out from land to remain unobserved; but observed it was – though not visually. Beneath the tall masts at station after station, the RAF operators watched the stately progress of LZ130 as the biggest blip they had yet seen on their radar.

On board the airship, General Martini and his crew were still only receiving static, their cathode-ray tubes showing a meaningless clutter of random radio noise. Near Hull, the Graf Zeppelin transmitted its position back to Germany – incorrectly; the radar men below knew it was some miles out but, although sorely tempted, thought in the circumstances it was better not to transmit a correction. . . .

Another Zeppelin flight was made in August; again no pulse signals were detected and the Germans therefore concluded that the British had as yet no operational radar. At that moment the Battle of Britain was half won.

Just why the German interrogation flights failed to detect the British radar, which had gone on to a continuous 24-hour watch on Good Friday 1939, remains one of the minor mysteries of the Second World War. It is true they had had trouble with some of the equipment aboard the Zeppelins, but that could only be a partial explanation. The real reason is probably very simple: German radar operated between $1\frac{1}{2}$ metres and 50 centimetres; British on the (to the Germans) unbelievably long wavelength of 10 metres. General Martini's men had been searching the wrong wavebands.

British radar had begun as a concept in 1934. Dr H. E. Wimperis, then Director of Scientific Research, Air Ministry, was only too well aware that little was being done in the way of scientific research for defence against air attack. The RAF fighter squadrons of the day were fabric-covered, wire-braced biplanes, operating out of neat grass airfields dotted around the country: they looked well enough, those Gloster Gauntlets, Bristol Bulldogs, Hawker Furies and Demons, brightly painted with checkerboard squadron markings, as they went through their aerobatics over Hendon at the annual Air Displays. But, however well flown, they were in essentials simply improved versions of the fighters that had flown over the Western Front twenty years earlier, and their tactics were as obsolete as the aircraft.

Air defence in the 1930s relied on the concept of the 'standing patrol' – that is, squadrons of fighter aircraft patrolling areas through which it was assumed enemy bombers would have to pass. When the fuel of the patrol was running low, and a typical endurance would be only about one hour at operational height, then another squadron would take over the patrol while the first one refuelled, and so on.

Such an inefficient system was very costly in aircraft, engine hours and, of course, fuel. To overcome the obvious and inherent weakness an alternative was proposed: the fast-climbing 'Interceptor' fighter. These were fast fighter aircraft which could wait on their airfields until enemy bombers were approaching, then take off and climb rapidly to intercept the enemy formations. The first of these interceptors was the Hawker Fury, an elegant biplane that could climb to 10,000 feet in $4\frac{1}{2}$ minutes and which was, by the standards of the day, fast, being the first RAF fighter to exceed 200 mph in level flight (its

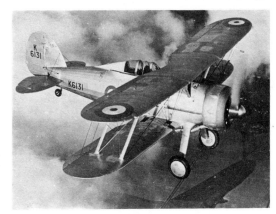

Between the wars RAF aircraft were largely biplanes, differing little from the machines that had fought in the last years of the 1914–18 War. Though now constructed from steel instead of wood, they were still fabric-covered and wire-braced. All the Hawker aircraft above came from the drawing board of Sidney Camm, who went on to design the Hurricane.

Top left: The Hawker Fury Mk I was powered by a 525-hp Rolls-Royce Kestrel engine, giving it a maximum speed of 207 mph.

Top right: The 'High Speed' Hawker Fury, K3586, was an experimental fighter with a maximum speed – in 1933 – of 220 mph.

Middle left: The Hawker Hart, a light day bomber. This highly successful aircraft, designed round the Kestrel engine, was to be adapted by the RAF to numerous other roles.

Middle right: The Hawker Audax, one of the 'Hart variants', was primarily equipped for army co-operation but was also used for training.

Bottom left: The Hawker Demon, another Hart variant, revived the concept of the two-seater fighter which had successfully been used in 1914–18.

Bottom right: The Gloster Gladiator, the last of the biplane fighters to take part in the war. It was powered by an 840-hp Bristol Mercury engine with a maximum speed of 253 mph.

maximum speed was 207 mph at 14,000 feet). These aircraft served as front-line fighters from 1931, until replaced by the Hurricane in 1939, and were thought to be fast enough to catch the slow, lumbering bombers of an attacking enemy. Just how that enemy would first be located was not clear, nor what would happen if they came in bad weather or at night.

Radio and navigation equipment was rudimentary in RAF fighters between the wars. Blind-flying instruments were by no means universal, and the radio sets installed were, in the words of Dr (now Sir Robert) Cockburn,

'beyond belief; the standard airborne set consisted of a box which had a 120-volt battery and two bright emitter valves and I remember the way you tested these parts, before you put them back in the aircraft, was to take the two valves out and drop them on the table and bounce them, Boing! and catch them and if they did not break you put them back and the sets would pass as serviceable. It was almost unbelievable how naïve and elementary the equipment was.'[1]

If the aids for the fighter pilots were limited, then those of the Army's anti-aircraft gunners were even more so. It had been planned that, when enemy aircraft approached, the AA batteries would receive an 'area warning' from visual spotters – men with telescopes who presumably spent their time gazing at the sky. Even when the weather was fine the maximum range they could hope to achieve was unlikely to exceed 12,000 feet. When a target was located and speed and bearing worked out from mechanical predictors, the next task was to determine height and range; this was achieved, weather permitting, with an optical rangefinder, which even under ideal conditions was subject to the immutable law that the error in a given range-reading is proportional to the square of the range: which meant that a range reading on a single aircraft could be in error by as much as 2250 feet.

Gloster Gauntlets. From 1935 to 1937 they were the fastest fighters in service, their Bristol Mercury radial engines giving a top speed of 230 mph. Gauntlets were used in the earliest radar experiments from Biggin Hill.

At night or in bad weather the only possible detection of approaching aircraft was by sound location. This method, essentially a microphone in a parabolic reflector, had been developed during the 1930s to the highest possible degree and remained next to useless. In the first place, any wind caused difficulty, as did extraneous noise from railways or traffic; but the most crippling disadvantage was the simple fact that sound travels at more or less 750 mph and, by the time the aircraft's engine noise had reached the locator, it was largely historical. An aircraft flying at a range of 12,000 yards, the theoretical limit of the system, would have its engine noise detected – in round figures – thirty seconds later: if the bomber was flying at only 150 mph, it would have travelled $1\frac{1}{4}$ miles in that time. Add to this the unknown variables caused by temperature, humidity and wind, and one can begin to appreciate the considerable flaws inherent in sound location as a detection system.

By the mid 1930s the Germans were openly rearming and in America a new generation of all-metal monoplane airliners with retractable undercarriages, the Boeing 247 and the Douglas DC2, were breaking records and flying at speeds and heights that would make them virtually impossible to intercept with the standard fighters and detecting techniques of the day. Not that the Americans were regarded as a potential enemy, but the trends in aircraft design were obvious, and would not be lost elsewhere.

It was against this background that Dr Wimperis was urgently pursuing any possible methods of improving British defences against air attack – a possibility that was becoming daily less unlikely.

The popular press in the 1930s made much of the radio 'Death Ray': stories were written about mad professors stopping motor cars and destroying aircraft. It was all nonsense, of course – or was it? Seeking enlightenment, or

A sound locator, typical of those still in use in the early years of the war, possibly as a cover for radar rather than a practical aircraft-warning system. Its operator had to judge the direction of enemy aircraft from the strength of the engine noise.

possible reassurance, Harry Wimperis wrote to the best possible man, Robert Watson Watt, who in 1934 was heading a group of young scientists at the Radio Research Station, Slough, a department of the National Physical Laboratory. Wimperis asked Watson Watt's opinion on the possibility of 'destruction by radio'.

Watson Watt asked one of his scientists, Arnold Wilkins, to make certain calculations:

> 'I received the request on a piece of torn off calendar. Watson Watt liked using that sort of thing being an economical Scotsman. The request I soon deduced was to assess the feasibility of a Death Ray, as he was asking me to calculate the amount of radio energy which must be radiated to raise the temperature of a man's blood to fever heat at a certain distance.'[2]

It took Arnold Wilkins less than half an hour to work out that the amount of energy required would be impossibly large. He took the calculations back to Watson Watt, who agreed with the conclusion and asked Wilkins if there was any other way they could help the Air Ministry.

Arnold Wilkins remembered that a year or so earlier he had heard of a report from the Post Office that aircraft flying in the path of an early and experimental VHF radio telephone link had caused severe fluctuations and fading of the signal. He suggested to Watson Watt that this effect might form the basis of a possible aircraft detection system. Watson Watt thought the proposal interesting and sent Wilkins away to make further calculations.

An important factor in the solving of the problem was the size of the aircraft that the system would have to detect. This Wilkins based on a typical heavy bomber then in service with the RAF, the Handley Page Heyford which, although it was fabric-covered, had a metal structure; Arnold Wilkins assumed that in a radio beam of around 50 metres, the 75-foot wings of the Heyford would act as a half-wave dipole aerial. His calculations soon showed that the amount of radio energy likely to be reflected back by such an aircraft would be very large, much larger than he at first had supposed. He took the unexpectedly favourable result back to Watson Watt, who checked the figures and then replied to Wimperis that, although Radio *Destruction* was a non-starter, Radio *Detection* was a distinct possibility.

Grasping at this timely straw, the Air Ministry Defence Committee requested Watson Watt to pursue the theme of radio detection, which he then outlined in a remarkable document, dated 12 February 1935 and entitled 'Detection and Location of Aircraft by Radio Methods'. His proposals included using a pulse technique to measure the three vital parameters required for a practical radar – range, bearing and elevation – and he even anticipated IFF – Identification Friend or Foe – a method of differentiating by coding the radar echoes as to whether a trace was from a hostile or friendly aircraft. Watson Watt foresaw the need for high-powered transmitters to give echoes from up to 100 miles and suggested that 'radio location' could be made to track a contact automatically. All this before a single echo had been received.

Evidently the Air Ministry were most impressed, for only days later they requested a demonstration 'to prove the mathematics'. A simple demonstration was arranged for 26 February 1935, with Wilkins conducting the experiment. Whether he received his brief on another page of a torn-off calendar he cannot now remember, but a vein of economy still ran through Slough; for this important occasion Watson Watt had 'borrowed' one of the BBC's powerful short-wave transmitters at Daventry.

It had been arranged that the transmitter would radiate a signal on 49 metres (6 mHz) and a suitable receiver was to be placed a mile or so away, the object of the experiment being to see if an aircraft flying through the radio field would reflect the signal. A great deal of work had been undertaken previously at Slough under the direction of Sir Edward Appleton into an investigation of the ionosphere, and although Sir Edward always used a receiver driving a galvanometer for his work, later workers were using a cathode-ray oscilloscope, then a very new and expensive instrument. It was connected to a special receiver that had been designed and built for the purpose of detecting radio pulses back from the ionosphere, and this enormous receiver with its fragile oscilloscope, complete with the necessary heavy lead acid batteries, was loaded into an (even then) ancient Morris commercial van, which was rather grandly known as the 'Travelling Laboratory'. Slowly the overloaded van made its way to Weedon, near Daventry, on a wet, cold 25 February.

The BBC short-wave 'Empire' transmitting station at Daventry as it was at the time of the 'radar' experiment in 1935. *Inset:* Sir Robert Watson Watt

Wilkins was assisted by a man named Dyer, who also drove the van. Together they set up the aerials in the gathering gloom and succeeded in getting the receiver and oscilloscope operational ready for the demonstration. The next morning Watson Watt, together with an Air Ministry observer, A. P. Rowe, arrived at the Weedon field and waited for the aircraft which was due from Farnborough. The pilot of the Heyford was Flight Lieutenant Blucke – the same man who was to be involved five years later in the Knickebein beams. He did not know the purpose of the flight, he had simply been briefed to fly at 6000 feet along a line between the BBC transmitters at Daventry and the town of Weedon, which he duly did, or at least thought he did – in fact he was slightly off course, which was to cause some apprehension below.

Down in the van, Wilkins, Watson Watt and Rowe watched the tiny green spot on the tube of the oscilloscope which represented the direct signal from the BBC transmitter. If the aircraft reflected the signal, it would cause the spot to move vertically.

The stationary spot glowed in the darkened van. Then the occupants heard the faint hum of the lumbering Heyford approaching at a stately 90 mph. On the face of the cathode-ray tube the spot began to move slowly up the screen. As the bomber flew over, 'well to one side', Wilkins remembers, the spot moved up and down, oscillating faster and faster. The oscillation was caused by the signal reflected back from the aircraft arriving at the Weedon receiver, because of the longer path taken, with a different phase relationship, or timing, from the direct signal. Since the aircraft was moving, this reflected path was continually altering in length, and therefore the phase shift, or timing, was not constant, one moment adding to the direct signal, at another subtracting from it. The varying output from the receiver caused the spot to oscillate, which it continued to do until, when it was about eight miles away, the Heyford flew out of range and the three delighted observers were left looking at the stationary green spot.

According to some sources, Watson Watt then said: 'Britain is once more an island'; Wilkins only remembers Rowe declaring that it was the most convincing demonstration he'd ever seen. The simple Weedon experiment with improvised equipment had proved that an aircraft could be detected at night or in cloud at a distance of at least eight miles. It was a very encouraging start, though a long way from practical 'Radiolocation'.

The BBC transmitter had been radiating a constant signal. Watson Watt had proposed in his paper that pulsed – or short – bursts of radio energy would be required for radiolocation. This was the technique which had been used at Slough to measure the height of the ionosphere, a layer of ionised gas which reflects radio waves from some sixty miles above the earth. A short duration pulse was sent up to the ionosphere and then received back; the transit time was measured and the height of the reflecting layer computed. The technique was essentially radar in slow motion.

In simple terms, Watson Watt was proposing in his paper a continuous train of pulses radiated to form a broad 'floodlight' extending for 100 miles in

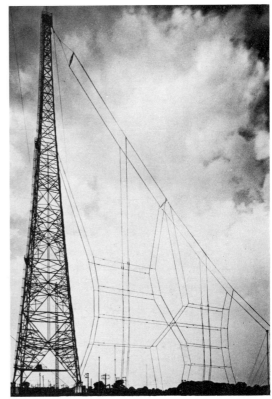

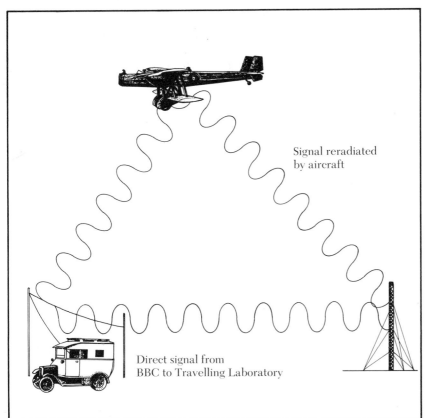

Signal reradiated by aircraft

Direct signal from BBC to Travelling Laboratory

Above: The 49-metre beam aerials at Daventry which radiated the historic signal which proved radar to be a practical proposition.

Top left: A Handley Page Heyford.

Middle left: The Travelling Laboratory.

Left: The Daventry experiment.

front of the station. Each pulse would be accurately timed and would travel at the constant speed of all radio signals of 186,240 miles per second (3.0×10^{10} cms per second), which is near enough the speed of light. In early radar the number of pulses per second was twenty-five; subsequently they were very much faster, but the principle remained the same.

Once the transmitter had sent a pulse it would shut itself down and a receiver, tuned to the same frequency, would stand by to detect any reflected signal. If the pulse encountered an aircraft, for example, then a portion of its radio energy would be reflected back to the receiver. The signals were to be displayed on a cathode-ray monitor; indeed, the whole system relied on a cathode-ray tube display – without that device any radar is impossible.

The cathode-ray tube had a circuit called a time-base which caused its spot to move so rapidly across the face of the tube that it appeared as a solid line. The time-base circuits were so arranged that it took the spot exactly the same time to travel from the left-hand to the right-hand side of the tube as the gap between the transmitter's successive pulses, during which time each single pulse had travelled a distance of 200 miles.

If none of the pulses was returned, then the trace on the face of the tube would remain as a straight line, since the receiver would detect no signal; if, however, an aircraft reflected a pulse, then when the receiver detected it, it would show on the tube as a 'blip' – that is a peak on the straight line of the trace – as the moving spot recorded the reflected signal. Since the spot's journey across the tube took the same time as the pulse to travel 200 miles, it follows that if a target was encountered at the range of, say, 100 miles, the maximum Watson Watt had envisaged, the reflected pulse would arrive back at the receiver just as the spot had completed its journey and the resulting peak on the tube would be at the very end of the horizontal trace. If, however, the echo came from an aircraft at a range of, say, fifty miles, then the spot would only be half-way across the tube when the peak occurred; at twenty-five miles a quarter, and so on. The face of the tube was calibrated in miles and the peaks therefore gave the range of the targets continuously, moving along the line as the aircraft reflecting the pulses moved either nearer or farther away.

Although the determination of range, as outlined above, was to prove relatively straightforward, there were still many problems to be resolved. For example, no one had yet been able to receive a pulse from nearer than thirty miles: to achieve this the transmitted pulses would have to be measured in tenths of a millionth of a second (rather than twenty-five per second, as was the case), and the cathode-ray tube's time-base accurately synchronised with these extremely short pulses.

At the time of Watson Watt's proposal, the questions of determining elevation and bearing were as yet no more than ideas on paper. But such was the urgency of the need to provide some form of early warning against air attack that the Air Ministry, with only the paper proposals backed by a crude demonstration, made available £10,000 for further experimental work almost within days. In 1935 £10,000 was a very considerable sum; it would have provided three or four fighter aircraft, which senior RAF officers could see and understand. Instead, the money was going secretly to finance an experiment that few of the Air Staff could comprehend, at a time when the defence budget was desperately inadequate.

On 13 May, with this backing, a small picked team from the Slough laboratory moved to an old artillery range at Orfordness, Suffolk. It was officially renamed the 'Ionospheric Research Station' to conceal its true purpose. To ensure privacy, the site chosen was a desolate coastal location on a long peninsula joined to the mainland only by a narrow strip of land at the northern end: it was practically an island and the scientists became known to the men at a nearby RAF airfield as the 'Islanders'.

Under the direction of Watson Watt, the team at once set up a 70-foot wooden mast and, drawing on their experience of cathode-ray displays and time-base generators, quickly set up a pulse transmitter and receiver with associated aerials on the tower. Within just three days of arrival the transmitter was working and a week later the receiver was operational and echoes from the ionosphere were observed.

The 'Islanders' must have been working round the clock, for during the next fifteen days they were able to 'see' aircraft on their experimental radiolocation equipment; these early contacts were using pulses of around ten to fifteen microseconds duration and already the ranges achieved were far in excess of any sound locators, but the team did not bother to record them officially. They were, they said, 'not worth writing home about' – not at that stage, for they knew that far better results would soon be available. Their confidence was such that, on 16 June, a demonstration was laid on for members of the Air Defence Committee – the men who had had the foresight to back the venture financially. Radio conditions that day were very poor – violent thunderstorms were causing severe atmospherics, yet the Committee watched an aircraft being tracked for seventeen miles. The aircraft used for these demonstrations, a Westland Wallace, was, of course, specially briefed and flying a prearranged course. On 24 July a new landmark was reached: while the 'tame' target aircraft was being tracked, suddenly another blip appeared at twenty miles range; it was diagnosed as a formation of three aircraft and, as the scientists watched the shimmering green trace, a smaller blip broke away: one of the aircraft had left the formation. The two remaining blips were tracked until out of range. Later the pilot of the Wallace confirmed that he had seen a formation of three RAF Hawker Harts, one of which had broken away, leaving the other two to continue on their way. The experimenters at Orfordness now knew that they could plot more than one aircraft simultaneously.

By August, height was being measured by comparing the received signal on two vertical aerials spaced a known distance apart, and a month later an aircraft flying at 7000 feet fifteen miles away was plotted with only 1° error in elevation: this after only three months work.

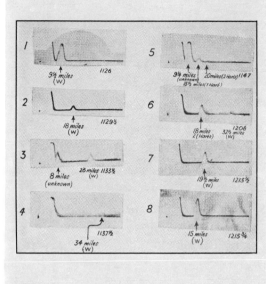

Above: A very rare photograph of the original 70-ft wooden mast at Orfordness which supported the aerials of the first British radar. Within three months aircraft were being plotted fifteen miles away.

Above right: Photographs of the oscillograph screen, showing the first radar observation, on 24 July 1935, of more than one aircraft. (The echo from the Wallace is marked W.)

The third dimension promised by Watson Watt – bearing, or direction – now alone remained. At the time this was considered to be the most difficult achievement of all; indeed, it was thought that it might take up to two years to solve the problem. So great was the pessimism on this point that the whole radiolocation development had been officially coded as 'RDF', the intention being to give the impression that the work at Orfordness was simply an improvement on the existing *Radio Direction Finding* systems.

The solution to the direction problem was in fact solved by January 1936 – in a similar way to that of elevation, but by comparing the received signal as detected by two crossed aerials. So the cover 'RDF' was no longer very obscure, and it was soon taken to mean Range and Direction Finding. But RDF remained as the general name for radiolocation until replaced by a clever and appropriate palindrome 'RADAR' – *Radio Direction And Ranging* – which was coined by the Americans.

By the beginning of 1936, the success at Orfordness was such that another station was required to test the linking of a chain of overlapping stations. A new site was chosen at Bawdsey Manor, near Felixstowe. The height of the masts above sea level determined the ultimate range of these early radars, and the masts at Bawdsey were self-supporting wooden towers of 240 feet, built at a cost of £94. Using these towers, a new radar record was established on 13 March 1936, when a Hawker Hart, flying at a height of 1500 feet 75 miles out to sea, was located. By September, Bawdsey was taking part in the annual Air Exercise – the first to incorporate radar. Pilots, who of course knew nothing of the highly secret developments, were amazed when told that they had flown incorrect courses; one flight was even detected dropping into a nearby airfield for an early tea, to the amusement of the Bawdsey observers.

Intense development work at Bawdsey settled the design of the standard coastal radar stations, and soon contracts were issued to industry for the high-powered transmitters, valves and associated equipment. In February 1937, Bawdsey became the training centre for university graduates, who would be required in time of war to develop radar techniques, and for the RAF signals personnel who would operate the equipment. At that time it was assumed that the operators would all be male, but a month earlier three secretaries from the Bawdsey station had been trained as operators, a job which they had done extremely well, and the three girls were the first of many hundreds of operators of the Women's Auxiliary Air Force (WAAF) who would eventually outnumber the men on the coastal radar sites during the Second World War.

By May 1937, Bawdsey had ceased to be purely experimental: it was now a fully operational Radar Station – the first one of the 'Chain Home' network. Preparations were put in hand to extend that chain, eventually comprising twenty linked stations to give continuous cover from the Solent to the Tay and able to detect an aircraft forty miles away if it was flying at 5000 feet, and 140 miles at 30,000 feet.

During 1937 scientists began the search for suitable sites. The ideal location was near the coast with a gentle slope down to the sea; this gave good height finding and good range. Hills were avoided where possible, as these caused undesirable 'permanent echoes'. The chosen sites had to have reasonable road access for the heavy equipment; the subsoil had to be able to sustain 350-foot steel masts and, most important in 1937, the masts must not 'interfere unduly with grouse shooting'.

The first part of the chain completed were the five stations guarding the Thames Estuary: Dover, Dunkirk (near Canterbury), Canewden (near Southend), Great Bromley (near Colchester) and Bawdsey. They were all operational in time to track Neville Chamberlain's flight to Munich in September 1938. By that time the five stations were on a continuous watch and the remainder were under construction. In the summer of 1939, as we know, the operators were able to watch the progress of the Graf Zeppelin as it flew around the English coast. A few weeks later, the entire operational chain was alerted when the screens suddenly showed over fifty aircraft crossing the North Sea straight for Britain. Just as the alarm bells were being rung, the entire formation, when only seven miles from the Norfolk coast, turned round and flew back east. Later it was realised that the CH Radars had participated, informally, in the 1939 Luftwaffe air exercises.

The Chain Home Radar worked on the 'floodlight' principle, on the long wavelength (for radar) of between 10 and 13.5 metres (22–30 mHz); the transmitters were 200 kilowatts and the maximum range was 120 miles. Incidentally, the wavelength included a band allocated to radio amateurs and

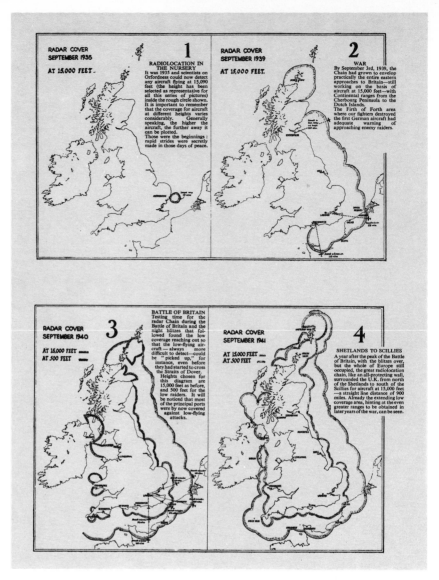

the Radio Society of Great Britain was discreetly asked by the Government to refrain from publishing in their Bulletin letters from amateurs on the subject of the strange pulse signals heard on 10 metres.

The use of the 'long' wavelength, though excellent for the purpose of watching an extensive coastline, had one grave shortcoming: it could not detect low-flying aircraft. This problem had been appreciated as early as 1936 and it was solved by an additional chain, Chain Home Low (CHL). This radar was in fact an adaptation – the result of work at Bawdsey to develop a gunlaying set. It used the overlapping or 'split' beam technique and could give a bearing to within a few minutes of arc; to achieve this, it operated on a much shorter wavelength than the main 'CH' station, 1.5 metres (200 mHz). This enabled a compact, steerable aerial array to be used, in effect, as a radio 'searchlight', able to pinpoint an individual aircraft and to direct a gun or searchlight on to it.

The experimental gunlaying set at Bawdsey had been one of the show-pieces of the establishment for visiting senior officers and politicians. The set was in a small hut, with the aerial array on the roof, the whole thing being on a turntable. The hut was windowless but a small telescope was fitted in the front wall and visitors were invited to look through this at the 'Butter Boat' – a small coaster that plied daily between Esbjerg and Harwich, and which was tracked by the radar. The visitors in the darkened hut would be amazed, on looking through the telescope, to find the cross-hairs plumb between the small grey ship's masts. The staff at Bawdsey nearly overdid this demonstration on 20 June 1939: Winston Churchill was the distinguished visitor on that occasion and, since the Butter Boat's sailings did not coincide with his timetable, an RAF flying boat from nearby Felixstowe was laid on and briefed to fly across the radar. At the appointed hour, the aircraft duly appeared and, although rather further out than requested, it was being accurately tracked. Churchill was invited to look through the telescope. He peered into it and growled, 'I can't see a – thing.' A scientist looked through the telescope and asked the operator to track slightly ahead of the target: 'No wonder you could not see it, sir, it was obscured by the telescope's cross-hair.' Churchill had another look: 'Marvellous,' he said; 'we must have this on His Majesty's ships.' Next day Admiral Somerville came down for a demonstration.

Production versions of the 200 mHz gunlaying radar were placed at the top of 185-foot towers, their 20-foot aerial gantries sweeping a wide arc and able to detect any low-flying aircraft trying to slip under the main radars. They had an effective range of fifty miles.

While the scientists were working on the construction of the stations, new tactics for Fighter Command were being worked out. It says a good deal for the foresight of the Air Council that these new techniques were evolved before the radar network was established. The tactical research was carried out at Biggin Hill, largely at the instigation of Henry Tizard, a scientist who was to contribute much to the defence of the country.

Tizard realised that radar would render all the old concepts of fighter defence obsolete – the 'standing patrol' in particular. He took the view that the amount of early warning to be expected from the radar network would be such that fighter pilots could wait on the ground until it was clear which course the attackers were taking; the nearest fighter squadrons would then take off in good time to climb and intercept.

The new tactics called for a form of ground-controlled interception – that is, men in control rooms instructing the fighter pilots by radio telephone to fly such and such a course to enable them to intercept the bombers. There was at first considerable opposition to this from the Squadron Commanders, who saw it as a challenge to the initiative of the pilots, subjecting them to the control of somebody on the ground 'flying a desk'.

It was during the summer of 1936 that the experiments began at Biggin Hill. Tizard was rather handicapped since he was not at liberty to reveal the

Above: A CH radar station. The 350-ft masts had the transmitter aerials slung between them. The receiver aerials were supported by smaller masts.

Above right: A CHL radar scanner on top of its 185-ft tower. This radar could detect low-flying aircraft up to 50 miles away.

existence of radar, merely informing the participants that they had to assume that range, bearing and height were to be available. This must have seemed, at that time, a rather large assumption. For these exercises the radar plots were simulated by the participating aircraft transmitting a radio signal which was picked up by a normal direction-finding station, the positions being telephoned to Biggin Hill. Gloster Gauntlets of No. 32F Squadron were the fighters and three Hawker Harts, based at Biggin Hill, were to act as 'enemy bombers'. The Harts were ordered to fly at a known height, speed and direction and, over the next few weeks, the radio-directed Gauntlets were able to intercept with nearly 100% certainty. It was then realised that this success was in part due to the known flight pattern of the obliging 'bombers'; the pilots of the Harts were therefore briefed to choose their own heading and height, with the result that the interception rate dropped dramatically.

One of the problems was the difficulty of keeping the simulated 'radar' plots up to date; by the time the D/F stations had telephoned their information, it was largely out of date and the complicated tracking of course and airspeed, which then had to be converted into visual 'vectors' on a blackboard, was time-consuming and inaccurate. To try to solve the problem, a collection of weird navigation computers was employed, without conspicuous success. At last the Station Commander at Biggin Hill, Wing Commander E. O. Grenfell, an experienced pilot, exasperated by the long-winded trigonometry of the 'experts', said he could do better by eye. He was frostily invited to try. Looking at the blackboard plot, he quickly gave his orders over the radio link to the fighter pilots to steer 150 degrees, and then gave the necessary adjustments to the course. To everyone's amazement, the Gauntlets and the Harts met.

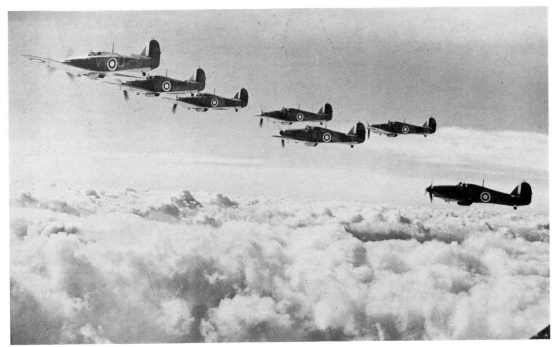

Hurricanes of 85 Squadron during the Battle of Britain. Part of 12 Group, they were based at Church Fenton. (This is one of very few air-to-air pictures taken during the Battle.)

Tizard immediately saw that this was the solution, and he rationalised the technique as the 'Principle of Equal Angles'. It was based on the assumption that fighters are faster than bombers and that being so, if one draws a straight line from the bombers to the fighters and makes this the base of an isosceles triangle, with the angle of the fighters' course made equal to that of the bombers, they will always meet at the triangle's apex. This simple technique, known as 'the Tizzy Angle', became the standard plotting procedure and would remain so until the 1960s, when electronic computers took over in the supersonic age.

From 1936, during the three years of peace that were left, both the radar network and the techniques of interception were finalised and resulted in the world's first complete air defensive system based on radar.

The early work at Biggin Hill was to evolve into the Filter Rooms, Sector Controls and the huge table maps with the WAAF operators moving the symbols for friend and foe – a familiar scene in films of the Second World War – together with the new vocabulary that was coined: Tally Ho!, Scramble, Angels One Five, Bandits and Vector, which were in reality, of course, a simple code for the pilots listening to their crackling HF radios in their noisy cockpits. The defence network enabled the RAF Fighter Controller, sitting above the large maps, to direct this most modern form of mechanised war and to watch the battle developing at his feet, much as a medieval king could watch his armies from a hilltop.

By the outbreak of the Second World War on 3 September 1939, the whole of the vulnerable East Coast was under continuous radar watch. It could detect an enemy aircraft 100 miles away, by day or night, in cloud or the thickest weather. It had taken four years of unremitting work, carried out

Above: WAAFs
operated the CH
radars during the
Battle of Britain.
They frequently
came under fire.

Top right: The
target of both radar
and fighters:
Heinkels of KG51.

Right: The plots
from the radars
were passed to the
Operations Room,
where the Fighter
Controller could
assess the situation
and deploy his
forces.

in the greatest secrecy, and it had cost £10 million. It was soon to prove very cheap at the price.

The Battle of Britain, which was fought during August/September 1940, was to prove the worth of the CH Radar network. Without it, Goering's boast that the Luftwaffe would smash the RAF's fighters within a month might well have been fulfilled. The Luftwaffe had some 3000 aircraft ranged against 600 Spitfires and Hurricanes. As it was, whenever the enemy planes took off and assembled for the daily raids, their every move was plotted by the ever-watchful radar operators, who soon became very skilled at estimating numbers from the flickering waveforms on their cathode-ray monitors. Height, bearing and range were built into the sets, but the number of aircraft detected was still very much an art rather than a science. The young WAAFs who operated the radars and manned the sector rooms were to fulfil the early promise shown and they were the first servicewomen to find themselves in the front line.

Early in the Battle, on 12 August, Ju87 and Ju88 dive-bombers attacked several of the CH Radar stations. Dover was the first, but little damage was done; at Rye huts were destroyed but the main transmitting and receiving buildings escaped. The heaviest attack was made by fifteen Ju88 dive-bombers of KG51 on the Ventnor, Isle of Wight, station. This station was to be the only one put off the air, the WAAF plotters remaining on duty until that moment.

Because of the overlapping of adjacent stations, German Signals Intelligence did not detect that the Ventnor station had been silenced and from then on the attacks against the stations diminished and became half-hearted. They were very difficult targets: the tall masts protected the stations to some extent from dive-bombers and, deprived of that most accurate form of bombing, the Luftwaffe seems to have more or less given up any decisive blow against those vital installations. That this was so was largely because of faulty intelligence appreciation of their importance.

General Adolf Galland recalled, in 1976:

'The reason for this may have been that we in Germany had not managed to develop our radar as quickly as the British and we mistakenly considered that the principal use for radar was as an anti-shipping weapon. It was not until later, when we had it working operationally, that we noticed it was effective against aircraft as well.

'We did attack British radar stations in Kent [during the Battle of Britain] but perhaps not enough; firstly because we had underestimated their importance, secondly because we did not know their exact positions, and thirdly because however much one tries to knock out such stations, one cannot do much harm, and anyway it is easy to repair them.'[3]

In fact many, if not all, of the original CH stations had what was known as a 'Buried Reserve'. This was a duplicate station, on the main site but, as the name implies, buried underground. Although these reserve stations used the same transmitters and receivers as the main stations, the aerials were supported on smaller 120-foot wooden towers and therefore operated on the shorter wavelengths of between 6 and 7 metres (42.5–50.5 mHz).

It is not proposed to give a detailed account of the Battle of Britain here, for there are many excellent accounts in print. Suffice it to say that the CH and CHL networks were of decisive importance: the controllers were able to husband the resources of Fighter Command, only putting aircraft into the air when the size and direction of the enemy formations had been evaluated. In this way, the relatively small number of RAF fighters available was able to be as effective as a force many times its size.

The hard-pressed German fighter pilots were unable to understand where the RAF got the apparently inexhaustible numbers of fighters from. Werner Schoerer, a German fighter pilot during the Battle of Britain, confirms this:

'I remember that I was astonished to find that each time we crossed the Channel, there was always an enemy fighter force in position. We thought that this was because we flew at a great height and that our assembly points were spied on; we were after all in occupied territory and there were agents enough who could inform and report on our movements. Another reason, we felt, was the very fine weather, which would enable British observers to see us coming from a great distance. However, even when we crossed the Channel at very low altitudes the RAF were still ready for us. We had no idea that anything resembling 'Radar' existed and could not imagine that [aircraft] could be seen directly on a screen.'[4]

The outcome of the Battle of Britain is now, of course, history. The all-conquering Luftwaffe, which had up to that time swept all before it in a series of unbroken victories, was for the first time halted. Although the figures of German losses were greatly exaggerated by the RAF at the time, the official postwar figures confirm the RAF victory:

German losses: 1736 aircraft destroyed.

RAF losses: 915 aircraft destroyed.

The object of the Battle, the destruction of the RAF's Fighter Command and the establishment of German air superiority as a prelude to Operation Sealion – the invasion of the British Isles – was not achieved. Operation Sealion was postponed – indefinitely – and the Germans were forced to change to night-bombing.

The victory in that summer of 1940 was not, of course, solely due to the radar network, but its contribution, together with that of the RAF fighter pilots in the Spitfires and the Hurricanes, and also the still largely unpublished role that was played by the breaking of the German Enigma codes, proved decisive.

After the Battle of Britain, the RAF turned to the offensive and began to bomb Germany. They bombed at night, for like the Luftwaffe they had found by bitter experience that daylight attacks against determined fighter defence were a costly business. On 18 December 1939, twenty-four Wellington bombers had attacked Wilhelmshaven; they were intercepted by a force of German Me109 and Me110 fighters and ten of the bombers were shot down

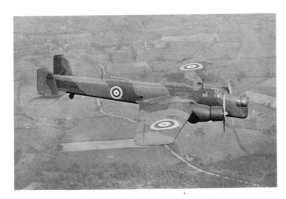

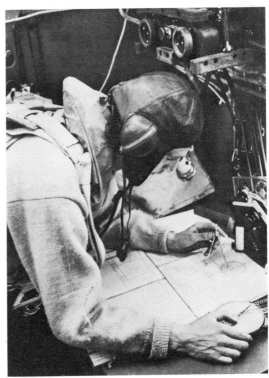

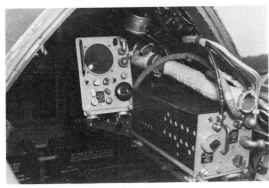

and a further three badly damaged. From then on the RAF bombed by night.

The fundamental problem of night bombing really came down to a question of navigation. To navigate over a blacked-out and hostile continent without specialised aids was virtually impossible. Dead Reckoning and Astro-Navigation – traditional position-finding by compass and sextant – could, under ideal conditions and on the bridge of a large ship, give a position accurate to within a mile. An airborne navigator at night would be lucky to establish his position to within eight miles.

James McCloy was an RAF navigator flying in Whitleys in 1941 and he remembers clearly the limitations of bubble sextant and star tables:

'We used to climb up with the sextant to the perspex astrodome and take a star shot. We would take six shots and average them out and then, with the aid of tables, of the sort that mariners had been using for years, one worked out where one was, *if* one was lucky. Personally I had no faith in the damn things at all.

'In fact on the *ground* I found the best I could do was to fix the position of the aerodrome within five miles: in the air I would have been lucky if I got to within twenty miles.'[5]

The basic difficulty of aircraft navigation is quite simply the wind. Air is to an aircraft as water to a ship: move the air in the form of wind and the aircraft is carried along with it. If the wind strength and direction are known, then the pilot or navigator can compensate for it; if it is not known, or simply guessed at (called forecasting), then unless the position of the aircraft can be checked regularly against a ground feature or – less reliably – a star, the aircraft will

Above: During 1940/41 navigation to and from targets was by Dead Reckoning. There were few radio aids (and no radar) and many aircraft had difficulty in locating their target.

Top left: An Armstrong-Whitworth Whitley, a typical twin-engined bomber of 1941. Used exclusively for night bombing, it equipped no fewer than eleven RAF squadrons.

Bottom left: A Gee set, probably in a Beaufighter.

The Vickers Wellington, known to its crews as the 'Wimpy', was the mainstay of RAF Bomber Command in 1940/41. It was the first aircraft to benefit from the use of Gee, and was the first RAF bomber to attack Berlin, on the night of 25 August 1940.

drift off its intended course. Flying at night, often in cloud, it was found to be virtually impossible to check position with ground features and the star shots with a sextant – assuming that stars were visible – were often woefully inaccurate. The sad fact that emerged in 1941 was that, of 44,700 tons of bombs dropped over German targets in a given period, over 90% landed in open countryside. Bomber Command's Operational Research Section discovered, from an examination of post-raid photographic reconnaissance and other evidence, that in one attack on 15/16 May 1940 only twenty-four out of ninety-six aircraft even located the correct target, let alone hit it.

Apart from finding their targets, many bombers were unable even to find their home bases on returning after raids and a number were flying into hills, again through faulty navigation.

The Germans, perhaps less handicapped by maritime traditions, had realised long before the war that Dead Reckoning navigation was best left to the birds and had developed their 'beams'.

One of the drawbacks from the German point of view was that, since they were actually 'beams', they gave a good indication of the intended target to the defenders. What the RAF required was a form of beam which would lead bombers to their targets without giving away to the enemy any indications of that target.

There was an admirable institution at the Telecommunications Research Establishment (TRE) known as the 'Sunday Soviet': people attending these informal gatherings would include scientists, Air Staff officers, junior research workers and serving officers. There was a tradition that anyone invited could speak his mind freely and many an eminent Fellow of the Royal Society was told by a junior officer that he was talking rubbish – which, in the light of the officer's operational experience, he probably was.

The object of the meetings was to get the 'users' and the scientists together, and very successful the Soviets were. At one of them, in June 1940, Air Marshal Joubert of the Air Staff deplored the poor bombing results due to RAF navigational difficulties. Watson Watt was present and he remembered a proposal for a blind-landing aid, based on a pulse system, that had been put to him at Bawdsey in 1937 by one of his scientists, Robert Dippy.

Following the June 'Soviet', Dippy was requested to develop his plan into a radio navigation system. The system, which became known as 'Gee', is not easy to describe, but in the simplest terms it consisted of three linked transmitters, A, B and C, each about 100 miles apart.

Transmitter A was the master station: it transmitted a train of radar-like pulses. Transmitters B and C, slave stations, picked up A's pulses and reradiated them. The three transmitters were therefore continuously radiating synchronised pulses, though with a known time interval between them: the time the pulses had taken to get from A to B and from A to C.

Since the pulses from the three stations would all be travelling at exactly the same speed, an observer looking at the pulses on a cathode-ray tube would see a different time relationship between them, dependent on his geographical position: if he happened to be near C, then C's pulses would appear first, followed by the others: if nearer to B, then the B station pulses would be leading. If the observer happened to be exactly the same distance from, say, A and B, then he would see the pulses with the same time interval as transmitted by those two stations.

This was the fundamental principle of Gee. A line could be drawn on a map showing where the pulses could be received, with the same time interval between each pair of stations as transmitted; these lines were called isochrones and, in the same way as an isobar joins up areas of equal pressure on a weather chart, the isochrones joined up equal time intervals between the pulses. They were not in general straight lines, but curving 'Hyperbolae': a whole family of hyperbolae can be drawn, each representing a known distance from the transmitters, forming a lattice or grid (hence the name Gee) and superimposed on the navigational charts. These families of lines were known to the scientists as 'confocal hyperbolae'.

A 1943 Gee map. The grid was colour-coded, making it very easy to use, and gave a position over Germany accurate to ±2 miles in 350. Gee was the first navigation aid to make accurate bombing on a large scale possible.

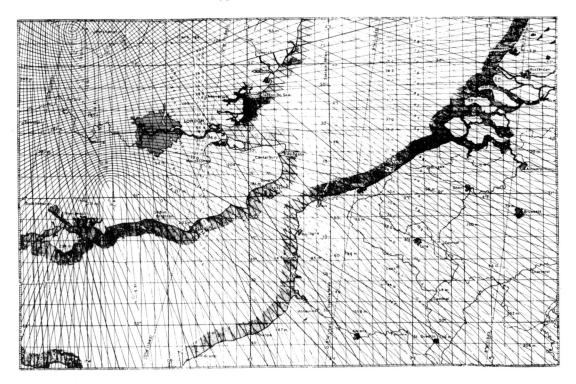

Fortunately, the navigator in his aircraft did not need to concern himself with these terms. The lines were colour-coded and numbered on his chart; to use Gee, all he had to do was to identify and measure the time intervals of the pulses on a special cathode-ray indicator and then refer to his Gee chart, following, say, 'Blue 20' with his pencil until it crossed 'Red 18'; he would then know his position accurately to within two miles in 350.

The great advantage of the Gee system was that it was entirely passive – that is, it did not require any signals from the aircraft which could compromise its position. It could also be used simultaneously by an unlimited number of aircraft. Unlike the German beams of 1940, the Gee Lattice pointed everywhere and yet nowhere; without the special receiving equipment and charts, the Gee pulses were useless and it was hoped that the Germans, on hearing them, would conclude that they were ordinary radar signals, which they were deliberately made to resemble.

RAF Bomber Command were, not unnaturally, very anxious to get Gee operational as soon as possible and, following test flights over Britain during the spring and summer of 1941, operational flights were made with twelve hand-built sets over Germany in August: the results were excellent and promised to transform night navigation, the navigators using their Gee sets not only to pinpoint their position, but also using them as the Germans had used their beams, to assess wind drift over the continent, and as 'homing' beacons to guide them back to their base airfields.

There was, of course, some risk in sending these highly secret prototype sets over enemy territory and, sure enough, on the night of 13 August 1941, an aircraft carrying an early Gee set failed to return from a raid over Germany. There was an immediate inquiry into the loss of this aircraft; it was thought, after questioning other aircrew, that it had crashed and exploded, but even if this were so, there was the possibility that members of its crew could have baled out and would now be under interrogation.

The matter was referred to Dr R. V. Jones. He did not think German Intelligence would have got much from the crashed aircraft, since it was unlikely that either the special map or receiver would have survived the impact. He was equally sure that the crew would not give anything away in direct questioning, but there was always a chance that they might fall for the bugged-room ploy – after all, Jones himself had got a great deal of information about Knickebein in just that way. He therefore decided to accept that German eavesdroppers would have picked up some reference to Gee from aircrews talking among themselves. Now G and J sound very similar in German, so Jones, a renowned practical joker himself, decided that here was a magnificent opportunity for a gigantic hoax against the Germans.

The first thing to do, Jones has said, was:

'. . . obliterate all traces of "Gee". Henceforth it was to be referred to as "J", so if the Germans heard prisoners talking about "J" they would think that they had mistaken "J" for "G" in their earlier eavesdropping. The next step was to conjure up a new system which would give body to "J".

Accepting it is inevitable that the Germans would realise that we were going to bring into operation some new radio aid, what better than to flatter them by letting them think that we had copied their beams? And so we invented the "J" beams and actually set up some "J" beam transmitters on our East Coast.'[6]

Jones also had the type number of the Gee sets changed. Originally these had been in the 5000 series, a sure indication that they were a radar pulse device. It was arranged that the racks in the bombers and all new sets had the label 'TR 1335'; TR – Transmitter/Receiver – indicated a radio, not a radar, device.

There was yet another gambit that could be employed. Many German agents had been arrested and some 'turned' – that is they now operated for the British. One of these agents was required to transmit to his German Control a fake conversation he was supposed to have overheard in the bar of the Savoy Hotel between two RAF officers, discussing the Honours List and how a well-known scientist 'had got the GCB, when all he had done was to copy the Jerry beams, and a year late at that!' Another message sent back to the ever-receptive German Intelligence was to the effect that 'Professor "Ekkerley" was reported as giving lectures to RAF Units in which he described the new "Jerry" radio navigation system using Lorenz-type beams.'[6] Jones left it to the Germans to work out if 'J' stood for 'Jerry'.

As to the effectiveness of these intelligence moves, the spoof 'J' Beams went on the air and were duly jammed, while the real aid, Gee, went unjammed for five months – a very long time indeed.

Gee lived up to its early promise and, with its aid, RAF bombers were able to adopt the German KGr100 technique of 'Pathfinding', the Gee-equipped bombers marking the targets with flares and fires to guide the main force. The first full-scale Gee raid was made on the night of 8 March 1942, when eighty Pathfinder aircraft equipped with Gee led a force of some 350 aircraft attacking Essen, in the Ruhr.

The Essen raid was highly successful. On 30 May Gee was used to lead the largest attack ever mounted by the RAF – the 1000-bomber raid on Cologne. The fire-raisers arrived dead on time and the raid was soon over. The aircraft had been guided by a single chain of Gee transmitters sited on the East Coast of England.

The concentration of the attack on Cologne was another facet of Gee. When D/R navigation was used, bombers would take off and fly more or less any course the captain chose, arriving over the target – if they found it – at widely-spaced intervals: a big raid would take hours. Now, with Gee, raids were concentrated into minutes, which tended to overwhelm the defenders.

Gee was not to be jammed by the Germans to any extent until early 1943. Eventual jamming had been foreseen and a Mk II set, TR1355, was ready. This had a very wide frequency coverage, as did the transmitters, enabling rapid changes to be made to nullify enemy jamming. Thus, by waiting until the 'Pathfinders' were near the target before suddenly switching to a new transmission, synchronised with the original (jammed) one but on an entirely

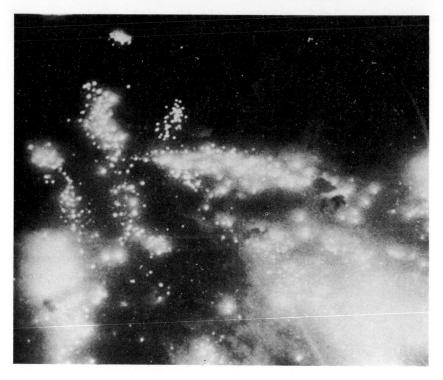

'Pathfinder' flares (left) float down to mark a target. They were dropped by Gee-equipped aircraft and were coloured according to a prearranged plan. The following aircraft simply dropped their bombs as indicated by the flares.

different frequency, the fire-raising bombers would get their 'fix' before the Germans had discovered the new channel and netted their jammers on to it. The reserve frequencies were of course known to the crews in advance: these tactics, called 'Latched K' working, were successful and enabled Gee to be used for far longer than anyone had dared to hope.

Even had the system been completely countered over Germany, however, it would still have been worth the effort for the aid it rendered to bombers returning home. Incidentally, the spoof 'J' beams were also used for this purpose. But Gee was not only of use to the RAF; the Navy found it invaluable, especially in the Channel, and its accuracy here was such that both mine-laying and sweeping were done with its aid. Gee's finest hour, so to speak, was its use during the D-day landings – so much so that one Commander suggested that it should have been renamed 'G'-day.

By that time there were five Gee chains in operation covering most of Europe from Norway to the Bay of Biscay. The Americans adopted Gee, but used it on much lower frequencies – 2 mHz – and called it 'Loran': *Long Range Navigation*. The range, under favourable conditions, was around 1200 miles and it is still in operation today as a general maritime navigation aid.

An official assessment of the role of Gee was included in a paper issued by TRE just at the end of the war:

'The Gee system was the most important of all the radar contributions to the offensive. In its application to Bomber Command, it permitted those close concentrations in time and space which were essential to the defeat of the enemy ground defences; it was essential to the "thousand bomber raid"; it made practicable . . . close relative timing of separate attacks, real and feint; and it gave valuable aid in bringing the great bomber formations, and their individual aircraft, back by the most suitable routes, and under close time control, to their bases, an aid which was invaluable in bad weather.'[7]

There is a postscript to the Gee story. On 24 February 1944, a German Ju188 reconnaissance aircraft was shot down over Britain. When RAF Intelligence officers inspected the wreckage, they found a radio set labelled FuG 122; it had a familiar look to it and further investigation revealed that it was in fact a TR1335 – a captured RAF Gee receiver. The Germans had also collected the Gee maps from crashed aircraft and were using the system as a replacement for their own jammed beams to navigate over Britain.

The RAF had done a similar thing with a long-range German radio aid called Elektra Sonne, which covered the Bay of Biscay and the Western Approaches. This system too had a number of linked transmitters, including one at Stavanger, in Norway: Coastal Command found the system so useful that when the Germans retreated from Norway towards the end of the war, the British Government actually paid the Norwegians to continue the service. Electra Sonne is still in operation, though now under the name 'Consol', and is much used by weekend yachtsmen, since it is one of the very few radio navigation aids that can be used with a simple broadcast receiver; like Gee, however, it does require a special chart.

Gee accuracy over the Ruhr was such that it was used principally as a navigation aid, not a precise blind-bombing aid: that there was the need for such a device was evident and scientists at TRE at Worth Matravers (and later at Malvern) were working on the problem, even before Gee became operational.

The brief was to develop a radio aid that would enable a bomber flying in cloud to drop its bombs not just on a given area of a given city – Gee could do that – but on a single factory or a specific military installation. To achieve that order of accuracy, an application of pulse techniques was essential to measure the range, for this measurement was the most precise feature of radar pulse systems.

The blind-bombing system which was adopted was called Oboe. It had been developed by A. H. Reeves and Dr F. E. Jones during 1941–42. It consisted of two converted radar transmitters, operating on $1\frac{1}{2}$ metres (220 mHz). They were situated on the East coast, some distance apart: one at Trimmingham in Norfolk, the tracker station coded 'Cat'; the other near Walmer in Kent, coded 'Mouse'. The two stations were linked by land-lines and transmitted synchronised pulses; these pulses were retransmitted by the aircraft back to the ground stations.

Cat kept the aircraft flying along a circular track that would take it over the target. In general terms this circular track was centred on Cat, and if the aircraft deviated from its track away from the centre, the pilot would hear a series of morse dashes in his headphones, or a series of dots if he were drifting towards Cat. When on the correct track, a continuous note would be heard, a

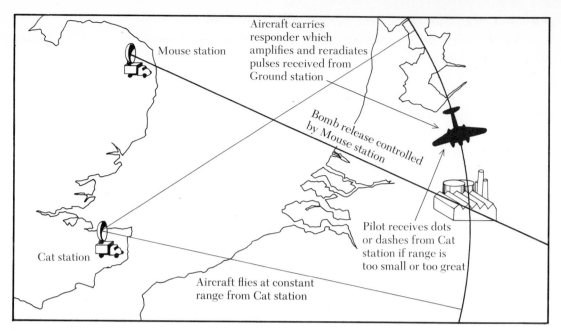

Oboe.

 labels within figure:

Mouse station

Aircraft carries responder which amplifies and reradiates pulses received from Ground station

Bomb release controlled by Mouse station

Pilot receives dots or dashes from Cat station if range is too small or too great

Cat station

Aircraft flies at constant range from Cat station

familiar presentation for a qualified beam-approach pilot. These left/right signals were sent out automatically by the ground station.

The function of Mouse was to assess the aircraft's ground speed and height and to plot the distance the aircraft was from the target; then the operators, knowing the ballistic characteristics of the bombs, could transmit a bomb-release signal. This signal, usually a break in the transmission preceded by a warning in the form of a prearranged group of morse letters, was heard only by the navigator. The pilot could thus concentrate on keeping on course by listening solely to Cat.

The range of Oboe was about 250 miles, which covered the vital targets in the Ruhr: at that range the accuracy of the system was within 100 yards, good enough for Pathfinders to mark individual factories. Tests carried out on bombing ranges in England were so impressive that a new problem was posed by the almost uncanny accuracy of the Oboe system: it was more accurate than the geodetic alignment of the British Ordnance Survey and prewar Continental Maps.

In order to test and calibrate the grids, Dr R. V. Jones was asked to nominate a target from which his agents could be relied on to report on the precise impact point of the bombs. He suggested the Headquarters of Sector 7 of the German night-fighter organisation, which was located in the Novitiate near the Belgian town of Florennes, where there were several active and reliable agents. On 20 December 1942 a small force of Mosquitoes, fitted with hand-built Oboe sets, took off for Florennes. The fast bombers flew at 30,000 feet, well out of the range of effective flak, and, tracked by the Cat and Mouse stations, dropped their bombs on the unseen target five miles below. Within twenty-four hours the Belgian agents had reported that one bomb had been a direct hit on the Novitiate, another had fallen on the entrance, and the mean error of the others was within 150 yards of the aiming point. This from aircraft flying at 300 mph; Gee could not have done better than $\pm$ 2 miles at that range of 250 miles.

The bomb plots revealed that small corrections *were* needed to align the two geodetic grids. During February 1943, the Oboe techniques were perfected and by March of that year, the Pathfinder Mosquitoes were leading a force of 860 heavy bombers to attack Düsseldorf, followed by raids on Dortmund, Cologne, Duisberg and Wuppertal. Before the advent of Oboe, even when aided by Gee only some 23% of bombs dropped were on the actual target: with Oboe, the figure rose to 70%, which meant that Bomber Command's force had been effectively trebled.

Prophets are ever without honour in their own country. Reeves and Jones were to be no exception: early in the work on Oboe, a 'high-ranking official' of the Ministry of Aircraft Production wrote:

'I regret having to do this, but I am sure it is time to say quite bluntly that these disquisitions from TRE on Oboe are becoming ridiculous.

'If they came as inventions from the outside public, and not from official sources, they would be rejected without hesitation. . . . If I had the power I would discover the man responsible for this latest Oboe effort and sack him, so that he could no longer waste not only his time and effort, but ours also, by his vain imaginings.'[8]

The Oboe Mosquitoes had very low losses indeed: only one was shot down in the first 600 sorties, and their overall losses were less than $\frac{1}{4}$% for the whole war.

The Oboe system on $1\frac{1}{2}$ metres was first jammed by the Germans in October 1943, so it, like Gee, had a good run free of jamming; anti-jamming measures were employed by the RAF which kept the original Oboe operational until November, when new developments enabled it to operate on centimetric wavelengths. The quest for centimetric radar is a story in itself.

The navigational aid Gee had a range of 450 miles from the British Coast: Oboe about 250. What was required now was some equally effective system that could be used anywhere over German or German-occupied territory.

The range of Oboe could theoretically have been extended by using a flying repeater station; but this was discounted as impractical. The only solution would be some form of self-contained aid – that is, one carried by the aircraft. The first radar to be carried by aircraft had been the Airborne Interception Set, which by the end of 1940 was in use with night fighters. These sets, which operated on $1\frac{1}{2}$ metres, had severe limitations, the most serious being the problem of ground returns – the radar pulses which were reflected back from the ground to the aircraft, blocking out most of the screens. These returns reduced the forward range of the Airborne Interception to the equivalent of the aircraft's height above the ground, limiting the maximum range to about $3\frac{1}{2}$ miles.

However, the sea did not reflect radar pulses back in this way. Water, unless very rough, acted like an optical mirror, the pulses bouncing off the sea *away* from the aircraft: 1½-metre radars fitted to Fleet Air Arm Swordfish were highly effective in detecting surfaced U-boats. As early as the summer of 1939, when the first experimental work was being conducted with these 1½-metre sets, it was realised that these ground returns and the absence of returns from the sea might form the basis of an airborne 'Town Finder'.

A Blenheim bomber, with a modified 1½-metre AI set, flew from Martlesham Heath to the west coast of Wales in 1939 and the scientist operating the radar had been able to give the pilot an accurate account of the route flown simply on the information presented by the radar which the aircraft carried. Other experiments were made during the winter of 1939/40, but it was obvious that much shorter wavelengths were required to make 'Town Finding' by radar a practical proposition.

The shortest wavelength on which appreciable power could be generated was around 50 centimetres; anything below this was, in 1939, virtually impossible because of the high-powered valves required. Neither British nor German scientists had succeeded in getting any high power on shorter wavelengths than 50 centimetres from the valves then developed; it was, however, desirable to get radar working on wavelengths around 10 centimetres, for generally speaking the shorter the wavelength the more precise the radar will be.

The Royal Navy required a centimetric radar for gunlaying and in 1939 had commissioned a group of scientists at Birmingham University, working under Professor Marcus Oliphant, to investigate 10-centimetre equipment. They were trying to develop a special valve called a *Klystron*, which could produce oscillations on 10 centimetres, but only at very low power – far too low for effective radar transmission. Among Oliphant's team were a research fellow John Randall (now Sir John) and a postgraduate student Harry Boot. These two men had been working on a coastal CH radar site and when they returned to Birmingham found themselves on the outskirts of the Klystron team, working in the corner of a teaching laboratory on a device called a Barkhausen-Kurz oscillator, which it was hoped could be used in a centimetric receiver. It did not take them long to prove that the Barkhausen-Kurz tube would not work as had been hoped and the pair turned their attention to the primary problem: the generation of radio power on low centimetric wavelengths.

Randall and Boot came to the conclusion that the Klystron was never going to produce the power needed and looked into another possible centimetric valve, the split-anode *Magnetron*, which was at that time little more than an interesting laboratory curiosity. It too could produce centimetric oscillations but was unstable, being incapable of working on a fixed frequency. However, the two physicists came to the conclusion that it might offer better prospects of centimetric development than the Klystron.

The Klystron, which incidentally was designed by two Americans, the Varian brothers, employed two resonators called Rhumbatons (from the Greek 'Rhumba', meaning rhythmic oscillation). These resonators, which

A wartime
Klystron.

Below: Sir John
Randall (right) and
Harry Boot in 1976,
during the filming
of the television
programme.
Dr Boot is holding
one of the original
Magnetron blocks.

were hollow structures, acted as electrical oscillators at the frequency of the
Klystron. They were thought to be the key to any centimetric valve and
Randall and Boot took the idea of a resonator a step further, hoping to
combine it with the principle of the Magnetron.

It was an afternoon in November 1939 when Randall began to sketch his
ideas: what emerged was a solid copper cylindrical block, with six resonator
cavities machined into it, surrounding a cathode. Boot made the calculations
on the traditional back of an envelope. The basic dimensions for the resonators were based on the work of Heinrich Hertz, who had first demonstrated the existence of radio waves with loops of wire in the 1880s;

ironically these first steps into radio were made on wavelengths around 10 centimetres. The loops Hertz made were extrapolated into the copper cylinder which was to be the heart of the new Magnetron.

Dr Boot explained recently that the idea was that this copper cylinder 'was to be put in a strong magnetic field and a high voltage applied between the copper cylinder and the cathode, so that the stream of electrons coming off the central cathode, instead of being attracted straight across to the anode [the copper cylinder], would rapidly rotate past the machined slots and, if this happened at the right speed, it would cause the slots to act as resonators and tuned circuits, oscillating in step, together [at a frequency of 3000 mHz].'

This was the theory. In practice they had to get approval from Professor Oliphant in order to proceed with the making of a prototype 'Cavity Magnetron', as they called their brainchild. Oliphant was not altogether enthusiastic but, possibly in view of the depressing results from the Klystrons, agreed that they could give the Cavity Magnetron a try.

The work had hardly any backing. Randall and Boot had to borrow transformers from the Admiralty at Portsmouth; a very old teaching electromagnet was found in a corner of one of the university's laboratories; other parts, including the high-tension rectifiers, they made themselves. The copper cylinder was turned up by a laboratory assistant in the mechanical workshop and a vacuum pump rigged up: the ends of the Magnetron were sealed by halfpenny pieces held in place with sealing wax.

Dr Boot well remembers the day it was ready to switch on:
'It was 21 February 1940 when all the gear was serviceable; we got rid of all the leaks in the vacuum equipment and I turned up the magnetic field, switched on the High Tension and gradually turned it up to 10 or 15 kilovolts . . .'[9]

As a load this first cavity magnetron had a car headlamp bulb, its base removed, wired to the output. As the high voltage was applied the two physicists anxiously watched the bulb for signs of life: it began to glow brighter and brighter and then burned out. Another, larger, lamp was produced: it too burned out, as did a succession of lamps, until eventually the output was measured at a staggering 400 watts.

That the Cavity Magnetron was producing power there could be no doubt, but as the two men watched the sizzling Heath Robinson lash-up, the question they hardly liked asking was whether the power being produced was on the elusive 10-centimetre wavelength. The only method of wavelength measurement available in that ill-equipped laboratory was by Lecher Wires. Two parallel wires, an inch or two apart, with a metric scale alongside were connected to the output of the magnetron; a small flashlight bulb was slid along the wires and it lit up at every half wavelength. By counting the number of times the bulb lit, the wavelengths could be accurately measured. Harry Boot slid the bulb along the wires and 'to our second great surprise, it was 9.87 centimetres: we had been aiming for 10!'[9]

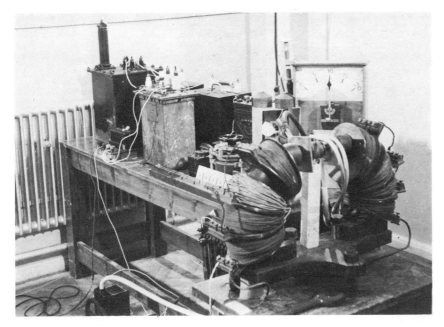

A reconstruction of Randall and Boot's laboratory, made for BBC television by the Admiralty Surface Weapons Establishment at Portsmouth. Much of the equipment, including the huge magnet, is original. The Lecher wires, used to measure the frequency, can be seen to the left of the magnet.

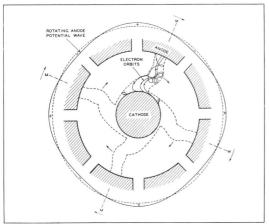

It is impossible to exaggerate the importance of Randall and Boot's work; it lifted radar from an electronic stone age to the present day. The lead it gave to the Allies during World War Two was incalculable. The Germans were certainly never able to catch up in the field where it was to confer the greatest advantage: Airborne Radar. Including the two halfpennies used to seal the end plates, the prototype Cavity Magnetron cost an estimated £200: had it cost £2 million it would still have been a bargain.

Before the magnetron could be used operationally a great deal of development remained to be done, much of it at the GEC laboratories at Wembley, led by E.C.S. Megaw. An improved version of the Birmingham magnetron was produced there during May 1940. This valve, which had much more effective sealing using a gold-fusion technique, was too large for airborne use and, like the original, was water-cooled; but it was followed by another, NT98, which was air-cooled, and when that was first operated on 29 June 1940, it gave a pulse output of 10 kilowatts at 10 centimetres, using a small 6 lb

Above left: Diagram of the path of electrons in an early magnetron. It was not until long after the successful practical application of the magnetron to radar that theoretical studies of the device were made.

Above: The original magnetron, now in the Science Museum, London.

Above: A Bristol Beaufighter with 10-cm radar, AI Mk VIII, inside the plastic covering on the nose.

magnet. NT98 no. 2 went, five days later, to Professor Dee's group at Air Ministry Research Establishment at Worth Matravers, for use in an experimental Airborne Interception set. The demand for those experimental valves was such that GEC made several copies using the chamber from a Colt revolver as a drilling jig for the copper anodes. No. 12 went to the still neutral USA in August 1940 with the Tizard mission; it was later described by the Americans as 'the most valuable cargo ever to reach these shores'.

The early magnetrons worked beyond expectation but they exhibited a tendency to jump from one wavelength to another, which led to many being rejected. This 'mode jumping' was largely cured by Dr J. Sayers at Birmingham University; he 'strapped' each alternate segment of the copper block, which made the cavities oscillate in phase and turned the magnetron into a reliable, stable, operational device.

The first airborne use of the early magnetron was in a new centimetric radar which was a much improved equipment for night fighters. This set, the AI Mk VII, went into service in Beaufighters towards the end of 1941. It was an immediate success; the much narrower beam of the new 10-cm radar was no longer plagued by ground returns which had so severely limited the range of the earlier 1½-metre radar. The Mk VII was quickly developed into the Mk VIII which used the production 'strapped' magnetron, the CV64. This small valve generated a pulse of 25 kilowatts on 9.1 cms and, using a small parabolic aerial which produced a helical scan, gave a maximum range of six miles and a minimum of 400 feet.

The operators using this AI radar noticed that although the general ground returns that were observed on the older sets were now absent, they could get discrete returns – coastlines and built-up areas – on their sets. When this became known to the scientists the old question of a 'Town Finder' as a self-contained airborne radar was revived.

In November 1941 a Blenheim bomber was flown from Christchurch, near Bournemouth, with the centimetric beam tilted downwards: the aerial was rotated at 30 rpm and responses were immediately observed, not only from built-up areas but other features on the ground. At a meeting on 23 December the Secretary of State for Air instructed that six flights should be made to 'determine whether the signals obtained . . . could be definitely associated with specific ground objects'. The flights duly took place and the results were sufficiently encouraging for a group to be set up under Professor Dee. It was led by a young scientist, Bernard Lovell.

Sir Bernard remembers that the work was at first coded 'BN' for Blind Navigation. This was soon changed to H2S, the name the system was ulti-mately known by, so called, according to his recollection, because of Lord Cherwell's remark on being shown H2S that 'it was stinking because it ought to have been done years before'.[10]

The H2S radar operated a magnetron transmitter on ten centimetres: the rotating aerial under the aircraft sent out a very narrow beam which scanned the ground below the aircraft. Water and very flat open country did not reflect pulses back but vertical buildings in built-up areas did. The result was a map-like presentation which could be followed by the navigator. The actual picture on the tube was known as PPI (Plan Position Indicator); the line of the scanning beam rotated continuously and 'painted' the ground details as it scanned them. The tube had a long-persistence phosphor so that the outlines of the returns remained until repainted by the next orbit of the rotating beam.

But the road from the first experiments to H2S being fitted to Bomber Command aircraft was to prove particularly stony. The first step was to fit the rotating scanning aerial into a heavy bomber – the Blenheim had only carried a modified AI Mk VII aerial which was unsatisfactory for the proposed H2S. Contact was made with the Handley Page Company and a perspex cupola was to be installed under a Halifax in the position originally designed for a gun-turret. This work was initiated on 4 January 1942 and the Halifax, V9977, landed at Hurn (Bournemouth) on 22 March 1942.

Opposite
Top left: An early 'strapped' magnetron, cut away to show the strapping of the anode.

Middle left: An X-ray photograph of the CV64 magnetron, which was given to the Americans in 1940 and was to found an industry in the USA.

Top right: When the 10-cm aerial scanner was tilted down it formed the basis of H2S, the self-contained navigation radar used by Bomber Command.

The bomber was then fitted with the first experimental H2S set, using the magnetron section of an AI Mk VII. The pace of development in those days is astonishing now, for the first flight with the H2S was made in the evening of 16 April. Unfortunately a hidden switch in a power supply prevented the radar from working but the next morning's flight was successful and towns were identified at six miles range from 8000 feet.

This early success was, however, not to last and for some time the small H2S team were to suffer setback after setback. One of the first problems was the effect of altitude on the new radar. The early flights in the Blenheim and later the Halifax had been made at around 8000 feet: when the flights were made at the high altitudes that would be used operationally, all kinds of problems arose. While these were being solved, the whole organisation of TRE was moved from Worth Matravers to Malvern. (This was because of the vulnerability of the coastal site near Swanage, it being feared that, following the Bruneval raid, the Germans might try a similar enterprise against TRE.)

A new obstacle now arose: it was decided at Air Staff level that the magnetron, which was vital to the success of H2S, was too secret to be flown over enemy territory. This decision had been influenced by tests which showed that the copper anode which held the secret of the device was virtually indestructible – at least by a charge that would destroy it and not the aircraft as well. It had therefore been ordered that the discarded Klystron, a device believed to be known to the Germans and, anyway, easily destroyed, was to be used as an alternative to the Magnetron. Valuable time was lost in proving that the Klystron as it then existed was a poor substitute. Moreover, though now hard to believe, there was considerable opposition to H2S: for some time its opponents outnumbered its protagonists.

The Air Staff convened on 19 May to review the whole question. It should be remembered that at that time Gee was operational and Oboe showing high promise. What probably saved H2S was the fact that these other aids were restricted by range to the Ruhr, whereas H2S was only limited by the range of the aircraft itself. The Air Staff gave H2S a reprieve, provided that:

'(a) The system should be accurate enough to guarantee that bombs would fall within an industrial or other area selected as a target.

(b) The Air Staff would be satisfied in the first instance if the range of the device enabled the aircraft to home on a built-up area from 15 miles at 15,000 feet.'[11]

This reassuring directive from the Air Staff did little to lessen the team's troubles. The next blow was the worst. In the late afternoon of 7 June, the Halifax bomber that was the test-bed for H2S took off from TRE's new airfield at Defford. Bernard Lovell should have been on board for the trials:

'. . . there was no respite, the pressure was enormous, and either I or some members of my group were flying every day in this Halifax – V-Victor 9977. I even remember the number of that plane clearly to this day. On Sunday 7 June I was taking a day off, tired of flying.'

On board were five of the key members of the H2S team, including A. D.

Above: An H2S scanner under a Halifax, with the protective cover removed.

Top left: A Halifax heavy bomber with the H2S blister clearly visible underneath it.

Left: An RAF navigator adjusts his H2S radar.

Blumlein, a brilliant scientist from the EMI Company, who was making a valuable contribution to the project and whose Company was about to undertake the large-scale production of H2S.

Lovell watched the Halifax take off:

'. . . I then returned to Malvern. About 7 o'clock that evening I had a telephone call from Defford Airfield to say that the Halifax had not returned.

'Then reports of a crash in South Wales began to come in. The rest of that night was a nightmare: I was driven by the CO of Defford, winding through those lanes near Ross-on-Wye, searching for the wreckage and then we found the field with the burnt-out Halifax.

'It was wartime, and no time for emotions; our first duty was to search for the highly secret equipment and collect the bits and pieces up.

'It was a very tragic event which I think under normal circumstances would have knocked us out completely.' [12]

There were no survivors from the crash: the RAF crew and the H2S team had perished. The effect on those remaining can well be imagined.

By now, such were the pressures to provide H2S for the RAF that the work continued: within days a replacement Halifax was made available and on 3 July Churchill himself ordered an all-out effort to equip two squadrons of RAF heavy bombers with operational H2S by October.

In spite of the sceptics and the difficulties, the work went on and a 'crash programme' was mounted with manufacturers and service units to get H2S operational. One of the most enthusiastic supporters was Air Vice Marshal D. C. T. Bennett, who was then the newly-appointed Commander of the Pathfinder Force and who had spent some time at Defford test-flying the new radar.

By the end of 1942, sets were installed in twelve Halifaxes of 38 Squadron and twelve Stirlings of 7 Squadron. After an intensive period of training the crews were judged ready for an operational flight. The first H2S operation was on the night of 30/31 January 1943, when in appalling weather six H2S-equipped bombers (four Stirlings and two Halifaxes) successfully marked the target, Hamburg, for the main force.

That raid was followed by others on Cologne, Turin and again Hamburg, on each occasion a small number of H2S aircraft of the Pathfinder units marking the targets. By February, Bomber Command issued a memorandum on the use of H2S:

'H2S in its present form fully meets Air Staff requirements and has exceeded expectations in that towns have proved easy to identify both by shape and relative positions.

'In addition to the exceptional value of H2S for identification and bombing of the target, its great navigational value has been proved beyond all doubt.

'The recognition of islands, coast-lines, estuaries and lakes has been particularly easy.

'In fact the problem of accurate navigation under almost any weather conditions is solved by H2S when operated by a trained navigator.' [13]

Continual development work went on, and by the end of 1943 an improved H2S, working on three centimetres, was able to give details of a densely built-up area, such as Berlin, and with the 'X'-band H2S, as it was called, that city was heavily attacked on 22 November – the opening of the 'Battle of Berlin'.

The most successful raid with the 3-centimetre H2S was on the night of 3/4 December 1943, when 500 RAF bombers made the first heavy attack of the war on Leipzig. The Pathfinders using H2S – Leipzig was well out of range of Oboe and Gee – marked with great precision, and the raid was later regarded as the most precise 'Pathfinding' of the war. The development of the X-band, 3-cm H2S was such that bombing through cloud and at night achieved accuracies near to that of visual bomb sights in daylight.

Gee, Oboe and H2S, the three main aids of the RAF night offensive

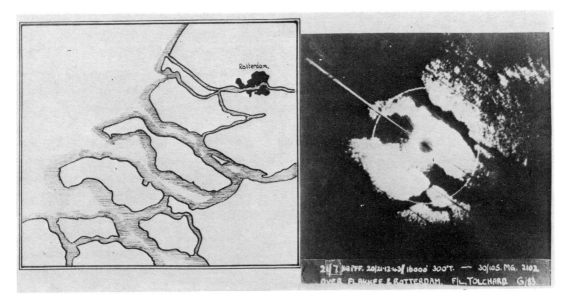

against Germany, did not go unchallenged. During the winter of 1942–3, an unremitting war of electronic countermeasures was fought out in the night sky over Germany. It was a battle that was to sway from one side to the other.

As the RAF bombers took off and assembled for the near-nightly raids, German radar would be waiting, listening for the first echoes that would give the clue to the target for that particular night. The enemy radar was the front line of a complex defence organisation.

British Air Intelligence had, one way and another, discovered a good deal about German radar: just how these secrets had been penetrated is an intriguing story. It began in December 1939 when, following the Battle of the River Plate, the German battleship *Graf Spee* was scuttled by her crew in shallow waters off Montevideo. Pictures of the stricken ship were published in newspapers throughout the world, many of which clearly showed an unusual aerial array high on the battleship's mast.

An H2S return photographed from the indicator tube in a Lancaster over Holland.

The unusual aerial array above the optical rangefinder on top of *Graf Spee*'s superstructure. This was the first positive proof of the existence of German gunlaying radar.

British Intelligence sent a radar scientist from Watson Watt's team – Bainbridge Bell – to Montevideo to try to examine the aerial. He duly arrived and climbed the mast of the listing wreck, reporting that the vessel had been equipped with a form of rotating radar aerial, probably for gunlaying use and working on either 57 or 114 centimetres.

An examination of prewar photographs of the *Graf Spee* and other similar German battleships revealed that the aerial structure, though hidden under canvas covers, was to be found on photographs taken as early as 1938. This was a surprise to British Intelligence: Royal Navy ships had no gunlaying radar at that time and would not have until 1941; but strangely, the Bainbridge Bell report seems to have been pigeon-holed and not a great deal of attention paid to it.

Dr R. V. Jones was now to be involved in the search for German radar and once again the Oslo Report gave a clue. One of the items in it referred to

'an aircraft detector system with a range of 120 km [75 miles], in which 20-kW short-wave transmitters were arranged along the German frontier, emitting 10-microsecond pulses which were reflected by aircraft and observed on a cathode-ray tube. Similar transmitters were to be installed all over Germany by April 1940.'

The anonymous author did not know the wavelength, though he did state that another system, using parabolic reflectors and operating on fifty centimetres, was being developed.

This was quoted by Jones in his Air Scientific Intelligence Report no. 7 of 17 July 1940.[14] The report went on to consider a new German code name 'Freya', which had been mentioned by a 'source', probably an Enigma intercept, dated 5 July 1940, to the effect that:

'. . . German aircraft were able to intercept [on 30 June] British armed reconnaissance owing to excellent Freya-Meldung [Freya Reports].'

Further Enigma intercepts were decoded and one mentioned:

'On 14 July . . . a request from Flakbrigade VII to Luftgau West for Flugmeldtrupp 20311 [Aircraft Reporting Troop] to be moved close to the Freya Geräte.'

'20311', Jones discovered, was a map reference for a point on the Cap de la Hague, on the extremity of the Cherbourg Peninsula near the small village of Auderville. There was yet another message which dealt with the establishment of a 3.7-cm Flak battery at Lannion, thought to be another Freya site, on the Brittany coast overlooking the sea.

A summary of the 'Freya' intelligence was that:

1) The Germans have an aircraft detection system, which

2) is an aid to interception and

3) which depends on the 'Freya Geräte' which

4) merits protection by 3.7-cm Flak.

5) Two positions have been given, both of which are on the coast.

At the end of July 1940 a Royal Navy destroyer, HMS *Delight*, had been sunk by Stuka dive-bombers some twenty miles south of Portland Bill. An

Enigma message reported that the ship 'had been sunk with the aid of Freya reports'. This message, Jones thought, confirmed the existence of a radar called 'Freya', sited on the Cherbourg Peninsula. He then decided to look into the provenance of Freya in Norse mythology:

'I got on to the idea that Freya was the Nordic Venus who had not merely sacrificed, but massacred her honour to gain possession of a magic necklace, Brisinga-men.

'The necklace was guarded by Heimdall, the watchman of the Gods, who could see *a hundred miles by day or night*.'

Though Heimdall would have been the most appropriate name for a radar, it was, Jones thought, too obvious, but he concluded that the next best choice, by association, would be 'Freya'.

There were two possible methods open to intelligence in 1940 for obtaining further information. One was a listening watch to try to identify pulse transmissions and to D/F them. The second was photographic reconnaissance. The first method was for a time unfortunately nullified by overlapping signals from British services; the second was also initially unsuccessful, due to the lack of detail available on the early short-focus cameras. However, new 20-inch lens cameras were coming into service and on 22 November 1940, Pilot Officer W. K. Manifold photographed several areas on the Hague peninsula.

When the prints were examined, there were two small unexplained circles to the north-west of a small village; about twenty feet across, they were too close together to be gun sites and were at first thought to be for some agricultural purpose.

The prints – they were a stereo pair – were enlarged and sent to Dr Charles Frank, a physicist on Jones's staff. The two photographs had been taken about ten seconds apart and, as he looked at them through a stereoscope, Frank noticed that they were not identical: the shadow cast by one of the 'objects' had moved between the first and second photographs. Jones asked him the name of the village. 'Auderville' was the reply.

A later low-level sortie flown over the site by Pilot Officer Manifold produced a magnificent oblique which clearly showed two rotating, directional-aerial arrays. The next problem was to try to identify the signals from the sites.

A scientific officer from TRE, Derek Gerrard, who had been posted to Jones's Air Intelligence staff had grown tired of sitting in a Whitehall office, and had enterprisingly fitted a VHF receiver into his car and drove along the South Coast listening for signs of enemy radar transmissions. Although arrested from time to time as a spy, he was able to detect pulse signals around 120 mHz ($2\frac{1}{2}$ metres). These signals, the ones which the RAF 'Y' Service had mistaken for British transmissions, were displayed on a cathode-ray tube at RAF Hawkinge and quickly confirmed as radar pulses with a 500-per-second repetition rate. Bearings indicated their source of origin as the Hague peninsula. The search for Freya was over.

Above: A German photograph of a Freya, *c.* 1941. On top of the main structure is the IFF aerial.

Above right: Pilot Officer Manifold's low-level pictures of the site, revealing the two Freya radar aerials.

Right: The original print of the unexplained structures at Auderville (circled).

Jones got the report of the successful detection of the Freya signals in the morning of the same day as the oblique photographs and was then able to report the discovery of Freya to the Air Ministry Staff that afternoon.

TRE continued to hunt for further radar signals using a mobile listening vehicle and, by October 1941, was able to issue a detailed report on an extensive 'Freya' coastal chain.[16] As a result of this initial success in uncovering at least a part of the German radar network Jones was asked to try to discover details of the enemy's entire radar defences.

From the outset, it was obvious to Air Scientific Intelligence that the Freya radar was only part of the story. From the nature of the aerials and the relatively long wavelength, it was concluded that Freya was an early warning radar corresponding to the British CH Chain and giving only range and bearing. There must, therefore, be much more precise and unknown radars to supplement it. The problem was how to find them.

As the RAF began to step up the attack on Germany, the need for such intelligence was growing. It was also becoming obvious that sooner or later the continent would have to be invaded.

Earlier it was said that the search for German radar was conducted in two ways: photographic reconnaissance and listening. There was of course a third option: reports from agents on the ground. It was from the reports of agents and other sources that a new code name began to appear in connection with enemy radar: 'Würzburg'. This, it was thought, must be the much more precise equipment necessary to give height and to direct searchlights, flak or night fighters on to an individual aircraft. To achieve that sort of accuracy, the radar responsible would be required to work on a much shorter wavelength than the Freyas, which would not normally be detectable in England. So a Wellington of 109 Squadron, equipped with a suitable receiver operated by TRE personnel, took off from Boscombe Down on the evening of 8 May 1941 on an electronic intelligence flight.[17]

The aircraft flew over Brittany and picked up radar signals on 53 cms (between 558 and 560 mHz) over nine locations: the enemy radar was noted as being able to track the aircraft for about twenty-five miles. The crew also reported powerful searchlights suddenly being switched on and directed to the Wellington; these lights 'followed the aircraft with good accuracy' and seemed to act as masters for other groups of searchlights. The crew concluded that the master lights were being directed by the radar.

The Wellington had been fitted with an omni-directional aerial for the search flight; the operators therefore could do no more than indicate the general area of the source of the radar signals they heard.

Jones knew that these 53-cm radars would be very difficult to find: because of their short wavelength they would be much smaller than the Freya, and that had been hard enough to locate. To try to solve the dilemma, Jones put himself in the position of the German commanders of the radar stations: they were, after all, working in hostile occupied country; with each new site, new problems of security and guarding would arise. Any existing Freya stations would have the required communications, power supplies, a secure perimeter and accommodation; the obvious choice was, therefore, to set up any new or additional radar on an existing site. Known Freya stations were rephotographed and very carefully examined.

In August 1941, a Freya was photographed on a coastal site on top of the cliffs at Cap d'Antifer, near the village of Bruneval. Charles Frank examined the prints and noticed that there was a narrow path from the Freya site which appeared to lead to a large château; but the path stopped about twenty yards short of the house, ending in a loop. Beside the loop was a small dot. Jones

Left: The lonely house on the cliffs at Cap d'Antifer, near Bruneval. The arrow points to the small dot which Jones thought might be the elusive Würzburg radar. This picture gives some idea of the difficulties faced by photographic interpreters.

Right: Tony Hill's magnificent low-level oblique, showing the Würzburg paraboloid. Jones described this shot as 'one of the great pictures of the war'.

remembers that the dot was so small that they had to get several prints made to prove it was not just a speck of dust. Could this tiny object be the parabolic aerial of a Würzburg radar?

One of the most brilliant photographic reconnaissance pilots, Flight Lieutenant Tony Hill, hearing of the inadequately small-scale photographs, quite unofficially took off from Benson in his PR Spitfire to get a low-level photograph of the Bruneval site. It was a far from easy sortie. The oblique cameras in Spitfires took their pictures through a porthole in the side of the fuselage: taking a picture of a small, heavily defended object at right angles to the line of flight, at something approaching 350 mph, called for fine judgment and great courage. As Tony Hill flashed over the radar station at about 300 feet his camera jammed, but he reported to Squadron Leader Wavell, of the 'G' Section, RAF Medmenham, that he had seen the object and 'it looks like an electric bowl fire about 10 feet across'.

Next day, 15 December, Tony Hill again took his Spitfire to Bruneval and this time returned with two of the great photographs of the Second World War. The exceptional prints showed in detail the small Würzburg radar parabola, almost certainly the source of the 53-cm transmissions that had been detected; the photographs showed additionally that, although the site was perched on the top of 400-foot cliffs, there was a small beach close by. After looking at the beach on the print, Jones turned to Charles Frank, and said, 'Look, I think we could get in there. . . .' The result was the now famous Bruneval raid, Operation Biting, which was mounted on the night of 27/28 March 1942.

At the suggestion of Lord Louis Mountbatten, Combined Operations decided not to make a seaborne raid but an airborne attack; the raiding party with, it was hoped, parts of the Würzburg and prisoners would be evacuated by sea from the small beach. The raid was to be made by C Company of the 2nd Battalion of the Parachute Regiment, led by Lieutenant Vernon of the Royal Engineers; it included one RAF man, a skilled radar mechanic, Flight

Sergeant C. W. H. Cox, who had volunteered for the operation, though he had never before been up in an aircraft, much less parachuted at night from one.

The primary object of the raid was to remove the aerial from the centre of the parabolic reflector; this would enable experts to ascertain if the wavelength was 53 cms. As a precaution, in case the raid turned out to be militarily unsuccessful, a receiver operated by a scientific officer from TRE, D. H. Priest, was to be carried in one of the seaborne vessels to check the frequency of any transmissions from the Bruneval site.[18] The secondary objective was to capture the radar receiver and the cathode-ray tube presentation: this should, on examination, reveal any anti-jamming measures that the Germans had built into the Würzburg. It was also hoped that the transmitter would reveal the extent of the enemy techniques on 50 cms; therefore, if possible, the transmitter itself should be brought back. A third objective was the capture of at least one, preferably two, German operators, so that some idea of the method of operation of the radar network might be established through interrogation.

General Intelligence could be gained simply from the labels on the equipment, since the serial numbers, dates and modification records would give a fair picture of German radar production. Such importance was attached to this aspect of the raid that the dismantling party were instructed to remove only the labels if the actual apparatus proved impossible to bring back. The raiders were also to make sketches and take photographs of the inside of the radar control cabin.

The timetable of the raid allowed the dismantling party, led by Lt Vernon and Flight Sgt Cox, only half an hour. They trained on a British 50-cm gunlaying radar, as this was thought to be the nearest equivalent to the German Würzburg, first taking the photographs, then dismantling the apparatus systematically, starting with the aerial then working backwards through the receiver and transmitter to the presentation equipment. After practice, the dismantling was achieved in the allotted thirty minutes.

Before the actual raid, Jones made efforts to have Flight Sgt Cox transferred to the Army, if only for this operation: as the only RAF man in the raiding party, if captured it would be obvious to the Germans that he must be a radar expert. He knew a great deal about British radar and would undoubtedly be rigorously and skilfully interrogated. Although this combined operation was a major undertaking and was to involve the three services, it nevertheless proved impossible to get Cox into Army uniform, even on a temporary basis: bureaucracy triumphed and he went on the raid as 955754 Flight Sergeant Cox C. W. H., Royal Air Force.

On 27 March, the raiders took off in RAF Whitleys from Thruxton and jumped near the site at around midnight. They achieved complete surprise, which does not say much for the operational efficiency of that particular radar station. Here is part of Lt Vernon's report, which he made just after the raid:

'Having landed successfully, I went over the crest of the hill to the forming-up point to collect the sappers. I waited for 5 to 10 minutes for the other two sapper detachments to reach the place appointed. They had brought trolleys with them to carry the tools and equipment.

'We all set off . . . and made our way up the other side of the valley in the direction of the house skirting right round the side of the hill until we reached three machine gun positions on the edge of the cliff.

'These we assaulted. We then made our way up to the equipment [the Würzburg].'[18]

There was a full moon and the ground was snow-covered. Flight Sgt Cox had jumped with a different stick and in his report he stated:

'I met Mr Vernon at the forming-up point at approximately 1235. We proceeded under Mr Vernon's direction to pull the trolleys up towards the house over various barbed-wire defences and through snow, which was rather rough going.

'Mr Vernon went on to the house and said we must make our way to the left hand side of the house and conceal ourselves until he whistled or shouted for us. This we did, and lay in a small ridge for what seemed a long time. . . . Then we all went through some more barbed wire to the equipment. I saw Mr Vernon and he said "This is it!"

'I surveyed the apparatus and found it to my surprise just like the photograph.'[18]

Cox then began to dismantle the aerial, assisted by one of the sappers; it was not all that easy and

'During the whole period of working at the equipment, bullets were flying much too close to be pleasant, but while we were working on the parabola we were protected by the metal of the parabola itself.

'By this time the soldiers were getting impatient and we were told to withdraw.'

Since part of the raiding party had landed some distance away, the timing of the attack went awry and consequently the dismantling party had only ten minutes instead of the thirty planned; however, although under fire, during that short time they did succeed in removing the vital parts of the Würzburg, as Jones revealed in his post-raid report:

'Lt Vernon's party removed the aerial by cutting through its base with a hacksaw. Cox traced the aerial lead back to the transmitter and proceeded systematically to remove the boxes of equipment found behind the para-boloid. In this way the party captured the transmitter, receiver, the pulse generator and the intermediate frequency amplifier, which represented all the important equipment housed in the pedestal behind the paraboloid.

'Had there been a little more time, they would undoubtedly have captured the only remaining important item, the presentation gear . . . which was inside the operator's cabin. . . .

'Three prisoners were taken; two were from the military guard at the beach, and the third was a reserve operator for the Würzburg apparatus . . . by skilful handling he might be led to tell us the important facts about the missing items. . . .'[19]

The raiders withdrew to the small beach with the captured radar and returned safely by sea to England. When the equipment was evaluated at TRE it was noted that:

'the outstanding feature of the equipment was its beautiful construction, while its date of design [1939, confirmed from the labels attached] shows that Germany was then ahead of us in the technique on 53 cms.

'Valuable knowledge has been gained for devising counter measures.'

There were several unforeseen repercussions following the raid. The Germans blew up the conspicuous house at Bruneval, which was ironic because the house, as the apparent reason for the path seen in the original high-level photograph, nearly resulted in Intelligence missing the Würzburg altogether. Every other German radar station was now surrounded by dense barbed wire, which prevented grass and vegetation under it being cut or grazed. This made the sites much easier to spot on aerial photographs, and several other Würzburgs were in fact identified in this way.

As mentioned earlier, it was feared that a similar raid might be mounted by the Germans on TRE, near Swanage. The RAF took a high-level photograph of the Establishment and it proved to be a photographic interpreter's paradise. The whole of TRE was therefore moved to Malvern, in Worcestershire, to be out of harm's way – though not without a good deal of disruption of the research work being done at the time, including that of H2S. It was learned after the war that high-ranking German Parachute officers had been greatly impressed by the Bruneval operation and would doubtless have been only too eager to emulate it. So perhaps the decision to move TRE from its relatively exposed coastal site was a prudent one.

Although the Bruneval raid was a success, it was soon apparent that the Würzburg radar was only part of the story. From interrogation of prisoners, agents' reports and information from 'other sources', Air Scientific Intelligence began to hear of 'Würzburg Riese' – Giant Würzburg. Dr Jones had received a rather poor photograph of a large structure in the Tiergarten in Berlin, taken by someone in the American Embassy there and smuggled out to London. (The United States at that time, 1941, were still officially at peace with Germany.)

For some time it was thought that the object – only half of which was visible – was a searchlight, but then by chance a Chinese physicist, who had been in Berlin and had seen the Tiergarten structure, came through London and was able to tell Jones that the object was in fact a large radar paraboloid. By that time, Photographic Reconnaissance had photographed Berlin and, from these pictures, Jones was able to scale the dish at 20-ft diameter. Almost at the same time an agent reported a similar 20-ft dish – this one on the Dutch island of Walchern, near Domberg. On 2 May 1942, Tony Hill took his Spitfire there and produced yet another set of superb low-level oblique photographs showing the Giant Würzburg. One print was even nicely scaled by a Luftwaffe man, frozen by the camera in the act of climbing up to the cabin.

Jones now had the evidence he needed to piece together the elements of

Another low-level photograph taken by Tony Hill, showing the Giant Würzburg on Walchern.

the German defensive radar networks: the Freyas for early warning of approaching bombers; the small 'Bruneval' 53-cm radar for searchlight and flak direction; and the Giant Würzburgs for tracking individual bombers and guiding night fighters on to them.

At this time a Belgian agent managed to steal a map of the entire radar disposition of a sector in Belgium. This map showed clearly the ranges of the various radars and gave Scientific Intelligence valuable details of the 'Kammhuber' line – a defence 'wall' of radars stretching from Alsace to Norway, so called by British Intelligence after the General in charge of German night fighters at that time, Generalmajor Josef Kammhuber. (The map incidentally was taken out of Belgium by a courier who was the fireman on the Brussels-Lyons Express. He carried his dispatches hidden in the coal on the locomotive's tender; if the train had been stopped and searched, all he had to do was to pop the evidence into the engine's firebox!)

The Kammhuber line or, to give it its German name, Himmelbett (four-poster bed) consisted of a number of adjacent boxes of radar, each comprising a Freya and two Giant Würzburgs. The Luftwaffe had a system of fighter control and radar reporting rooms much like the RAF. The plotting of the tracks of bombers and the intercepting night fighters, based on information from the radar, was carried out in the operation room for each sector. After the Freyas had given advance warning of the approach of enemy bombers, a Würzburg would isolate an individual aircraft. Meanwhile,

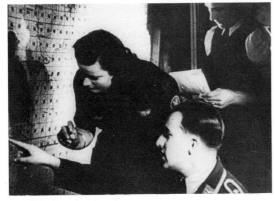

German night fighters would have been scrambled as soon as the Freyas had picked up the approaching raid, and one of the fighters would be followed by the second Würzburg. The actual plotting was done at each sector's control room by female auxiliaries – Luftwaffe Hilferin. The girls were known in Luftwaffe slang as 'Blitzmädel' (literally 'Lightning Maidens'). Three girls were allocated to track the plots of each of the Giant Würzburgs. This was done on a large, translucent glass plate known as a 'Seeburg Tisch' (table). The radar position of both the bomber and the night fighter were displayed on the table as moving spots of light – a red spot for the bomber and a green spot for the fighter. The table was divided up with a section of the German Fighter Grid: in this Grid, one square measured half a degree of longitude by a quarter degree of latitude. The squares were identified with two-letter designations, and were themselves subdivided into nine smaller squares, numbered from 1 to 9. On the Seeburg Table, aircraft were plotted to the nearest square, representing an airspace of roughly 9 × 11 kilometres – well within the search capability of the fighters' airborne-interception radar. Each Seeburg Table would represent the airspace covered by the sector's radar.

The girls would get information on range, bearing and height of the bomber continuously and, as the red light moved over the table, its track would be traced in chinagraph on the glass. A Luftwaffe officer acting as the Fighter Controller sat on a dais overlooking the table and directed the fighter by an HF radio link: as the night fighter closed with the bomber, its track was also

A German night-fighter sector control room (this one was for Jagddivision 2 in Denmark). Blitzmädel working on plots on a Seeburg Table keep the tracks of bombers and night fighters up to date on a large translucent screen. The Fighter Controller studies the radar tracks of RAF bombers before giving an interception course to his fighters.

traced on the table. The fighter pilot's airborne radar set, code named 'Lichtenstein', operating on 62 cms, would enable him to close with the bomber from about three miles down to visual range.

Once the existence of the Kammhuber line was known to British Intelligence, countermeasures were deployed. The 'Line', being a series of linked and overlapping sectors, had little depth, so an immediate counter-measure was to channel the bomber stream through one sector in as compact a formation as was possible with heavy bombers flying at night. The object was to swamp the Würzburg radars which could only track one bomber at a time. Once through the Line, the bombers would be relatively free from the German night fighters which were causing very heavy losses. The Germans countered the move by deepening the Line so that a bomber had to fly through several sectors; there were also heavy radar-controlled flak and searchlight defences round all likely industrial targets.

Since the Germans were using a form of ground-controlled interception for their night fighters, an obvious countermove was to jam the controllers' radio link and the night fighters' radar, but before any of this could be achieved, the exact wavelengths had to be ascertained.

RAF 'Y' Listening Stations had detected faint pulse signals on 490 mHz (62 centimetres) and they also heard German controllers directing their fighters, but there was no positive evidence that the 62-cm signals heard were in fact from the night fighters' radar. There was only one certain way of confirming this: that was by deliberately flying a 'ferret' aircraft, equipped with a radar receiver, into a night-fighter sector in the hope that it would be attacked by a radar-equipped fighter: a very dangerous mission.

To give the crew a chance, efforts were made to get the fastest aircraft available – a Mosquito, but although this was agreed by Bomber Command there was some delay, so instead of a 380 mph Mosquito a Wellington bomber, with a maximum speed of 255 mph, had to be used. On the night of 3/4 December 1942, the Wellington (DV819), piloted by Pilot Officer Paulton with Flying Officer Harold Jordan as the special radio observer, took off from Gransden Lodge and flew with the bombers that were to attack Frankfurt that night. At 0430 hours, when near Mainz, the Wellington left the main bomber stream and flew northwards alone. Very shortly after, Jordan picked up weak pulses on 490 kHz; for some minutes he monitored the signals and, as they were getting ominously louder, he transmitted the details of the intercept back to base in England. There then began a running battle with the night fighter, identified as a Ju88. Jordan was hit in the head but kept at his set and was able, by judging the position of the fighter from the strength and direction of the radar signals, to give his pilot warning enough to enable him to take violent evasive action. In this way they survived eleven attacks; every member of the crew was wounded and the Wellington was a flying sieve by the time it limped home, losing height and so badly damaged that the pilot considered that they had no hope of landing safely and decided to ditch the aircraft. Unfortunately the Wireless Operator/Air Gunner was so badly

injured that it was not thought he would survive the ditching, so Jordan's log of the night's interception was stuffed into a pocket of the gunner's flying suit and he was parachuted out of the aircraft over Canterbury. He landed safely (and later recovered); the Wellington came down in the sea off Deal and happily all the remaining crew were rescued. Jordan received an immediate DSO.

The secrets of Lichtenstein were further revealed when, on 9 May 1943, a Ju88, D5+EV, of 10/NJG3, landed at Dyce Airfield, Aberdeen, equipped with the FuG 202 Lichtenstein radar.[20] There remains a mystery about this aircraft, which is preserved at RAF St Athen: it appears that the crew had defected and that not only was its arrival expected but, according to one report, it even had an escort of RAF Spitfires. Whatever the reason, the gift of an operational Ju88 was a windfall for TRE and the radar was soon evaluated and found to be comparable with the British Mk VII AI, although the TRE report found certain deficiencies, noting that: '. . . efficient and quick interception is possible only by a fighter which has been vectored to within 30° of its target'.

The need for countermeasures was now very great, as the loss rate to German night fighters was reaching unacceptable proportions. In an effort to reduce these losses, a bewildering number of jammers, and counters, and counters to counters, in the battle against German radar, were developed. It was to be no quick and easy victory, for the enemy, in the words of a TRE report, was 'to show himself extremely resourceful in defence and a battle of wits developed between the scientists on each side'.

The techniques varied. 'Tinsel' called for the radio operators in the bombers to net their 1154/1155 standard airborne communication sets on to the German night-fighter controllers' RT link, jamming it by radiating engine noise from a microphone in one of the engine bays. 'Mandrel' was an airborne jammer for Freya, and was for a time operated from single-engine Defiant aircraft flying with the bombers. 'Jostle' and 'Airborne Cigar' were high-

Above left: Luftwaffe radar operators inside the control hut of a Giant Würzburg.

Above right: The indicator tube of a Giant Würzburg, showing returns from 3–5 kms.

powered airborne transmitters which superseded 'Tinsel' for jamming the controllers. 'Piperack' was an airborne jammer used against the Lichtenstein radar.

As well as straight noise-barrage jamming, more subtle methods were devised. 'Moonshine' was a transponder which made a single decoy aircraft appear on enemy radar as a large formation; 'Perfectos' was a device which triggered German fighters' IFF sets, revealing their position.

There was, too, later in the battle, Operation Corona, a counter in which the German night-fighter controllers were impersonated by German-speaking RAF men, who gave false instructions to the fighters. For a very short time these men operated from RAF bombers over Germany, but the Germans countered this by using women to direct the fighters, believing correctly that the RAF would not send WAAFs up in operational aircraft. This stratagem had been foreseen and German-speaking WAAFs were ready; they did not fly in the bombers, but operated from Hollywood Manor at Kingsdown in Kent, the transmitters being on the East Coast and beamed over Germany.

Many of these girls had come to Britain as refugees at the beginning of the war and thus spoke perfect German. One was Ruth Tosek, a Czech from the Sudetenland, who remembers Operation Corona well, particularly the reaction of the real German female controllers: [21]

'. . . They would say, "Das ist eine feind Stimme – an enemy voice, don't listen to it! Don't listen to it!" And we would reply, "Wir sind die richtige Stimme – *We* are the real voice." This would go on until the pilot became completely confused and didn't know who was who.'

To obtain the frequencies of the German radars and high-frequency communications networks, 'ferret' aircraft – Halifaxes and B17 Fortresses of the

highly secret 192 and 214 Radio Counter Measures Squadrons – flew with the main force, carrying sophisticated receivers: 'Bagful', an automatic wide-band receiver which searched the spectrum to locate German signals, and 'Blond', which analysed and recorded the nature of the signals found by 'Bagful'. These aircraft also carried many of the countermeasure jammers, such as 'Piperack', 'Mandrel' and 'Airborne Cigar'.

In spite of the countermeasures, by mid-1943 the loss rate of Bomber Command's aircraft was approaching the maximum that was considered to be acceptable: 200 four-engined bombers with their seven-man crews a month.

The German night fighters were twin-engined Me110s and Ju88s, carrying a pilot and a radar operator. Once they had been guided to within about two miles of the bomber by the ground controllers, the radar operator would then establish contact on his set and would 'talk' his pilot into visual range; the pilot would then manoeuvre his fighter under the bomber, which was the

Above left: A Revi sight, used for aiming the 'Schräge Musik' cannon on to the fuel tanks of RAF bombers.

Above right: The tube of the indicator unit of a German night-fighter interception radar. The blip is an RAF heavy bomber about a mile ahead of the fighter.

blind spot on most British types, gently pull the nose of his fighter up, and aim the guns at the fuel tanks. The night fighters were armed with three 7.9-mm MG17 machine guns and three 20-mm cannon. A short burst of this lethal armament usually resulted in the bomber immediately exploding into flames. Later versions of the Ju88 night fighter were fitted with two 20-mm MG151 cannon mounted in the top of the fuselage and firing upwards at an angle of between 70° and 80°. Using this armament, nicknamed 'Schräge Musik' (Jazz Music), the pilots simply formated underneath the bomber and aimed the guns through a special 'Revi' reflector site.

So successful was the Himmelbett system of controlling the night fighters that in mid-1943 Generalmajor Kammhuber argued that the number of his night-fighter groups (Nachtjagdgeschwader)† should be increased from six to eighteen and the Himmelbett zones increased to cover virtually all German airspace. Unfortunately Reichsmarschall Goering did not like Kammhuber and his plan was rejected; in the subsequent row, Kammhuber was replaced by Generalmajor Josef Schmid. The question of interception techniques, however, was to be drastically revised by events of the night of 24/25 July 1943.

Amongst all the countermeasures there was one device which would today doubtless be described as a 'Doomsday Weapon'. It carried the code-name 'Window' and was simply short strips of aluminium. These innocent-looking bundles of foil were in fact a weapon so deadly that Window became the subject of controversy at Cabinet level. The principle was very simple and was known from the earliest days of radar; it was that a piece of metal cut to half the wavelength of a radar acts as a resonating dipole aerial and will therefore reradiate much more of the radar pulse than the random structure of an aircraft. If the Window strips were cut to half the known German radar wavelength of 53 cms, i.e. 26.5 cms, each strip as it floated down would return a strong radar 'echo'. If dropped in large bundles, the cloud of Window would block the German radar network completely, while leaving the RAF's H2S 10-cm radar largely unaffected.

Opposite left: German airborne radar, similar to that fitted to night fighters – in this case an anti-shipping radar, Hohentwiel. These large arrays caused considerable drag, unlike the streamlined British 10-cm airborne radar (see p. 96).

But Window was a double-edged sword: the moment the RAF used it, the Germans could copy it and use it against British radar. So ran the argument among the scientists and the Air Staff. In fact the Germans had Window too, though they called it 'Düppel' and they too were afraid to use it: indeed when General Martini, the Luftwaffe Head of Signals, reported in 1942 the results of tests of Düppel, Goering was horrified and ordered that all copies of the report be destroyed and that no mention of the name was ever to be made again.

In England, one of the most outspoken opponents of Window was Sir Robert Watson Watt, who, Professor Jones has said,

'. . . was almost like Alec Guiness in the film *The Bridge on the River Kwai,*

---

†Each group was nominally equipped with 120 fighters.

in that, having built this great structure of radar, he did not want to see it ruined, even if it was German radar!'[22]

Jones was himself all for using Window, though Lord Cherwell, who had originally sponsored its trials, now was against using it.

The argument for and against continued and, on at least one occasion, the foil was actually loaded into the aircraft, then removed. Meanwhile the RAF bomber losses mounted until eventually, about a year later than it could have gone into operation, the Prime Minister gave the order 'Open the Window'.

Window was first used on the night of 24 July 1943, on Operation Gomorrah: the destruction by bombing of the German port of Hamburg. 746 heavy bombers took off from bases in eastern England, carrying, in addition to incendiaries and high explosive bombs, forty tons, ninety-two million strips, of Window. The effect on the German precision-radar defences was total and catastrophic: the cathode-ray tubes were alive with shimmering false echoes

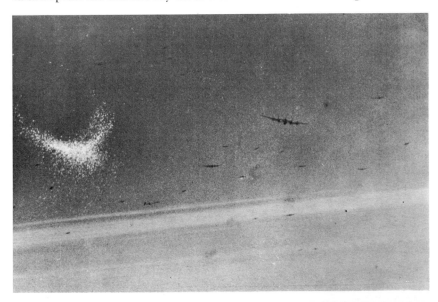

Lancaster bombers dropping Window over Germany.

Below: A German photograph showing the effect of Window on a Giant Würzburg radar (cf. the normal return on p. 113).

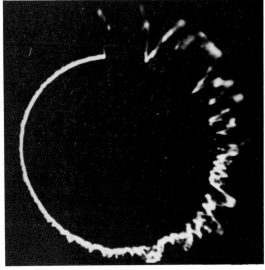

which blocked out everything; master searchlights, their radar useless, groped around the sky; the flak batteries simply fired blind in the vague hope of hitting a bomber. For the night fighters, the effect was even worse: many found themselves flying through enemy bomber formations that suddenly they could not detect; others were directed to contacts that melted away from them as they flew through the clouds of metal foil.

The H2S of the Pathfinders being unaffected by Window led the main force. It had been exceptionally dry that summer of 1943 and the city was like tinder; the incendiary bombs soon started fires that developed into an horrific firestorm, which virtually burned out Hamburg and caused the deaths of 51,000 of the port's inhabitants.

That night the RAF lost twelve bombers; without Window the losses statistically would have been around fifty, so some 280 aircrew had lived to fight another night. Albert Speer, then Hitler's Minister of Armaments, has said that if attacks on the scale of the Hamburg raid had been made against five other German towns, the war would have ended there and then in mid-1943.

Attacks on the Hamburg scale were not followed up: in the Secret War success was rarely absolute and the Germans reacted very quickly indeed to the changed situation caused by Window. Firstly, the Kammhuber Line, or Himmelbett system, was discarded, to be replaced by a new tactic, 'Wilde Sau' (Wild Boar). This strategy was very simple: as soon as the bombers' target had been identified, the night fighters would fly over it and rely on visual contact, seeing the bombers silhouetted against the fires and search-lights below. The very intensity of the RAF raids aided the fighters and the Wilde Sau tactics achieved considerable success. But there was a price to pay: to achieve visual contact, the German fighters were dependent on good weather; the RAF bombers, on the other hand, were largely equipped with H2S and able to operate in all weathers.

Another factor worked against the defenders: the Wilde Sau tactics called for much longer endurance; instead of operating in the relatively small 'boxes' of the Himmelbett system, fighters now had to range far and wide. The Me110 – a somewhat undistinguished fighter which had proved un-satisfactory during the Battle of Britain – had found a new lease of life: now with the changed conditions, its short range was severely curtailing its use. The Ju88, originally designed as a bomber, had sufficient endurance, but the fighters often had to fly from one end of Germany to the other, chasing feints and real raids; this resulted in exhausted crews having to land, when down to the last drop of fuel, on ill-lit and unfamiliar airfields, with the inevitable consequence of a growing number of accidents. Many fighters crashed simply from running out of fuel.

The Wild Boar tactics were only an interim measure, however. German scientists now began their countermeasures against Window. Many of the Himmelbett radar bases were moved into Germany and were fitted with certain counters aimed at reducing the effect of Window. It had soon been noted that the Window foil, once dropped from the aircraft, quickly lost its forward speed, while the bombers continued at some 200 mph; that being so, provided that the wind was below about 15 mph a new device, Wurzlaus, could detect the 'Doppler Shift' – that is the minute difference in the frequency of the pulses returned from the fast-moving bomber, compared with the virtually stationary Window.

There was also another aid, code-named 'Nuremburg', which could detect the slight modulation present on genuine echoes caused by the aircraft's propellers. Some skilled radar operators could actually hear this modulation without the Nuremburg. In addition, unknown to the RAF, the Germans had set up a network of special receiving stations equipped with 'Korfu', a set which could track the course of bombers from their H2S centimetric transmissions. With a range of 125 miles, the Korfu receivers could pick up British bombers as they took off from their bases.

These techniques and the 'Wild Boar' fighter patrols caused the losses sustained by the RAF night bombers again to creep up, only to drop a little as the winter of 1943/44 closed in. In early 1944, however, they suddenly rose dramatically to the worst losses yet.

On 21 January Bomber Command lost fifty-five aircraft out of a force of 648 attacking Magdeburg. Later that month, of 683 bombers raiding Berlin forty-three were lost. On 19 February seventy-eight heavy bombers failed to return from Leipzig. Worse was to come, for on the night of 30 March of the 795 bombers attacking Nuremberg no fewer than ninety-four were lost – nearly twelve per cent, the highest figures ever for a single night.

Losses on that scale could not be sustained; they were outstripping replacement crew training and aircraft production; it was becoming only too clear that the German scientists had developed some unknown and highly effective countermeasures to Window, for numerous crews were now reporting running battles with night fighters all the way to and from the targets.

The first hint came in the spring of 1944: an American Air Force long-range fighter caught a Ju88 night fighter in daylight. It was shot down; when the camera-gun film was examined, it revealed a cluster of long radar aerials on the nose of the aircraft. The photograph was not sufficiently clear for the radar aerials to be measured and there, for the moment, the matter rested; but in the small hours of 13 July, there came an incredible stroke of luck: a nearly new Ju88G of 7/NJG2, coded 4R + UR, landed by mistake at an RAF airfield – Woodbridge, in Essex. The unfortunate pilot had made the classic error of flying a reciprocal compass course. Daylight revealed that this night fighter had the same long aerials, known as 'Hirschgeweih' – stags' antlers – to the German crews, that had been seen in the American photograph. These aerials were part of an unknown radar, FuG220 or Lichtenstein SN2: the equipment operated on $3\frac{1}{2}$ metres (90 mHz) and was therefore unaffected by the Window the RAF had been dropping, which was cut for 50-cm radar.

In addition to this new radar, the aircraft carried two other significant devices: an FuG 227 'Flensburg' and FuG 350 'Naxos'. The first of these was

4R + UR, the
Ju88G-1 which
inadvertently
landed at
Woodbridge.

a radar receiver tuned to the frequency of a tail-warning radar, coded Monica, with which most RAF bombers were then fitted. The other set, Naxos, was tuned to the H2S radars. When the captured Ju88 was test-flown from Farnborough, the RAF pilot had no difficulty in 'homing' into a firing position on a Lancaster from forty-five miles away just by using the Flensburg receiver tuned to the bomber's Monica radar. The Naxos set also proved capable of 'homing' on to H2S 10-cm transmissions.

It was now clear how the Germans had nullified the effect of Window: they had devised new techniques to utilise the SN2 and the homing radars. These tactics were called 'Zahme Sau' (Tame Boar): aircraft circled round radio beacons and were then directed to the bomber streams from Freya and a PPI version of Freya, coded Jagdschloss (Huntingcastle), an enormous device operating on 150 mHz (and thus immune to 50-cm Window), its 2-metre aerials slowly rotating on top of a castle-like structure, driven by a motor of at least 140 hp. This radar had a range of between two and 120 kilometres, but gave no height indication.

The effectiveness of the new measures was the cause of the very heavy losses in the early part of 1944 and they had enabled German fighter pilots to amass very high scores against RAF bombers, the most successful being Major Prince Heinrich zu Saya Wittgenstein, who shot down eighty-four bombers – four in a single night. He was himself shot down and killed by an unknown air gunner, probably in a Lancaster, on 21 January 1944: that was the night the RAF lost fifty-five bombers in raiding Magdeburg.

The repercussions of the unexpected gift of the Ju88 were immediate: within ten days a new long Window (coded 'Rope') was in use, which was to prove as effective against the new SN2 Lichtenstein as against the earlier radars. Monica was removed from all operational Bomber Command aircraft and crews, who had been in the habit of leaving the H2S on from take-off to landing, were now instructed to use the H2S only when strictly necessary.

With SN2, Naxos and Flensburg countered, the German night-fighter force was in reality spent. True, new radars were put into service: Neptune, operating on 170 mHz, which was soon 'Windowed', and finally the FuG240

Above left: The radar operator's position in 4R+UR. The large sloping unit (right) is the FuG220 SN2 Lichtenstein radar, then unknown to RAF Intelligence. Behind it is the FuG277 Flensburg receiver, which could home on to Monica.

Above right: The huge Jagdschloss radar.

Left: Major Prince Heinrich zu Saya Wittgenstein.

Berlin, a 10-cm radar built around copies of a magnetron captured from a crashed Stirling's H2S. Only about ten of these sets were ever built. But by now RAF Mosquito night fighters were flying with the bomber streams and attacking the German night fighters. The hunters had become the hunted.

From late 1944 an additional, and ultimately fatal, factor working against the German night fighters was fuel. Shortage of aviation spirit, caused by the daylight bombing of the oil refineries, was curtailing training and operational flying; many serviceable fighters were simply grounded for want of fuel and its shortage reduced the number of fighter sorties from 200 to fifty per night – a situation which became steadily worse until the inevitable end of the war.

When peace came to Europe, scientific teams picked their way through the rubble and collected some of the superbly engineered Giant Würzburgs: they were given new electronics and allocated to universities. One of them was to discover the Hydrogen line on 23 centimetres, founding the new science of radio astronomy which has since discovered Pulsars, Quasars and Black Holes and reached to the very limits of space.

A German wartime photograph of a V1 just after launching.

Below: A wartime reconstruction of the layout of the V1, based on British Intelligence information and the examination of fragments. Operational V1s did not have tapered wings.

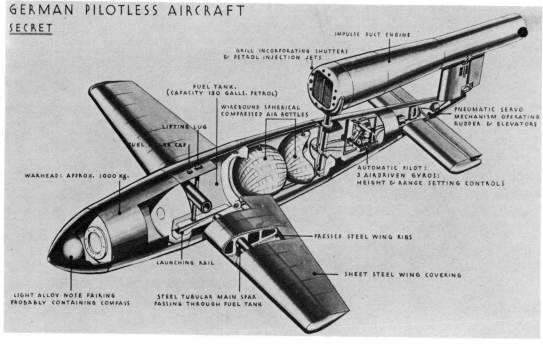

GERMAN PILOTLESS AIRCRAFT
SECRET

IMPULSE DUCT ENGINE

GRILL INCORPORATING SHUTTERS
& PETROL INJECTION JETS

FUEL TANK,
(CAPACITY 130 GALLS, PETROL)

WIREBOUND SPHERICAL
COMPRESSED AIR BOTTLES

PNEUMATIC SERVO
MECHANISM OPERATING
RUDDER & ELEVATORS

LIFTING LUG

FUEL FILLER CAP

AUTOMATIC PILOT:
3 AIRDRIVEN GYROS:
HEIGHT & RANGE SETTING CONTROLS

WARHEAD: APPROX. 1000 Kg.

PRESSED STEEL WING RIBS

LAUNCHING RAIL

SHEET STEEL WING COVERING

LIGHT ALLOY NOSE FAIRING
PROBABLY CONTAINING COMPASS

STEEL TUBULAR MAIN SPAR
PASSING THROUGH FUEL TANK

3. TERROR WEAPONS

In the early hours of 13 June 1944, just one week after the D-day landings, a small aircraft crossed the English coast, flying low and very fast towards London. It was making a noise like a large motorcycle without a silencer; it also appeared to be on fire. On reaching the capital the engine suddenly cut and the plane dived and exploded in Grove Road, Bethnal Green, killing six people, destroying a number of houses and badly damaging a railway bridge. Rescue workers were quickly on the scene and, after tending the injured, they searched the debris for the crew of the aircraft that had crashed. They searched in vain and found none: there were none.

The unfortunate civilians killed that morning in June 1944 were the first casualties of a new era of warfare: the long-range guided missile. The incident at Grove Road was not the only one: four of these pilotless planes had crossed the coast, but the only one to penetrate into inner London was also the only one that night to cause casualties. It would not be the last: within the next twenty-four hours 393 were fired, and before the bombardment was over 6000 people were to be killed, and a further 18,000 seriously injured, mostly in London.

The Press at first called them 'Robot Planes' but they became known as 'Buzz Bombs' or 'Doodlebugs': the Germans simply called them the V1 – 'Vergeltungswaffen Eins' (Revenge Weapon One).

Although the general public knew nothing of the V1s until they actually began to arrive, they were known to the Government as early as the previous September; and not only flying bombs, but also long-range rockets. Dr Jones had warned in a report dated 25 September 1943:

'Much information has been collected. Allowing for the inaccuracies which often occur in individual accounts, they form a coherent picture which despite the bewildering effect of propaganda has but one explanation: the Germans have been conducting an extensive research into long-range rockets. . . . Their experiments have naturally encountered difficulties, which may still be holding up production. Although Hitler would press the rockets into service at the earliest possible moment, that moment is probably some months ahead.

'It is probable that the German Air Force has also been developing a pilotless aircraft for long range bombardment in competition with the [Army] rocket.'

Jones's summary of the available intelligence was very accurate: the pilotless aircraft, the V1, was not in fact discovered until the existence of the potentially much more dangerous rockets had been proved. The story of the uncovering of the secrets of these most secret of German weapons is one involving espionage, cloak and dagger operations, disagreements between scientists at the highest level, photographic reconnaissance on a vast scale, and scientific intelligence.

The first hint that the Germans were experimenting with long-range rockets was contained, as we have seen, in the Oslo Report, which also mentioned a Secret Research Establishment at a place called Peenemunde. There was additionally Hitler's Danzig speech in September 1939, in which he had threatened 'Secret Weapons with which we ourselves could not be attacked'.

There was virtually no further evidence until mid-December 1942, when a Danish chemical engineer reported to British Intelligence a conversation overheard in a Berlin restaurant about the trials of a 'large rocket' at a site near Swinemunde, on the Baltic coast. The rocket was reported to have a range of 130 miles and to carry a 5-ton warhead. A further report from another source in February 1943 stated that 'the rocket could carry ten tons of explosive over a 70 mile range', adding that the experiments were being conducted at Peenemunde on the Baltic coast. This was the first confirmation of the place mentioned in the Oslo Report: all the evidence until then had come from doubtful sources; the Oslo Report, for example, had been dismissed by many as a 'plant' and the Danish engineer's reliability was, at that time, untested.

On 22 March 1943 there came further evidence of the existence of some sort of long-range rocket which could not be dismissed; it came from a high-ranking German General, Ritter von Thoma, one of Rommel's staff. He and

General Ritter von
Thoma (left).

124

another Afrika Korps Commander, General Cruewell, had both been captured in North Africa and, in November 1942, brought to London, where they had fallen for one of the oldest Intelligence tricks: after being interrogated the two men, who knew and trusted each other, were placed together in a room, where they talked freely, not suspecting that the room was bugged. Dr Jones, who, it will be remembered, had received vital clues in the search for the nature of the beams by just such a method, remembers that:

> 'General von Thoma said something like "Well, you know, something must have gone wrong with those rockets because I saw them eighteen months ago with Field Marshal von Brauchitch and the Major in charge had said that they would have been ready [operational] in a few months. Here we are near London and we've heard no bangs, nothing seems to have happened . . .".' [1]

Jones had been reading a report of this conversation with an Intelligence colleague, who said, 'Look, we had better take these rockets seriously'. Jones agreed, for it seemed very unlikely that von Thoma was deliberately planting false information, and the generals' unguarded conversation corroborated information from the other sources. From then on the existence of the German rockets began to be taken seriously.

The immediate result was unfortunate, in Jones's view, because he felt that more concrete information should be obtained in order to present a coherent account to the Chiefs of Staff. War Office Intelligence, however, took the view that the rockets were potentially so dangerous that the information should not be confined to Intelligence circles, but passed on at once. The result was that when Lt General Nye, Vice Chief of the Imperial General Staff, received a summary of all the available intelligence, he immediately consulted Dr A. D. Crow, a scientist from the Ministry of Supply who was concerned with the development of British rocket projectiles, and Professor C. D. Ellis, who was Scientific Adviser to the Army Council. This resulted in a report to the Chiefs of Staff of 11 April 1943, entitled 'German Long Range Rocket Development', which considered all the available evidence and went on to envisage the potential of a German long-range missile, suggesting possible countermeasures.

The most unfortunate feature of the document was a technical appreciation which postulated a two-stage rocket with a range of 130 miles, weighing $9\frac{1}{2}$ tons, 95 feet in length and carrying a warhead of $1\frac{1}{4}$ tons of high explosive. The rocket was to be fired from a large projector, unless 'an extremely accurate method of directional control has been developed'. No consideration was given to the method of propulsion: any statement as to range and payload could therefore only be conjecture.

In view of the state of British rockets at that time and Dr Crow's experience, it was assumed that the German missile would be propelled by solid fuel, cordite being the only one considered possible; the possibility that it could be using a liquid fuel was apparently ruled out. This omission was to cause endless trouble later on in the investigation.

The report recommended immediate photographic reconnaissance and air attacks on the 'projectors'; and that the Prime Minister and Minister for Home Security be warned that large rockets could fall on the country with little or no warning. Dr Jones, in his capacity as Head of Air Ministry Scientific Intelligence, felt such a release of information was premature: while conceding that it was a correct interpretation of the known facts, in that a German long-range rocket was a possibility, he took the view that all that had been achieved was to raise the alarm that an attack on London by enemy rockets was due in a few weeks, at a time when no one knew enough about the rocket to take any countermeasures. Far better, he argued, not to raise any alarm but to let it be known discreetly that Intelligence was after a rocket at Peenemunde and seek further facts.

The Chiefs of Staff had agreed that the Prime Minister should be informed, that scientific investigations would be mounted and that an individual should be appointed to take charge of a review of all the evidence for German Long-Range Rocket Developments. The man appointed (on 20 April 1943) was Duncan (now Lord) Sandys.

The day before his appointment, the Air Ministry had instructed the Photographic Interpretation Unit at RAF Medmenham, near Henley-on-Thames, to commence an investigation into German secret weapons:

Duncan Sandys.

'1. No specific locations in connection with this weapon can be given, but the following suggestions as to its nature have been made:

(a) It is a long-range gun.

(b) It is a rocket aircraft controlled on the 'Queen Bee' principle [i.e. by radio: Queen Bee was the name of a British radio-controlled target drone].

(c) It is some sort of tube located in a disused mine out of which a rocket could be squirted.

2. The investigation at the P.I. Unit should aim at solving the following points:

(a) Where the weapon is being constructed.

(b) Where the experiments are taking place.

(c) The nature of the weapon.

(d) What constructions or implacements within 130 miles of London and Southampton are capable of being used for its launching.

3. A search is to be made of the areas within 130 miles of London and Southampton, using photographs not earlier than January 1943. All gaps in the flying are to be made up at once by arranging for additional flights.

4. The highest possible priority is to be allotted to this investigation.'

Duncan Sandys was at that time Deputy Minister of Supply. He had served with an anti-aircraft unit in Norway at the beginning of the war and had later commanded an experimental anti-aircraft rocket unit, but he had been involved in a car crash that had resulted in his being invalided out of the army to become Under-Secretary at the Ministry of Supply – a post in which he gained considerable experience in weapon development. He argued that, in addition to the photographic coverage of likely launching sites in northern France, coverage should also extend to possible experimental stations, which would probably be on coastal sites, away from populated areas and out of the normal range of allied bombers: a likely place was Peenemunde on the Baltic island of Usedom. He requested the Interpretation Unit at RAF Medmenham to re-examine existing cover of Peenemunde and to mount new photographic sorties over it.

The first photographs of Peenemunde had been taken casually in May 1942 by a pilot on the way to Kiel. 'Heavy construction work and some strange elliptical earthworks' were noted and the pictures were filed away. Four new sorties had been flown over the site by 22 April 1943, on which day coverage of the whole of the Peenemunde peninsula was taken from a high-flying PRU Mosquito from Benson.

After examination, the interpreters at Medmenham prepared their report. Some long structures at the northern end of the Peenemunde site were considered to be some sort of sludge pumps working on land reclamation; two very large factory-like buildings were noted to the south-east; there were some elliptical earthworks near the northern tip of the peninsula; and the photographs also showed a power station on the western shore and three large circular earthworks to the south. The tentative interpretation of the tall buildings was that they were 'possibly a nitration plant'. Another building was thought to resemble an ammonia plant, being similar to other such known buildings at other sites. The general appearance of the site suggested the manufacture of explosives. The report concluded:

'A large cloud of white smoke or steam can be seen drifting in a north-westerly direction from the area. On photograph 5010, an object about twenty-five feet long can be seen projecting in a north-westerly direction from the seaward end of the building. When photograph 5011 was taken four seconds later this object had disappeared, and a small puff of white smoke or steam was issuing from the seaward end of the building.'

What the photographic interpreters could not know was that they had a photograph of the twenty-first A4 rocket being run up on test stand 7 and, before the Mosquito had landed at RAF Benson, that rocket was successfully test-fired into the Baltic.

A Mosquito of No. 1 PRU. These wooden aircraft roamed widely over Germany in daylight on photographic reconnaissance missions, including the vital cover of Peenemunde. Unarmed, they relied on their speed – over 400 mph – to evade German fighters.

A group of scientists and engineers from the Ministry of Supply visited Medmenham to discuss the nature of the weapon being tested; by this time the whole emphasis was inclined towards a rocket. At a subsequent meeting on 29 April in Sandys's office, the following conclusions were reached:

'1. The whole site is probably an experimental station.

2. The whole area is not yet in full use and is probably an explosive works.

3. The circular and elliptical constructions are probably for the testing of explosives and projectiles.

4. If rocket projectiles are in fact being tested here, their use has not gone beyond the experimental stage so far. The area must however be watched by frequent photographic reconnaissance.

5. In view of the above it is clear that a heavy long-range rocket is not yet an immediate menace.'

On 14 May Sandys asked for further photographic cover of Peenemunde. Two sorties were flown and the interpreters at Medmenham discovered that a great deal of activity had been going on five miles below the PRU Mosquitoes. There was much movement of vehicles and one was apparently carrying a 'cylindrical object thirty feet by eight feet, which projects over the next truck'. The second sortie that day revealed another of these 'objects'. (The high level of activity observed by the RAF was perhaps slightly atypical; that day, 14 May, a high-ranking party official, Gauleiter Fritz Sauckel, the Reich Director of Manpower, was visiting the rocket establishment and the Army CO, Colonel Stegmier, was naturally anxious to create a good impression.)

Two days later, as the result of sorties over northern France, the interpreters were able to report considerable activity at a site in the Bois d'Eperlecques, a mile from Watten, near Calais. The photographs showed a huge concrete structure under construction in a clearing in the woods in what resembled a gravel pit: the structure was served by a railway. The interpreters could not connect this strange building with any conventional

military purpose. It therefore came under suspicion as a potential rocket-firing site.

A drawing made by Intelligence officers, based on evidence of the Watten site.

On the strength of aircrews' evidence, as well as additional information from agents, Sandys issued his first report: it was to lead to immediate controversy, as Lord Sandys recounted in a 1976 interview:

'I advised the War Cabinet that in my opinion the Germans were developing a long-range rocket. But that opinion was not readily accepted. In particular Churchill's principal scientific adviser, Professor Lindemann [by now Lord Cherwell and Paymaster General] argued strongly that any such rocket would have to be propelled by cordite and that cordite would have to be burnt in a thick steel case which would mean that the rocket would weigh somewhere between sixty and 100 tons and that wasn't a feasible proposition.

'Not being a scientist myself, I refused to be drawn into a scientific argument. I took the very simple view that even if Professor Lindemann did not know how to make a long-range rocket, it did not necessarily mean that the Germans did not know how to do so.

'It was quite clear that the Germans were putting an enormous effort into this project and it must therefore be taken seriously.'[2]

The reaction of Lord Cherwell to the Sandys report was the beginning of a long-fought struggle that was to dog the scientific inquiry from then on. In simple terms it was that a cordite or solid-fuel rocket would be too large to be a practical proposition and that any alternative, particularly a liquid fuel, was beyond the technology of the time. Therefore the rocket was an elaborate hoax to conceal some other weapon, possibly a flying bomb. History was to prove Lord Cherwell both right and wrong; in the meantime his opposition to Sandys was complicated by other than purely scientific disagreement.

Lord Sandys will not to this day comment publicly on this; others, however, do not share his reticence. Professor Jones, for example, stated (in 1977):

'Well, the complication of course was that Lord Cherwell did not like Duncan Sandys, and once Duncan Sandys had begun to believe the evidence and say that it was a very serious danger, Cherwell reacted the other way and started to argue that there was no such thing as a rocket.'[1]

It is probably true that Lord Cherwell, a distinguished scientist, felt that he, rather than Duncan Sandys, who disclaimed any scientific pretensions, should have led the inquiry.

A great deal of the evidence for the long-range rocket had so far been obtained by photographic reconnaissance, and tribute should be given to the men who flew these long, lonely flights in unarmed aircraft over enemy territory in daylight. They developed techniques that were far in advance of any other nation's at that time. The Germans, until late in the war, had not photographed England to any extent. In contrast, by the war's end allied photographic reconnaissance had covered all of Germany and German-held territory twice. If mistakes in interpretation were made in the quest for the German V Weapons, this was a very new field for the interpreters, who had been trained to look for conventional military hardware and movements.

Peenemunde was now being photographed by Mosquitoes twice a week, and cover secured on 12 June 1943 by Sortie N/853 showed that the foreshore had been levelled and on it 'about 470 feet from the most south-easterly buttress [there was] a vertical column about 40 feet high and 4 feet thick'.

Jones got hold of the prints and saw 'what seemed to me to be the outline of a rocket, somewhere around 38 feet long, with a tail fin perhaps 10 feet long and perhaps 10 feet across at the near end. . . .' At this the report from the photographic interpreters was amended to read:

'The object is 35′ long and appears to have a blunt point at one end. The appearance presented by this object on the photographs is not incompatible with its being a cylinder tapered at one end and provided with three radial fins.'

Even with this pictorial evidence in front of them the interpreters were remarkably reluctant to label the 'objects' as rockets.

In the light of this new interpretation by Jones, a re-examination of all the earlier cover of Peenemunde was made. It revealed that similar-shaped 'objects' were to be found on railway flatcars together with – most significantly – a number of railway tankers.

Lord Cherwell was still maintaining that the whole site was a hoax to mislead, even when shown the photograph which clearly showed a rocket-like shape. Jones meanwhile was collecting intelligence information from other sources. His work was to prove that in intelligence the obtaining of information is only half the story: it is the use which is made of the information that is important. In his establishing the provenance of Peenemunde the point was admirably made.

Jones took the view that if, as Lord Cherwell maintained, the whole Peenemunde site was a gigantic hoax, then the best that the Germans could hope for would be that the Allies would bomb it. They would hardly do this if the area was in fact a genuine experimental station. He managed to prove that this was so from a very small piece of ('Ultra') evidence that he acquired from another investigation. It was a circular, sent by a lowly clerk in the administrative bureaucracy of the Luftwaffe to all the German Air Force research stations, setting out the procedures for the allocation of petrol. This seemingly trivial document made no direct mention of Peenemunde but there was a distribution list at the foot of the memorandum which listed recipients in order of importance: Peenemunde was second only to Rechlin, the German Farnborough. As Jones later said: 'It showed that Peenemunde was as genuine as our own Farnborough, and whatever hard things may have been said about the latter establishment, few of us would actually have liked to see it bombed.'

Jones now produced further evidence that proved the nature of the work at Peenemunde. He was aware that the Germans must use radar to track the missiles and that the most likely unit for this work would be the 14th and 15th Companies of the Luft Nachrichten Versuchs Regiment (Experimental Signals Unit). He was right: an 'Ultra' signal showed that a detachment of this regiment had been sent to set up a radar station on Rügen Island, north of Peenemunde and another detachment to Bornholm Island in the Baltic, ninety-five miles east of Peenemunde. This deduction was to prove vital later on in the V Weapon story.

As if to corroborate this intelligence, there now became available a brilliantly clear set of photographs taken on the most successful sortie yet, flown on 23 June by Flight Sergeant Peek. These showed beyond any reasonable doubt that there were rockets close to the firing point. Sandys was now convinced and, following a report in which he summarised all the evidence, he recommended the immediate bombing of the Peenemunde complex. At a Cabinet meeting on 29 June it was decided that it would be bombed with the heaviest-possible precision night attack that Bomber Command could muster. However the distance ruled out an immediate raid: the nights in June/July were simply not long enough.

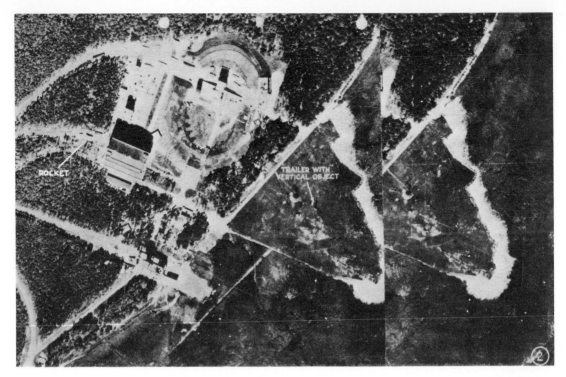

ROCKET

TRAILER WITH VERTICAL OBJECT

A stereo pair: one of a series of remarkably clear shots taken by Flight Sgt Peek on his sortie over Peenemunde on 23 June. A trailer with 'a vertical object' and a rocket can be seen.

A conference at HQ Bomber Command considered the best way to attack this difficult and distant target. Air Chief Marshal Sir Arthur Harris wrote:

'It must be remembered that at that time our only successful attacks on single factories in Germany had been made by small forces of exceptionally experienced crews, either in daylight or when there was an unusually good chance of identifying the target by night. In the attack on Peenemunde, I knew that I should have to use the main force to ensure the destruction of a target of such great strategic importance; and that the attack would have to be made in moonlight; there could be no question of trusting only to H2S [Radar] for the identification and the marking of a target of this nature and Peenemunde was far beyond the Oboe range. Even in moonlight, it would be an extremely difficult task to destroy the whole establishment.

'Its buildings lay scattered in a narrow strip along the coastline . . . there would clearly have to be several aiming points with different sections of the force assigned to each. . . .'.[3]

The raid was to be mounted on the night of 16/17 August. In the intervening fortnight the tactics were worked out: Pathfinders and experienced crews from No. 5 Group were to lead the attack, with a Master Bomber orbiting the target to inform the main force by radio of the accuracy of the target-marking indicators. There was some worry that smoke could obscure the aiming points, so it was arranged that Lancasters from No. 5 Group would make a timed run from Rügen Island, which would show well on their H2S radar. Practice runs were made over a similar stretch of coast in Britain and the accuracy improved from 1000 to 300 yards.

The threat of the German rockets was still a closely guarded secret as far as the British public was concerned. The true nature of the target was not revealed even to the RAF bomber crews: they were simply told that the target was concerned with radar and was of such importance that it would have to be attacked again the next night if the first operation failed. The crews were then briefed that the bombing runs would be made from only 8000 feet – far below normal bombing height – to ensure accuracy.

To help reduce the inevitable losses on this raid, being made at extreme range and in bright moonlight, a deception plan was drawn up. It relied to some extent on the fact that Peenemunde had never been attacked before and that the route taken by the bombers would be in a large measure the same as that for Berlin, which of course was often bombed. A small force of Mosquitoes would in reality attack the city and, by dropping 'Window', hope to deceive the German night-fighter controllers that the main attack was on Berlin.

Six hundred aircraft took off for the raid: the deception plan worked; all the signs on the German radar screens were of a massive raid on the capital. Night fighters headed into the attack and, as they orbited beacons near Berlin, the main bomber force, protected from radar surveillance by 'Window', turned for the real target: Peenemunde.

The first bombs were to be aimed, not on the test stands or even the laboratories, but on the living quarters of the scientists: these men were irreplaceable, the other targets were secondary. It was just a minute or two before midnight when the Pathfinder flares floated down, followed by the high explosives and incendiaries; Peenemunde was soon a sea of flames.

As the raid progressed there were still no night fighters, although the local flak opened up and smoke screens were seen. The bombs were dropping on the Pathfinder coloured marker-flares. The raid took longer than planned, however, and the last wave of bombers was attacked by the German night fighters, which had seen the fires whilst over Berlin, 110 miles away to the south, and had made for the target area. Forty heavy bombers were shot down but, without the feint attack and the 'Window' countermeasure, the losses would have been much heavier.

On returning to base the Pathfinder crews were certain that they had marked the target successfully; over 450 night photographs had been taken and it was claimed that the majority of the main force had bombed within one mile of the aiming point. Confirmation would have to wait until a photo reconnaissance aircraft, piloted by Wing Commander Gordon Hughes, flew over the target at 10 o'clock the next morning. When analysed, his photographs showed that fifty out of eighty permanent buildings of the experimental station were destroyed, including the design offices; and the scientists' quarters were almost totally destroyed. However, there had been an error in one target-marking which was to have tragic consequences and proved a setback for Air Intelligence: some target indicators had fallen on a nearby Concentration Camp, which was heavily bombed. Professor Jones said recently:

High-altitude photograph of Peenemunde, showing the disposition of the V Weapon sites. It was taken after the RAF raid – a number of bomb craters can be seen.

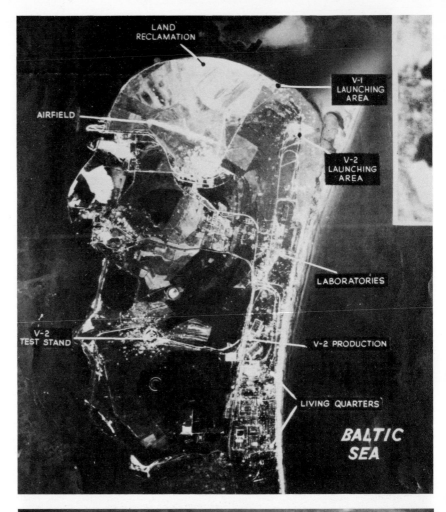

The scientists' living quarters on the morning following the RAF attack.

'The whole attack was of the order of two miles overshot . . . and unfortunately in that very position was the hutted camp in which all the conscripted men from the occupied countries were.'[1]

Some of these men – from Luxemburg – had been British agents and had been able to warn Jones about the nature of Peenemunde: they were now silenced.

In spite of this error, a great deal of damage had been done. Many scientists had been killed, including Dr Thiel, one of the chief designers of the project: in all, 735 people lost their lives, including the foreign labourers. After the war the Germans admitted that the raid had put the V2 project back by several months.

Albert Speer, Hitler's Minister of Armaments, remembers that night well: 'I was in Berlin in a Flaktower and I saw a glow in the sky on the horizon. I heard then that it was a big raid on Peenemunde – next morning I was flown there. Everyone was very excited by this setback, but later that day it became apparent that the consequences of the raid were not as heavy as at first supposed. Many engineers and scientists had been killed, but parts of the works producing test rockets were not too badly hit.

'It is true that the project was set back for several months. Although, to be frank, I would say that they [the experimental staff] needed an excuse, because they had been modifying the rockets and were behind schedule anyway by several months.'[4]

In the weeks prior to the Peenemunde raid, reconnaissance had been kept to a minimum to avoid alerting the German defences. The suspect sites in

Albert Speer with Hitler.

northern France, however, had been photographed with increasing frequency. The site at Watten in particular was watched; in addition to photographic evidence, an agent reported that there was 'German long-range rocket activity'. Fresh cover showed the site was now a hive of activity: new railways were being laid that led to a very heavy construction, and what had previously looked like a gravel pit was now shuttered and appeared ready for concrete pouring.

The reality of the rockets – now code-named Bodyline – was being assumed in Government departments. It had been estimated by the Ministry of Home Security that up to 4000 casualties could be caused by one rocket falling in a heavily built-up area. To meet this contingency, discreet plans were being drawn up for a partial evacuation of London: these included 100,000 priority cases, mothers and children, to leave the city at the rate of 10,000 a day. Herbert Morrison asked the Cabinet to consider the allocation of enough steel to make 100,000 of the family air-raid shelters that bore his name. Plans for evacuation were later extended to other possible targets for the rockets – Portsmouth and Southampton.

From various sources more intelligence was coming in of other unexplained constructions at Wissant, Noires, Bernes and Marquisse, in addition to the site at Watten, where it was now known from agents that over 6000 workers were employed. Ten days after the Peenemunde raid, the 8th United States Army Air Force made a very heavy attack on this site. 370 tons of bombs were dropped by 185 B17 Flying Fortresses and the effect of this precision daylight

The Watten site, surveyed by the Royal Engineers after occupation.

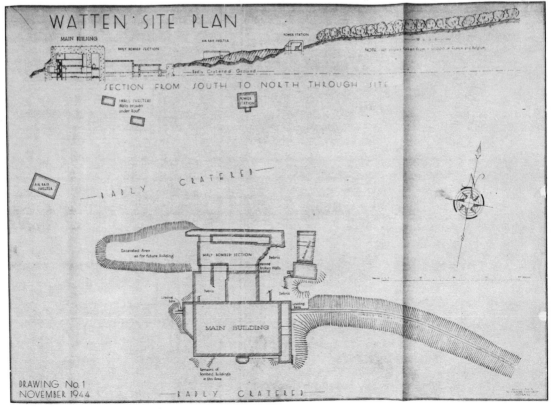

raid was devastating. Photographs taken after that attack were shown to the civil engineer, Sir Robert MacAlpine: his verdict was that 'it would be easier for the Germans to begin again somewhere else. . .'. Reichminister Albert Speer seems to have come to the same conclusion, for work started on a new rocket bunker at a place called Wizerns.

In the meantime a message from a well-placed 'source', high in the Army Weapons Department of the German War Office, had been received on 27 August 1943. It was circulated to the Chiefs of Staff by Duncan Sandys as an Appendix to his Interim Report No. 11, with the following introduction:

'Intelligence.

'A detailed report about the state of development of German long-range weapons and of the enemy's plans for an attack of this kind against England has been received from a quite unusually well-placed and hitherto most reliable source. . . . .

'1. There were two distinct weapons in existence: a pilotless aircraft known as "Phi 7" being tested at Peenemunde, and a rocket projectile known as A.4 (Aggregate 4) 16 metres long and 4.5 metres in diameter, its warhead equivalent to a 4-ton British bomb. . . . Its range was 200 km and its altitude was 35 km. The Siemens Company of Berlin were said to be making the radio control equipment for both. . . . Important parts were made at the Zeppelin works at Friedrichshafen [this had previously been bombed by the RAF, as it was thought to be making "Würzburg" radars]. Other parts were made all over Germany but the rockets had been assembled and test-fired at Peenemunde.

'So far [the report continued] about 100 had been fired but their accuracy had been poor. . . .

'2. In addition, concrete emplacements for the rockets were stated to be ready near Le Havre and Cherbourg, more were under construction, for storage only, *the rockets could be fired from open fields if necessary*.†

'3. A4s were launched under their own power from easily constructed [bases] of iron rails. . . . 100 had been constructed. . . . They [the rockets] were fired vertically and the noise was deafening.

'4. On 10 June Hitler had told military leaders that London would be levelled and Britain forced to capitulate. . . . 30 October [1943] was the zero date for the rocket attacks to begin. . . . 30,000 A4s had been ordered, 1500 skilled workers had been transferred to the project.'[5]

The identity of this 'source' has never been revealed; it could well be yet another example of the work of the code-breakers at Bletchley Park – though there is, as is so often the case with 'Ultra', as yet no direct evidence for this.

A Chiefs of Staff Meeting to discuss this information was held on 31 August:

'Mr Duncan Sandys said [that the report] . . . largely confirmed his previous conclusions. The information concerning the range and accuracy of

†My italics.

the rocket was, however, still uncertain. It was doubtful if we should be able to detect by air reconnaissance the firing points. . . . They were relatively small and might even be concealed inside large buildings in towns.'[5]

Lord Cherwell was still sceptical: many of the reports were 'inconsistent and some of them scientifically incorrect'; there was also the question of the rockets in the photographs having rounded, not pointed noses. (It is interesting to note that the archive copy, No. 67, of the minutes of this conference, in the Public Records Office, has the word 'rocket' in Lord Cherwell's transcript crossed out and the handwritten word 'object' substituted, possibly at his insistence; he was still far from convinced that the 'rockets' existed.)

Sandys said that there was a steady flow of German propaganda referring to secret weapons; the German press often discussed a rocket attack; a wide variety of reports from a number of sources had been received, all pointing to the fact that the Germans were developing a long-range rocket, although he admitted he could not as yet prove this.

Air Chief Marshal Sir Charles Portal, Chief of Air Staff, then brought up a new point. He reminded the meeting that Lord Cherwell had previously suggested that the rockets could be a cover for another quite different weapon, and pointed out that the Navy had been attacked in the Bay of Biscay recently by a 'Glider Bomb'. (This was the Henschel 293, not strictly speaking a glider bomb: it was rocket-powered for the initial stages of its flight – see page 298.)

On 22 August, Portal revealed, a pilotless aircraft had been seen at Bornholm Island, flying from the general direction of Peenemunde. The aircraft was larger than the glider bomb (HS293); it had crashed, and a sketch of it had been made by an agent who was able to examine it for some ten

A sketch of a V1 made by an agent.

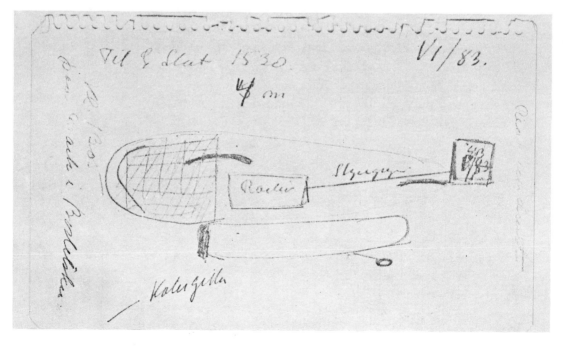

minutes before the Germans arrived on the scene. It appeared to be a bomb fitted with wings and rocket propulsion. Might this not be the weapon referred to as 'Phi 7' in the report under consideration? Portal suggested that, if it was the same, it was of far more immediate concern than the long-range rocket.

Even though this new evidence seemed to vindicate him, Cherwell immediately poured cold water on it, as the minutes reveal:

'He said that from the dimensions indicated in the sketch the explosive charge carried would be of the order of 1000 lbs. He thought that a pilotless aircraft would be an expensive method of dropping such a relatively small amount of explosive.'[6]

Nevertheless there was general agreement from the meeting that every effort was to be made to assess the potentialities of this new weapon reported from Bornholm.

The position by the beginning of September was that the 'objects' seen at Peenemunde were the only direct evidence of the existence of a German long-range rocket. For the moment it would seem the 'Phi 7' was considered a side issue to the main preoccupation – the A4 long-range rocket. Scientific opinion as expressed through Lord Cherwell, who was after all adviser to the Prime Minister, was that the German rocket, on the basis of the photographic evidence, was virtually impossible and that all the other evidence was 'planted'.

Sandys was not to be deflected, however. He requested that further scientific opinion be sought, and received authorisation from the Prime Minister to set up a Scientific Committee to examine all the evidence for and against the rocket. The Committee was expected to come to a definite conclusion.

Now began a bitter internecine dispute between the scientists. On 29 September 1943, a scientific questionnaire to 'establish the practicability, or otherwise of the German long-range rocket' was drawn up in collaboration between Sandys, Lord Cherwell and Herbert Morrison.[7] Cherwell wanted the document to be sent to a small committee consisting of Professor G. I. Taylor, FRS, Sir Frank Smith, FRS, Dr A. D. Crow, and Professor Sir Ralph Fowler. Sandys, however, pointed out that he had already appointed a Panel of Scientists, largely to investigate the question of the fuel aspect of the rocket. This panel included Professor Taylor and Sir Frank Smith, as well as Professor J. E. Lennard Jones, FRS, Professor C. D. Ellis, FRS, Dr H. L. Guy, FRS, and Professor W. E. Garner, FRS. It was agreed that Lord Cherwell's nominees, Dr Crow and Professor Fowler, would also be circularised. In the event, as Cherwell discovered, they never either received or heard of it. He was furious, virtually accusing Sandys of deliberately withholding the document from the two scientists.

The questionnaire began:

'Rumours have been in circulation about a large long-range rocket alleged to carry many tons of explosive over a range of about 130 miles. . . . A number of objects . . . have been photographed at a German experimental station . . .'

A drawing was reproduced based on the aerial photographs which showed a blunt-nosed rocket between 36 and 40 feet long, 5 to 7 feet across, with three 12- to 14-foot fins. The document continued:

'It would help the Government to form an opinion as to whether these objects are long-range rockets of approximately the performance described, if you would kindly answer the following questions . . . .'

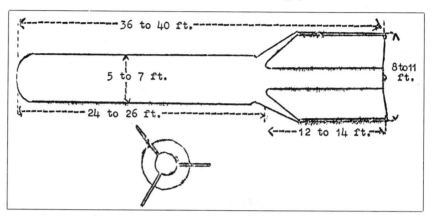

The drawing of the Peenemunde 'object' as it appeared in the questionnaire which was placed before the Scientific Committee.

There then followed seventeen highly technical questions, put to test the feasibility of the rockets. These queried the likely range; whether it would be a multi- or single-stage rocket; the problems of the velocity of the effluent gases and their temperature; the question of launching – would a projector or mortar be feasible; could such a mortar, with its heavy cranes, be visible from the air; would the flash be visible; what would the size of the warhead be; what would be the likely effect of its destructive power; and finally:

'(17) Do you believe that the production of such a rocket is a practical possibility from a technical point of view?'

Following the issue of the questionnaire, the Committee then considered the single most important aspect of the existence of a rocket – the question of the fuel. It was simply not possible that the Peenemunde 'object' could be a long-range, single-stage rocket if it was powered by cordite – this was the only rocket fuel used in Britain at that time due to the problems of pumping the very large quantities of suitable liquid fuel, which was the only possible alternative to cordite. However, that did not take into account the work of Isaac Lubbock, Chief Engineer of the Asiatic Petroleum Company (a subsidiary of Shell): he knew a great deal about *liquid fuel* as a rocket propellant. For reasons not entirely clear, he was not brought into the enquiry until that time (October 1943), although as far back as early 1941 his work was well known to at least one of the scientists on the Committee, Dr Crow, who was the Controller of Projectile Developments at the Ministry of Supply and in charge of all official rocket research in Britain.

The Shell Company had been given a research contract to try to develop an aircraft-assisted take-off rocket, using any fuel other than cordite, which was then in short supply. Lubbock began to experiment at the Petroleum Warfare Establishment near Horsham in Sussex with a liquid fuel based on aviation spirit and oxygen. By mid 1942, working on a very small (£10,000) budget, test-runs of half a minute had been obtained. Lubbock and his chief assistant, Geoffrey Gollin, were confident that they were well on the way to producing a lightweight rocket for aircraft take-off purposes. A demonstration was given to Crow in October 1942, and a further demonstration in May 1943 was before a larger audience including Professor Sir Alfred Egerton (a brother-in-law of Sir Stafford Cripps, the Minister of Aircraft Production) and Crow.

According to David Irving:

'The rocket motor was put through a perfect 23-second test, the howl of the exhaust echoing over the Sussex countryside and the trees trembling in the blast. Sir Alfred Egerton warmly shook Lubbock's hand and exclaimed: "It amazes me that you can bring a flame of that size under control using liquid oxygen and petrol. I congratulate you!"

'Crow made no similar gesture. . . . When he returned to London that day he made no attempt to bring these developments to Mr Sandys's attention, and the belief that the Peenemunde rocket must be solid-fuelled – like Dr Crow's own 3-inch anti-aircraft "UP" (Unrifled Projectile) rockets – persisted until late September.' [8]

Dr Crow's refusal to acknowledge that a small liquid-fuel rocket was producing more thrust than an equivalent cordite one was a serious omission, and without this information Lord Cherwell's faction were able to persuade other scientists that the German rocket must run on solid fuel and therefore be so large as to be a virtual impossibility. In scientific terms, a rocket's viability is expressed in its 'Alpha ratio', which is the ratio of the calorific value of the fuel – its 'heat' content – to the total weight of the rocket.

A solid-fuel rocket is essentially the same as a bonfire-night rocket: the body of the rocket not only contains the solid fuel, but also has to withstand the very high pressures and temperatures of combustion – with a large rocket, fuelled by cordite, up to $2100°$ Centigrade. A long-range rocket would have to withstand such temperatures for perhaps fifty seconds and would therefore require a very thick steel casing, which would comprise most of the structure, making it very heavy with a poor Alpha ratio and limited range. This assumption led the inquiry to believe that any German long-range rocket would be massive, requiring very heavy handling equipment, some sort of mortar to fire it, and – a very important point – a firing site that had to be served by a railway. These conditions were to mislead the photographic interpreters, who were briefed to look for firing sites with large cranes and served by a railway.

A liquid-fuelled rocket was a different proposition: in this the body of the rocket was largely a fuel tank, with a separate motor in which the actual combustion took place. This meant that the rocket could be a far lighter structure, manufactured with aircraft technology in lightweight alloys. The consequent reduction of the 'clothing' weight, together with a high-efficiency fuel –

alcohol and liquid oxygen – would offer a much more favourable 'Alpha' ratio. For a given warhead, the range could be as much as doubled against that for a solid-fuelled rocket. Had that information been available to Duncan Sandys at the beginning of his inquiry – as it could have been had Lubbock been consulted – the Peenemunde 'objects' would have been seen for what in reality they were: long-range, *liquid-fuelled* rockets.

Colonel Post, Sandys's Scientific Adviser, then drew attention to the question of liquid fuels and the work of Isaac Lubbock. Unfortunately, Lubbock was at this time away in the United States studying American assisted-take-off, liquid-fuelled rockets, but his chief assistant, Geoffrey Gollin, who had been concerned with the earlier trials at Horsham, was asked to attend a meeting of the Fuel Panel on 20 September. Gollin had been informed, presumably by Lubbock, of the latest work on liquid fuels that was taking place in America. He therefore could report to the Fuel Panel that, in the light of new developments, it should be possible to reduce the 'clothing' of a rocket to only half the weight of the fuel: this represented an 'Alpha' ratio of 0.67 (which was roughly what the Germans were to achieve with the operational V2).

At the meeting Dr Crow opposed this assertion; the best figure for the rockets that he had designed – solid-fuel ones – was only 0.25 and consequently the Peenemunde object was part of a multi-stage cordite rocket. He said that he had in mind a four-stage rocket and that his Department had prepared a hypothetical design for such a rocket.

There were further meetings on 30 September and 4 October. Gollin's claim that alcohol and oxygen were a practicable fuel for a single-stage rocket was rejected by the Panel, which was influenced by Dr Crow to conclude that:

> 'We are of the opinion that the necessary range cannot be achieved by a single-stage rocket, and that the possibility of such a development in Germany can be ruled out.' [9]

The meeting decided to express a final opinion as to the nature of the Peenemunde objects at their next meeting on 11 October, which would have Lord Cherwell in attendance.

This premature rejection of the case for the liquid-fuelled rocket was unfortunate. To help a new presentation of that case, Gollin had sent a cable to Lubbock informing him that 'Factors in Sussex' required his immediate return to London.

Isaac Lubbock, who knew more about liquid-fuelled rockets than anyone else in Britain, arrived back from America on 10 October. He was presumably briefed by Gollin and probably shown the scientific questionnaire; in any event, he and Colonel Post, assisted by two ballistic experts from the Ministry of Supply, sat down in Post's office in Shell Mex House in the Strand that afternoon and began to draw up a tentative design for a liquid-fuelled rocket that would conform to the outline of the Peenemunde object which they, correctly, concluded was a single-stage, liquid-fuelled rocket without its warhead. [10]

In his original work with alcohol and liquid oxygen, Lubbock had been faced with the problem of forcing this potentially explosive fuel into the combustion chambers under high pressure. In his Sussex experiments he had used compressed nitrogen from heavy-pressure vessels. Whilst in the United States, he had found that the Americans were using a different and apparently more attractive method, which employed centrifugal pumps to fuel the rocket motors. Liquid oxygen is disastrously incompatible with any form of grease lubricant, so the Americans were using nitric acid and aniline, and with an ordinary car engine to drive the pumps had achieved good results, experimentally, with high 'Alphas' of 0.57 and 0.64.

Based on this American work, the theoretical design emerged as a 54-ton missile with a range of 140 miles; the 42 tons of fuel was to be fed to the engines either by a turbine pump or driven out by gases generated by burning cordite within the tanks.

The next day, 11 October, at 2.30, the Fuel Panel met in Shell Mex House. The meeting was in many ways difficult: on the long table were enlargements of the photographs of the Peenemunde objects. Lord Cherwell, although he had informed Sandys that he did not 'think there is any object in my going to the meeting', was nevertheless present, as was Dr Crow. Gollin and Lubbock were also there, seated opposite Cherwell. David Irving has written an account of what followed:

'When Colonel Post described the tentative rocket design prepared by Lubbock and himself on the previous day, there were strong protests that this was being introduced as new evidence, before anybody had had the opportunity of examining it.

'Lord Cherwell was not impressed by Isaac Lubbock, whom he regarded, for all his qualifications – the Shell engineer had taken a double first at Cambridge – as a usurper in the investigation. The Professor stoutly declared that nobody could teach him anything about rockets: he could safely say that he and Dr Crow knew more about rocket design than any man in Great Britain.

'After hearing Mr Lubbock's proposals, Sir Frank Smith asked each member present if the Peenemunde object could be a rocket. Only Lord Cherwell and Dr Crow dissented, Dr Crow maintaining that the objects were "barrage balloons". Colonel Post then asked him why in that event did the Germans find it necessary to transport their balloons on railway wagons; were they perhaps heavier-than-air balloons?

'Crow did not reply.'[11]

The Lubbock design was examined by F. E. Smith, Chief Engineer of Armament Design, on 20 October. He found that 'there was no single major engineering factor which had not been considered and for which an answer was not forthcoming'. The report convinced Sandys and a meeting of the full Scientific Committee considered the design the next day. There was some doubt about the method of forcing the fuel into the combustion chamber and Professor Garner thought that there was a high probability that the cordite gases could cause an explosion of the nitric acid. Lubbock conceded the point: 'If we had to build the projectile we should use pumps', he said.

Dr Crow was finding himself increasingly isolated. He protested he had not had enough time to study the Lubbock/Post design; nevertheless he considered it to be impracticable. He was still arguing the case for a cordite rocket, although now opinion was moving perceptibly against him and towards the liquid-fuel camp.

The next crucial meeting was held on 29 October in the underground War Cabinet room in Whitehall.[12] Churchill was in the chair and the full War Cabinet had the Lubbock/Post design before them. Sandys reported on the design and the possibility that liquid fuel was employed by the Germans. Cherwell would have none of it; looking straight at Lubbock he said it was a great pity that Dr Crow, who knew more about rockets than anyone else in the country, was not present to give his views as to whether or not the Lubbock/Post design was a practical proposition. According to Irving, he dismissed Lubbock as 'a third-rate engineer', although this statement does not appear in the official minutes. He then made the remark that he was to live to regret: 'At the end of the war, when we know the full story, we shall find that the rocket was a mare's nest'.

Lubbock, enraged by his treatment by Lord Cherwell, then put his case – according to Professor Jones's recollection, 'very badly'. He was further handicapped in that he could not, for security reasons, reveal that he had consulted Wing Commander Frank Whittle, who had agreed that the gas turbine engine that he was developing for jet aircraft could easily pump the fuel (in fact, the Germans had a more elegant solution to this problem). In spite of this, the meeting was convinced and the German long-range rocket was now accepted as a reality and a very dangerous one at that, although nothing was known of the weight, method of launching, guidance, or the fuel used.

The only countermeasure possible at this stage was the rephotographing of an area of northern France within a 150-mile radius of London (over 1,200,000 photographs were to be taken on this search for the rocket-launching locations). All likely factories were to be attacked and a close watch kept on any likely experimental sites. Finally the Prime Minister decided to place the facts before the House in a secret session.

By the beginning of November 1943, new evidence became available that was to put the rocket inquiries further and further into the background. A French agent had, towards the end of October, reported the locations near Abbeville of six 'secret weapon sites'. An examination of previous cover revealed nothing, but on 28 October a photographic reconnaissance pilot managed to photograph one of the sites in a wood – Bois Carré – about ten miles north-east of Abbeville. (The remaining five sites reported by the agent were obscured by cloud; they were covered on 3 November.)

When the photographs were examined at Medmenham, the strange sites all showed common features: each had one square building, a long concrete ramp, a sunken building protected from blast, and three long, narrow buildings, each shaped like a giant ski on its side. The most disturbing feature was the ramp: each of the six sites had the ramp aligned in precisely the same direction – towards London. There was little doubt in the minds of the photographic interpreters at Medmenham that these strange structures were part of the 'Bodyline' threat, but they had been briefed that any rocket site

RAF Medmenham, near Henley-on-Thames, HQ of Photographic Reconnaissance during the war. (The topiary was maintained even in the war.)

would have to be served by a railway and none of the Bois Carré 'ski' sites (as they were now known) had railways anywhere near them. The concrete paths which connected the buildings were not strong enough to bear 60-ton projectiles; there was no sign of heavy lifting-machinery; and the electrical supplies to the sites, judged by the size of the transformers, were only enough to supply lighting and light power loads. But there were the ramps and the ski-shaped buildings.

A particularly clear low-level oblique photograph of the original Bois Carré site, showing it in great detail, was taken by a Spitfire of a Canadian Squadron, No. 400 City of Toronto. The ski-shaped buildings were unlike any seen before: two were identical – 268 feet long including the bend, the third only 241 feet. The buildings had no windows and were constructed from pre-cast concrete blocks. Photographs of other sites showed that the precise location of the 'skis' differed from site to site, to take advantage of any natural cover from trees. The radius of the curve was such that the Peenemunde 'object' would not pass through. In any case rockets are launched straight up, or nearly so: the ramps were clearly pointed on London and equally clearly unsuitable for a rocket, but they would be ideal for launching a small pilotless aircraft.

The excellent low obliques taken at Bois Carré also showed in some detail the square building that was always present on the sites, of which nineteen had now been photographed. It measured 44 feet by 44 feet and was always

FIRST V1 LAUNCHING SITE
in France to be assessed by photographic interpretation

The low-level picture taken by a Canadian Spitfire pilot of one of the 'skis' at Bois Carré, the first V1 launching site discovered.

aligned exactly parallel to, but a little to one side of, the ramp that was now regarded as the firing point. The square buildings each had an entrance just 22 feet wide. Assuming that these sites were for flying bombs – and no other purpose could be envisaged – then it was logical to suppose that the weapons were stored in the 'ski' buildings without their wings – the entrance to the skis was too narrow. The bombs could be wheeled to the square building where they could have the wings fitted and the missile prepared for launching from the ramp.

Some confirmation of the role of the square building came in from an agent, a Frenchman employed by a contractor. He stated that the Germans were very particular about that building: it was to be constructed entirely without ferrous metal; even the door-hinges were imported from Germany, made from a non-magnetic material called, so the agent reported, 'Zinquat'. This report suggested that the square building might be used to set up a sensitive magnetic compass that could form part of the missile-guidance system.

The expected accuracy of the missile had been rather overestimated by British Intelligence, due to the German obsession with thoroughness. The ramps had been aligned on London with great accuracy, but French maps were based on a different geodetic grid from the British. (Napoleon had refused to accept Greenwich as the zero meridian and had instead based all French maps and charts with the zero running through Paris!) German Army engineers had therefore undertaken a completely new geodetic survey to match their maps of northern France with those of Great Britain. This, unbelievably, was observed by photographic reconnaissance, a task made possible because the German Army surveyors used a standard tower for their trig. points. By plotting their positions, the new grid, which matched the British, emerged.

The number of 'ski' sites discovered by Photographic Reconnaissance grew until, by the end of November 1943, no fewer than seventy-two had been found. The vital missing link was the aircraft for which it was assumed the sites were being prepared; so far none had been seen. The aircraft section at Medmenham had been briefed to look for a small aircraft with a wingspan of about 20 feet, on the assumption that it would have to pass through the 22-foot doorway of the square building.

Flight Officer Constance Babington Smith was the interpreter of 'L' Section at Medmenham, which was responsible for watching enemy airfields and aircraft factories. She re-examined all the previous cover of Peenemunde and found a small aircraft behind some hangars on the Karlshagen airfield. The photographs had been taken nearly six months previously and overlooked at that time. The scale was too small for any detail, but the strange aircraft had a wingspan of about 20 feet and Constance Babington Smith designated it as 'Peenemunde 20'.

On 28 November, one of the most brilliant Photographic Reconnaissance pilots, Squadron Leader Merifield, took off with his observer, Flying Officer Whalley, in a Mosquito to photograph bomb damage on Berlin. They found solid cloud over the German capital, so they flew north and photographed the Baltic ports of Greifswald, Stettin and Swinemunde. They then turned south-east to Usedom and Peenemunde, and on to Zinnowitz, another experimental station about eight miles from Peenemunde, which was thought to be a radar site and which had never been photographed before. Six hours later Merifield landed back at base.

When the photographic interpreters got the prints, they found little of interest in the Peenemunde cover but Zinnowitz was far more rewarding; the photographs taken on the off-chance showed a complete 'Bois Carré' type of site, with the launching ramps pointing straight out to the Baltic. There were, however, no ski-shaped buildings, which tended to confirm that they were for storage of missiles on an operational site. Zinnowitz was obviously for testing or training and needed no storage facilities. The ramps were complete – unlike the Bois Carré sites which were still under construction; when examined under a stereoscope, they were seen to be inclined at ten degrees and 125 feet long. These excellent photographs were only disappointing in one respect; there was no sign of the small aircraft.

The Peenemunde photographs which Merifield had taken on the same flight were passed through various departments at Medmenham and eventually reached Section 'L', for Constance Babington Smith to make a routine examination of the Luftwaffe Peenemunde Airfield, Karlshagen. She found nothing of interest on the airfield itself, but since on one of the previous covers she had spotted some odd-looking structures which she did not understand, on land which had been reclaimed for extending the airfield, she decided to follow once again the road to the edge of the sea and take a further look at the three unidentified structures. She already suspected that they were meant for launching missiles of some kind, although the Industry Section at Medmenham, which was responsible for interpreting the area of Peenemunde in question, had dismissed them as unimportant and probably something to do with the dredging operation.

The new set of photographs only just covered the shoreline site – in fact the 'unidentified structures' had nearly not been photographed at all: there was not even a stereo pair – the single print was the very last of the run. But it so happened that this one exposure had been made at a vital moment. Looking at it carefully under a magnifier, Constance Babington Smith noticed on the central structure a tiny cruciform shape: a small pilotless aircraft sitting on the end of a firing ramp awaiting launch. Its wingspan she measured as 19 feet.

One man in Britain who was not unduly surprised at the discovery of the aircraft was R. V. Jones, who it will be remembered had discovered that certain radar units were plotting the flight of missiles over the Baltic. These units were now operational and were transmitting by radio the results of their plots in a simple code, which substituted letters for figures. This code Jones had broken:

Constance Babington Smith with an enlargement of the famous photograph of Peenemunde, showing (arrowed) the V1 on its launching ramp which she discovered.

148

'Money for jam as it turned out – it was a very simple code and it didn't take long to put the whole thing together – the [radar] stations were warned in advance when the trials were taking place and the aiming point, so we were able to build up complete tracks . . . right up to impact.' [1]

By studying the tracks of these missiles, Jones found they came from two points: one at Peenemunde itself, another from a site a few miles along the coast at a place called Zempin (Zinnowitz). He had requested that a photographic reconnaissance flight be made, and Squadron Leader Merifield had had this request as a secondary target for 28 November.

Jones now knew that the radar tracks he had been able to plot were those of a small winged missile and he had been able to gather a good deal of information about its range, accuracy, height and frequency of firing. In a sense, however, the discovery of the pilotless aircraft on the ramp posed more questions than it answered. How was it powered? Was it radio-controlled? What was the weight of its warhead? Was it the only device to be launched from the ski sites?

A new name for the bomb, which was tentatively thought to be the one called 'Phi 7' by the agent on Bornholm Island, was obtained from an 'Ultra' intercept: FZG76, which stood for Flak Ziel Geräte, or anti-aircraft target device, and was obviously a cover name. (Later the 'Phi 7' was cleared up – it was a mistake by the agent: the missile's manufacturer was the Fiesler Company and they had designated it Fi.103.)

Once the nature of the ramps was understood, a search of all the past photographs taken over Peenemunde revealed that there were four ramps on the reclaimed land at the water's edge which represented various stages of prototype development. The first had been photographed in 1942; it had been joined by a second one in September 1943, so it was concluded that the prototype testing had been completed sometime in August of that year. Construction of the Bois Carré sites had also begun in September 1943.

In the light of the new discovery at Peenemunde, intensified reconnaissance over northern France was made which resulted in a further twenty-four sites being located; no fewer than ninety-six ski sites were now identified.

This new threat was to be the main preoccupation of the Chiefs of Staff. The codename 'Bodyline' was changed to 'Crossbow' and now included any missile, since it was obvious that the large rocket was not the only new weapon the Germans were developing for use against Britain. However, it did little to moderate the difference of scientific opinion, which at times seems to have overshadowed the battle with the enemy.

To try to resolve the disputes, at the end of October Churchill set up a Committee of Inquiry to decide once and for all the nature of the rockets. He had invited Lord Cherwell to preside but the latter declined. Sir Stafford Cripps accepted, but soon the growing evidence of the ski sites caused the inquiry to be adjourned. On 16 November the War Cabinet Defence Committee was advised of the latest developments by Sir Stafford:

'There is little reliable evidence to connect the sites with any long-range weapon though the impossibility of explaining their use . . . leads to the assumption that there may well be some connection . . . .'[13]

The report went on to note the existence of the Henschel 293, and to consider that the sites could be used for a larger version of it – or of some other pilotless aircraft. There was also the possibility of some other small rocket being fired from the sites. Cripps concluded that the order of probability of the nature of the secret weapons was:

'1.   Larger size Hs 293 glider bomb.

2.   Pilotless aircraft.

3.   Long-range rocket, smaller than A4.

4.   Rocket A4.

    'Whatever the use to which they [the ski sites] are put it is apparently something to be operated by a special unit of the German Air Force, and it is clear that the Germans attach importance to it. It is therefore wise for us to destroy these structures as soon as possible.'

Lord Cherwell wrote a long minute to the Prime Minister, again dismissing the A4 long-range rocket as 'extremely improbable'.[14] On the ski sites, he remarked,

    'the significant point seems to be the curious distribution of these sites – 120 odd miles from London when there is plenty of room in the Calais region, only 90 miles away. It seems extremely odd, if the enemy's object is to bombard London, that he should . . . site his projects 30 miles further away than he need. . . .

A Henschel 293 radio-controlled flying bomb. The conical shapes on its wingtips are to restrict its maximum speed (see p. 298).

'If a secret weapon exists at all, some form of pilotless aircraft or propelled bomb – which is much the same thing – is by far most likely. But I should be surprised if the scale of attack were serious.'

His Lordship was due for a surprise.

The decision to attack the ski sites was taken. There was some resistance to this, since it meant diverting bombers from the strategic attack of Germany. Most of the Bois Carré sites were still under construction, and as it was estimated that each site took approximately 130 days to build, it was decided to attack sites as they were nearly completed. This was done by giving each site a number of points as it progressed: 10 points each for the ski buildings, 10 points for the square building, 10 for the launching platform, and so on up to 100. When 70 was reached, the site was attacked.

By 19 December 1943, fifty-four of the sites had the required number of points. Two days later the first location was bombed. The effort was shared by RAF Bomber Command, US 8th and 9th Air Forces and the Second Tactical Air Force. Eventually over 23,000 tons of bombs were dropped in 1053 sorties on the ninety-six known sites. To the credit of Photographic Reconnaissance, they had discovered every one: only ninety-six were in fact constructed.

Raids took place throughout January 1944, and by February the Germans had apparently decided to abandon the sites. Closer examination of air photographs had revealed that twenty-eight of the attacked sites had been partially rebuilt, the Germans leaving craters and other damage untouched as a blind. It was a double deception however, the Germans hoping that the sites would be bombed again, when in fact they had already been abandoned.

A V1 launching ramp. Many sites were left unrepaired and new ramps built instead, concealed by natural camouflage.

Deception or not, all ninety-six ski sites were now just rubble. Despite this apparent success, however, the battle was far from won.

On 27 April 1944 an Army Photographic Interpreter, Captain Robert Powell, examining some photographs taken over the Cherbourg Peninsula, noticed between two farm buildings near the village of Belhamelin the now-familiar launching ramp for a flying bomb.

The conclusion following this discovery was disconcerting: this and other new sites, named 'Modified' or 'Belhamelin', were much simpler than the originals. The ramp was prefabricated, only requiring to be bolted together; it and the square buildings were often concealed in woods or within existing farm buildings. The photographs revealed a lack of the 'skis', which indicated that the missiles would arrive at the site fuelled, armed and ready to fly. In addition, some of the abandoned Bois Carré sites were being prepared for use in the same way.

The Chiefs of Staff were disturbed. The flying-bomb threat which they had considered eradicated by the destruction of the ski sites was once again a reality – and this a bare month from the Normandy D-day landings. By 13 May twenty of these 'modified' sites had been discovered, most so close to French villages that bombing would be difficult, if not impossible. All that could be done was to alert the defences, bomb possible supply centres, and keep up a close photographic watch. Whenever a site appeared to be ready to fire, a warning would be issued, the codeword for which was 'Diver'.

The weather around D-day, 6 June, was uniformly bad, and it was not until 11 June that photographic reconnaissance coverage was resumed. Sixty-six modified sites were photographed, of which six were deemed to be ready for firing. Two days earlier an agent had reported a train of thirty-three wagons loaded with 'rockets' passing through Belgium towards northern France.

The 'Diver' codeword was issued, but inexplicably not passed on. Someone in the Air Ministry simply filed the agent's report and the 'Diver' warning. The result was that Air Marshal Hill, the man responsible for alerting the air defences against the flying bomb, knew no more of the imminent attack than anyone else.

For Colonel Max Wachtel of Flak Regiment 155(W), the German unit that was to fire the bombs, 13 June had been a most frustrating day. He had hoped that a great salvo of his V1s would be launched against London. Each site had been planned to hold in readiness twenty operational bombs: since there were originally ninety-six sites, nearly 2000 tons of high explosive could have been dropping on London every twenty-four hours. Incidentally the twenty missiles 'issued' to each site was the reason for one of the 'skis' being shorter than the other two; since it contained six bombs rather than seven, the thorough Germans saved material by making it shorter. The characteristic ski shape was simply a precaution against blast, not so much from Allied bombing as from inevitable misfires of the V1s themselves. However, with the original sites all flattened, and due to supply difficulties, only eleven bombs were launched that night, of which four reached England.

Up to the moment that the first V1 landed, the British knew little about this weapon. Just what was this FZG 76, Fi 103, V1?

It was a simple, all-metal monoplane, with a wingspan of 18 feet, length 25'4", weight 4750 lbs, powered by an ingenious Pulse Jet engine. Speed varied a good deal but a typical performance was 360 mph at 3000 feet. The

One of the modified 'Belhamelin' sites (this one at Vignacourt). The launching ramp is concealed in an orchard and the 'square building' in the meadow is exactly aligned with it. Another point of interest is the supply building, at the bottom of the picture, partly concealed by an existing barn.

warhead was 1874 lbs of Amatol. The missile was not radio-controlled, although a number of the V1s carried a small radio transmitter to enable direction-finding stations to track the bombs and ascertain the accuracy of the guidance system.

The guidance system and the power plant were very interesting and I propose to examine them both in some detail. The mechanics of a pulse jet are very simple. Take a test tube, put in a drop or two of petrol, shake the tube and ignite; the petrol will not burn continuously, but with a rhythmic pulse. This elementary phenomenon was well known as early as 1906, when an engineer named Karavodine had constructed and run a simple tube pulse jet. Between 1928 and 1930 a young German fluid dynamics engineer, Paul Schmidt, was experimenting with a pulse jet. This too was a simple open tube, with spring-loaded flap valves, rather like a venetian blind, at one end. A combustible mixture of fuel and air was introduced and the mixture ignited by a sparking plug; the expanding gases then shut the valves and accelerated down the tube to give thrust, the gases leaving an area of low pressure at the inlet end of the tube which caused the valves to open and a fresh fuel/air mixture to be drawn in. The cycle repeated at a rate determined largely by the resonance of the tube.

Schmidt applied for a patent in 1931, not for the tube itself, but for a vertical take-off aircraft with three Schmidt tubes arranged with outlets under each wingtip and the tail, the object being simply to lift the aircraft into the air, a conventional propeller engine being used to provide the forward movement.

This very early VTOL was not built, however. The snag was the problem of ignition, but after further work, in particular an investigation into using the shock waves of the expanding gases to give compression ignition to the fresh charge, some success was achieved, and in 1934 Schmidt received financial support from the German Air Ministry. He even submitted a proposal for what was, in essence, the flying bomb, but this was turned down, although he continued to work on his pulse engines. (It is interesting to note that he was granted two British patents – 368,564 (1931) and 737,555 – in connection with his work on pulse jets.)

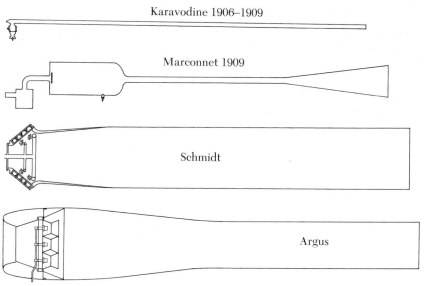

The historical development of the pulse jet from 1909 to 1945.

Karavodine 1906–1909

Marconnet 1909

Schmidt

Argus

In 1939 the German Air Ministry decided to look seriously into the question of jet propulsion. Various aero-engine firms were approached and one of them, Argus Motoren Gesellschaft of Berlin, was asked to develop a pulse jet. Rather strangely they were not aware of the earlier work of Schmidt, so they started from first principles.

The first principle was simply that, if one of the two components needed for combustion, the air, enters intermittently, then the other, the fuel, can be supplied continuously. The first experimental model had a rather complex reflex arrangement using what is called a Borda mouth, which was not very satisfactory. The second engine, tested on 13 November 1939, proved very promising: it had a good steady pulse and exhibited the strange ability of pulse jets to go on working with the ignition switched off. These early engines had no mechanical parts at all; the flow of the expanding gases was dictated by the shape of the combustion chamber. It was superseded by a third engine which, like the Schmidt design, had spring-shutter valves; it was not a straight tube, however – there were two chambers, one for mixing and the other for combustion. There was a 'pinch' in the tube between the two chambers which prevented the expanding hot gases reaching the flap valves.

This third model engine performed satisfactorily on the bench and, considering that only three months had elapsed from the start of the work, things

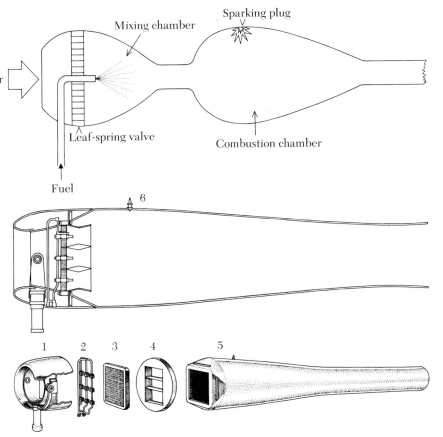

Mixing chamber

Sparking plug

Air

Leaf-spring valve

Combustion chamber

Fuel

The third Argus pulse-jet engine. The pinch in the combustion chamber was to prevent ignition of the fuel in the mixing chamber.

The Argus 014.
1   Air intake and fairing.
2   Fuel spray bar.
3   Flap-valve assemblies.
4   Baffle.
5   Jet pipe.
6   Sparking plug.

were going rather well. At this point, someone in the German Air Ministry remembered Paul Schmidt and a meeting was arranged between him and the Argus men. The outcome was that the Argus engine was able to use Schmidt's spring-flap valves, which had been developed considerably and were sturdy enough to allow the use of a straight tube.

By 30 April 1941 a full-size engine was flight-tested under a training biplane. Work progressed and on 19 June 1942 the Argus Company was ordered to build a high-performance pulse jet for an unmanned long-distance missile. The operation of these extremely simple engines was now clearly understood and an operational jet was soon developed – the Argus 014 – giving 660 lbs thrust on low-grade petrol at 3000 feet.

This engine was a sheet-steel tube about twelve feet long with a gentle taper from the combustion chamber for about a third of its length, when it continued as a straight tube. There were only five units to the assembly: an air intake, which also contained a diffuser with provision for the attaching of a compressed air-line for starting purposes; three spray-bars carrying nine atomising fuel jets; the flap-valve assembly; a cast-alloy baffle to prevent the combustion flames reaching the flap-valves; and finally the duct itself. To start the engine a press-button starter allowed a measured quantity of petrol and compressed air to enter the combustion chamber, a sparking plug ignited the mixture violently, and the pulse cycle began. (There is some evidence that the open end of the jet pipe was covered with a paper diaphragm to contain the starting mixture within the tube.) The engine would run satisfactorily in a static condition, though the ram-air effect as it flew gave increased efficiency.

Once running, the sparking plug played no further part in the ignition. This self-ignition phenomenon had been observed from the earliest experiments with pulse jets and was at first thought to be due to the thin walls of the jet pipe, which ran cherry red, igniting the charge. The Argus team proved this assumption incorrect: they ran static engines on endurance runs in a test-rig with water jets playing on the duct to cool it, and the engine still ran with the ignition switched off. Eventually they rediscovered Schmidt's theory that the expanding gases were analogous to a mechanical piston in a cylinder and that, as the high-velocity gas left the tube, a secondary pressure-wave travelled back down the jet-pipe and compression ignited the new charge.

These simple engines seem to have been reliable – the only moving parts were the spring-loaded flap-valves – but they were rather inefficient. In particular the fuel consumption was high, but this was compensated for to some extent by the use of low-grade petrol. There was little control over the engine's output, though by varying the pressure in the fuel system, a degree of control could be obtained. The 680-litre fuel tank was pressurised to about seven atmospheres prior to take-off, the pressure being obtained from a spherical compressed-air bottle within the fuselage. The control of the fuel nozzle-pressure had to be adjusted automatically for take-off, climb and cruise. It was accomplished by a governor which could vary the nozzle pressure between about 1.2 and 2.6 atmospheres, the difference between static running and take-off; intermediate pressures were controlled by the governor for climbing and cruising.

This engine with its control systems was ready for the airframe that

The fuel supply to the V1.
1 Spherical compressed-air vessel.
2 Pressure-reducing valve.
3 680-litre fuel tank.
4 Fuel governor.
5 Spray bar containing fuel vessels.
6 Pulse-jet pipe.
7 Compressed-air flight-control gyros.

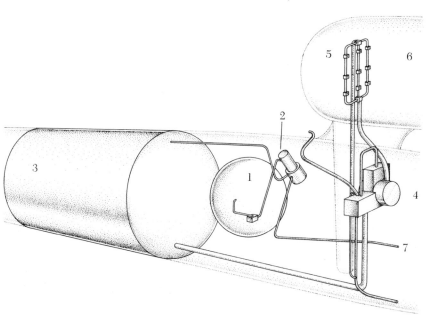

the Fiesler Company had built and the first test flight took place from Peenemunde six months after the initial order – a very considerable achievement. The autopilot for the FZG76 was designed by Askania Company, who called it the Steuergerät (steering device), and it was based on a displacement gyroscope mounted in two gimbals at right angles. This gyroscope had pickups which detected pitch, yaw, heading, roll and attitude. Movement in these planes was sensed and used to actuate pneumatic servo units that moved the rudder and elevators: there were no ailerons.

The heading of the missile was maintained by the aircraft's compass, which allowed the gyro to precess slowly at $3°$ a minute until the direction of flight coincided with the setting of the compass. The main gyro (there were also two smaller, 'rate' gyros) and the pneumatic servos were driven from a second compressed-air bottle similar to the one which pressurised the fuel tank. Total air consumption in flight for the control unit was 300 litres a minute.

This autopilot was required to:

1. Maintain lateral stability.
2. Control heading for 25 minutes.
3. Compensate for a change of launching direction of $\pm 60°$.
4. Maintain a fixed altitude between 300 and 2500 metres.
5. Get the missile down after a given distance flown.

This last was not, strictly speaking, part of the autopilot's task. A small propeller on the nose of the FZG76 turned a log which measured the distance flown and could be preset; at a given distance the elevators were fully deflected, and the aircraft dived. (This sudden application of negative 'G' caused the engine to cut out, giving some warning to those on the ground; it was unintentional and when they learned of it, late in the campaign, the German designers of the V1 altered the control so that the elevators were slowly deflected: the bomb then dived under power.)

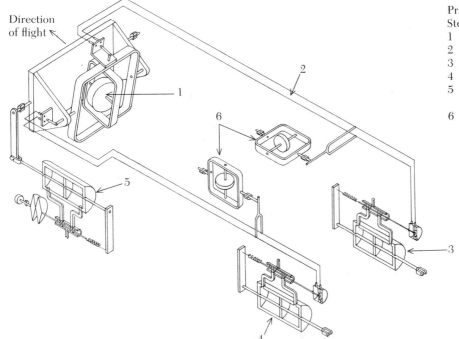

Direction of flight

Principle of the Steuergerät.
1 Main gyroscope.
2 Air lines.
3 Rudder servo.
4 Elevator servo.
5 Altimeter and altitude servo.
6 Rate gyros.

The thrust from the pulse jet was insufficient to launch the V1 unaided. The launching was from the ramps that had been so conspicuous in the air photographs. These were 125 feet long and consisted of a long tube, with a slot cut into its upper surface running the entire length of the ramp. A piston with a fin-like projection was placed in this tube at the firing end, the fin sticking up through the open slot and engaging a collar under the missile. A sealing strip of just sufficient size to close the opening ran inside the length of the split tube and was fed through the piston.

When the missile was ready for firing, the pulse jet was started and high-pressure steam, generated by decomposing hydrogen peroxide with potassium permanganate, forced the piston along the tube, carrying the V1 with it, the steam pressure in the tube apparently being sufficient to hold the sealing strip in the opening. According to German figures, the launching velocity of an operational V1 was 340 feet (105 metres) per second; thus the V1 was launched in something under one second, using some 220 lbs of hydrogen peroxide for each launch.

At the far end of the ramp the piston shot out, disengaging from the missile and hitting the ground some distance away. (It could then be recovered and, if undamaged, used again.) Photographic-reconnaissance interpreters used the marks made by the pistons to count the number of bombs launched from each site. This very ingenious steam catapult was to be re-invented with much acclaim several years later by the Royal Navy, for use on aircraft carriers, using conventional steam from the ship's boilers.

The development of the V1 missile was not all plain sailing: over 300 test flights were made from Peenemunde. To help assess the aerodynamic behaviour, some forty V1s were fitted with a low-powered telemetry transmitter on 4 mHz, monitoring attitude, altitude and the positions of the controls. A

A still from a film of a V1 launching. This frame was taken 2.5 seconds after the firing button was pressed. The flame from the pulse jet can be seen, surrounded by steam from the catapult; a second later the missile was leaving the ramp at the top of the picture.

number of test aircraft rolled over and crashed shortly after take-off. At first the autopilot was suspected, but the cause was traced to the high 'G' loads on launching, which twisted the wings out of alignment and caused a severe rolling movement which the autopilot could not counteract. Other missiles flew with a constant bank of up to 7°, causing skidding and a loss of heading. This fault was due to the haste with which the airframes had been manufactured. Eventually a small trim tab on one wing, pneumatically operated and actuated by a pendulum, was added to compensate for any asymmetry.

The design team's biggest headache was the effect on the airframe of the hammer blows from the pulse jet. The compass in particular was initially very badly affected and course errors of up to 10° were common. This was cured by suspending the compass from lengths of rubber within a wooden sphere, which was in turn suspended from the airframe by additional springs. The heading error was then reduced to less than one degree.

There was another initial problem with the compass. All ferrous-metal structures have magnetic properties. The V1 was fabricated from sheet steel and during manufacture, particularly when being riveted or hammered, the molecules in the steel would align themselves with the earth's magnetic field. The polarity of this imprinted magnetism would be dependent on the heading, relative to magnetic North, of the assembly during construction – this is true of any aircraft or ship. This built-in magnetism will, of course, affect any compass that the aircraft may carry. Normally it is corrected by a rather laborious process known as 'swinging the compass': the aircraft is slowly turned through 360° and the compass reading compared with known headings. Small magnets are fitted to aircraft (and ships') compasses to compensate for any error, or deviation, as it is called. (Very small residual errors are displayed on a 'Deviation Card' near the compass.)

Even if the Germans had had the time for this correction of deviation, it would have been pointless in the case of the V1. In the sheet-steel structure the errors would be very large and, even had they been compensated for on the ground before flight, once airborne the hammering from the pulse jet would have caused the airframe's magnetism to change again to that of the missile heading. Any compensation magnets would then cause large and unforeseeable errors and the missile would fly off its intended course.

This was overcome in a very simple way. When the missile was finally assembled and armed at the launching point, it was taken into the 'square' building which, it will be remembered, was always parallel to the ramp and direction of flight and was built from non-magnetic materials. Inside this small hangar the airframe was carefully aligned on to the magnetic heading it was intended to fly. Those parts of the fuselage around and near the compass were beaten with wooden mallets, causing the molecules of the sheet-steel structure to realign themselves with the Earth's magnetic field, but now in the direction of the line of flight. (Any further realignment during flight from the pulse jet would not matter, since the heading would be unchanged.) In this way the deviation was reduced to one degree or less. This, then, was the main function of the 'square buildings'. Whilst in this building, the compass would be set to compensate for wind drift and the ground speed calculated to enable the flight log to be adjusted to control the missile's range.

The V1 attack began on the night of 13/14 June 1944 and ended when, on 29 March 1945, the last one to fall on Britain was shot down by gunners in Suffolk. A total of 10,500 missiles was launched, of which 3957 were destroyed by the defences; 3531 reached England, 2420 falling in the London area; 6184 people were killed and 17,981 were seriously injured; damage to property was enormous. Roughly two people were killed and five seriously injured by each bomb that evaded the defences.

It could have been far worse: by the end of the war, the Germans had manufactured between 30,000 and 32,000 flying bombs. Although they had planned an assault of some 2000 bombs each twenty-four hours from the ninety-six ski sites, all the launchings now were from the 'modified' sites. These were of a makeshift nature, without storage facilities, yet the second attack on London came on 15 June and, by noon the next day, 244 V1s had been launched from fifty-five sites in two main areas – the Somme/Calais area, where photographic reconnaissance had located forty-eight sites, and the Seine area, where no sites had been found. In spite of the shortage of photographic aircraft, which were now flying almost continuous sorties to support the invasion, a considerable number of new V1 launching ramps were found. (Eventually 156 were covered, which turned out to be the total actually built – a considerable achievement, for these 'modified' sites were not easy to see: the Germans took great care not to disturb the existing cover.)

Once a site had been used, it was a great deal easier to find; apart from the launching piston's tell-tale skid marks on the ground, many of the missiles, either through trouble with the catapult or engine failure, stalled as they left the ramp and exploded, leaving large craters and often stripping the leaves from the camouflaging trees.

Finding the sites was one thing; attacking them was another. This was difficult for two reasons: they were often located in or around French villages, and the bombers could not be spared. The Battle of Normandy was at that time at a critical phase and diverting tactical bombers would have been prejudicial to success in the vital land battles. The main defences against the V1 were therefore fighter aircraft, anti-aircraft guns, barrage balloons and, finally, bombing of the bases which kept the firing points supplied with the missiles.

The man responsible for the defence against the V1, Duncan Sandys, was not in England when the attack started:

'I happened to be on the other side of the Channel seeing the Mulberry Harbour, which had been damaged by a recent storm.

'I was immediately recalled to London and appointed Chairman of a Committee of Service Chiefs and Scientists to co-ordinate the defence of London and Southern England against the flying bombs. Several months earlier the Chiefs of Staff had prepared a contingency plan to deal with this situation, should it arise.

'This gave the main responsibility to the fighter aircraft along the coast; behind them there was a belt of anti-aircraft guns and around London a belt of barrage balloons. This plan didn't work well in practice, for the simple reason that when the flying bombs came over it was found that they flew a good deal faster than most of our fighter aircraft. The aircraft chased the bombs over the gun belt, which prevented the guns from firing.

'General Pile [AA Commander], Air Marshal Hill [C-in-C fighter de-fences] and I came to the conclusion that we would do a lot better if we were to move the guns down to the coast and give them prime respon-sibility for the defence.

'We ought of course to have asked the Chiefs of Staff before tearing up their plan but, no doubt improperly, we decided to act on our own authority and gave the orders for the guns to move down [to] the coast.'[15]

The decision to move the guns was taken on 13 July, and four days later 23,000 men and women with their guns, radar and communication networks, were installed on new coastal sites. Lord Sandys remembers that:

'The Chiefs of Staff were naturally furious. London inevitably was left undefended for about forty-eight hours while the guns were on the move and there were quite high casualties.'

But the decision was quickly seen to be justified as the number of bombs destroyed rose dramatically; during the first week over 50% of all the bombs crossing the coast. The percentage rose steadily and by the last week in August stood at 83%.

The gunners were achieving much better figures for three reasons. The new coastal sites were a much better environment for the new American SCR 584 gun-laying radar – there was far less 'clutter' or radar interference and permanent echoes in open country. The shells were fused with a new 'prox-imity fuse' – a miniature radar set, designed to withstand the tremendous forces when fired and exploding when within lethal range of its target, turning a near miss into a hit. This was a British invention which had been developed in America and was available in quantity just in time. Finally, the gunners had a clear area to shoot in. Allied fighters were banned from it, and the guns could work on an 'if it moves hit it' basis.

The fighters had two main zones – over the Channel in front of the gun-belts and behind the guns. They, too, had considerable success, although at first the small size and high speed of the V1s made them difficult targets; there was also the danger of exploding the 1800-lb warhead at too close range: several pilots did just that and, although some of them got away with it, it could lead to damage or the loss of the aircraft. Many pilots, however, continued to close with the V1s and shoot them down.

Wing Commander Roland Beamont flew Hawker Tempests, the fastest piston-engined RAF fighter of the day, against the V1:

'For the first few days it was rather interesting because none of us knew

During the V1
attacks Hawker
Tempests shot
down 638 out of the
RAF's total of 1771.

exactly what was going to happen; they were bombs, after all, and they
were expected to blow up. We first of all started opening fire on them from
about 400 yards, for safety, from astern; they were a tiny target and we
used to miss them rather consistently, and so we halved the range to about
200 yards. When you fired at that range and the thing exploded in front of
you, you were travelling at 400 mph or more and you'd have no time to
avoid the explosion, and as soon as you saw it you were in it and you'd go
through the centre of the fire ball and come out the other side and always
come out upside down. It was some time before we could figure this one out
but you were in fact going through a partial vacuum as you went through
the centre of the explosion. In a partial vacuum the torque of this enormous
propeller had the effect of twisting the aeroplane over. It was rather
extraordinary. The only adverse effects were fire damage to the outside of
the aeroplane – the rudder and the elevator of the Tempest were fabric-
covered and quite often this used to burn, and the other problem was that
the pilots used to come back with a burn blister on their left arm. In the
cockpit of the Tempest you had two air ventilators, one on either side, and
the left-hand one was immediately over your left arm and in hot summer
weather we were all flying in shirt-sleeves and the flame was coming
through the ventilator and burning our arms, so we shut the ventilator.'[16]
There was another method of attack, even more dangerous, pioneered by
Wing Commander Beamont:

'I had used up my ammunition on one V1 and saw another and decided to
do something about it. The idea was to get my wingtip close under the
wingtip of the V1 but not touching it, then gradually raising my wing
causing the airflow over it to make the V1 bank. This affected the gyro-
stabilisation of the missile, causing it to go out of control, toppling over and
crashing.'

One of the only Allied jet fighters to see service during World War II, the Gloster Meteor, also tipped over a V1. On 4 August Flying Officer Dean of 616 Squadron had closed on a V1, but his guns had jammed, so he overtook the missile and tipped it over as described by Wing Commander Beamont. This was the first time an enemy aircraft had been destroyed by a jet and the first jet versus jet encounter: the Meteor was a Mk I, EE216. Later that same day another Meteor of 616 Squadron shot down a V1: altogether 616, the only jet squadron in the RAF, destroyed thirteen V1s.

The most successful day for the defences was 28 August when, of the ninety-four bombs successfully launched, sixty-five were destroyed by the anti-aircraft guns, twenty-three by fighters and two by the last-ditch defence, the balloon barrage. Only four got to London.

As the ground forces consolidated their foothold on Europe the priority for bombing effort was such that aircraft could be spared for attacks against the V1. Rocket-firing fighters and bombers attacked the 'modified' sites, though these were difficult to knock out permanently. The supply depots were attacked by heavy bombers, but first they had to be located. Once again photographic reconnaissance was responsible. Considerable activity had been seen in an area near Paris at a place named Creil, where there was known to be an extensive system of underground tunnels, used prewar for mushroom cultivation. From agents' reports and further air reconnaissance, it was learned that the caves had been greatly enlarged by the Germans; the entrances had been strengthened and a new railway spur ran into them. There were similar caves at St Leu d'Esserat: there two sites were so heavily bombed that underground passages caved in and the entrances were blocked by landslides.

During the V1s' offensive, mainly against London, the Germans were concerned to know just where their bombs were falling, so their agents in

Britain were ordered by their controllers to signal back the fall of shot. So far as is known, all German agents in Britain were arrested and some were 'turned': that is, they were given the simple alternative of either being shot or working to MI5 instructions. Most, if not all, chose the latter course and continued to send information back to Germany, but now operating their clandestine radios from cells in Wandsworth jail – on instructions from their captors. They were ordered to signal that the V1s were landing to the north of London and that many were overshooting; in fact, the tendency was to undershoot. The Germans at the firing points therefore reduced the range, causing the missiles to undershoot still further. The interesting thing is that, even though the radio-equipped V1s were being accurately tracked by direction finders and reported as undershoots, such was the faith of the Germans in their agents, who were allowed to send genuine information from time to time, that the D/F reports from the radio men were disregarded as mistakes.

Flying Bomb damage in London. Because of their relatively low speed on impact, V1s caused a great deal of blast damage and were more effective than V2s, which tended to bury themselves before exploding. In a densely built-up area most damage was caused by blast.

Wherever they fell in built-up areas, the V1s caused a great deal of damage and loss of life. Being in London at the time was to be in a city under siege. Most people remember the attack as an experience heard rather than seen: the V1s flew low at about 3000 feet and the buildings in the city areas prevented one from seeing any distance; the first warning would be the deep-throated throb of the pulse jet, growing rapidly louder. In the streets people would stop and look upwards, trying to judge the direction of the bomb and praying it would fly over and away to somewhere else. But if the engine suddenly cut, then everyone would dash for the cover of doorways or even lie flat on the pavements: there would be a wait that could seem an eternity, then a shattering explosion followed by a deep roar as some building or other dissolved into rubble; then silence. Smoke would billow up behind the skyline and then the bells of the fire engines and rescue services would be heard and probably the distant deep throb of another bomb.

The sight of a V1 was unforgettable: they flew at a very high speed – some at 400 mph – and their small size tended to make it look even faster. What many people remember is the eerie way they kept going straight on, indifferent to guns, fighters and balloons; their blind robot purpose was itself chilling. Evelyn Waugh summed it up well in *Unconditional Surrender*: 'It was as impersonal as a plague . . . as though the city were infested with enormous venomous insects.'

Gradually the bombing of the supply depots reduced the intensity of the attack, and in the first weeks of September Allied troops overran the launching sites in the Pas de Calais. The Germans then resorted to air-launching the missiles from Heinkel 111s and 177s: about 1200 were launched against Portsmouth and Southampton and about fifty against Manchester, the majority being shot down. A few longer-range V1s were launched in March 1945 from bases in Holland but only a dozen got through to London.

The reality of the V1 had diverted attention from the rockets, although during the spring and summer of 1944 the evidence for their existence had been mounting. Dr Jones had been receiving intelligence reports about the German work on the long-range rocket throughout the winter of 1943–4. In March 1944, he had received reports from Polish sources that there was considerable new activity at an SS Artillery Range that had existed near the village of Blizna since 1941. Forced labour arrived; some 2000 workers began to make a new road; a railway was extended to the site, and new buildings and concrete structures were built. The villagers were evacuated; barbed wire surrounded the site and anyone approaching within half a mile was shot.

Further intelligence proving the importance of Blizna came, probably from 'Ultra', in the same form of petrol allocation that had enabled Jones to prove that Peenemunde was genuine. The Polish Underground was now able to report that 'aerial torpedoes' were being fired from the site and London had been notified of the size and location of craters made.

Following these reports it was decided to photograph the Blizna area. A

Photographic Reconnaissance Mosquito flew the 600 miles from San Severo in Italy on 15 April and the resulting cover revealed the familiar 'modified' Belhamelin type of flying-bomb ramp. Another sortie, flown three weeks later, showed that the V1 ramp had disappeared and, most significant, there was great activity, including a train of 'Peenemunde'-type fuel wagons, a number of heavy road trailers and, once again left lying in the open, a large rocket – this one with four fins. The most disturbing feature of the Blizna photographs, however, was the complete absence of any sign of heavy-launching structure or even of the large elliptical earthworks seen at Peenemunde.

The Home Army Section of the Polish Underground had been busy trying to get to the wreckage of the missiles fired overland from Blizna. They were lucky when, on 20 May 1944, a V2 rocket fell in the river Bug, near the village of Sarnaki, eighty miles north-west of Warsaw. The missile had not exploded and was lying in shallow water near the bank of the river, with the fins sticking above the water.

The Underground men got to the scene before the Germans and managed to get the tell-tale fins out of sight by pushing the rocket deeper into the soft river-bed, concealing the outline by driving cattle into the river to disturb the mud. They were successful, for after three days the German search parties gave up. The Poles then removed the rocket with a team of horses, transported it on two heavy farm wagons, and hid it in a barn in the village of Holowczyce-Kolonia. Engineers from Warsaw, led by Jerzy Chmielewski (code-named Raphael), began to dismantle the V2 and parts were smuggled to Warsaw for detailed examination by scientists, one of whom was Antoni Kocian, a young aerodynamicist.

Another expert was Professor Greszkowski of the Warsaw Polytechnic, who made a detailed survey of the radio equipment found in the rocket in the flat of the German Commander of the Luftwaffe's airfield at Warsaw. While

Members of the Polish Home Army, photographed on 23 May 1944 while removing the V2 rocket engine from the river Bug.

the German was away at his office during the day, his Polish housekeeper used to ring him up to enquire what he would require for dinner and at what time; in this way she knew his movements and, therefore, when it would be safe for Professor Greszkowski to continue his work. Each day just before the German returned to the flat and his conscientious cook, the radios and other equipment were hidden – in one of the German's own suitcases!

London was informed by radio about the Polish Underground's find and immediate arrangements were made to fly the vital parts of the rocket out of Poland, but before that could be done, yet another rocket was to become available. This one, however, was not fired from Blizna.

An A4 (V2) rocket was launched from Peenemunde on 13 June 1944; it went off course and at 1608 hours there was a violent explosion at low altitude over Gräsdals Gäro in Sweden. The rocket, which it was subsequently discovered had not carried a warhead, had exploded in mid-air, probably due to structural failure rupturing the fuel tanks. The main debris landed 200 metres from a farm and was to be found in a crater, according to a contemporary report in the Swedish paper *Svenska Dagbladgt*, 'five metres wide and two to three metres deep. Big rocks had been thrown more than ten metres and the tree-tops had been broken like sticks.'[17]

What the paper did not reveal was that the wreckage had been quickly removed from the farm by the Swedish Military and was examined by them with more than casual interest. Diplomatic activity in Stockholm was considerable: the Germans not unnaturally wanted their rocket back and the British even more desperately wanted either the remains, or at least a report on the investigation that Swedish scientists were already busy drafting. The British offered some mobile radar sets in exchange – a tempting bargain: the Swedes had no radar at that time. The offer was accepted. (Some sources stated that a Squadron of Spitfires was to be the fee but this was not so: the Swedish Air Force did not acquire any Spitfires until after the war, when in

A farmer's wife and three soldiers pose behind the engine casing of the V2 which came down in Sweden.

1948 they bought seventy Photographic Reconnaissance Mk XIXs (PR19), which remained in service until 1954.)

British Intelligence Officers flew to Stockholm and examined the remains. With these findings as well as the information from Poland, Jones felt able on 16 July to issue an Intelligence Report. The main dimensions of the rockets were a little over forty feet long and six feet in diameter; they had four fins and the liquid fuel was hydrogen peroxide. Although the launching weight was unknown, it was estimated that the warhead was probably between three and six tons.[18]

Jones thought the evidence pointed to gyroscopic control but added that a radio guidance system could also be involved. The range of the rocket was now known, to the extent that the Swedish A4 had flown some 200 miles from Peenemunde and the Blizna rockets, from information supplied by the Polish Underground, had a range of about 185 miles. The most important single piece of evidence in the intelligence report was a statement from a prisoner of war which claimed that the rockets could be launched from a 'simple concrete slab'.

The British experts who examined the Swedish rocket concluded from the serial number of the assemblies that it was one of a production batch, which meant that quantity production was under way and that perhaps up to 1000 missiles had been manufactured.

Two days later the full 'Crossbow' Committee, with the Prime Minister in the chair, considered the report. The minutes revealed that opinion was now as follows:

'Evidence from Sweden.

Certain radio parts of the rocket which had fallen in Sweden had just been received in this country on loan for a month. . . . It was definitely established that the rocket was radio-controlled, and the wiring was of immense complexity.'[18]

Jones's statement that the control was primarily gyroscopic was not mentioned.

In fact the Swedish rocket was unfortunately a red herring; it *had* been radio-controlled but had been used as a test vehicle for trials of the radio-guidance system of a quite different rocket: a ground-to-air missile coded 'Wasserfall', which was also being developed at Peenemunde. This not unreasonable misunderstanding was to lead to the false hope that a radio-jamming countermeasure might be employed against the missiles.

The Committee decided (on evidence from Poland) that the probable accuracy of the rockets would be of the order of fifty per cent falling within ten miles of the aiming point. There was now no doubt that a rocket attack on London was possible, even probable, as the minutes reveal:

'In summing up the Prime Minister said that, if rocket attacks should develop, he was prepared after consultation with the United States and the USSR to threaten the enemy with large-scale gas attacks in retaliation should such a course appear profitable. . . .'

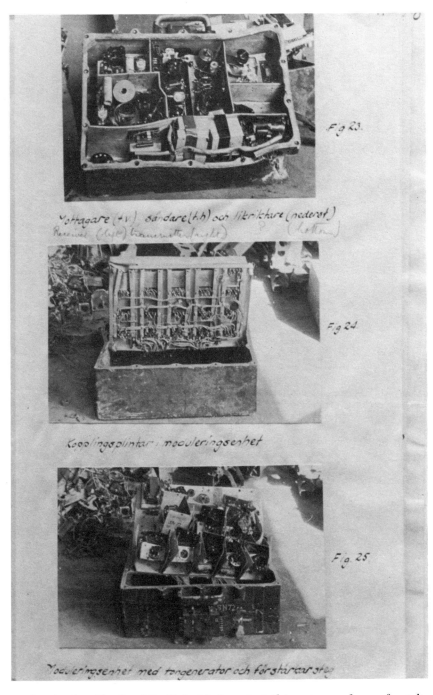

Evidently the Chiefs of Staff decided against this extreme form of retaliation, though according to the minutes of this meeting no one at that time raised objections.

At a subsequent War Cabinet meeting on 25 July, Churchill was critical of the way the intelligence had been presented:

'he . . . had been very surprised at the information suddenly produced a week ago, and felt that this information should not have been withheld.

'It had suddenly been brought to light that the Germans had made a thousand of these rockets, and that instead of a complicated and bulky edifice for firing them, all that was required was . . . a simple bed of concrete.

'[The Prime Minister] felt that he should have been kept more fully informed on these matters.'

Jones then pointed out that much of the information had become known to him only during the week previous to his report and the question arose as to whether, in fact, a rocket attack *was* imminent:

'There was no sign whatever so far of the large movement westward of men or stores which would correspond with a big offensive.'

The whole picture of the rocket now stood in a new light. By far the most disquieting disclosures were the fact that up to 1000 rockets existed and that the launching did not require any complicated and heavy equipment, or even a fixed site.

The photographic interpreters at Medmenham now complained that they had been misled: they had been briefed to look for large structures, which they claimed – with some justification – were considered by the scientists to be indispensable to the launching of the rockets. Whatever the validity of this charge, the fact remains that the photographic interpreters *had* seen the very large, fan-shaped asphalt area by the shore at Peenemunde and had not asked themselves why the German military engineers had gone to the trouble of reclaiming the land and laying such a piece of hard standing on a beach. Furthermore, a year earlier a PRU sortie had revealed 'a vertical column about 40 feet high and 4 feet thick' (see page 130). This had not been interpreted as a rocket; had it been seen for what it was – a rocket sitting on its fins – then the nature of the launching sites would have been obvious.

By mid-July 1944 a detailed report on the Swedish rocket was available and it was now known that control of the vital initial ascent was effected by graphite vanes in the rocket's efflux, which enabled it to take off unaided from any simple, level site ('a bit of planking on a forest track, or the overgrown track itself', General Dornberger wrote in his postwar book *V2*).

A test-stand at Peenemunde before and after the USAAF daylight raid.

The Peenemunde and Zinnowitz sites were heavily attacked by the United States 8th Air Force on 18 July, just eleven months after the RAF attack on Peenemunde. General Spaatz, C-in-C 8th USAAF, said that the daylight raid

was 'the finest example of precision bombing I have ever seen'.

By 24 July, Blizna was in danger of being over-run by the advancing Russian Army and on that day the Germans fired the last V2 before blowing up the site and abandoning it. Churchill cabled Stalin requesting that, when the area was occupied, a British scientific mission would be allowed access to examine any material left behind by the Germans. (Later, a British Scientific Mission was allowed by Stalin to visit the Blizna area. They collected together a large quantity of components from the rockets, which were crated up and arrangements were made with the Russians to fly the material to England. However, when the crates were eventually opened at Farnborough, they were found to contain only pieces of crashed German aircraft.)

On 25 July, an RAF Dakota took off from Brindisi in Italy, and flew over Hungary heading for a large meadow near Tarnow in Poland. There it was to be met by a reception party from the Polish Underground with fifty kilos of components from the stolen rocket and by the young Polish engineer, Jerzy Chmielewski, who was to accompany the finds to London.

400 Polish partisans of the Home Army were scattered around the large meadow and surrounding woods: it was raining but during the afternoon the steady drizzle stopped and, to the consternation of the Poles, two German aircraft landed on the soggy field, which was occasionally used by the Luftwaffe. Knowing that the Dakota was already airborne and making for Tarnov, there was nothing that the partisans could do but wait, as the two German pilots, probably on a cross-country exercise, strolled about chatting and smoking cigarettes. After what must have seemed an eternity, the pilots climbed into their aircraft and took off. It was now almost night and within the hour it was dark and the engines of the Dakota could be heard approaching. Lights were displayed to indicate the direction of the wind and the large transport landed safely, taxiing on the wet grass towards the waiting Poles.

The pilot of the Dakota, Flight Lieutenant Culliford, and his Polish co-pilot, F/O Szajer, were naturally keen to get their aircraft away as soon as possible. German units were in the area, so with the engine ticking over and the rocket components and Jerzy Chmielewski on board, the door was shut and the throttles opened up. A Dakota is not exactly a light aeroplane and it would not

The landing strip near Tarnow with Polish partisans waiting for the RAF Dakota.

171

budge, having become bogged in the soft meadow in the middle of German-occupied Europe. Desperately Culliford tried all he knew, opening up first one engine then the other to try to unstick the 11-ton aircraft. The Poles heaved against the wheels and both engines were opened flat out. Still the plane would not move and the reception party were all for dowsing it with petrol and setting it on fire; they were talked out of this by the Dakota's crew, who suggested dismantling a farm cart to put some boards under the aircraft's wheels. Again Culliford opened the throttles: the noise must have been audible for miles but if the German patrols heard it, it is possible that they thought it wise to turn a deaf ear; the lonely Polish countryside at night, with 400 partisans about, was not the place for a small party of Germans, armed only with light weapons, to be heroic. Eventually the reluctant Dakota, its cylinder-head temperatures well in the red, pulled itself to firmer ground and took off for the long flight home, landing safely at Hendon.

Jerzy Chmielewski stayed in Britain and gave much useful information to British Intelligence about the Blizna site. He was a Captain in the Polish Home Army and had enjoyed something of a charmed life, having been arrested accidentally by the Gestapo in 1942 and sent to Auschwitz Concentration Camp, from which he was released in March 1944 (a very rare occurrence). Anton Kozian, who had supervised the dismantling of the rocket, was not so lucky: he was arrested by the Gestapo and shot during the Warsaw Rising of 1944.

A few days after the Polish rocket parts had arrived in London, on 31 July, a Halifax bomber landed at the Royal Aircraft Establishment, Farnborough, with twelve large packing cases, containing two tons of wreckage from the V2 that had crashed in Sweden. These were unpacked under conditions of great secrecy in a hangar of the Aircraft Crash Investigation Unit.

Gradually the rocket took shape as the twisted metal parts were laid out in their correct order in just the same way as a crashed aircraft is reconstructed. One of the largest areas of dispute had, as we have seen, centred around the question of the fuel. The RAE experts cleared up the problem very quickly.[19] It was found that the fuel tanks and associated pipes were stained by two dyes. These were analysed, and identified as methyl violet and fluorescein.

The nature of these dyes suggested that methyl violet, an aniline dye, had been dissolved in alcohol, and that therefore the main fuel was alcohol. The traces of fluorescein led from another fuel tank to a pump which was found to bear certain tell-tale evidence that pointed to its being used to pump oxygen. Liquid oxygen is a very low-temperature fluid, typically $-183\,°C$; the pump and associated piping were lagged, but more convincing evidence was found: a screw in the pump was found to be fractured and the break proved to be crystalline, indicating a very low temperature at the time of the fracture. The pump also had very large clearances (.014″) in its plain bearings, which were lubricated by the fluid that was being pumped. The lack of any normal lubricant based on oil or grease was an almost certain pointer to liquid oxygen.

As the pieces of this giant jigsaw were fitted together the picture became clear. Although the Farnborough investigators only had the remains, by no means complete, of a 12-ton missile that had crashed at around 2500 feet per second (1700 mph), they were able to issue a report (EA 228/1) which included weights and principal dimensions and a general-arrangement drawing.[19]

	Farnborough Figures	German (Postwar) Figures
Overall Length:	45′ 10″	46′
Diameter of Body:	5′ 5¼″	5′ 5″
Diameter over fins:	11′ 8″	11′ 7″
Take-off weight:	12.2 tons	12.7 tons
Take-off thrust:	30 tons	25 tons
	for 65 secs.	for 65 secs.
Warhead:	1 ton	1 ton

It was now clear that the V2 rocket was a most brilliant scientific achievement. The Germans had solved a number of very complex problems and were years ahead of any other nation in long-range rockets. The value of such a missile as a military weapon with a conventional warhead was another matter.

However, the question that had for over a year divided scientific opinion so bitterly was now settled, to the embarrassment of some, though Lubbock in particular was vindicated in his prediction about the fuel pump (although not the fuel itself). This was now revealed as a most elegant solution to the problem: it was a steam turbine driving a dual pump cast in light alloy. The

The fuel pump of the Swedish rocket – which proved that the V2s were liquid-fuelled.

steam was generated by decomposing 80% hydrogen peroxide (H_2O_2) with potassium permanganate ($KMnO_4$); the two-stage 500-hp turbine drove two centrifugal pumps at approximately 4300 rpm, pumping alcohol and liquid oxygen at pressures around 350 lbs/in², with a temperature differential between the steam at 425 °C and liquid oxygen at −183 °C of 608 °C. The pumps were only about a foot in diameter.

The actual rocket motor was a steel structure, six feet long and double-walled for cooling by the alcohol fuel. It had eighteen burners arranged around its top end, each with three rows of jets which mixed the alcohol and oxygen before burning them at a temperature of 2700 °C. It produced a thrust of 25 tons for 65 seconds, with an exhaust gas velocity of 6700 feet per second, propelling the 12.7-ton missile up to a height of 100,000 feet at a maximum speed of 3600 mph and a horizontal range of some 200 miles.

A report on the findings made at Farnborough was presented at a meeting of the Crossbow Committee on 31 August 1944, exactly one month after the remains had arrived at the RAE.[20]

As mentioned earlier, the Swedish V2 was carrying radio equipment which was not typical of the operational weapons. This was included in the report which identified a receiver, E230, found in the wreckage, as identical to that which was employed in the Henschel 293 flying bomb to control that much smaller missile. The receiver was known to the Germans as *Strassburg* or FuG230: when employed to guide the HS293, it was known to operate on nine channels around either 60 mHz or 27 mHz.

The set recovered from Sweden, however, had the vital frequency-determining components missing. In addition to this receiver there was also part of a transmitter/receiver which was thought to be some sort of transponder, for speed and range measurement. There were other fragments of electronic instruments and the wiring harness was noted to be extremely intricate.

The evidence[20] led the Crossbow Committee to grasp at the straw of radio countermeasures which had defeated the German beams three years earlier. On receiving the early Swedish reports that radio control of the V2, now coded 'Big Ben', was a possibility, radio countermeasures were deployed. A special listening watch was organised to determine the frequencies of the radio-control signals and sixty receivers of the S27 and AR88 type were listening round the clock.

Four USAAF P38 Lightning long-range, twin-engine fighters were equipped with suitable receivers and were to fly over the Blizna area, refuelling in Russia. 192 Squadron of the RAF was also to carry out listening flights nearer home. By 15 August sixty jamming transmitters (including the BBC Television transmitter at Alexandra Palace) were ready and waiting. A radar watch was also mounted to plot any rockets, with the dual purpose of establishing the launching point and also to warn of the rocket's arrival, though not much more than two minutes' warning could be given of its approach. There was also a proposal to fire a curtain of anti-aircraft shells into the radar-predicted path of the V2s, but this in the end was discarded as the effect was thought to be 'minimal'.

The best, and indeed the only, countermeasure that could be in any way effective was the bombing of the supply, distribution and firing sites. This commenced on 4 August: the 'heavy' sites in northern France at Siracourt, Watten, Wizerns and Mimoyecques were bombed by USAAF B17s. (Mimoyecques was to prove later to be for a totally different weapon.) Over 3000 tons of bombs were dropped on suspected storage areas in France.

During August 1944, the threat of the V2 seemed to diminish. The ground battle was going well: the Allied armies had broken out of Normandy and by 19 August had reached the Seine; Paris was liberated by the 25th and by the end of the month the armies were rolling through Belgium. The war seemed as good as won. All the flying-bomb sites had now been overrun, as had the suspected 'heavy' V2 sites. Operation Market Garden, the Arnhem landing, was being planned and would, if successful, liberate Holland.

Since the V2 had roughly the same range as the V1, which, apart from a small number of air-launched missiles, had virtually ceased operating against London (although Antwerp was now under heavy V1 fire), how could the Germans use the vastly more sophisticated V2 which required much more precision in its launching? Germany was now under a tremendous air attack by day and night; railways and roads were constantly bombed and attacked by rocket-firing fighters.

Optimism grew to such an extent that by 5 September Sir Charles Portal, Chief of Air Staff, advised that attacks on rocket storage depots should be

Another extract from the 'Swedish Report', showing the main rocket engine.

abandoned, releasing the tactical bombers to support the ground forces. Plans to evacuate London were dropped. On 7 September Duncan Sandys and Herbert Morrison held a Press Conference and announced: 'Except possibly for a few last shots, the Battle of London is over. . . .'

The existence of the V2 had not been revealed to the public; the reality of the V1 had been bad enough, without causing further anxiety by warning of a new threat which might not materialise. The timing of events, therefore, was doubly unfortunate. The very next day, 8 September 1944, at 1843 Double British Summer Time, there was a tremendous explosion at Chiswick, London. There had been no warning; no aircraft, pilotless or otherwise, had flown over. The first German long-range rocket to fall on Britain had arrived; it had been fired just five minutes earlier from the eastern outskirts of the Hague.

That rocket on Chiswick was not, in fact, the first one to be launched operationally; earlier that day, Batterie der Artillerie Abteilung 485 had launched a V2 against newly-liberated Paris: it had fallen on the outskirts of the French capital. Another unit, Lehr und Versuchs Artillerie Batterie 444 (Experimental and Testing Battery) now joined 485 in the attack on London.

Both these units were withdrawn east on 18 September, after firing thirty-five rockets, to await the outcome of the ill-fated Arnhem landings. This gave London a respite from 18 September until 3 October, although Batterie 444 fired forty-four missiles from Frisland (Denmark), aimed at Norwich and Ipswich. Only one was anywhere near the target, falling on the outskirts of Norwich; of the rest, twelve never arrived, five fell offshore, the remainder in open country. When it became plain to the Germans that the Arnhem operation had failed, the two units returned to Holland and on 3 October resumed the bombardment of London.

There was no defence against the V2. Although the rockets which landed in the first few days did have a form of radio control, it was quickly realised from examination of the wreckage that later ones did not. Basically, all the V2s were guided by an inertial platform – an arrangement of three gyroscopes which controlled the rocket in pitch, yaw and roll. If the rocket deviated from its intended course or attitude, the gyroscopes would be displaced; this displacement or precession was sensed and caused servo-motors to operate the control surfaces, correcting the errors. The control surfaces were of two forms: one, as previously noted, in the form of graphite vanes in the rocket jet, the other parallel (though operating at a different rate) aerodynamic surfaces at the extremity of the four fins.

The range of the rocket was determined by cutting off the fuel at a given moment when the required velocity had been reached. In the early rockets this *was* controlled by radio signals, which were used to work out the velocity of the missile for any given moment. At the precise moment the desired velocity was achieved, a transmitter sent a coded signal which shut off the fuel.

Only a small number of early missiles used this radio system; after 18 October, rockets that fell on London were found to have a self-contained

'Integrating Accelerometer', based again on gyroscopic precession, which cut off the fuel and determined the range. A Farnborough report on this accelerometer concluded that 'errors due to the instrument alone are not likely to be more than about $\pm 1\%$: that is ± 2 miles in 200'.[21] In practice, due to other factors, the V2 never achieved anything approaching that order of accuracy.

The discovery that the control of the V2 was independent of radio removed any hope of radio countermeasures, not that it was ever a practical possibility. Even the early rockets only required radio range-guidance for some sixty seconds following launching; the receivers were multiple-channel and at the high frequency – 60 mHz – used, the range of the required jamming would have posed difficult problems. In any event, postwar statements by the Germans indicate that the range signals were in fact never jammed.

The only remaining countermeasure to the V2 was to attack the supply depots and the launching sites. The problem was to identify these sites; radar tracking gave some indication and Allied pilots saw the ascending vapour trails, enabling the general areas to be established.

The Allied Air Forces now began to attack any suspicious area where movement likely to be associated with the rockets had been seen and reported. Wing Commander Roland Beamont remembers one of the few successful sorties of this nature, flown on 4 August 1944:

'. . . we were told to attack the corner of a wood, by a junction between two roads. We found this and went in. . . . A tremendous barrage of defensive fire came up, which indicated that they were trying to defend something and after about three of the Tempests had made their firing passes I looked back and a great ball of fire came up in the middle of where we had been firing, so we had hit something. Whether it was a V2, I don't know. We lost one of our planes on that target. . . . We were employed on these attacks for about three weeks, but we were not doing any good. The Germans were very good at camouflage and you never stood a chance of actually seeing one of these V2s on its launching pad.'[16]

The rockets were in fact launched by mobile units which could set up a V2 and fuel, arm and fire it in about four hours. They only needed road access and a piece of reasonably level ground to achieve this. A convoy of vehicles comprised the launching unit; the rocket on a special trailer called a 'meillerwagen', fuel tankers, an armoured control vehicle and troop carriers. After firing, the unit would move on to another site. To be able to launch a sophisticated missile in this way was an extraordinary achievement and it explains why the rockets were next to impossible to find and attack.

During October and November, many of the rockets were launched from Holland. A clearing in a wood at Rijs was seen in an aerial photograph, after radar had pinpointed a possible firing site, but it was by then abandoned. Other used sites were found, but it was not until 29 December 1944 that V2 operational rockets were seen on the ground. By that time the number of areas open to the enemy with adequate road and rail facilities and in range of England were becoming very limited.

A V2 being raised to a vertical position on its launching pad, the Meillerwagen.

The Germans were now once more back in the Hague, based in a wooded park called the Haagsche Bosch, where some thirteen V2 rockets had been concealed under trees, but the leaves had fallen and the rockets were found on air reconnaissance photographs. The Haagsche Bosch was immediately attacked by RAF fighter-bombers; over 400 sorties were flown by Spitfires dropping some sixty tons of bombs and shooting up buildings known to house German troops. These attacks went on into the New Year and one Spitfire pilot, Raymond Baxter, recalls vividly one such sortie[27] he led with his Squadron, No. 602 (City of Glasgow):

'We flew from Coltishall in Norfolk and had been briefed to make life as difficult as possible for the V2 operators. We carried a thousand pounds of bombs under our Spitfire XVIs and dived and skip-bombed roads, railways, bridges, and straffed anything that moved.

'The most memorable occasion was 14 February 1945. I led one attack on a wood just north of The Hague [the Haagsche Bosch]. We dive-bombed it then after that attack turned back to shoot up the anti-aircraft gunners who had been firing at us; just as we got back to the target there rose up from the centre of the wood right before our eyes the unmistakable shape of a V2 that had just left its launching pad. It was the first one any of us had actually seen.

'I could not do much about it as I was in the middle of a rather unpleasant

argument with the gunners on the ground but my number four, a little Scotsman called Cupid Love, who was away and low to my right, actually fired his guns at the V2 as it flew through his sights.

'I think this must have been the most optimistic shot of the entire war. On reflection it is perhaps just as well he did not blow it up; that could have been most embarrassing for the rest of us, but I am certain that the occasion was the first and only time a conventional aircraft engaged an airborne rocket missile.'

A rocket-firing Typhoon severs a German railway line, disrupting the supply of V2s and their fuel. Many V Weapons were actually destroyed in transit by air attacks on railways.

Soon after that attack, bad weather hampered further low-level raids, but high-level bombers of the 2nd Tactical Air Force dropped seventy tons on the Haagsche Bosch on 3 March. Unfortunately most of the bombs fell a mile away, killing many Dutch civilians.

During March, the Germans moved out of the Haagsche Bosch and for some days no rockets were fired. When the attack resumed it was from the Duindicht racecourse, also near the Hague. There was little cover here and, due to the lack of time and the high water-table in Holland, no underground storage was possible and rockets with their attendant servicing vehicles were seen by reconnaissance aircraft. The Duindicht site was soon attacked by fighter-bombers.

The Germans were by now finding it very difficult to maintain supplies of rockets and fuel, due to the scale of air attacks on their communications. The rocket units were withdrawn east, eventually to Germany itself, from where they attacked Antwerp and Liège. On 27 March 1945 the last two rounds were launched against London; the first of these was to cause very heavy casualties, falling on a block of flats in Stepney and killing 134 people. At 1400 hours that day, the last V2 fired against England fell on Orpington. The Battle of London really was over.

Of the V2s successfully launched against England, 1115 actually arrived, 517 in the London area. In all, 2754 people had been killed and 6523 seriously injured by them. The figures for 'conventional' bombing of Britain were 51,500 killed and 61,400 injured. To put these figures in perspective: the V2 campaign against London had lasted seven months; in just fourteen *hours* the German city of Dresden suffered 135,000 killed in a combined RAF/USAAF raid on 14/15 February 1945.

What had these German 'Terror Weapons', the V1 and the V2, achieved? In military terms, practically nothing: the V1 was in effect a small aircraft and, as such, relatively easily shot down, to such an extent that the weight of the attack was only a fraction of what the Germans had envisaged. Also the timing of the attack was wrong: by 1944 the population of London had endured four long years of war, had survived the Blitz, and had lived through a time when death and disaster had become commonplace. Once the D-day landings had succeeded, the war was obviously going to end in an Allied victory; on every front the Germans were retreating; German towns and cities were suffering far worse destruction than British towns and cities had ever sustained. It would have been a different story in 1940, if the V1 had been used then; there would have been no aircraft fast enough to catch them; no proximity fuses to help shoot them down.

The V2, which seems today the more terrifying, was not so in reality. It is true it gave no warning, but in a way this was a psychological advantage: if you heard the bang then you had survived; if not, then you had no further problems. London was a vast target and the 'incidents', as they were called, were few and far between. It could be argued that in the long run the V2 actually did more harm to the Germans than the British: Albert Speer thought so; he took the view – after the war – that the immense effort of highly skilled men, scarce raw materials and fuels could have produced a large number of jet fighters which, as we shall later consider, could have been decisive in the air war. The one-ton warhead of the V2 (about the same as the V1) did not justify its cost; that it went into production at all was probably due to Hitler's love of the romantic – Speer had shown him a colour film of an early V2 launch and that had been enough for him to decide to sanction the rockets.

The Germans had long been attracted to rockets and the idea of interplanetary travel. Early experiments had met with some success. In 1932 the German Military took an interest and a Captain Walter Dornberger and a young scientist, Wernher von Braun, were soon working at Kummersdorf, near Berlin, for the Heereswaffenamt-Prüfwesen (Army Ordnance Research and Development Department). They had by 1937 developed a liquid-

Opposite: A V2 'incident' in London.

fuelled rocket, the A1 (Aggregat 1), running on alcohol and liquid oxygen; the engine developed 660 lbs of static thrust and the rocket was gyro-stabilised. It blew up, but the next two, named 'Max' and 'Moritz', after two German comic characters, flew to 6500 feet from a test site on the North Sea island of Borkum.

The success of the Borkum flights loosened the military purse strings and a new experimental establishment was acquired well away from prying eyes, near the small town of Wolgast on Usedom Island. This secret establishment was named Heeresversuchsstelle Peenemunde (Army Experimental Station). A wind tunnel was built and work progressed on a series of larger rockets, the A3s, which were twenty-one feet long with 3300-lb alcohol/liquid oxygen motors. These were fired in 1937 from the nearby island of Greifswalder Oie: the rockets failed, not because of engine trouble, but due to faults in the inertial guidance system; it took two years to get that to work.

By 1938 the German Army had issued a specification for a new long-range rocket capable of flying reliably up to 200 miles with a one-ton warhead. It had to be transportable and therefore conform to the German railway loading gauge. The Peenemunde team got to work and the result was the A4, but an interim vehicle was built – the A5 – to test the troublesome guidance systems. Three of these rockets were tested with the designation V1, V2 and V3, the 'V' standing for 'Vorschlag' (proposal). This nomenclature was to cause confusion later when, during the war, the A4 became the V2 – the 'V' then standing for Vergeltungswaffe (reprisal weapon).

The A5s were fired with complete success from Greifswalder Oie, and the new guidance system functioned perfectly when test-flown during the summer of 1939.

During 1940 and 1941, Peenemunde was a hive of activity, a team of brilliant scientists and engineers under Dr von Braun producing the first A4 rockets. The first test-firing was on 13 June 1942 and failed; the trouble was the fuel feed causing the engine to flame out soon after lift-off. A second launch a month later was a partial success; the rocket at least was airborne for long enough to be the first guided missile to exceed the speed of sound.

The third launch, on 3 October 1942, was a complete success and full production was authorised at Peenemunde. After the RAF raid which badly damaged the production centre, a new factory, known simply as Mittelwerke (Central Works), took over the production of the V2. This was an underground complex in the Harz mountains near Nordhausen and it was to turn out 900 V2s a month in addition to V1s.

This factory had been located by Photographic Reconnaissance, by the relatively simple process of tracing the route taken by the trains that serviced the forward launching sites in Holland. Photographic interpreters skilled in railway workings regularly studied the types of wagons and their loads, whether military or civil, in order to determine the nature of the traffic and whether, for example, Allied bombing was causing congestion or rerouting. In the course of this routine surveillance, the Railway section at RAF

The V2 rocket engine-erecting shop in the Mittelwerke. Nearly complete engines can be seen on the right. The photograph gives a good idea of the size of the underground workshops.

One of the two V2s fired on Operation Backfire is transported on its Meillerwagen.

Medmenham had identified several special vehicles used for the V2s, including the 60-foot liquid-oxygen fuel tankers, as well as examples of the 'triple flat' which carried the V2 rockets themselves. These specialised trucks were seen in numerous locations between Holland and an underground industrial plant at Niedersachswerfen, near Nordhausen, in the Harz mountains.

From a study of the railway sidings and reports from agents and prisoners of war, it was concluded that this was the factory that was concerned with the manufacture of both the V1 and V2. The extent of the underground factory, which was itself invisible from the air, was judged from the disposition of the entrances and the scale of the manufacture by the electrical power fed to the sites by the German grid system, the size of the transformers in the sub-stations giving experts in these matters enough information to calculate the power requirements of the factory.

Photographic Reconnaissance also tracked down thirteen liquid-oxygen and twelve hydrogen-peroxide plants: for some reason difficult now to fathom, none of these plants or the Harz mountain factory were ever heavily attacked. The absence of attacks on the factory (which it was learned after the war was the only one engaged on V2 assembly) was to prove of price-less value to the United States and Russia after the war.

In late January 1945, it was obvious to von Braun and his colleagues that the war was lost and they had to make up their minds whether to stay put at Peenemunde and be captured by the Russians or to move south and contact the Western Allies – or, more specifically, the Americans. It will come as no surprise that the overwhelming majority chose the latter course of action.

One directive from Berlin had charged the Peenemunde staff 'to stand and defend the holy ground of Pomerania'; another to make for the Nordhausen area to continue their work there 'until ultimate victory was assured'. In February a convoy with the entire Peenemunde technical archive, all four-teen tons of it, von Braun, his closest associates and 500 engineers set out southwards and were eventually installed in a vacant army camp at Bleicherode, near Oberammergau, part of the famed 'Last Redoubt', where the Nazis were to fight to the last.

On receiving news of Hitler's death on 30 April, von Braun, who had now been joined by General Dornberger, sent Magnus von Braun, his English-speaking brother, to make contact with the approaching Americans. Magnus von Braun gave himself up to an American private, Fred P. Schneiker, in the Austrian town of Reutte, informing him of the group of scientists he repre-sented who wished to turn themselves over to the US Forces. Intelligence Officers quickly arranged for the surrender and the scientists were moved to a captured German Army barracks in Garmisch Partenkirchen for interro-gation.

Von Braun soon came to the point: they had decided to offer their services to the Americans because they were well disposed to America and Americans generally, and, perhaps more cogently, they realised that only America could offer the resources required to enable them to continue their true work – the exploration of space.

Thus the Americans now had a head start in the Anglo-American-Russian race for the rocket scientists. It must be admitted that they played their unexpectedly dealt hand very well, though not perhaps strictly according to Hoyle.

Colonel Holger N. Toftoy, Chief of the US Army's Ordnance Technical Intelligence team in Paris, was ordered by Washington to get to the Nordhausen Mittelwerke plant as soon as it was captured and try to salvage V2 assemblies. The factory was entered by US Forces on 11 April: the soldiers found to their amazement that it was absolutely intact; the production lines of V1s and V2s had been left undisturbed when the 4500 workers had fled. An American Intelligence team, under Major Robert Staver, made arrangements to remove as much of this priceless booty as they could, and as quickly as possible. There was no time to indulge in protocol with Allies, as one of them – Russia – was to have control of the Nordhausen area as part of the Yalta Agreement, which had drawn up the postwar division of Germany.

The war in Europe ended on 8 May 1945; the Russian occupation was to start on 1 June. Between 22 May and 1 June the Americans removed from Nordhausen 341 wagon loads, comprising at least 100 V2s, and tons of parts and ancillary equipment. The trains went straight to Antwerp docks, where the material was loaded on to no fewer than sixteen Liberty Ships bound for New Orleans; from there the cargo was transported to the White Sands Proving Grounds of the US Army Ordnance Corps in New Mexico.

Under an existing agreement between Britain and the United States, Britain had been entitled to half of the Nordhausen V2s; Colonel Toftoy had decided not to share this priceless haul with his allies, not even to inform them

A nearly complete V2 at Nordhausen, guarded by an American military policeman. This rocket was almost certainly one of those removed to White Sands.

185

about it. British Intelligence got wind of the nature of the loading operations at Antwerp Docks, but by the time British officers on Eisenhower's staff had obtained authorisation to stop the movement, the Liberty Ships were safely on the high seas.

But one prize still eluded the Americans: the Peenemunde archive. Von Braun had realised that this priceless collection of drawings, test reports and scientific papers was the record of all German rocket research work from 1932 to 1945; he would require access to it if his work was to continue. Very much aware of Hitler's 'scorched earth' orders, he had prudently charged two trusted associates, Dieter Huzel and Bernhard Tessmann, to hide the 14-ton dossier. After various adventures the two men finally hid the documents in a disused mineshaft near the town of Dörnten, north of the Harz mountain region, an area most fortuitiously just being occupied by the US Ninth Army.

Major Staver, with a man from General Electric and armed with information gleaned from British Intelligence, ran several former Peenemunde men to ground and, with their assistance, on 26 May the cache at Dörnten was found. It was just in time: the next day at 10 am, the area became part of the British Zone of Occupation.

When Huzel and Tessman had hidden the papers in the mineshaft, they had had the entrance dynamited. As the Americans were digging the debris clear to remove the documents, a British Army party arrived on the scene. The Americans posed as German geologists and claimed that they were assessing the iron ore with a view to reopening the mine. The ruse succeeded and the British soldiers went away. At first light next morning the excavation continued and the documents, which were by now technically in the British Zone, were recovered, loaded on to US Army lorries and driven past groups of British soldiers who were just setting up their road blocks. Once inside American-occupied territory, the documents were discreetly shipped to the United States. All the British got was a disused mine and a box of low-grade iron-ore samples.

The next part of the operation was the questioning of the key scientists themselves. 115 of them including Wernher von Braun were offered immediate contracts to work for one year for the US Ordnance Corps in America; they all accepted the offer. General Dornberger had been handed over to the British who had, most inconveniently, put him in jail; he had to serve two years before signing his American contract.

The whole operation, which was coded 'Overcast' later 'Paperclip', saved the United States twenty years of research and several millions of dollars – it was to prove 'one large step'.

The Russians too came out of it quite well: they had the entire Nordhausen complex, with its wind tunnels and laboratories, and the residue of the German scientists led by Helmut Gröttup. Britain, the country which, with Belgium, had suffered most from the V weapons, got two V2s to test; these were fired (with German aid) into the North Sea from Cuxhaven, a project with the not inappropriate name of 'Operation Backfire'.

The Peenemunde papers revealed much. There was in existence the A4b – a winged version of the V2 with a range of 400 miles: two had been tested. The A6 was a completed design with a new engine using nitric acid as an oxidant and vinyl isobutyl ether as the fuel (which would store better and be easier to handle and transport than hydrogen peroxide); it did not, however, get beyond the design stage.

Then there was the A9/A10 proposal: a huge two-stage rocket, powered by a fuel of nitric acid and diesel oil, with a range of 2500 miles: there was even a three-stage rocket visualised, with a giant A11 rocket under the A9/A10 combination; this could have placed the A9 into orbit, or into New York. It was the blueprint for the exploration of Space.

'I aim for the stars', Wernher von Braun often said. A cynic might add: 'But I sometimes hit London'.

Operation Backfire.

SS *Athenia*.

4. THE BATTLE OF THE ATLANTIC

'The only thing that ever really
frightened me during the war was
the U-boat peril. . . .'

WINSTON CHURCHILL

Within a few hours of the outbreak of the Second World War U30, a German submarine, torpedoed and sank the passenger liner *Athenia* off Rockall. There had been no warning: 128 of the passengers and crew went down with the ship. In vain the Germans protested that the liner had been sunk in error by an overzealous officer who had mistaken the vessel for a troopship. The sinking was taken by the Admiralty as a resumption of the unrestricted torpedoing of unarmed merchant ships on the high seas that had nearly cost Britain the war in 1917.

The convoy system – large groups of ships sailing together protected by escorting anti-submarine vessels – had proved effective when introduced in 1917 and the German submarines were eventually defeated by it. Following the sinking of the *Athenia*, the convoy system was reintroduced and the Royal Navy prepared for another struggle against its old enemy, the German U-boat.

It was to prove a long and bitter struggle, fought without quarter between two ruthless opponents. It was to span the entire European War from the first day to the last and involve not only thousands of sailors, airmen and merchant seamen, but also some of the ablest scientists on both sides, in a see-saw struggle for technical supremacy. Known as the Battle of the Atlantic, it was one of the decisive battles of the Second World War.

The submerged U-boat, when sinking an unarmed merchant ship without prior warning – an act which the Treaty-makers between the wars had naively tried to ban – had all the advantage of surprise and, to a very large extent, invisibility; U-boats fired their torpedoes from periscope depth and then dived deep. The only defence then possible was a counterattack by the surface anti-submarine vessels of the convoy escort.

In fact, there was at that time not a great deal British escorts could do against the submerged submarine. The only method of detection was ASDIC, a secret British underwater device which was rather similar to radar in concept, the difference being that sound pulses rather than radio waves were reflected from the submerged U-boat.

The idea of using sound to detect submerged objects at sea goes back to 1912, when a British engineer named Richardson had suggested, after the liner *Titanic* had sunk with heavy loss of life following a collision with an iceberg, that icebergs might be detected by echoes of sound waves sent from an approaching ship. The idea was never put into practice as an iceberg warning,† but in 1915 the Admiralty Board of Invention and Research set up an anti-submarine committee, which eventually became the 'Allied Submarine *D*etection *I*nvestigation *C*ommittee', or ASDIC, to consider all possible methods of detecting submerged submarines. The Committee had the services of some of the most distinguished scientists of the day, including Professors W. H. Bragg and Sir Ernest Rutherford.

The Hydrophone was an early candidate; it was essentially an underwater microphone which could pick up the sound of the submarine's propellers and machinery, provided they were turning and provided the ship using the hydrophone had stopped her own engines. No accurate range of the under-water sound was given.

The Committee pressed on, testing – in Hackney Municipal Baths and Scottish lochs – many strange ideas, including trained seals; there was even a serious proposal to feed estuary seagulls from a dummy submarine periscope in the hope that they would flock towards an enemy submarine the moment its periscope appeared.

During their work, ASDIC were co-operating with the French Navy who had a similar group in Toulon, under Professor Langevin. Both groups appre-ciated that very high-frequency sound waves would be necessary for under-water detection, to concentrate them into the narrow beam required to enable the direction of the submerged submarine to be ascertained. The problem was the generation of ultra-sonic sound pulses. Several methods were tried, without success, until Langevin applied the 'piezo-electric effect', which had been discovered by Pierre Curie: a crystal of quartz, when cut in a certain way, will oscillate at an ultra-sonic frequency if a voltage is applied to the crystal. Conversely, if the crystal is compressed or stretched mechanically, it will produce an electrical charge. (Modern flintless lighters use the piezo-electric effect of a small quartz crystal to generate the spark.)

Langevin had solved the problem of the generation of the high-frequency pulses and work began to develop the 'effect' into an anti-submarine weapon. The idea of the detection system was that, if such a crystal were suspended in the sea, it could be made to send a pulse of high-frequency sound through the water by applying an alternating current to it, for the duration of the pulse. If the pulse was returned by an object – a submarine, for example – it would, on reaching the crystal, reverse the piezo-electric effect and produce a voltage which could be turned into an aural warning.

There were many difficulties in getting the system to work. Tests in the Firth

†The Americans tested a 'Fessenden oscillator' on an iceberg, but the usable range proved to be so short that it was of no practical value and the experiment was discontinued.

of Forth using a British D Class submarine were unsuccessful; the scientists even had difficulty in getting information relating to the number of U-boats sunk, how the attacks were made, and other details. In spite of endless conferences, they felt they were getting nowhere. It was in declining to attend what he considered to be yet another interminable and pointless meeting at the Admiralty that Rutherford sent his famous apology:

> 'I have been engaged in experiments which suggest that the atom can be artificially disintegrated. If it is true, it is of far greater importance than a war.'[1]

The delays imposed by authority on the scientists were such that it was not until the last year of the war, spring 1918, that experimental ASDIC equipment was able to obtain the first echoes from a submarine submerged off the Admiralty Experimental Station at Harwich. The range obtained was a 'few hundred yards'.

The measurement of range of the ASDIC signal was by the same method as used for radar – the time taken for a transmitted pulse to return from the submarine. The speed of sound through salt water is more or less 1600 yards a second: thus, if an echo was received one second after it was transmitted, then the object reflecting it would be 800 yards away.

Between the wars, the menace of the submarine was appreciated and a good deal of development work on ASDIC was done and many problems overcome. One of the most besetting was the protection of the quartz transmitter: it had obviously to be under the ship and to have a clear all-round acoustic vision; equally obviously it needed some sort of protection, otherwise the turbulence of the water as it swirled around the transmitter would act as a barrier scattering the sound pulses and generating false echoes. It was to prove one of the most difficult obstacles to a practical submarine-detection system.

The quartz crystal was placed inside a dome, which had to be thin enough to allow the sound pulses to pass through, yet strong enough to stand up to the pressure of the water as the ship travelled at twenty knots. The dome needed to be full of water and fixed to the bottom of the hull in order to transmit and receive the pulses, and the ASDIC transmitter/receiver had to be able to turn through 360° and nod up and down inside the dome in order to detect bearing and depth of target. One of the main difficulties, Admiralty scientists discovered, was the shape of this cover: clearly it had to be streamlined, but the various configurations tested either collapsed due to suction, or produced a turbulence which drowned the vital echoes in a tremendous roar. J. Anderson, a scientist from the Anti-Submarine Establishment, actually made many trips *inside* a transparent dome under the hull of HMS *Devonshire* so that he could observe the effect on various-shaped structures while the cruiser was travelling at thirty knots.

By 1931 the shape and position of the ASDIC cover had been established as a straight-sided teardrop, this being the best compromise of maximum mechanical strength and minimum turbulence. The best position was found

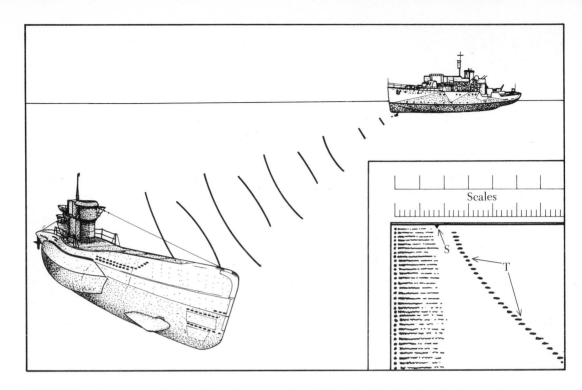

Scales

S

T

ASDIC. The ultra-sonic pulses from the escort vessel rebounded off the target, giving range and bearing which were shown (*inset*) on a recorder. The stylus (S) continuously recorded on the moving sensitised paper the distance of the target (T) from the hunting vessel.

to be exactly on the centre line of the ship's hull and as far forward as possible, and the optimum frequency of the pulses had also been established at 20,000 Hz. At that frequency a 250-watt transmitter could get usable echoes from between 200 and 5000 yards. After years of operational trials from the Arctic to the Pacific, ASDIC was slowly improved. The name was officially adopted and it became a vital part of the Royal Navy's anti-submarine weapons system.†

At the start of experimental work the actual detection of the echoes was at first interpreted on a pair of simple headphones, but in 1930 a visual pre-sentation was introduced. It was based on a device known as a Fultograph, which was used for facsimile reception in the early days of radio press-picture transmission. The Fultograph was an electro-chemical recorder con-sisting of a moving roll of paper impregnated with potassium iodide, which became discoloured when an electrical current was passed through it.

The display was a mechanical analogy of an early radar presentation; instead of the cathode-ray tube with its travelling spot, however, there was an electrode which was conveyed across the sensitised paper in synchronisation with the sound pulses. At the start of its journey a spot was recorded on the left-hand side of the paper as the pulse was transmitted. If an echo was received during the transit, a second spot would appear on the paper, caused by a voltage from the detector discolouring the special surface. The distance between the spots was proportional to the distance to the target. With each pulse the paper was moved, in a way similar to a typewriter's line feed, and a

†The US Navy called the system Sonar, which was adopted by NATO in the 1950s.

new pair of dots recorded. During a search, if contact was maintained and the ship closed with the submarine, the dots would get closer and closer together as the distance decreased.

The minimum range in bearing was 200 yards; from then on the Captain leading the attack had to rely on a stopwatch and his experience to judge the moment when to fire his depth charges.

In practice, there could be difficulties with ASDIC. In the first place, U-boats were fitted with hydrophones which picked up the ASDIC and also the sound of the hunting ship's propellers: using his hydrophones, a skilled submarine captain could take evasive action beneath the surface. Additionally, many things could affect the echoes: turbulence from the wake of ships or depth charges; layers of water of a different temperature or density; fish; and even, later in the war, deliberate countermeasures from the U-boats. Many, many long hours were spent searching for contacts. The monotonous pings from the repeaters on the rain- and spray-swept bridges of corvettes, pitching and rolling in a heavy swell on a winter's night in the North Atlantic, are only too well remembered by those who fought that grim battle.

When everything went well, however, it was a different story. One of the most successful submarine hunters was Captain Donald Macintyre, RN. His ship, HMS *Walker*, had been hunting a U-boat with ASDIC: the submarine, U100, had been rammed by another ship of the escort group, HMS *Vanoc*. Here is part of Captain Macintyre's account of what followed:

'... as we circled *Vanoc*, I was electrified to hear the ASDIC operator, Able Seaman Backhouse, excitedly reporting "Contact. Contact." But I could hardly credit it, for not only was it unbelievable that in all the wide waste of

HMS *Vanoc*, the escort destroyer which rammed and sank U100, commanded by Kapitänleutnant Joachim Schepke, one of Doenitz's 'aces'. The object in the foreground is a standard depth charge on its launcher.

ASDIC operators. The officer is pressing his headset to his ears to try to distinguish the vital echo. The Royal Navy had overestimated the performance of ASDIC in peacetime; under operational conditions the disturbance in the water caused by depth charges and the wakes of surface ships created difficulties which the U-boats exploited.

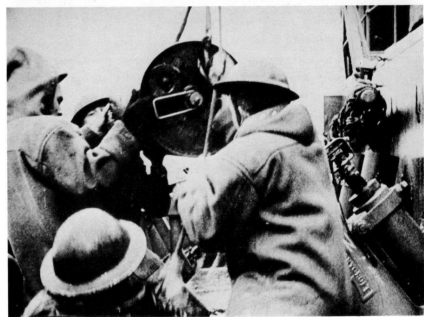

Manhandling a standard depth charge – a difficult and dangerous task on the heaving deck of a corvette in the North Atlantic.

the Atlantic a second U-boat should turn up just where another had gone to the bottom, but I knew that there were sure to be areas of disturbed water persisting in the vicinity from our own and *Vanoc*'s wakes.

'The echo was not very clear and I expressed my doubts . . . but Backhouse was not to be disheartened. "Contact definitely submarine," he reported, and as I listened to the ping the echo sharpened and there could be no further doubt. . . .

'A pattern of six depth-charges – all that could be got ready in time – went down. As they exploded, *Walker* ran on to get sea-room to turn for further attacks, but as we turned came the thrilling signal from *Vanoc* – "U-boat surfaced astern of me".

'A searchlight beam stabbed into the night from *Vanoc*, illuminating the submarine U99 which lay stopped. The guns' crews in both ships sprang into action and the blinding flashes from the four-inch guns and tracers from the smaller weapons made a great display, though I fear their accuracy was not remarkable. . . . But fortunately we were able very soon to cease fire as a signal lamp flashing from the U-boat: "We are sunking" (sic), made it clear that the action was over.'[2]

HMS *Walker* picked up the survivers from the U99, including her captain, who turned out to be Kapitänleutnant Otto Kretschmer, who had been credited with sinking more than 250,000 tons of Allied shipping.[3] U100, the U-boat rammed and sunk by *Vanoc*, had been commanded by Joachim Schepke, who had also been credited with 250,000 tons, though, less fortunate than Kretschmer, he had perished with his submarine.

The action in which U99 was sunk was fought in 1941, before the U-boat war had reached its climax. Germany began the war with fifty-seven submarines in commission; thirty-two of these, however, were Type II, small coastal boats of 250 tons, which did not have the range for long-distance ocean patrols. The remaining boats were mainly the Type VII† which displaced 626 tons and had a surfaced cruising range of 6800 nautical miles at ten knots (fourteen for short periods) or a submerged range of ninety nautical miles at four knots. They carried eleven torpedoes and were manned by a crew of forty-four. The Type VII, universally considered a good submarine, was the most numerous of the German Navy's U-boats; 705 were constructed and it became the standard 'Atlantic' boat.

By the end of 1940, the small number of German operational U-boats had been extremely successful. They had already sunk 443 merchant ships, totalling 2.5 million tons, a British aircraft carrier, HMS *Courageous*, the battleship *Royal Oak*, sunk, to the embarrassment of the Royal Navy, at her moorings in Scapa Flow by Gunther Prien's U47, and twenty-six lesser naval vessels. All for the loss of thirty-one U-boats.

But it was only the start, for with the fall of France the U-boat commander-in-chief, Admiral Karl Doenitz, himself a World War I U-boat Captain, quickly set up bases on the Biscay Coast. This shortened the journey to the North Atlantic and the convoy routes. In the spring of 1941, just two months of unrestricted warfare against the Allied merchant convoys saw 142 ships, totalling 815,000 tons, sunk with their vital cargoes of food and war materials.

Successful though these individual U-boats had undoubtedly been, a new strategy was devised against the convoys, the 'Rüdeltaktik', or 'Wolf Pack' to the Allies. As many U-boats as possible were concentrated to make a co-ordinated attack, swamping the convoy's meagre defences and then sinking the merchant ships almost at will. There were simply not enough escort

†Actual figures were: 2 Type I, 32 Type II, 17 Type VII, and 6 Type IX.

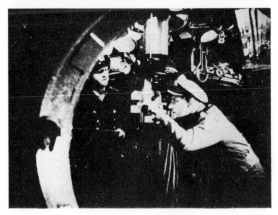

Top left: A Type VII U-boat. These 'Atlantic' boats were highly successful; they varied according to Mark, but later ones were typically 760 tons' displacement with a crew of 44 and 14 torpedoes. Their 2800-hp diesels gave them a surface speed of upto 17 knots – fast enough to outrun a Flower Class corvette.

Top right: Grosser Admiral Erich Raeder (left), C-in-C German Navy, was a 'big ship' man. He was supplanted by Admiral Karl Doenitz (centre), a U-boat commander in the 1914–18 war, who had built up the U-boat arm into a formidable weapon.

Middle left: Gunther Prien returns to base in U47 after an Atlantic cruise. His sinking of the battleship

Royal Oak in the Scapa Flow anchorage made him a national hero. U47 was later sunk by the British corvettes *Arbutus* and *Camellia* in the North Atlantic.

Middle right: A U-boat commander at his periscope. His First Lieutenant stands by to work out the deflection for the torpedoes. The submarine has been trimmed a little high, so the captain has to bend down to the periscope rather than raise it and show more than a few inches above water.

Bottom left: A still from a cine film shot through the periscope of a U-boat. An American Liberty ship has been torpedoed and is down at the stern. The crew

Continued opposite

vessels to guard the convoys against large numbers of U-boats and, in any case, a submerged submarine was – and remains – very difficult to detect before it has revealed its presence by attacking.

During 1941, the year they were introduced, the wolf-pack tactics, controlled by Doenitz's staff from their HQ at Lorient, were simple enough. A U-boat or a long-range Focke-Wulfe Condor aircraft would sight a convoy; its course, speed and the number of escorts would be radioed to Lorient. Signals would be sent to other U-boats in the vicinity to converge on the convoy; up to ten might form a patrol line, usually ahead of the merchant ships, which plodded along at the speed of the slowest ship.

Strictly speaking, the U-boats of World War Two were not true submarines, but submersibles; they had to come up for air to run the diesels to recharge the batteries that powered the electric underwater-propulsion motors. Because the capacity of the batteries limited the range of the electric motors, U-boats cruised to their patrol stations at night at high speed on the surface, using their diesel engines. This was a weakness of the early U-boats, for detecting a U-boat on the surface was a far better proposition than when it was submerged, and it was clearly an application for shipborne radar.

The story of radar in the Royal Navy really dates from a meeting held in March 1935 to discuss what means were available on HM Ships to detect aircraft. The answer given was 'a pair of × 7 binoculars'.

As soon as the Radar Research Station at Orfordness began its work, the Royal Navy was involved and, indeed, the contribution made by the Royal Naval Signal School in the early days of radar was invaluable, particularly in the provision of high-powered silica valves, which had been developed for radio telegraphy purposes by the Navy and were used in the early CH Radars. The urgent need, as far as the Navy was concerned, was to have a reliable form of aircraft warning aboard their ships. But although the early work of the Watson Watt team at Orfordness was showing high promise, the requirements of a shipboard radar were to be quite different from those of shore-based installations.

The initial problem, which was to be the keynote to naval thinking on radar, was simply a physical one: the size of aerial that could be accommodated, even on a battleship, was clearly limited; also, since ships are free to move, the radar aerials, being directional, had to be rotatable. The Navy were, by these requirements, more or less compelled to pursue their early research on very short wavelengths from the outset, since such wavelengths would permit the use of physically small aerials, and the narrow beam which resulted promised not only good directional properties against aircraft, but also detection of surface vessels.

During 1937, work was concentrated on a naval radar operating on the shortest wavelength that was possible with a rotatable masthead dipole aerial. The compromise between what was – at that time – electronically attainable and physically possible suggested a wavelength of around 7 metres

Opposite, continued
in one of the ship's lifeboats rows past the U-boat's periscope. Wartime stories of survivors being machine-gunned by German submarines were, with one exception, untrue. The sole U-boat commander who did shoot survivors was himself tried and executed on Doenitz's orders. *Bottom right:* The U-boat pens at the Biscay port of Lorient. These massive ferro-concrete structures proved all but indestructible and are still standing. Many bombers were lost attacking them, and, although there were hits, not one U-boat was destroyed inside them.

(45 mHz). It was envisaged that one of the ship's masts would carry the transmitting aerial and another the receiver's, the two aerials rotating synchronously. Some idea of the size of these aerials can be gauged from the fact that they were almost exactly the same as the old Band I BBC television aerials – those 'H's which were common on chimneys during the 1950s and 1960s.

The early work was done at HM Signal School in Eastney Barracks, Portsmouth, in close collaboration with developments at Orfordness and Bawdsey. A very small but enthusiastic team worked throughout 1937 and soon echoes were being returned from electricity pylons on Portsdown Hill. By the summer of 1938, HMS *Rodney* and HMS *Sheffield* had been fitted with this aircraft-warning radar. From sea trials with these ships, it quickly became apparent that a battleship mast was, to say the least, an unsuitable environment for a radar aerial. However, the sets worked and not only detected aircraft but also, in certain favourable circumstances, located surface vessels.

The early experimental sets were much improved by new valves, and a series of redesigned sets of roughly three times the power of the originals were made at the Signal School and fitted to ships just before the war. Hundreds were subsequently installed, many to serve throughout the war.

Simply detecting an enemy ship was one thing: to do something about it was another. Before radar, naval gunnery had been sighted by optical rangefinders, which were dependent on good visibility, were easily countered by smoke screens, and could only be used at night by illuminating the target with star shells. Their biggest drawback, however, was that they were subject to certain errors which increased in proportion to the square of the range.

The next logical step, therefore, was the development of 50-cm gunnery radar sets: Type 282 for anti-aircraft fire; Type 283 for long-range, heavy-barrage anti-aircraft fire; and finally Type 284 for surface gunnery. These sets were fitted by the beginning of 1941, and HMS *Sheffield* was able to locate and shadow the German battleship *Bismarck* successfully with her 284 radar.

Since range-finding with radar was simply a matter of the time taken for the pulses to return from the target, any errors were constant and predictable. Range-finding was now no longer dependent on good visibility, neither darkness nor smoke-screens protecting the target. Radar operators could even follow the flight of the 14″ shells from their battleship's main armament – which was fascinating, but less so when watching the return fire curving towards their ship.

It was the Royal Navy, in pursuing the shortest possible wavelength for its radar, which had commissioned the Birmingham University 'Centimetric' group which produced the cavity magnetron. The news of the successes of Randall and Boot was received about the same time as it was realised that the Navy was going to have to fight a long, hard battle against the U-boats: 50-cm radar, excellent for gunnery against other warships, was because of its long wavelength of little use for detecting a submarine – a small target even when surfaced. With the cavity magnetron, 10-cm radar was now a possibility: in September 1940 scientists and naval officers from the Signal School at Eastney went to TRE at Worth Matravers for a demonstration of a prototype magnetron-powered 10-cm radar, which had been set up on the cliffs near Swanage. The set was able to follow a surfaced British submarine for seven miles out to sea.

The Eastney team, under the direction of Dr Landale, began to work on a prototype 10-cm radar which was small enough to be fitted into a new class of convoy escort vessel – the Flower Class corvette – built for the express purpose of detecting U-boats. The first experimental set was ready for installation in HMS *Orchis* in March 1941. It did not prove easy: with the ultra-high frequencies involved – 3000 kHz – losses in the aerial feeders then available meant that the actual transmitter and receiver had to be mounted on the ship's mast behind the aerials, the whole assembly being protected from wind and spray by a structure with perspex windows which resembled a small lighthouse lantern. *Orchis* sailed from the Clyde to test the new radar at sea a few weeks later. There were several unknown factors: the effect of the necessary screening of the aerial, the vibration and rolling of the small ship, to say nothing of what would happen to the radar when the corvette's guns were fired. However, the results were encouraging beyond expectation: surfaced 'tame' submarines were detected at 5000 yards; even when submerged their periscopes gave useful returns. 10-cm radar offered the prospect of being at least one answer to the U-boat.

The problem now was time. In mid-1940 ships were being sunk faster than the yards could replace them; there was fearful loss of life and of the vital supplies on which the continuation of the war depended. So urgent was the need to fit as many escort vessels with 10-cm radar as possible that com-

HMS *Alisma*, a typical Flower Class corvette. The class was developed from a prewar whaler, *Southern Pride*, and was built solely for convoy escort duties. Corvettes were excellent sea boats, although those who served in them in the winter gales of the North Atlantic swore that they rolled even in dry dock. The 'lantern' between the mast and funnel is the housing for the 271 radar scanner. In 1942 25 of these vessels were supplied, under reverse Lease-lend, to the US Navy.

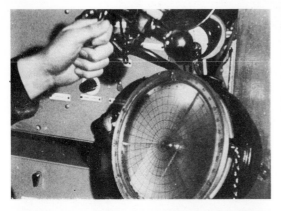

271 Radar. The aerial scanner was hand-trained and the display *(top right)* was a simple horizontal timebase. This photograph shows a U-boat contact at 6½ nautical miles.
Bottom left: The contact is plotted by the operator on a translucent bearing-indicator.
Bottom right: A Type VII U-boat dives. Within 20 seconds it would be completely submerged.

ponents were immediately ordered for 150 sets, which were now officially named the Type 271. The first were actually hand-built at Eastney by the Admiralty Signals Establishment staff. To save time, indicator units of the 50-cm gunnery radar were gutted and rebuilt as 271s. By July 1941, twenty-five corvettes were fitted with the type 271 – the first operational, magnetron-powered centimetric radar in the world.

The sensitivity of the 271 sets was a revelation in surface radar; it was soon found that the detection of a submerged submarine periscope by HMS *Orchis* was no freak. Escort vessels were able to pick up such small radar targets as wooden rafts and ships' lifeboats at night, enabling survivors from torpedoed ships, who otherwise might not have been seen, to be rescued.

The early sets used the first production 10-cm magnetron, the NT98. Later sets were fitted with the first 'strapped' magnetron, the CV 56, which gave a much larger output: unfortunately, the primitive aerial feeders of the time could not cope with the increased power and continually burned out. As an alternative, a highly accurate copper, rectangular tube, known as a waveguide, was employed; its dimensions were related to the wavelength and it could pass the signals from the transmitter to the aerial without any appreciable loss of power.

The escort vessels with the 271 radar were now at least able to fight surfaced U-boats on something approaching equal terms. Up to that time the German submarines were having a run of success that was only limited by their small numbers – a defect that the German shipyards were soon to remedy. With the introduction of Type 271 radar, the war at sea was entering a new phase which was to be a struggle for technological supremacy. 'The Happy Time', 'Die glückliche Zeit', as the German U-boat crews called them, the days of easy victories, had ended. Of the 'Aces' of that period – Gunther Prien (U47), Joachim Schepke (U99) and Otto Kretschmer (U100), each credited with sinking more than 250,000 tons – Prien and Schepke were now dead and Kretschmer captured. The Battle of the Atlantic was, however, far from over.

Before the advent of radar, U-boats favoured night attacks on convoys. They were then able to shadow the ships while surfaced – essential due to the low speed and limited range of the U-boats when submerged. When running on its diesels on the surface a Type VII U-boat could not only keep pace with a fast convoy, but could outrun the escorting Flower Class corvettes. An aggressive and experienced U-boat commander would have little difficulty in slipping undetected past the widely-spaced escorts in the dark, selecting a target (usually a tanker) and getting into an attacking position inside the convoy while on the surface. The first intimation of the presence of a U-boat was often a tanker exploding into a sea of fire, usually followed by several other vessels being torpedoed by other U-boats of the 'wolf pack'.

As soon as the ships were attacked, brilliant flares known as 'snowflake' would be sent up in the hope that the escorts could sight a submarine. More often than not all they could do was to estimate the position of the submerged U-boat and begin an ASDIC sweep. Occasionally a U-boat would be spotted on the surface within the convoy and one of the escort vessels would immediately attack it by gunfire or by ramming, to which U-boats were particularly vulnerable: once the relatively thin pressure hull was pierced, the submarine was doomed.

The difficulty lay in sighting the U-boats in the first place. All too often they would remain undetected until they had torpedoed a ship. Radar changed all that. The escort vessels with 271 radar could now fight at night and the surfaced U-boats could be tracked and then, as they crash-dived – and a Type VII boat, well handled, could disappear in some twenty seconds – the ASDIC could be brought to bear with some accuracy and the submarines attacked by the only method open to the commanders of the surface fleet: depth charges.

The Mark VII depth charge contained 300 lbs of Amatol which was detonated by hydrostatic pistols as it sank. The pistols could be set to fire at any of six depth settings from fifty to 500 feet. 'Dustbins' (as they were known to the sailors) were laid in a diamond-shaped pattern of five – three dropped over the ship's stern at 150-foot intervals and two projected by explosive throwers from either side of the ship. (Later in the war depth charges were dropped in groups of ten or fourteen.) The charges sank at sixteen feet a second, allowing time for the ship to get clear (this was vital, for a depth charge could easily blow the stern off a corvette). The lethal range was about twenty-five feet from the submarine, though severe damage could be inflicted from up to fifty feet and the cumulative effect of 'near misses' was considerable, many U-boats being forced to surface and, using their single 88-mm guns, fight it out with the escorts – a battle as one-sided as that between a U-boat and a merchant ship.

Over 200,000 depth charges were discharged and about one in sixteen attacks were successful, 158 U-boats being sunk by depth charges from British ships.

The basic tactic of a depth-charge attack had been evolved during the First World War. There were disadvantages, particularly the method of laying the charges astern of the corvette. In the first place, ASDIC's minimum range of 200 yards meant that, if the contact was ahead of the hunting ship, it would lose touch as it passed over its target, having to drop the depth charges by stopwatch. This momentary loss of contact gave a skilled U-boat captain a chance to slip away and, once the target was lost, it could be very difficult for ASDIC to regain it in the disturbed water caused by the exploding charges and the wakes of the hunting ships. Another disadvantage was simply that, since the depth charges exploded by hydrostatic pressure whether they hit anything or not, unless the submarine was forced to the surface, there was no certain way of knowing if the attack had been successful. Some U-boat crews released oil and debris to give the impression of a hit; the captain of the escort had to use his experience and 'feel' to judge if he had been successful. Many of the escort commanders had this ability, some to an exceptional extent. Captain Donald Macintyre was one; another was Captain F. J. Walker, RN, whose Second Escort Group sank six U-boats in a single patrol.

It was obvious that the chances of a successful depth-charge attack would be much greater if ASDIC contact could be maintained up to the point where depth charges were dropped. Much thought had been given to the possibility of a *forward*-throwing depth-charge launcher, and this was eventually developed by the Department of Miscellaneous Weapons Development as a multiple mortar, consisting of twenty-four bombs, each with a charge of 31 lbs of high explosive. The bombs were designed to be stable aerodynamically, and to dive quickly and accurately in the sea. They were fired electrically from a platform on the ship's deck from inclined spigots; it was the appearance of the twenty-four spigots that gave the weapon its name: Hedgehog. The mortars were 'ripple'-fired and described a graceful arc 215 yards ahead of the anti-submarine vessel, landing in a 130-ft circle and sinking at twenty-three feet a second.

Since these bombs were fitted with contact fuses, if an explosion occurred it would be almost certain that they had hit a submarine: one unforeseen result of this was that crews, used to the enormous water upheavals from the 'dustbins', whether they hit anything or not, were highly disappointed when no contact was made; and, of course, there was no 'near-miss' damage to U-boats. However, Hedgehog was fitted to ships from January 1942, and fifty U-boats were claimed as sunk by it.

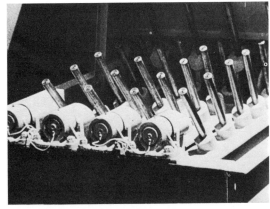

A later development in this forward-throwing technique was Squid. This was a three-barrel device which projected the full-size depth charges, with hydrostatic instead of contact fuses; however, by the time Squid came into service in 1944, the war against the U-boat was all but won, though eighteen U-boats were sunk by them.

Although the Type 271 radar had given the escort vessels an invaluable weapon against U-boats, its range in practical terms in the rough waters of the North Atlantic against the small target of a U-boat's conning tower was seldom more than three miles. But since the beginning of the war there had been considerable developments taking place in *airborne* anti-submarine tactics.

At the outbreak of war Admiral Doenitz, in addressing U-boat commanders, had said, 'The U-boat has no more to fear from aircraft than a mole from a crow'. He was wrong. By 1945, 289 German, eleven Italian and twelve Japanese submarines would have been sunk by aircraft. Even during the First World War small coastal airships were so respected by U-boat commanders that not a single ship was sunk while in a convoy protected by them, as the Americans were to find during World War II with their blimps. (Because of the longer range of enemy fighter aircraft in the Second World War, there could be no question of Coastal Command using vulnerable airships.) At the outbreak of war RAF anti-submarine aircraft were woefully inadequate.

Top left: The twenty-four Hedgehog mortars before firing.

Top right: The spigots which guided the mortars. It was their appearance which gave the name Hedgehog to the weapon.

Bottom left: Hedgehog mortars in the air an instant after firing. Their splashes as they hit the sea (*bottom right*) show an excellent grouping.

Nevertheless, the presence of such obsolete and short-range aircraft as Avro Ansons could cause a U-boat to dive. Indeed in 1940 206 Squadron, desperately short of any aircraft, formed No. 3 Coastal Patrol Flight with nine Tiger Moth trainers flying 'scarecrow patrols', in the hope that even these inoffensive biplanes would cause U-boats to dive for safety.

Coastal Command's anti-submarine armament in the early months of the war, a 100-lb bomb, was soon found to be inadequate. In December 1939 a Royal Navy submarine, HMS *Snapper*, was attacked while on the surface by an aircraft from a discreetly unnamed squadron of Coastal Command; the attack was accurate enough and the '100-lb anti-submarine bomb' hit *Snapper* square on the base of the conning tower, causing total devastation – to four of the submarine's electric light bulbs.

The results of the *Snapper* incident were threefold: the development of an efficient airborne 250-lb depth charge; a redoubling of the Admiralty's efforts to gain control of Coastal Command from the RAF; and a tendency from then on for HM Ships to fire at *all* approaching aircraft. But, as the tempo of the U-boat attacks increased, Coastal Command gradually received better aircraft, and it was soon to benefit from the introduction of a search radar, which would make the hunting of U-boats a much easier proposition.

Airborne radar was known to the Navy and RAF Coastal Command as ASV: Air to Surface Vessel. The first naval aircraft to be so fitted was a Fairey Swordfish – known throughout the Fleet Air Arm as the 'Stringbag'. These single-engined, open-cockpit biplanes were designed as torpedo and reconnaissance, carrier-based machines, and were to become legendary during the war through such actions as the sinking of the *Bismarck* and the Battle of Taranto. What is much less well known is the role these archaic-looking biplanes played in the development of ASV radar.

In the autumn of 1939 a very small experimental group of naval and civilian technicians were given a corner of a hangar at Lee-on-Solent, and a Swordfish, in order to fit a modified RAF Mk II AI (Airborne Interception) set in the hope that it would prove more satisfactory in detecting ships at sea than it was at detecting enemy bombers in the air. The group, which numbered seven, had very little in the way of equipment; most of it was, in time-honoured service fashion, 'won' in foraging round Portsmouth Dockyard: a DC motor to drive a high-tension generator, for example, had originally powered one of His Majesty's mincing machines aboard some forgotten battleship.

Apart from the difficulties of getting equipment, the problems of installing an airborne radar were considerable. The RAF AI sets were designed for twin-engined Blenheim night fighters – comparatively large aircraft; when fitted into the far smaller single-engined Swordfish, weight had to be kept to a minimum, or the operational aircraft would never get airborne from the decks of their carriers.

The ASV set was to operate on 1.7 metres (176 mHz), and a simple dipole transmitter aerial was mounted in front of the upper wing on the centre section. That was a fairly easy decision since there was really nowhere else;

the question of the receiving aerials was another matter altogether. The early RAF AI sets had two Yagi receiving aerials,† mounted near each wingtip: the Blenheims were metal monoplanes and the aerial fitting was not a very difficult problem; the 'Stringbag', however, was a fabric-covered biplane with struts and numerous bracing wires and, to complicate matters even further, all Swordfish had folding wings. In the end, the aerials were mounted midway on the front of the outer interplane strut, and set to 'look' slightly outwards.

The Swordfish took off from Lee-on-Solent on Boxing Day 1939. The airfield was covered with snow and it was bitingly cold in the aircrafts' open cockpits, but the primitive equipment worked: echoes were obtained from ships, though the ranges were depressingly short and it was obvious to the frozen crew that a great deal of work had to be done before the ASV radar could be considered an operational weapon.

During January 1940, in the cold of that bitter first winter of war, test flights were undertaken and improvements to the aerials were made until, towards the end of the month, a convoy in the Channel and the battleship, HMS *Rodney*, gave good echoes at ranges of several miles. The results were so encouraging that the small radar flight was expanded. The Swordfish was joined by two Supermarine Walrus amphibians. The Walrus, known as the 'Shagbat', was, like the Swordfish, a biplane in a monoplane era. It had, unbelievably, been designed by R. J. Mitchell, the creator of the Spitfire; anything further removed from that most graceful of aeroplanes would be hard to imagine, but it carried its three-man crew in a snug, enclosed cabin and was very strong and stable – an ideal test-bed for the ASV radar.

Among the myriad problems the team had to solve was the severe interference that their radar was causing to the aircraft's standard communication radio. Some suppression had been made, but a test flight revealed little improvement. It was on that flight that an unfamiliar aircraft flew alongside the Walrus for a short time, then banked away. Back at Lee-on-Solent as they taxied in people came running up to ask if they had seen the Junkers 88 that was in the vicinity. . . . The Walrus had been recalled soon after take-off but had not received the message since its radio was jammed by the experimental ASV.

With three aircraft (fortunately) still available, work progressed rapidly. Difficulties were overcome, ranges were increasing, and the equipment was proving to be reliable and consistent, so much so that within six months of the outbreak of the war design specifications were issued to contractors for operational Mk II ASV sets for issue to the Fleet Air Arm and Coastal Command.

The position of the aerials had now been finalised. In single-engined biplanes, such as the Swordfish, the transmitter aerial was fitted on the centre

†These aerials were named after a Japanese physicist and were slightly larger versions of the familiar UHF television aerials of today.

Above: 'Stringbags' – Fairey Swordfish – on the deck of an escort carrier. The aircraft on the left have their port wings folded to make more room on the narrow flightdeck for the aircraft waiting to take off. The $1\frac{1}{2}$-metre ASV receiving aerials can be clearly seen on the wing struts of the aircraft in the foreground. The transmitter aerial can just be distinguished on the upper wing's centre section.

Above right: A Coastal Command Wellington XIII (JA144), showing the stickleback ASV aerials on and around the fuselage.

section of the upper wing, as already noted; in later twin-engined types, the Beaufort and Hudson, it was on the nose. The receiving aerials were under the wings – near the tips – on monoplanes and on the interplane struts of biplanes; in either case these receiving aerials were set outwards to give maximum coverage. RAF Coastal Command later used the ASVs in larger aircraft: Whitleys, Wellingtons and Sunderland flying boats had additional aerials arranged along the top of the fuselage, which enabled a sideways search pattern to be carried out as well.

The transmitter aerial sent out its pulses on a wavelength of 1.7 metres in a broad, fan-shaped pattern ahead of the aircraft; any echoes returned from surface ships were detected by the two receiver aerials, which had overlapping directional lobes. Thus, if an echo was being returned from a target to

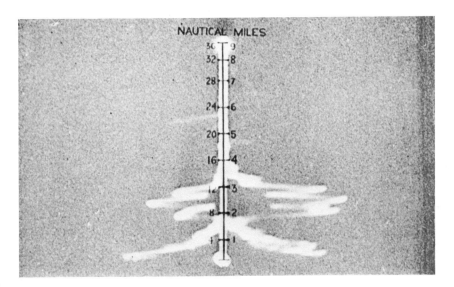

NAUTICAL MILES

The indicator of a 1½-metre ASV radar. The contact is a little to the right of the aircraft and at 2½ nautical miles' range. Although the signal is about to be submerged in the 'sea returns' at the bottom of the scan, the target would be in visual range in daylight.

one side of the aircraft, that aerial would pick up the signal; if straight ahead, then both aerials would receive the echo. The display in the aircraft was on a single tube, with a vertical time-base calibrated in miles (like the coastal CH stations). At the bottom of the trace would be the zero range, where the signal was masked by 'sea returns' from underneath the aircraft; the target would appear as a narrow elliptical blip some way up the trace, depending on its range, and across it or to one side, depending on its direction. As the range decreased, then the blip would move down the time-base.

The operational use of this relatively simple radar was equally straightforward. Once a contact had been established, the radar observer would tell the pilot the direction, and the aircraft would turn until the blip was centred on the trace and the range read off. The range of the early equipment was up to about twelve miles on surface craft, including a surfaced submarine, but coastlines would show up from fifty to seventy miles and transponder beacons up to ninety miles. The sets had switches which enabled the operators to select two ranges: 0–9, or 0–36 miles.

Though crude by later standards, the '1½-metre ASV' (as 1.7-metre ASV was called) was to prove very effective against U-boats. But why was it so much more effective at sea than when used as Airborne Interception in RAF night fighters? The answer is simple. Firstly, as ASV it was only required to give range and bearing: AI had to give height as well. Secondly, and most importantly, the problem of land returns, which limited 'metre' AI, was absent over the sea: water, unless very rough, does not return strong echoes. In practice, since the open sea was rarely completely calm, a certain amount of 'sea clutter' was present, but the radar observer could control this by adjusting the gain of the receiver.

The first, small pre-production batch of airborne ASV arrived from the contractors towards the end of July 1940. By then the Germans were stepping up the daylight air attacks which were to develop into the Battle of Britain. Lee-on-Solent was only a few miles from Portsmouth dockyard and obviously vulnerable, so the radar section was moved to the comparative safety of Arbroath, in Scotland. The two Walruses, the Swordfish and an Albacore took off with the precious experimental sets on a Thursday; on the Sunday Lee was heavily bombed.

As more and more aircraft of the Fleet Air Arm and RAF Coastal Command were fitted with ASV, they used it to locate surfaced submarines and attack them with newly-developed airborne depth charges. These had replaced the earlier, unsatisfactory anti-submarine bombs; weighing 250 lbs, they were fitted with aerodynamic tails to give a predictable and accurate flight; the warhead was 165 lbs of Amatol. These depth charges remained 'safe' until actually dropped, to prevent premature explosion in case the aircraft had to ditch, or crashed on take-off or landing on carriers.

In addition to direct attack, the main value of the early airborne radar was as a deterrent, in that it forced U-boats to remain submerged by day; no longer could they shadow a convoy in daylight, keeping out of range of the surface escort's radar, and then attack at nightfall.

At the end of 1941 two factors were dramatically to reduce convoy losses. Firstly, Doenitz had to send a large proportion of his operational U-boat force into the Mediterranean to try to stem the losses that the Royal Navy were inflicting on the German supply routes to the Afrika Korps. Then, on 9 December 1941, Germany declared war on the United States. This was seen by Doenitz as an opportunity for rich pickings. Hitler allowed him to send a few of his long-range, Type IX 1000-ton U-boats, which were armed with twenty-two torpedoes, to attack coastal shipping. To increase their range further they were refuelled at sea by the Type XIV tanker U-boats, nick-

A Milch Cow, a long-range Type XIV tanker U-boat, meets another U-boat in the South Atlantic. These huge submarines had a range of 12,300 miles at 10 knots.

named 'Milch Cows'. These submarine tankers, displacing nearly 2000 tons, could carry sufficient fuel, as well as provisions, spare torpedoes and other stores, to resupply fourteen operational U-boats.

The Americans, in spite of the appalling losses that the German submarines had inflicted on the Atlantic convoys, seemed to have learned very little from their allies' experience. Shipping off the Eastern Seaboard of the United States sailed as if it were still peacetime; there was no convoy system and anti-submarine patrols were ineffective; the coastal towns observed no blackout, so that offshore shipping was often silhouetted against the lights of towns. The results were predictable and disastrous: the seas off Cape Hatteras and Hampton Roads became a killing ground. Between January and July 1942, 460 ships, including tankers plying from the oilfields of Venezuela, were sunk – a total of 2.3 million tons. Many of the ships were attacked by gunfire from surfaced U-boats, which thereby conserved their torpedoes; they had little to fear on the surface for the lack of air cover at that time was such that they could meet their supply vessels in broad daylight to transfer oil and stores.

In spite of the heavy losses, the US Navy was reluctant to resort to the convoy system, considering it to be a defensive measure and inappropriate to the traditions of a Navy which had never known defeat on the high seas. Eventually the lack of success of their surface patrols and increasing shipping losses to U-boats forced them to adopt a convoy system, but this was not until April 1942. The Royal Navy also sent twenty-five escort vessels it could ill spare, and the loss-rate off the eastern seaboard dropped. The U-boats then intensified their operations in the Gulf of Mexico and the Caribbean. The

The lack of air cover off the American coast in early 1942 enabled U-boats to receive fuel and stores from their Milch Cows on the surface in broad daylight.

sinkings continued there until July, when the US Navy began to take defensive measures in that area.

Because there was no possibility of German aircraft off their coast, the Americans were able to use small airships with great success. K2 Class 'blimps' were developed by the Goodyear Company, which built about 150 during the war. Once they came into service they proved a most effective anti-submarine weapon; indeed, at the end of the war, US naval authorities stated that no American vessel was ever sunk by a U-boat while in a convoy escorted by these airships.

Once the American Navy had organised their defences in the summer of 1942, the U-boats' second and last 'happy time' ended. In any event, Doenitz knew that, however many ships his U-boats sank off the United States, the decisive battle was on the North Atlantic supply routes to Britain. As the U-

Below: A U-boat crew opens fire on an American merchant ship with its 88-mm gun. In the absence of convoys and effective anti-submarine forces, ships were attacked in daylight on the surface and sunk by gunfire to conserve torpedoes.

An American tanker from the oilfields of Venezuela blazes off Cape Hatteras. The picture is a frame from a German newsreel shot from the conning tower of the U-boat. Such was the lack of US escort ships in the winter of 1941–42 that the U-boat was able to remain on the surface filming although clearly visible in the light of the burning tanker.

boats concentrated once more on the Atlantic convoys, airborne ASV was beginning to make itself felt and it was joined in mid-1941 by another weapon, silent, unseen and deadly – 'Huff Duff', officially HF/DF, 'High-Frequency Direction-Finding'.

German U-boats, particularly when hunting in the 'wolf packs', depended greatly on radio to organise the attacks. A single U-boat or a long-range Focke Wulfe Condor reconnaissance aircraft would locate a convoy; its composition, number of ships and type of escort, the course and speed, would immediately be transmitted to U-boat HQ at Lorient. HQ operations room would then, by radio, direct other U-boats in the vicinity to assemble – perhaps as many as twenty for a large convoy. As each individual U-boat that was to form the wolf pack was contacted, it would signal acknowledgment and give its present position. These radio signals, which were of course enciphered, were intercepted by special Royal Navy listening watches. The cipher, usually five-letter groups in morse, was the German Navy's version of Enigma (Schlüssel M); it was not to be broken for over a year,† but as far as Huff Duff

†In fact U110 had been captured off Greenland on 9 May 1941 and its Enigma machine and code-keys recovered, although this has only recently been officially acknowledged. Even the capture of U110, which sank under tow, was not admitted until the mid-1960s.

was concerned, that did not matter: the signals themselves were betraying the position of the U-boats sending them.

Huff Duff was a very special system of direction-finding. Not only was it of very long range and able to plot the positions of the loquacious U-boats at distances of over 1000 miles, but the sets, Type FH4, incorporated a cathode-ray tube which gave an accurate visual bearing on any signal they picked up, and they did it very quickly, enabling a 'fix' to be obtained even on the shortest morse transmission. The Germans, suspecting that the Royal Navy would use direction-finding apparatus to locate U-boats, had devised special short code-groups for U-boat transmissions. The speed of transmission was such that a position message or routine report could be transmitted in less than thirty seconds. However, unlike conventional direction-finding apparatus which required manual adjustments, that was long enough for Huff Duff to get a 'fix'.

An escort destroyer, HMS *Hotspur*, in the Mersey. The 'Huff Duff' aerial (inset) can be seen at the top of the after mast.

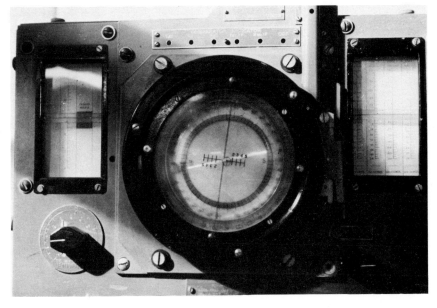

FH4 Huff Duff with a contact on the indicator tube.

For direction-finding a single bearing is, of course, next to useless: it gives direction but no range. It is only when a second bearing, or several bearings, cross the original bearing that an accurate fix is possible. The more stations, the more accurate the position. Under ideal conditions the position of a U-boat could be located to within a quarter of a mile.

Huff Duff was the result of pioneer research using cathode-ray tubes, at the National Physical Laboratory's Radio Research Station at Slough, under Watson Watt and Bainbridge Bell. The work, like radar itself, was another spin-off from research into the nature of the ionosphere. The CR/DF (cathode-ray direction-finding) technique had originally been devised to track thunderstorms. The Services became interested in the technique and, by 1939, the Royal Navy in particular had made considerable progress and experimental installations at Flowerdown, Portsmouth, and on Gibraltar were tracking not thunderstorms but enemy radio traffic. Several warships were fitted with CR/DF sets and it was certain that Britain was well ahead of any other power in the matter of rapid, accurate, radio direction-finding by the outbreak of the Second World War.

In 1940 Professor P. M. S. (later Lord) Blackett had suggested that a number of high-frequency direction-finding sets could be positioned along the western seaboard to locate U-boats. (By this time the prototype FH4 set had been developed by the Royal Navy Signal School, in close collaboration with the commercial firm of Plessey: this was the set that was compact enough to be installed aboard the small escort ships.) The bearings from ships and shore stations were sent to the Admiralty plotting-room and the information so gained was used to build up a picture of the movement of U-boats, enabling escort vessels and aircraft to attack individual submarines and, in the case of large formations of 'wolf packs' that were out of range of land-based aircraft, convoys could make alterations to their course to avoid them, whilst the escorting warships could get into position to attack.

The first detection of a U-boat by means of Huff Duff was in mid-1941 and, from then on, the success rate grew until the HF/DF sets vied with radar as the most successful submarine-detection system: a skilled operator at sea could estimate the distance of a U-boat from a single bearing.

In the summer of 1942, three examples of the FH4 sets were given to the US Naval Research Laboratory as prototypes and, by October of that year, the first American-built versions were fitted aboard US anti-submarine vessels.

In spite of new technical developments, the shipping losses due to U-boats continued. There is little doubt that they would have been far higher without the aid of radar and HF/DF, but German shipyards, using efficient production techniques, were simply building U-boats faster than the Allied navies could destroy them. In 1941 the Allies had lost two million tons of shipping, representing 429 ships, to U-boats; the Germans lost thirty-five submarines. In 1942 the figure appeared worse: 1155 ships, six million tons,

A U-boat hull under construction. Up to 1943 some sixteen yards were engaged in building U-boats. With conventional shipbuilding techniques it took about seven months to complete a Type VII. During 1942 212 U-boats were commissioned – and only 87 sunk.

An Allied merchant ship photographed through a U-boat's periscope in a heavy swell. The gun on the poop is unmanned. The vessel was obviously unaware of the presence of the submarine, and was torpedoed a few moments later.

sunk, and although eighty-seven U-boats failed to return to their French bases, whereas Doenitz had ninety-one operational U-boats in January 1942, by December that year German shipyards had given him 212. During 1942 U-boats were sinking some 650,000 tons of shipping a month -- a figure far beyond the capacity of British shipyards to replace. The German Naval staff had calculated that sinking 800,000 tons a month would bring Britain to her knees, by stemming the flow of food and war materials from the United States which was essential to the prosecution of the war. This figure appeared to be well within their reach. In fact, the tide – though it must have been far from obvious at the time – was about to turn against the U-boats.

American shipyards were turning out prefabricated all-welded, standardised merchant vessels – the famous 'Liberty Ships' – in large numbers and incredibly quickly. British shipyards were producing new fast escorts – the River Class frigates – able to cross the Atlantic without refuelling and, most important, with sufficient speed to outpace a surfaced U-boat – neither of which the earlier Flower Class corvettes could do. But perhaps the most telling weapons were the scientific ones, radar and HF/DF. Of these, radar was in the end to prove decisive, especially airborne radar.

As the war progressed and Coastal Command received better aircraft, equipped with ASV radar and efficient anti-submarine weapons, U-boats began to be sunk by them in significant numbers, particularly when crossing the Bay of Biscay in daylight. So much so that they submerged during the day and cruised to and from their bases only at night. They were safe enough at night, for although the $1\frac{1}{2}$-metre ASV could pick up a surfaced submarine at about five miles, it could not track it closer than about a mile in average sea conditions due to 'sea clutter' – that is returns from the waves on the surface. In daylight this limitation was of little consequence since the U-boat could be attacked visually. At night, however, this was impossible.

The problem of using ASV at night came – quite unofficially – to the notice of an RAF personnel officer at Coastal Command HQ. Wing Commander Leigh had been a pilot in the First World War and knew well enough the hazards of flying at night and the difficult task of finding such a small target as the conning tower of a U-boat. He thought about the problem and came to the conclusion that the only possible solution was to mount a small, lightweight but powerful searchlight in the nose of the searching aircraft. Now, although Leigh knew about aircraft, he knew nothing about searchlights.

Coastal Command HQ was at that time in the London suburb of Northwood, so Leigh simply went to a local anti-aircraft site and gathered a good deal of information from the officer in charge about his searchlights: their various sizes, the power and range, what they could and could not do. Based on this information, Leigh sketched out his ideas, which emerged as a 22-million-candlepower light with a $10°$ flat-topped beam.

The first thing was to enlist the support of experts at the RAE, Farnborough, whose job such an enterprise really was. Not surprisingly, they poured cold water on the idea; experts tend to do this with ideas that come from other people. Such a light, they said, would take up to two years to develop and anyway they had thought up another solution to the problem, which involved towing flares. In short, Leigh got no help at all. To be fair to the RAE, however, the winter of 1940/41 was hardly the best time to approach them; they had many other pressing problems.

In desperation, Leigh next went to see the C-in-C Coastal Command, Air Chief Marshal Sir Frederick Bowhill, who fortunately had been his Squadron Commander in the First World War. Bowhill liked the idea and said he would back it, which enabled Leigh – still an obscure officer in personnel – to get hold of an early Wellington, one of four which had been used for exploding

A long-range B24 Liberator illuminated by a Leigh Light from another aircraft.

magnetic mines. To do this they had a large coil suspended beneath them, energised by a generator driven by a Ford V8 car engine. Leigh explained that the generator was essential for his light and, since the aircraft were now stored and no longer required for their original purpose, it would be easy to start the experiment without much additional expenditure.

Using the 'old boy' network to the limit, Leigh persuaded Vickers, the gun turret manufacturers Frazer-Nash, and Savage & Parsons, who made searchlights at Watford, to start work – without official Air Ministry authority – and after about four months the first 'Leigh Light' was installed in a Wellington at Weybridge. The light was designed to be moved up and down and left to right by an operator using the controls and actuating gear from a standard Frazer-Nash gun turret with the guns removed. The light's movement was remotely controlled from the front gunner's turret; the light itself was in a retractable mounting under the aircraft's fuselage.

During trials – still largely unofficial – the Leigh Light was able to pick up a surfaced British submarine at night very well. So far so good: then came disaster. Bowhill, who had taken a somewhat Nelsonian view of Leigh's clandestine activities, was posted and a new C-in-C Coastal Command, Air Chief Marshal Sir Philip Joubert, appointed.

By coincidence, in his previous appointment at the Air Ministry Joubert had been concerned with another airborne searchlight, known then as the Helmore Light. Fitted into an American Douglas Havoc aircraft, its purpose was to illuminate enemy bombers so that night fighters, flying in formation with the Havoc (a twin-engined conversion of the Douglas Boston medium bomber), could see their target. This light, about which Leigh knew nothing, was fitted in the nose of the aircraft and fixed, being directed to its target by manoeuvring the aircraft.

Joubert not unnaturally told Leigh that, in view of the considerable development work already done, his unofficial light must be dropped. This was a bitter blow to Leigh: on the strength of the air tests with the Wellington, he had already, in collaboration with Major Savage of Savage & Parsons, designed an under-wing version of the light for use on the very long-range Catalina and Liberator aircraft that Coastal Command were receiving from the United States. Convinced that sooner or later his light would be required, he took Major Savage into his confidence, and the searchlight manufacturer took a chance and continued to work on the Leigh Light without any official sanction.

Two months went by, during which time tests of the Helmore Light proved, as far as Coastal Command were concerned, 'disappointing'. Joubert sent for Leigh who, thirty-five years later, remembers the conversation at their meeting:[4]

'. . . he wanted to know where the [Leigh Light] aircraft was. I told him it was at Vickers at Weybridge. He said he wanted to see it himself, told me to order his car the next day, and that we would go over together and see it.

'When we came back he said, "You know, Leigh, that light of yours might work all right, but what I really want is something that will go on a Catalina, and you can't stick a turret through the bottom of a flying boat."

A Leigh Light under the wing of a Catalina. A 1½-metre ASV Yagi receiving aerial and the wind-driven generator for the Light can also be seen. Behind the generator are the racks for airborne depth charges.

'I said, "No , Sir, but if you will come with me next week to Watford to Savage & Parsons, I will show you a light that will go on a Catalina."

'"Do you mean a proper searchlight?" he asked.

'I said, "Yes, Sir, an arclight".

'"Who authorised it?"

'I said, "Nobody Sir".

'"Who did it?"

'I said, "I did Sir".

Joubert then asked if the Air Ministry or the Ministry of Aircraft Production knew about the new light. Leigh replied that they did not:

'There was a bit of a pause and I wondered what was coming next. He said, "Right, let me know when it's ready and I will come and see it."

'I took him [to Watford] the next week and he played with the controls on the floor of Savage & Parsons' workshop.'

The happy result of this visit was that the Leigh Light was immediately ordered in very large numbers and was, as we shall see, vital in the struggle against the U-boats. As for Leigh, who had disobeyed direct orders to stop working on the light, he feared, in spite of its success, some form of official displeasure, but Sir Philip Joubert, who was soon to become Chief of the Air Staff, never mentioned the matter again until the war's end, when he admitted he had been mistaken in not adopting the Leigh Light in the first place. Leigh's persistence had saved about six months and the Navy and Coastal Command had acquired a most valuable weapon against the U-boats.

The Leigh Light called for a special attack technique, which was quickly developed by the first Coastal Command Squadron to be so equipped, No. 172, flying Wellington VIIIs from Chivenor. These aircraft had the Mk II ASV $1\frac{1}{2}$-metre radar which would detect a surfaced submarine at maximum range. The radar operator, having established contact, would then direct the pilot towards the U-boat and call the crew to action stations. The navigator would then lower the Leigh Light from its retractable turret under the Wellington and the co-pilot would climb into what would normally be the front gunner's turret: using similar controls to those originally fitted to train the guns, he would direct the light, on information from the radar, using two dials marked in degrees – one for up/down, the other for left/right.

The pilot was meanwhile easing the big aircraft down to a height of 250 feet above the sea, a hazardous manoeuvre on a dark night, since the flying was entirely on instruments and the pilot had to rely on the accuracy of a meteorological forecast giving him the correct barometric pressure to be set on the altimeter. The local sea-level pressure (QNH) would be set at so many millibars on the altimeter's subscale; any mistake could be fatal at such a low altitude and, since one millibar is equivalent to thirty feet, there was not much margin for error.†

---

†Later, Leigh Light aircraft were fitted with radio altimeters, which were accurate to a few feet and independent of pressure errors.

During the run in to the target, the Light-operator would be listening to the homing bearings being called by the ASV radar observer and applying these to the Light, using his dials while making corrections for wind drift and the movement of the target. The light, still unlit although bearing directly towards the contact, would be set to undershoot slightly. When within about a mile, the ASV would lose the target because of 'sea clutter': the light would then be switched on and the operator would tilt it upwards and, with a little luck, illuminate the U-boat dead ahead. If it was ahead, then and only then the pilot would be told 'target in the beam', and he would look up from his instruments and make the final stages of the attack visually, diving his aircraft to about fifty feet to drop a pattern of depth charges over the U-boat.

The effect of these surprise attacks on a U-boat crew was, as can be imagined, considerable. They would have been unable to hear the approaching aircraft, since its engine noise would have been masked by the roar of the submarine's diesel and the seawash. The first intimation of the attack would be the blinding 22-million-candlepower searchlight, followed by the depth charges. The first successful night attack resulted in the sinking on 5 July 1942 of U502 by a Wellington VIII of 172 Squadron.

The combination of ASV radar and the Leigh Light made it possible to attack surfaced U-boats as they crossed the Bay in what they had hitherto regarded as the 'safe' hours of darkness. The number of night interceptions during June and July 1942 were about twenty, and by August the German submarine commanders were sufficiently alarmed not to surface at night but during the day, and then only long enough to recharge their batteries, with lookouts on the conning towers quartering the sky for the first sight of approaching aircraft.

Referring to the Leigh Light attacks, Doenitz noted in his War Diary that: '. . . difficulties which confront us in the conduct of the war can only lead, in the normal course of events, to high, indeed intolerable, losses'.[5]

German scientists quickly realised from reports of U-boat captains who had survived that the accurate night attacks with the Light could only be guided by radar. Quickly they counterattacked by providing the U-boats with a special warning receiver, the FuMB1, 'Metox', which covered the frequency bands of all known British airborne radar, 113–560 mHz ($2\frac{1}{2}$ metres to 53 centimetres).

Thus it was able to detect the $1\frac{1}{2}$-metre radar pulses and so warned U-boats of an approaching ASV-equipped aircraft, which it did by giving a series of 'bleeps' of increasing frequency as the aircraft drew nearer, enabling the U-boat to have ample time to crash-dive to safety.

The aerial for the Metox set, however, was carried on a small wooden frame on the conning tower and was known as the 'Biscay Cross'; the snag was that the co-axial cable had to be led through the pressure-tight hatch, which meant the hatch could not be shut for diving until the Biscay Cross was safely inboard – a time-wasting procedure when every second counted. Nevertheless Metox proved very successful in countering the Leigh Light,

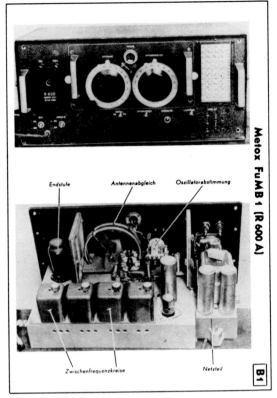

Metox FuMB 1 (R 600 A)

Endstufe   Antennenabgleich   Oszillatorabstimmung

Zwischenfrequenzkreise   Netzteil   B1

and in mid-1942 a large number of 'disappearing contacts' were reported by Coastal Command's crews.

Other factors also conspired against the Allies in the Battle of the Atlantic during 1942. From June the American Navy withdrew a large number of escort vessels, which were transferred to the Pacific, and many British escorts were also detached to the Mediterranean to support the military convoys for 'Operation Torch', the invasion of North Africa. The hard-pressed British and Canadian Navy escorts remaining did as best they could, as did aircraft flying from bases on the West Coast of England, Northern Ireland, Iceland and from Newfoundland, in providing cover over the convoys; but the aircraft then available were for the most part of limited range and there remained 'The Gap' – an area in mid-Atlantic where aircraft from east or west, other than those possessing very long range, could not patrol.

Only one squadron of Coastal Command, No. 120, had been equipped with very long-range aircraft, American Consolidated Liberators, which had the necessary range – 2400 miles – to close the Gap. A very small number had been operating since June 1941 from Nutts Corner in Northern Ireland, but there were simply not enough of them available. Although Coastal Command pressed for more of such aircraft, those that were available were being used by the RAF as bombers and the Gap, as far as shore-based aircraft were concerned, remained until 1943.

At the beginning of 1943 the Battle of the Atlantic was finely balanced:

Left: The Metox set. In addition to aural warning it also had a visual cathode-ray tube indicator which showed the approximate range of the attacking aircraft.

Right: The aerial for the Metox was called the 'Biscay cross'. It was not a fixture and had to be passed through the pressure hatch in the conning tower each time the U-boat dived.

both sides in the grim struggle were in a potentially winning position. The surviving U-boat commanders and crews were skilled, highly disciplined and well led, as were the Escort captains and their crews. They had all gained their experience in a very hard school and were backed by scientists whose work, one way or another, was in the end to prove decisive.

One of the British scientists, Professor Blackett, led the unglamorous-sounding department of 'Operational Research', whose scientists brought some highly original thinking to the war at sea. It was of these men that the C-in-C Coastal Command, Air Chief Marshal Sir John Slessor, said:

'A few years ago it would never have occurred to me, or I think to any officer of any fighting service, that what the RAF soon came to call a "Boffin", a gentleman in grey flannel bags, whose occupation in life had previously been something markedly unmilitary such as biology or physiology, would be able to teach us a great deal about our business. Yet so it was.'

One of the most effective examples of operational research was in the matter of the setting of aircraft depth charges. These were set to explode at a depth of 100 feet, on the assumption that, when a submarine was under air attack, it would have seen the aircraft approaching and crash-dived to a depth of from fifty to 100 feet by the time the aircraft was overhead and had dropped its charges. One of Blackett's 'Boffins', E. J. Williams, looked into what actually happened: he found that when aircraft sighted U-boats three

Below left: A Hurricane aboard a lighter is towed to its CAM ship.

Below right: A CAM ship with a Hurricane mounted on its catapult. Twelve cordite rockets were used to launch the fighter.

times out of four they were on the surface or just diving and could therefore be attacked with accuracy; if, on the other hand, the U-boat was already submerged when sighted, then in all probability it would turn under water and be lost. Williams showed that if a submerged U-boat was regarded as a lost target and attacks were concentrated on surfaced or diving submarines, a better 'kill'-rate could be achieved. All that was required was to alter the depth-setting on the charges from 100 to twenty-five feet. As soon as this was done, the success rate in U-boat sinkings went up by two to four times, a result so dramatic that survivors thought that the British depth charge had been given a double weight of explosive.

Another telling result of operational research was a brilliant analysis of the optimum size of convoys. It was found that the same number of ships were lost, roughly speaking, whether the convoy was large or small. The actual figures were an average loss of 2.6% for convoys of less than forty-five ships, and 1.7% for larger convoys. The number of escorts, about six, was the same in each case, since the area of a large convoy is only slightly larger than that of a small one. (The perimeter for a convoy of eighty ships would be only a seventh longer than that of a convoy of forty ships.) Even if a U-boat were to break through the screen of escorts, it would be unlikely to sink more ships in a large convoy than in a small one, since the limiting factor would not be the number of potential targets but the torpedo-reloading time and the number of torpedoes available.

By mid-1943, large-convoy techniques had reduced the number of close escorts needed by one third, allowing the formation of support escort groups, which could go to the aid of any convoy under attack and hunt for U-boats joining or leaving the area. In this way the convoy was not left unprotected as it had been previously when its escorts left to chase submarines.

However effective the escorts were they could not alone defeat the U-boats. Radar-equipped aircraft were essential, either working with the surface vessels or attacking U-boats directly, but there still remained the Gap, already referred to, which could not be effectively patrolled by shore-based aircraft, at least until sufficient numbers of long-range aircraft became available. The obvious answer was to use short-range anti-submarine aircraft operating from carriers, but the only aircraft carriers available were in desperately short supply: HMS *Courageous* and HMS *Glorious* had both been sunk in the first year of the war, and in November 1941 the most famous of them all, HMS *Ark Royal*, was torpedoed by U81 while transporting fighters to Malta. The few remaining Fleet carriers were far too valuable to be risked guarding merchant convoys.

The first British aircraft to fly over convoys in mid-Atlantic were Hurricane fighters which were catapulted from HMS *Pegasus* (formerly the first *Ark Royal* – a seaplane tender dating from the First World War), later supplemented by requisitioned and converted merchant ships which were fitted with a single catapult and a Hurricane or Fulmer fighter. They became operational in 1941, not to attack U-boats directly – the fighters carried no

Opposite

Bottom left: Gunners on lookout in a Catalina. Operational Research scientists showed that simply cleaning the perspex windows of Coastal Command aircraft significantly increased the sightings of U-boats.

Bottom right: Operational Research also showed that the number of escorts with a convoy could be safely reduced, thus enabling hunter/killer groups of corvettes to be formed.

depth charges – but the long-range Focke Wulfe 200 Condors of KG40, which were being used as reconnaissance and spotter aircraft for the U-boat wolf packs as well as bombing isolated ships. Catapulting fighters was a successful tactic – up to a point: the aircraft were unable to land back on the ship, and, if out of range of the nearest land, had to be ditched after their single flight.

On 3 August 1941 a Hurricane catapulted from HMS *Maplin* and piloted by Lt R. W. H. Everett, RNVR (who had won the Grand National in 1929 on Gregalach), shot down a FW200. Everett managed to ditch his Hurricane and was safely picked up by the destroyer HMS *Wanderer*. That was the first and only Condor actually shot down by a catapulted naval fighter, though they continued to be used and several merchant ships were later equipped with a Hurricane or Fulmer. These CAM ships (Catapult Armed Merchant Ships) carried a normal cargo and flew the Red Ensign. Two further Condors were damaged, and the fighters often managed to drive others off, which was sufficient to justify the existence of the CAM ships, for it denied the U-boats their long-range reconnaissance. CAM ships continued to operate until 1943, though they were only an emergency stop-gap: a return, in a way, to the Sopwith Camel fighters which took off from the gun turrets of battleships in the First World War.

The fact that a single short-range fighter could seemingly protect a large convoy from air attack revived the Navy's interest in the idea of the small Escort Carrier, which had first been considered before the war. A German prize-ship, *Hannover*, of 5600 tons, with its superstructure removed and a flight deck substituted, embarked six Grumman Martlet fighters and, re-named HMS *Audacity*, sailed operationally in September 1941. Because there was no hangar the six aircraft were permanently parked on the narrow deck and the first to take off only had a run of about 300 yards; it says much for the skill of the eight pilots, five of whom had never flown from a carrier, that they could operate from such a small flight deck.

Audacity was to have a brief career escorting two return convoys to Gibraltar, her Martlets shooting down five FW Condors, damaging another three and driving one away, as well as shooting up several U-boats – all for the loss of two aircraft shot down and one which went over the side when the small carrier was rolling 16 degrees and the flight deck was pitching up to 65 feet. *Audacity* was torpedoed by U741 on 21 December 1941 with heavy loss of life, but she had shown clearly that, even when operating under the most primitive conditions, an escort carrier could provide air cover in the Gap.

It was not until the spring of 1943, however, that largely American-built escort carriers (CVEs), nicknamed 'Jeep' or 'Woolworth', began sailing with the merchant convoys. Twenty-three CVEs were eventually used by the Royal Navy alone. They carried some twenty planes – Grumman Martlet fighters (now known by their American name, Wildcats) and Fairey Swordfish. In addition to these purpose-built ships there were several Merchant Aircraft Carriers – MAC ships – which were tankers or bulk grain-carriers with their superstructure removed and a short flight deck fitted. Like the CAM ships,

The escort carrier HMS *Biter*, photographed from a Swordfish which has just taken off. On the very short flightdeck Grumman Wildcat fighters are ranged.

they too flew the Red Ensign and carried a normal cargo in addition to their four Swordfish. From the time of their introduction in 1943 until the end of the war, not a single ship was sunk by a U-boat in any convoy with which these makeshift carriers sailed.

The Fairey Swordfish, with its open cockpit and slow speed, found a new lease of life aboard the small carriers. Fitted with $1\frac{1}{2}$-metre ASV radar, depth charges and rocket projectiles, they sank altogether some twenty-five enemy submarines (thirteen directly and the remainder shared with surface vessels). That these obsolete, fabric-covered biplanes, designed in 1936, were so successful is an indictment of those responsible for the provision of aircraft for the Fleet Air Arm, as well as a tribute to their aircrews, who had to endure hours of flying in the freezing temperatures of the North Atlantic in winter, operating from narrow decks that could be pitching sixty feet or more in driving rain and gale-force winds. Flying over the Atlantic convoys in winter is described by Hugh Popham, in his book on naval flying, *Into Wind*:[6]

'. . . to the airmen in the Swordfish, peering hour after hour for a periscope wake or the black amorphous outline, like a half-tide rock, of a surfaced boat or the blip on the ASV screen, one convoy run might be colder, more disagreeable, more dangerous, than another; but the quality they shared above all others was the feeling of interminability. This kind of warfare, like the trenches, lacked the solace of an imaginable conclusion.'

One possible replacement for the Swordfish which was considered was the Curtiss Seamew, known to the US Navy as the Seagull, or SO3C. 250 of these monoplanes were ordered for the Royal Navy and on paper they appeared to offer some advantage over the 'Stringbag'; they were faster, with a maximum

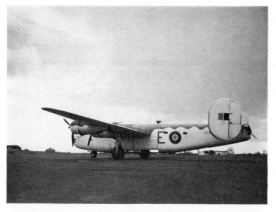

Aircraft that fought the Battle of the Atlantic.

Top left: A Coastal Command Liberator. These very long-range aircraft closed the 'gap' in the middle of the Atlantic.

Top right: An ASV-equipped Swordfish is ranged on an escort carrier. The men who flew these open-cockpit aircraft had to contend with biting cold and the prospect of landing on a heavily pitching deck. If their single engine failed and they ditched, their life expectation could be measured in minutes.

Middle left: An American Consolidated Catalina. With an exceptional endurance of seventeen hours, Catalinas served with Coastal Command from 1941.

To a Catalina of 210 Squadron fell the distinction of sinking Coastal Command's 196th and final U-boat on 7 May 1945.

Middle right: A Catalina dropping depth charges over a crash-diving U-boat.

Bottom left: By 1943 the Short Sunderland equipped nine Coastal Command squadrons, and it remained in service until 1957. The 'big boat' gave a good account of itself against enemy aircraft, earning the Luftwaffe nickname 'Flying Porcupine'.

Bottom right: Lockheed Hudsons were the first American aircraft to be used operationally by the RAF.

speed of 190 mph at 7500 feet against the Swordfish's 139 mph at 4750 feet, and they had an 8-hour endurance. Unfortunately they were powered by engines of monumental unreliability: they were rejected by the US Navy, and those that were delivered to Britain were relegated to training radio operators – over land.

Although the escort carriers did much to close the Gap, they were augmented, on the personal orders of President Roosevelt, by some sixty Consolidated B24 Liberators to supplement the small number already in service with 120 Squadron. These big, four-engined bombers had much of their normal defensive armour and weapons removed to make way for the maximum number of fuel tanks but they could fly far over the Atlantic and were still able to remain with a convoy for up to three hours.

There had been a struggle to get these additional B24 Liberators, for the requirements of the bombing offensive against Germany had taken priority. Coastal Command had been starved of four-engined aircraft, having to make do firstly, as we have seen, with inadequate types such as the Avro Anson, which lacked range and practically everything else required for anti-submarine work. The Sunderland Flying Boat helped, but it too had a relatively short range. The best of the early aircraft was the American Catalina; twin-engined Whitleys and Wellingtons were used, but they still lacked the vital range, and were anyway obsolete bombers converted for Coastal Command. Eventually, at the end of 1942, some four-engined Halifax IIs were received, later to be followed by a maritime version – the Halifax V, but no Lancasters were supplied until after the war.

The reason was that these four-engined British aircraft simply could not be spared from their primary role, the bombing of Germany. In any case, the Air Staff believed that the best form of attack against U-boats was to bomb their bases and the shipbuilding yards where they were built. In fact, not one U-boat was destroyed by bombing the U-boat pens on the French Atlantic Coast. The pens were hit all right – some 15,000 tons of bombs were dropped on the bases – but the massive reinforced-concrete structures were all but indestructible. Over 100 heavy bombers were lost in attacks on the U-boat bases in the first five months of 1943 alone.

In January 1943 British, Canadian and United States escorts and aircraft were faced with an *average* of 116 U-boats at sea each day. This large fleet was to be aided by the work of the German cryptanalysts, the B-Dienst whose code-breakers had penetrated the Allied convoy radio code. The U-boat high command could therefore plot the route of many of the convoys across the Atlantic.

In March, acting on information supplied by the cryptanalysts, thirty-nine U-boats were concentrated to intercept two convoys: SC122, a 'slow' convoy of fifty-two ships, and HX229, a 'fast' one of twenty-five. HX229 was attacked first and eight ships were sunk in as many hours. For three days the running battle continued, the two convoys joining to help their combined escorts fight the submarines; but in all nine ships, totalling 140,000 tons,

U-boats in their
pens, immune from
air attack.

were sunk – four of them by U338 alone – for the loss of only three U-boats.

That German success was to prove the high point of the battle; had they been able to sustain it, Doenitz's ambition of cutting the lifeline between Britain and America would have become a reality. It was not to be. The escort carriers and the long-range B24 aircraft now closed the Gap permanently, and – most significantly – the scientists were about to provide yet another weapon which would in the end prove decisive: 10-cm ASV radar.

It all began with Randall and Boot in their Birmingham University laboratory and the development of the cavity magnetron – work, it will be recalled, conducted under Admiralty patronage. The shipboard 271 radar had been the first operational 10-cm set and, following its success, work had begun on the 10-cm ASV as early as the winter of 1941; but pressure from the RAF had secured priority for H2S and that radar had been developed first. However, the H2S team under Dee at Malvern had designed an ASV capability into H2S. Indeed it was known at TRE as H2S/ASV.

The Metox countermeasure enabling the U-boat crews to be warned of the approach of the 1½-metre ASV-equipped aircraft had made a drastic change of wavelength essential. Since it was known that the Germans, lacking the magnetron, considered 10-cm radar impractical, it was thought unlikely that they would be expecting British aircraft to be using it. Ten centimetres was therefore the obvious answer.

There was some opposition: in the first place, Bomber Command were claiming total priority for H2S radar in the bombing of Berlin and, even at TRE itself, many people felt that 10-cm ASV was insufficiently developed, and that its introduction was premature. The adaptation of H2S to ASV was, as Sir Bernard Lovell remembers:

'. . . most bitterly opposed and we were not allowed to divert any H2S equipment from Bomber Command. In the end, we made the [ASV] equipment ourselves in TRE.'

The answer to the objections to ASV was provided by the tonnage of ships being sunk in 1942: 5,970,679 tons – 1354 ships – by September. The early success of airborne ASV and Leigh Lights had been nullified by Metox, so in the autumn of 1942 the decision was made to divert some H2S sets from Bomber Command for fitting as ASV Mk III in Leigh Light Wellingtons.

The main difference between ASV Mk III and H2S was in the scanner position: it was simply not possible, due to ground clearance and other structural problems, to mount the H2S cupola under a Wellington. The only possible alternative was in a 'chin' under the nose; this entailed a considerable redesign of the scanner, which in any case now had to work at an altitude of 2000 feet instead of 20,000, with a $40°$ blind spot behind the aircraft. Even when these problems had been solved, further delay was caused – at a time when shipping losses were running at around 600,000 tons a month – by the RAF insisting on unnecessary refinements such as blind-landing and homing-beacon facilities being incorporated in the sets.

In spite of all the difficulties and delays, two prototype ASV Mk III sets were hand-built at TRE and fitted to two Wellington VIIIs (LB129 and LB135) at Defford during December 1942. By the end of February 1943 twelve Wellingtons based at Chivenor, backed up by almost as many TRE scientists as airmen, had ASVs installed. On the evening of 1 March two Wellingtons took off from Chivenor for the first patrol with the new radar over the Bay of Biscay (it was just a month after the first H2S raid over Germany by Bomber Command). No contacts were reported but, to the relief of the scientists, the crews had no difficulties with the new set.

During the night of 17 March, the first U-boat contact was made by 10-cm ASV at a range of nine miles; unfortunately the Leigh Light jammed, and no attack was possible. The same aircraft, a Wellington XIII (HZ538), obtained another sighting the next night at seven miles; this time all went well and the U-boat was attacked with six depth charges, the crew reporting that 'the submarine was fully surfaced and under way, showing no signs of suspecting attacks'. This was, of course, the whole point of the 10-cm ASV; with Metox unable to detect the new radar, the success rate grew, particularly in the Bay of Biscay. In March thirteen submarines were caught at night, and there were twenty-four attacks in April. It was the same success that Coastal Command had enjoyed in June 1942 when the Leigh Light had first been introduced: the U-boats could no longer risk crossing the Bay at night, and had to run the gauntlet on the surface in daylight.

A Wellington with 10-cm radar and a Leigh Light. The scanner was in the 'chin' under the aircraft's nose. The Metox warning receiver was unable to detect this new radar, with the result that many U-boats were surprised on the surface, like U966 (*below*) which was bombed and sunk a few moments after this photograph was taken on 10 November 1943 off Cape Ortegal in the Bay of Biscay.

The success of the new ASV and the larger number of long-range aircraft were such that in May two convoys, ON184 and HX239, arrived in British ports without a single ship lost: the German Navy, on the other hand, lost six U-boats vainly trying to attack them. In all, no fewer than forty-one U-boats were sunk by escorts and land- and carrier-based aircraft that month. Faced with these increasing losses, Doenitz ordered his submarines to fight it out on the surface when attacked by aircraft in daylight. Additional flak weapons were added to the existing armament, and initially the heavily-armed U-boats had some success against unwary aircraft. But the RAF soon developed a very simple counter; aircraft finding a U-boat on the surface simply flew in circles, just out of range of the submarine's guns, and called up the nearest surface units. The U-boat was constantly watched and, as soon as the tell-tale plumes of spray indicated the submarine was blowing her tanks to dive, the plane would close for an attack. This developed into a grim race – the 'battle of the seconds'. With a highly trained crew it was possible to clear a U-boat's deck and dive in about thirty seconds. If they got down in that time they had a chance; many did not and were sunk by the aircraft's depth charges or rocket projectiles.

As more and more U-boats were sunk and the lucky ones that had limped back to base reported that the Metox sets were not giving any warning of aircraft attacks, German scientists were perplexed. They discounted 10-cm radar for the not very sound reason that they themselves had been unable to produce a practical one.

Then a captured RAF airman mentioned under interrogation that the attacking aircraft were homing on the U-boats by signals radiated by the Metox set itself. To this day, the identity of this man remains a mystery; also a mystery is his motive. Whatever the reason, the effect on the Germans of this bogus intelligence was dramatic.

Laboratory tests showed that the Metox receiver *did* radiate a small signal (most radio sets do). U-boat HQ immediately ordered the entire fleet to turn off their receivers at once. The sets were then extensively redesigned and completely screened, so that not the smallest signal was radiated. It made no difference, of course. The U-boats were still attacked out of black night skies; one moment sailing on the surface, secure and seemingly invisible, the next a blinding light heading straight for them, then the roar of four 1200-hp engines and the blast of the shallow-set depth charges as a B24 Liberator or a Sunderland flew over at fifty feet.

How were the aircraft finding their small targets now? The Metox sets were no longer radiating: infra-red was a possibility, but German scientists came to the conclusion that a new and unknown radar was far more likely. Its identity was not long in coming: an RAF Stirling night bomber, equipped with H2S, was shot down over Rotterdam. As British experts had feared, the magnetron was recovered intact and the Germans established its working frequency and wavelength: 10 centimetres. It was to be reconstructed as the 'Rotterdam Geräte', but for the moment the answer to the U-boats' problem was clear and simple: a new Metox-type warning receiver, but working on 10 centimetres.

Now to receive 10-cm radar pulses is a very much easier proposition than to transmit them, and a search receiver, the Telefunken FuMB7, 'Naxos', was quickly installed in Atlantic U-boats. A small dipole aerial was held up by a crewman on the conning tower whenever a U-boat was surfaced; any 10-cm pulses would be picked up and the receiver would give a warning on a cathode-ray tube below in the U-boat. The Naxos set covered the 'S' band, from 2500 to 3700 mHz (12 to 9 cms).

Naxos was not as effective as Metox for two reasons: it was omni-

Naxos. The hand-
held aerial is at the
top of the set.

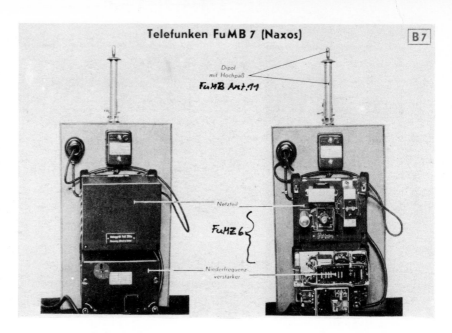

Telefunken FuMB 7 (Naxos)

directional – all it would do was to warn that an ASV-equipped aircraft was in
the vicinity; and that vicinity would be pretty near, since the simple dipole
aerial had no gain, and the set itself was insensitive. Early Naxos had an
additional disadvantage in that the aerial, small as it was, still had to be
brought down the conning tower so that its cable cleared the pressure-tight
hatch. The handling of a long length of co-axial cable often damaged it, with
the result that the receiver gave no warning at all.

The big worry on the Allied side was that the Germans would find an
effective warning receiver as good on 10 centimetres as Metox had been on $1\frac{1}{2}$
metres in September 1942. This problem had been much in the minds of the
H2S/ASV team at TRE, where there had been rather pessimistic estimates of
how long the ASV Mk III would be 'safe'. It was an axiom of those days that
any new device was considered to be safe from countermeasures for only a
matter of weeks and therefore, whenever possible, a second-generation
model was ready to take over. The obvious immediate counter, should Naxos
prove efficient, was a jump to another frequency; this meant even shorter
wavelengths – to 'X' band, 3 centimetres. An X-band H2S had been developed, and an ASV version was also produced. However, simply changing
the wavelength was only a short-term solution: sooner or later the Germans
would discover it and provide a suitable receiver. But there were other ways
of defeating the listening sets.

ASV Mk VI, which operated on 3 centimetres, was issued to Coastal Command in January 1944. It had two new features. Its range was increased
by stepping up the output from 50 kw to 200 kw – a staggering figure for an
airborne radar in those days. The anti-listening measure was the provision of
an attenuator control. The operator, once he had gained a contact, could then
reduce the output of the radar to a point where he could just maintain the

target on his screen as they flew towards the U-boat. The effect of this on the enemy listeners was that the pulses did not appear to get any stronger and they therefore assumed that the aircraft was not homing on them until it was too late to dive to safety.

The Germans went to extraordinary lengths to counter the 3-cm ASV: there was a new search receiver – FuMB36, the 'Tunis' – which covered from 15 to 3 centimetres; and the periscope standards, schnorkel trunking and even, in some cases, the entire conning tower were covered in a special material called 'Sumpf', a sandwich of rubber with carbon granules impregnated in it. The sandwich was composed of two types of Sumpf: one had the property of variable resistance over its area, the other variable dielectric or electrical density. The object of the coating, code-named 'Schornsteinfeger' (chimney-sweep), was to make the structures above the water absorb the radar pulses, reducing the strength of the echo and making them less 'visible' to radar. In tests under laboratory conditions, Sumpf appeared to offer some promise, but it was not really practical. The sea tended to remove the covering, salt deposits reduced its electrical properties, and finally, the permanent aerials now fitted to detect the 3-cm radars returned excellent echoes. So in spite of these measures the attacks on the U-boats continued. The Luftwaffe sent Ju88 fighters into the Bay of Biscay to intercept Coastal Command's aircraft; the RAF countered by escorting the anti-submarine patrols with Mosquitoes and Beaufighters, and the Royal Navy increased its surface 'Hunter Killer' groups.

A new phase of warfare then appeared: the radio-controlled glider bomb, the Henschel 293. This bomb achieved some success but was soon countered by jamming its simple radio-command link (see page 298). Throughout 1943 the Battle of the Bay of Biscay was fought out. It resulted in the sinking of forty U-boats. Referring to the use of 10-cm ASV, Hitler conceded:

One of the forty U-boats sunk in the Bay of Biscay in 1943 with the help of 10-cm ASV. A Mosquito attacks with cannon and rockets.

'The temporary setback to our U-boats is due to one single technical invention of our enemy.'[5]

The Germans too had new technical inventions, for example 'Pillenwerfer', or 'Bolde' – an abbreviation of the German word 'Lügenbold', meaning habitual liar. This was a canister of chemicals which, when released from a submarine, caused a cloud of fine bubbles which blocked the ASDIC: a marine version of 'Window'.

There was also an acoustic torpedo, the T5, Zaunkönig, which could 'home' on to the sound produced by the propellers of a ship travelling at between five and twenty-five knots. These torpedoes were known to the Allies as GNATs, German Naval Acoustic Torpedoes; they were first used operationally in September 1943 when the frigate *Lagen* and two merchant ships in convoy ONS18/ON202 were sunk. During the next six days three more merchant ships and two escorts were sunk by the new torpedoes, though the Germans lost three U-boats during the attack. Countermeasures were soon devised. First of all it was very slow for a torpedo – about twenty-five knots – and could therefore be avoided with alert lookouts; and then it was found that, at certain engine revolutions, the sound produced by the ship's propellers made the homing of the torpedoes ineffective. Disturbed water and the explosions produced by dropping depth charges also attracted the torpedoes; and finally a 'Foxer' was devised: a noise-producing decoy which consisted of two lengths of steel piping which banged together when towed some distance astern of the escorts and on to which the GNAT homed and harmlessly exploded. The countermeasures were so effective that the GNAT torpedoes were soon withdrawn.

The next German device was a half-forgotten Dutch invention, the Schnorkel – now familiar to skin divers. An air trunk on the conning tower remained above the surface when the U-boat was fully submerged, enabling it to cruise under water powered by its diesel engines. There was a float-operated valve at the top of the schnorkel just above the water line, which automatically closed the trunking when the submarine dived; unfortunately sea swell, waves or a badly trimmed boat could also close the valve, which had a most unpleasant effect on the crew since the big diesels immediately sucked the air out of the hull, creating a partial vacuum which caused severe discomfort as the boat depressurised. Another unpleasant aspect of a schnor-kelling submarine was the gale of freezing salt-laden air howling through the boat. There was also the uncomfortable feeling, while submerged, that the top of the schnorkel tube, with its tell-tale wake, was visible above the sea, inviting attack from aircraft whose 3-cm radar could detect even that small target. But the schnorkel did enable a submerged boat to travel more or less indefinitely under water at a far higher speed than possible on its electric motors. All newly constructed U-boats and many of the existing ones were fitted with schnorkels and they were used extensively when crossing the Bay of Biscay.

Useful though the schnorkel was, it was still a physical link with the surface:

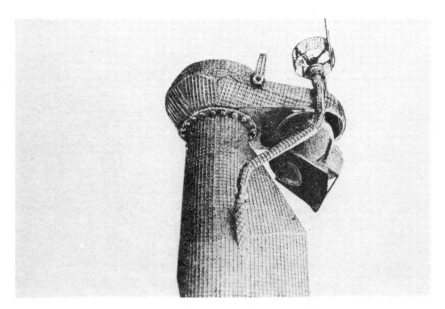

the boats that were fitted with it were still submersibles. But it was a step towards the true submarines which were now under construction in German shipyards. These were the revolutionary 'Walter' Type XVII boats. The main feature of this class was its very high underwater speed of twenty-five knots. This was achieved by a 'closed-circuit' system – that is, it was independent of external oxygen and therefore needed no schnorkel. The main propulsive motor was a Walter turbine, driven by gases created by the decomposition of a concentrated fuel of hydrogen peroxide called 'Ingolin' or 'Perhydrol'. Unfortunately, not only was this fuel difficult and very costly to make, it was also highly unstable and dangerous, and the Walter engine required such a vast amount of it that the Type XVII U-boat would have been restricted to a range of about eighty miles at full speed.

None of the XVIIs became operational, though one of them, U1407, which was scuttled at Cuxhaven at the end of the war, was salvaged and went to the Royal Navy as HMS *Meteorite*. It was used to evaluate the Walter system for four years but was scrapped in 1950, the British considering it to be 'highly dangerous'. Had the German Navy had time to develop the Walter boats, they could have proved highly successful; independent of outside air, they could have remained submerged for an indefinite period.

It is improbable that the Walter boats could have been developed in time to affect the outcome of the Atlantic battle, but another design, the Type XXI, first seriously considered in 1943, could well have done so, had it been put into production earlier. The Type XXI was known as the 'electro submarine' and had a much increased battery capacity, giving it a high underwater speed of sixteen knots. These large, very well-designed, 1800-ton submarines had a range of 11,000 miles and carried twenty-three torpedoes as standard. There was also a smaller coastal version, the XXIII, which displaced 256 tons and had a small 14-man crew.

The XXI U-boats were designed for mass production, being entirely

An airborne attack on a surfaced U-boat. Crewmen cling to the conning tower.

welded and extensively prefabricated in eight major assemblies, much of the construction being done by semi-skilled labour. Had it proved possible to produce the Type XXI in sufficient numbers, they might well have prolonged the U-boat offensive; but it was not to be. Materials, manpower and supply communication were increasingly affected by Allied 'round the clock' bombing; many Type XXI U-boats were bombed under construction in the shipyards. Even if the planned construction programmes of 634 U-boats could have been completed, the 62,000 trained crew members they would have required were non-existent. From late 1944 onwards the German Army took priority over all else. Another factor which has rarely been mentioned was the extensive RAF mining of the Baltic, which seriously disrupted U-boat training.

The war against the U-boat was in reality won by the summer of 1943. Ships were still being sunk, but not at anything like the replacement rate, and the cost to the German Navy in U-boats lost was very high. Crossing the Bay of Biscay became increasingly difficult and those that did get to the concrete havens at Brest, Lorient and St Nazaire heard only the bad news of other U-boats missing and sunk, of rumours of more and more Allied aircraft and escorts with new and deadly weapons. Gone were the days of the triumphant returns with flowers and bands playing, with the Admiral himself bestowing the Iron Crosses, the adoring German auxiliaries and the girls from the

5 May 1945: Doenitz had sent his last order to his U-boats, the Battle of the Atlantic was over, and the surviving U-boats surrendered.

A US Navy blimp accepts the surrender of a U-boat off the American coast.

The U-boat under the American flag.

A U-boat steams up the Thames – with a Royal Navy prize crew aboard.

Radar plots on a British destroyer. By the war's end superior radar and advanced weapons made the task of the U-boats almost impossible, countering any late developments the Germans made.

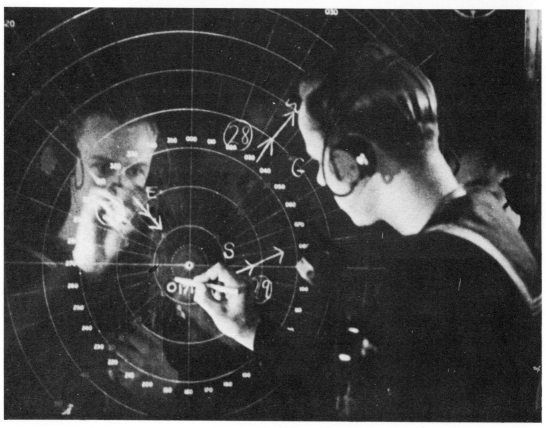

French *établissements*. Now everything was drab and grey in the shadow of defeat.

After the liberation of France, the U-boats withdrew to German bases at Kiel and Cuxhaven and still continued to sink Allied ships in the coastal waters off Normandy, the British Isles and in the North Sea. The cost, however, was heavy: 241 boats in 1944 and 153 in the first five months of 1945. Of the 39,000 officers and men enlisted in the German Navy's U-boat arm, 28,000 were lost at sea and 5000 captured: an 85% casualty rate; 1150 U-boats were commissioned, of which 842 were operational: 781 (or 93%) of these were sunk, the highest percentage losses of any section of armed forces anywhere.

The surviving U-boats continued to fight to the very last day of the war: thirty-four boats were sunk in March 1945; fifty-seven in April; twenty-eight in May. Then Doenitz, with the end of the European war, sent the following message:

'All U-boats. Cease fire at once. Stop all hostile action against Allied shipping. DOENITZ.'

It was 5 May 1945; Doenitz was now the last Führer of the Third Reich. Next day he sent a longer message to his U-boat crews; in it he claimed that the U-boat arm of the German Navy had been defeated by 'overwhelming material superiority'. This was only a partial truth for, although it was true that American production had enabled the ships to be replaced and aircraft and weapons provided in great numbers, quantity alone could not have won the Battle of the Atlantic. The U-boat had been defeated by superior science: Radar, HF/DF, ASDICs, the Leigh Light, and depth charges, and by the skill and courage of the men on board the escorts, the merchantmen and carriers and in patrolling aircraft.

As the surviving U-boats surfaced, flying a black flag while making their way to the nearest Allied base or warship to surrender, the Battle of the Atlantic was finally over. It had been a hard fight: in the Atlantic alone, 30,000 sailors had gone down with 2282 ships – a total of 14.5 million tons. Britain, as in 1917, had come very close to defeat in that cruel sea, the North Atlantic.

The Royal Navy
destroyer HMS
Blanche, an early
casualty of the
German magnetic
mine.

5. MISFORTUNES OF WAR

In the autumn of 1940 Hitler, not without reason, considered that the war was as good as won and therefore curtailed all long-term scientific research. Thus committed to a short war, German scientists were increasingly to find themselves trailing behind the Allies, for the time taken to develop new weapons and counters to electronic developments was never enough, and wrong decisions or mistakes could have far-reaching consequences.

Mines

One such weapon within two months of the outbreak of the Second World War had sunk twenty-nine merchant ships and the destroyer HMS *Blanche*. The cruiser, HMS *Belfast*, though not sunk, was so badly damaged that she was out of action for three years. The German secret weapon which had achieved this was the magnetic mine.

The German Navy had begun to lay mines on the first day of the war: they were the classic buoyant type and sank the first mine victims of the war, the SS *Goodwood* and *Magdepur*, just seven days after hostilities commenced.

The buoyant contact mine was a known technology, dating from the First World War; it was relatively easy to sweep and was not regarded as a serious menace. Very soon, however, the Germans began to lay a far more effective weapon – the influence or non-contact mine, actuated by the magnetic field that all steel ships possess.

The magnetic mine had been invented by the British in 1917 and was used in small numbers that year against German U-boat bases in Holland. But interest in mines had languished in Britain between the wars – largely, it is said, because high-ranking naval officers considered mine-laying to be the resort of second-class naval powers.

The German magnetic mines of 1939 were non-buoyant and virtually unsweepable. They were laid in harbours, estuaries and shallow coastal waters, sinking to the sea-bed undetected: waiting. During September many such mines were laid by U-boats, usually near the lightships which were still at that time working normally. U19 laid nine around the Inner Dowsing Lightship in the Humber: three ships were sunk. Such success was by no means isolated and the mines continued to cause heavy losses, until by November the Germans had all but succeeded in closing the Port of London.

Though the magnetic mines were initially laid by U-boats, E-boats and destroyers, by 17 September the Luftwaffe too was involved. Most airborne mines were laid by parachute, but one enterprising crew actually landed their Heinkel seaplane in Harwich harbour, deposited two or three mines, and took off again into the night.

November 1939 was the height of the crisis. Over 200,000 tons of British shipping were lost; it was vital that this new and unknown mine be countered. Before any countermeasures could even begin, however, it was clearly essential that an intact example be recovered. This proved easier said than done. HMS *Mastiff*, a trawler converted into a minesweeper, was blown up in an heroic attempt to land a mine which she had dredged up in a fishing net on 20 November. The very next night, however, another of the secret mines was to come within reach of Admiralty scientists. Around 10 pm on 21 November a soldier on duty at an artillery range on a desolate stretch of the Thames Estuary, near Shoeburyness, heard the characteristic desynchronised-engine throb of an approaching German bomber. The aircraft, a Heinkel 111, flew low over the water and the soldier saw an object, which he later described as 'looking like an army kitbag', parachute into the sea just offshore. The sighting was reported to the Admiralty where Lieutenant Commanders R. C. Lewis and F. W. Ouvry (the latter an expert from the Mine and Torpedo School, HMS *Vernon*) were waiting for just such a report.

The two officers arrived at Shoeburyness at around 3 am to learn that the tide was ebbing and that the 'object' should be visible. They quickly collected together a working party of soldiers armed with torches, stakes and ropes to secure the mine, if such it proved to be, against the ebbing tide.

Up to this time, it should be realised, no one in Britain knew if the mines were in fact magnetic; they could equally have been actuated acoustically,

On 17 September 1939 the Luftwaffe began to lay magnetic parachute mines. Here a Heinkel 111 flies over docks on a tidal estuary – a typical target for their nightly minelaying operations.

though magnetically was thought to be more probable. As a precaution, Ouvry and Lewis had removed all metal badges, buckles and buttons from their uniforms. They then walked across the mudflats towards the mine, led by the alert soldier who had made the first sighting and followed at a safe distance by the working party.

After a short time they saw the sinister, black cylindrical shape of the mine, looking to Commander Ouvry 'like a stranded whale', though he was now in no doubt that it was a mine of an unknown type. The soldiers were stopped and the two naval officers walked on alone, feeling, Lewis later said, 'very, very lonely'.[1]

The 8 ft-long mine was carefully examined by torchlight and Ouvry, the expert, noted that:

'. . . there were two fittings on top of the mine which obviously had to be removed to render it safe; one was made of brass, with a small brass spindle sticking out of it, pretty certainly a hydrostatic valve; the other was polished aluminium with a brass securing ring.'

To unscrew this fitting, a special pin-spanner was required, so Lewis made a rubbing of it on a signal pad as a pattern for a brass, non-magnetic spanner to be made in the nearby Army workshops.

The two men then returned to the Artillery Camp to await daylight and low tide. As they waited they planned the best way to deal with the dismantling of the mine. Soon after dawn they were joined by Chief Petty Officer Baldwin and Able Seaman Vearncombe, who had brought non-magnetic tools from HMS *Vernon* in Portsmouth.

On their return to the mudflats, low tide and daylight revealed a second mine about 400 yards from the first; it had obviously been dropped by the same aircraft. It was decided that Ouvry and Baldwin, as the most experien-

The Shoeburyness mine, photographed at first light as the tide receded.

ced, would tackle the first mine and Lewis and Vearncombe would watch through binoculars, making notes from a safe distance in case of accidents.

Carrying their non-magnetic toolkit, Ouvry and Baldwin approached the mine, making as little noise as possible in case it *was* acoustic. It must have required a great deal of cold courage calmly to walk up to the unknown mine, which was one of Germany's much-vaunted Secret Weapons and would almost certainly contain anti-handling devices. Nevertheless the two men, conscious of how vital it was that the mine's secrets be penetrated, began to dismantle it alone on the desolate mudflats – against time, for the tide had now turned.

They decided to tackle the aluminium fitting first: this was sealed with wax or tallow and had a small copper strip on the top which Ouvry thought was an arming device that the German aircrew had neglected to remove. To get the brass pin-spanner, which had been made in the Army workshop that night, to fit, it was necessary to bend the copper strip clear,

> '. . . so I told Baldwin to bend it back carefully, but being an old sailor he got hold of it and gave it a tremendous wrench and the thing came half off. I stopped him very quickly . . . and we fitted the pin spanner and started to unscrew. Off came the ring. I then got hold of the fitting with my hand and found it would come free. I thought it might be a magnetic needle, so I lifted it up very slowly so as not to move it quickly in the earth's magnetic field: I took about three minutes to get the cylinder, as it was, clear of the mine.'

Under the cylinder, which was a detonator, there were discs of explosive which were the primers for the main charge. The cylinder that Ouvry had removed later proved to be fitted in case the mine was to be used as a parachute bomb; the copper strip which Chief Petty Officer Baldwin had nearly torn off was an igniter for a delayed-action fuse.

In order to remove any remaining fittings, it was now necessary to roll the mine over. Lewis and Vearncombe came over to assist and a second detonator was revealed and removed; as this was being carried ashore, it began to tick loudly and the party dispersed very quickly. It later became apparent that Ouvry and Baldwin had been very lucky indeed: the ticking clock in the fitting that they had removed from under the mine was actuated hydrostatically by water pressure and was designed to keep the mine safe until it had settled on the sea-bed. Fortunately the clock had jammed: if it had not, the mine would have been fully armed by the time it was discovered.

The mine, stripped of its detonators and priming charges, but still containing 660 lbs of explosive, was towed ashore by a caterpillar tractor and taken by road to HMS *Vernon* for detailed examination in the non-magnetic laboratory. (The laboratory was full of interested officers and if the mine had contained a booby trap the Royal Navy would have lost practically its entire strength of mine and torpedo experts: fortunately it had no such device.) As the rear plate of the mine was removed there was much speculation among the onlookers as to whether an acoustic or magnetic mechanism or some totally new actuator would be revealed. Under the cover plate was a rubber dome; when this was removed a scale was seen: on it the single word 'GAUSS' – the unit of a magnetic field. The mechanism was removed and the main charge steamed out of the mine. Admiralty scientists worked through the next night on the magnetic actuating mechanism, and within eighteen hours had solved the riddle of its operation. It proved to be similar to the British 'M' mine of 1917 in that it was triggered by a passing ship altering the vertical component of the earth's magnetism.

In the northern hemisphere, if a magnetic needle is balanced horizontally, its north-seeking pole will dip downwards towards the earth's magnetic field. The German mine worked on this principle: it had a bar magnet which was pivoted and biased by a helical spring, which kept the north pole upwards. There was a contact on this pole which the spring kept open; the strength of

The interior of the magnetic mine. The scale marked Gauss proved that the mine was magnetic.

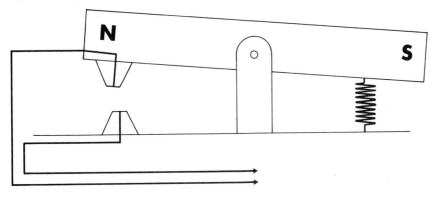

The basic arrangement of the actuator of a magnetic mine. The contacts were wired to an electrical firing mechanism.

the spring was adjustable so that the vertical component of the earth's magnetic field at the point where the mine was to be laid was just balanced: hence the scale calibrated in Gauss – the Shoeburyness mine had its setting at 0.02 Gauss. The whole of the beautifully-made actuator was set in gimbals, so no matter which way the mine rested on the sea-bed, the vital magnet was always in the correct plane, the spring just able to counteract the tendency of the north-seeking pole of the magnet to dip downwards.

Ships built in the northern hemisphere have a magnetic field with a downwards-pointing north pole and, as every schoolboy knows, 'like poles repel, unlike poles attract'. Thus when a ship passed over the mine, it repelled the mine magnet's north pole, enabling it to overcome the helical spring and close the electrical contact, thereby exploding the mine. A ship built in the southern hemisphere, on the other hand, would have its magnetism with a *south* pole pointing downwards; such a vessel could pass over the mine with impunity, since its south pole would attract the mine's north, aiding the spring and pulling the contacts further apart.

Once the principle of the operation was understood, countermeasures were soon devised. The work was the responsibility of scientists of the Royal Navy's Mine Design Department of HMS *Vernon* and a team from the Admiralty Research Laboratory, which included Dr C. F. Goodeve and Dr E. C. Bullard. There were two possible lines of attack. One could detonate the mine by safe means, or prevent the ship's magnetism actuating the detonator.

The first method was in many ways the most attractive, though there were no means at that time for achieving it. However, some work done in 1936 was found to be relevant; in that year Naval Intelligence had begun to get reports that the German Navy was experimenting with magnetically-fired torpedoes. A committee had been set up to investigate possible countermeasures and it had been decided that the best course of action would be to *increase* the magnetic field of a steel ship so that the torpedo would explode while at a safe distance from its target. In the course of experiments during 1937–8, HMS *Curacoa* was wound with coils of various sizes in order to produce a strong magnetic field. Admiralty scientists also made a magnetically-scaled model of the ship, and a great deal of information about induced magnetic fields was gathered. Although the work was not primarily intended to detonate magnetic mines, it could be relevant.

The immediate result was a very strange vessel indeed – HMS *Borde*, the world's first magnetic minesweeper. This ship carried an enormous electro-magnet weighing 400 tons, the core being a bundle of railway lines 200 feet long. *Borde* put to sea and detonated its first mine on Christmas Eve 1939: the shock waves were such that everyone on board had to stand on thick layers of rubber to avoid broken ankles.

No ship could withstand that sort of treatment for long and another, less dramatic, method was sought. Expendable barges were considered, but the idea was discarded as impractical; someone even suggested attaching small bar-magnets to fish in the hope that they would swim near enough to mines to detonate them, but after careful consideration this too was turned down.

One interesting method actually used resulted in one of the most bizarre aircraft of the Second World War. This was the DWI Wellington – 'DWI' standing for 'Directional Wireless Installation', to try – not very convincingly – to disguise the purpose of the 51'-diameter coil suspended beneath the bomber. Composed of strips of aluminium energised by a Ford V8 car engine driving a 35-kw generator, which put a current of 310 amps through it, the coil created a strong downwards-pointing magnetic field. The idea was that the aircraft would fly low over estuaries and detonate any mines below, without being shaken to bits like the unfortunate HMS *Borde*.

A Mk IA Wellington (P2516), fitted with the coil streamlined by a balsa-wood fairing, was found by test pilot Mutt Summers to handle surprisingly well. It was taken to Boscombe Down and flown over the actuating mechanism which had been recovered from Shoeburyness; for two hours the Wellington roared over the mechanism at heights from ten to 100 feet, while the scientists below plotted the polar diagram of the aircraft's magnetic field and were delighted to discover that the mine's magnet clicked away merrily. It was concluded that the DWI Wellington could detonate a mine safely, and in early January 1940 an operational trial flight was made over the Medway: almost immediately a mine blew up.

About a dozen DWI Wellingtons were commissioned; later types used a more powerful generator driven by a Gipsy Six aircraft engine, which enabled a slightly smaller ring to be used. Although they did explode mines successfully – the Germans paid the compliment of copying the idea, using Ju52s – they only 'swept' a very narrow channel, and an unmarked one at that, so they were used only until other methods became available, though several were employed in the Middle East to sweep the Suez Canal and small harbours. (It was, incidentally, one of these DWI Wellingtons with its engine-driven generators which was used for the first Leigh Light experiments.)

A DWI Wellington. The large ring made surprisingly little difference to the aircraft's handling.

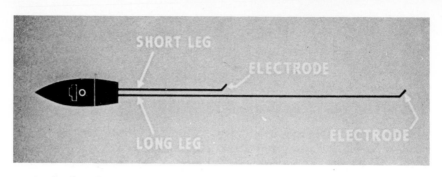

The final and entirely satisfactory solution to the problem was a method known as the double longitudinal, or Double L, sweep. This consisted of two wooden ships, which steamed on a parallel course about 300 yards apart, each towing two lengths of floating cable: one about a third of a mile long and the other much shorter. Each cable had electrodes at its end, and large lead acid accumulators on board the ships sent DC pulses of five seconds' duration at 3000 ampères down each pair of cables – one cable for the negative pole, the other for the positive. The salt water between the electrodes completed the electrical circuit. The pulses from each ship were precisely synchronised and an intense magnetic field of roughly ten acres was set up in the water. Any magnetic mines in that area would explode, and it was a continuous process: the ships steamed non-stop and another ten acres would be swept when the next pulses occurred.

The Double L sweep worked satisfactorily. Because of the length of the cables there was no danger to the sweeping ships, and a broad channel was quickly cleared and accurately plotted. It was operational from May 1940, and continued until after the war.

Work on developing this most efficient counter to the German mine had begun at the height of the crisis in November 1939. The theory was put forward by Dr Goodeve and others of the Mine Design Department, though several scientists (including Professor Lindemann) considered it unsound and unworkable.

A testing of the system took a somewhat unusual form. In November 1939, with ships being blown up and sunk daily, the inhabitants of Southsea were surprised to see a group of sailors apparently playing with toy ships on a children's boating pond. (It was hinted that it was an experiment to detect U-boats trying to slip into British harbours by placing wires on the sea-bed which picked up tiny currents induced by the submarine's magnetism. Though this was a cover story, just such a system had been tried between the wars.) What was really being tested was, of course, the Double L; the sailors pulling the model boat masked the real test. Goodeve had reversed the system: the 'floating' cables were lying on the bottom of the lake, chosen because it was salt-water, and Goodeve was being rowed over them with the magnetic firing mechanism from the Shoeburyness mine concealed on his lap. Power from batteries hidden in a van was pulsed to the cables and, to Goodeve's relief, actuated the mechanism satisfactorily.

A full-scale sea trial was arranged for Boxing Day 1939. Two tugs were loaded with numerous car batteries and a Ford V8 engine-driven generator to provide current for the cables. The cables were not self-buoyant but were lashed to logs and, although the trials were considered satisfactory, the day ended with one of the tugs aground on a sandbank with a cable wound round its propeller.

The problem of floating the cables now assumed some importance: it was obviously not practical to use logs and spars. A Canadian officer at HMS *Vernon* thought that the Americans were using a form of buoyant cable to

The first buoyant cable is reeled on to a drum at the BICC factory.

A Double L twin cable is paid over the stern of a magnetic minesweeper. The cables can be seen floating astern.

power dredgers on the Great Lakes. This was reported to the British Insulated Callender's Cable Company, who said, in effect, 'If the Americans can make buoyant cables so can we'. They did, in just a matter of weeks. The buoyancy was provided by modifying tennis-ball machinery to make cylindrical 'balls' which formed flotation elements for the cables. The first buoyant cable was delivered on 18 January 1940 – the first of over $1\frac{1}{2}$ million yards to be manufactured by the end of the war. It was in fact the first buoyant cable in the world – the Canadian had been mistaken: the Great Lakes dredgers were powered by cables lashed to logs.

By February the first magnetic mines had been swept by the Double L. Special wooden minesweepers, modelled on Yarmouth trawlers, were commissioned and they operated with great success, countering the magnetic mine effectively: seventy-four mines swept by March, nearly 300 by the end of June 1940.

While the Double L sweep was being developed, an alternative counter-measure to the magnetic mine was introduced. This reduced the magnetic field of steel ships so that they no longer triggered the mines. The technique became known as 'de-gaussing'.

A wooden non-magnetic minesweeper trailing its double L sweep.

De-gaussing was achieved by passing a direct current through a coil of heavy cable wound round a ship's hull. Just sufficient current was passed to neutralise the ship's magnetism, the residual field being too weak to influence a magnetic mine. At first the coils of heavy cable were simply suspended by ropes from the ship's deck, but this was far from satisfactory as many coils were washed away in a heavy sea. It was then discovered that the coils were just as effective if laid on the ship's deck, and later still, to the embarrassment of the responsible scientists, if laid inside steel tubes within the ship's hull.

The calculation of just how much neutralising magnetism any ship required depended on the character of its 'natural' magnetism. This was evaluated by stations in all major ports: ships passed slowly over a number of large coils on the sea-bed which detected the magnetic 'signature' of each individual ship. This signature was then plotted on a paper graph and the required counter or de-gaussing current worked out.

The character of a ship's natural magnetism depended to a large extent on the direction, relative to magnetic north, in which the keel was laid. This led to some very odd signatures, such as those of ships which had sailed from the northern hemisphere to the southern and back, and those of Liberty ships, which were prefabricated, the two halves of their hulls often being built in different directions. The readings taken were so accurate that, with increasing experience over the war years, the officers in charge could not only tell from which yard the vessel was launched, but often the actual slipway.

As a variation to de-gaussing, which was only effective as long as current was flowing through the coils, Goodeve suggested 'wiping' – a technique whereby a single coil of very heavy cable carrying several thousand ampères was slowly drawn up the sides of a ship by sailors with ropes. The cable with its heavy current actually clung to the ship's hull; the effect was to magnetise the ship in the opposite direction to its natural magnetism, so it became in effect a southern-hemisphere ship with a vertical south pole which would not detonate the early German magnetic mines.

The advantage of 'wiping', particularly for small vessels, was the absence of the bulky and heavy coils and associated generators. Many of the hundreds of small ships at Dunkirk were wiped and, so far as is known, only two were sunk by magnetic mines during that operation. The disadvantage was that

Joining together de-gaussing cables before fixing them round HMS *Repulse*'s hull. The size of the cables is a clear indication of the large current required.

wiping had to be repeated every three months, though a small ship could be done in an hour or two and even a large vessel in a day. Before wiping, all the ship's clocks and compasses had to be taken ashore, since the strong magnetic field would ruin them. (On one occasion, when an aircraft carrier was 'wiped', all the ship's compasses were duly removed ashore, but the compasses in its twenty-four aircraft were overlooked.)

During the six years of war, de-gaussing and wiping cost some £20 million and made heavy demands on scarce materials, particularly copper, but it prevented the sinking of many hundreds of ships. Much of the early work was improvised and made unusual demands on scientific resources: for example, a fluxmeter was found to be ideal in the assessment of the natural magnetism of ships. The firm who made these precise instruments was asked by an Admiralty representative to supply 500 – immediately; the firm's astonished manager replied that they had only made a dozen since 1898.

The final word on the success of de-gaussing is the story of the merchant ship's captain who, having sailed the Atlantic and safely reached port, thankfully rang 'finished with engines' and switched off the current in the de-gaussing coil. Immediately he did so his ship was blown up by a magnetic mine. . . .

The Germans continued to lay vertically-polarised mines, though of an increasing sophistication; the later types were bipolar, able to operate under the influence of either a north or south pole, and to counter de-gaussing they increased the sensitivity of their magnetic actuators. The Royal Navy was very grateful since this made the mines much easier to sweep. By the summer of 1940 the magnetic mine was, to all intents, beaten. After the war it became known that the Germans had come to the same conclusion: unused stocks of the early parachute mines were dropped on Britain during the 1940 Blitz as 'land mines'.

The Germans very soon developed an alternative to the magnetic mine. On the last day of August 1940 a motor launch exploded an unknown type of mine in the Firth of Forth. The next day the cruiser *Galatea* reported that a mine had exploded some distance ahead of her when she was near the Chequer Shoal Buoy in the Humber estuary. At about the same time several destroyers exploded mines up to half a mile away. The scientists at the Mine Design Department at HMS *Vernon* were not unduly surprised; they correctly assumed that the mysterious explosions were acoustic mines and waited for the German Air Force to present them with a specimen. In the meantime countermeasures were put into operation.

Since an acoustic mine was actuated by the sound of ships' propellers and engines, the obvious counter was to produce a sound effect that was stronger than the target's sound and thus trigger the mine. The destroyers, which had been steaming at above twenty knots, were unwittingly doing this; so was an unfortunate tramp steamer which blew itself up when starting a worn-out donkey engine to weigh anchor.

The first intentional counter to the acoustic mine was fitted to the trawler *Harwich*. The fish hold of the ship was filled with seawater and a pneumatic road drill was used to produce a loud hammering against a bulkhead; the result was that the *Harwich*, like HMS *Borde*, was badly shaken by the mines she exploded. Several other trawlers of the same class were used as acoustic sweepers and some were sunk by the mines they detonated.

Then the Luftwaffe, much to the anger of the German Navy, dropped acoustic mines in shoal waters and two were recovered intact – one off Cardiff and another in the Thames estuary. On examination at *Vernon* they were found to contain a reed which vibrated at 240 Hz per second: the vibrations were picked up by a microphone, amplified, and used to detonate the priming charge. They were fitted with anti-sweeping devices – delay circuits that would ignore five or six ships and explode on 'hearing' the seventh – and also contained clocks that could be set to immobilise them for days or weeks.

As a countermeasure, minesweepers and merchant ships were given special hammer boxes which were towed at a safe distance from the vessel. These boxes contained a modified 'Kango' road-drill which beat on a metal diaphragm in contact with the water, spreading a wide spectrum of frequencies. It was very effective, exploding acoustic mines up to a mile away. (The record was five miles.)

As a result of the magnetic and acoustic mines, a great deal of knowledge was gained by the scientists who had to counter them and who had to be ready to counter any further developments that the enemy might use. The de-gaussing

A hammer box containing a Kango road-drill about to be lowered over the side of a minesweeper.

work had provided new information about the natural magnetism of ships, and the acoustic mine was similarly to lead to research into just what sounds ships make. At Innellan on the Clyde a station was set up with a number of hydrophones to analyse the entire spectrum of underwater sound made by ships. The results were surprising: although, as expected, the propeller produced most of the sound, it covered a much larger range than at first supposed – from 1 Hz to 100 kHz. The unexpectedly low-frequency sound was caused by the bearings of the propeller shafts. Armed with the analysis of the possible range of ships' sounds, Admiralty scientists were ready for any variation the Germans could use.

Research into a possible third type of influence mine, the pressure mine, was also undertaken. This was detonated by the pressure-waves caused by a ship passing over it in shallow water. The work was a precaution since, at the time of the investigation, no German pressure mine was known to exist. The research was to prove timely, however, since shortly after D-day, on 14 June 1944, an Enigma intercept revealed that the Germans were about to lay an unidentified type of mine to try to stem the flow of supplies to the armies in Normandy. Five days later the Luftwaffe once again delivered two intact specimens to the Royal Navy, this time by dropping them on dry land occupied by Allied troops.

Within twenty-four hours the mines were being examined at *Vernon*. They proved to be pressure mines and by 22 June their secrets were known: they worked on a pressure difference equivalent to one inch of water. The counter was simple; since the pressure variation caused by a ship is proportional to the square of the speed of the vessel, all that had to be done was to decrease the speed of ships when in water of less than 25 fathoms. The actual figure depended on the size of the ship and the depth of water. Typical figures for 10–15 fathoms were:

Ships over 15,000 tons:	6 knots
Destroyers:	12 knots
Smaller craft:	no restrictions.

Although the pressure, or 'Oyster' mines as they were known, would have been difficult to sweep, the Atlantic swell did it very effectively and they failed to disrupt the flow of supplies.

Of the three basic types of non-contact mines, the magnetic was by far the most effective, causing serious losses and diverting much effort to counter it; yet it *was* countered, as were the other later types. The actual science involved could have been found in a school textbook; what was important was the way in which this elementary science was applied – service officers, civilian and uniformed scientists, and industry combining efficiently and singlemindedly to one end. The countering of the magnetic mine was the first example of how narrow the margin between victory and defeat was to be in fighting the Secret War, and the early recognition that the scientist was to play an increasingly important role in warfare.

The Giants of Leipheim

In the autumn of 1940 it seemed to the German people that the war was as good as won: a not unreasonable supposition. Much of Europe – Poland, Norway, the Low Countries and France – was under German occupation; Britain, it was true, remained undefeated, but that surely was only a question of time. Meanwhile the victorious troops were coming home: fifteen divisions were demobilised; peace – on German terms – was at hand.

Behind the parades and the cheering crowds, however, the prospect of peace was not all that immediate. The Luftwaffe's failure to smash the RAF during the Battle of Britain had forced Hitler to postpone Operation Sealion, the invasion of Britain, until the successful completion of Operation Barbarossa, the invasion of Russia. Hitler was convinced that the crushing of the Soviet Union could be accomplished in a lightning campaign and then he would be free to turn his undivided attention to his primary objective: Britain.

The original plans for Sealion, drawn up in the summer of 1940, had assumed that the RAF would be no match for the Luftwaffe and that total air superiority would have been quickly established over the Channel and the bridgeheads on the south coast of England. Clearly, in the light of the heavy losses inflicted on the Luftwaffe, plans for any future Sealion venture would require extensive revision. German staff planners concluded that the only hope of success lay in an overwhelming initial assault with heavy artillery, tanks and thousands of fully-armed troops.

Unlike the Luftwaffe, the German Navy did not make the mistake of under-estimating their opponents; they stated flatly that they could not guarantee to land the required forces in the face of Royal Navy opposition. So a bold decision was taken: the heavy assault guns, tanks and men would be landed as an *airborne* force. To achieve this, an armada of hundreds of the largest gliders ever built would carry the invading armies.

The concept of a glider-borne assault force was entirely German and had first been revealed to astonished military observers earlier in 1940 during the fighting in Belgium. At dawn on 10 May, forty-one DFS 230 gliders, towed behind Junkers Ju52s, crash-landed airborne troops who then successfully stormed the Eben-Emael forts, and took three vital bridges which were held until the arrival of the ground forces.

The gliders were cheaply made and expendable; each carried nine fully-armed men and was able to land precisely and silently behind enemy lines. The success of the DFS 230s made a profound impression on military thinking the world over and was to lead to the formation of Allied glider-airborne forces, which culminated in the Arnhem action. The biggest impression, however, was made on the Germans themselves, for immediately following the Belgian action the Reichluftfahrtministerium, which had previously been sceptical about the use of gliders, ordered the Gotha Go242, which could carry up to twenty-one fully-equipped troops or some 15,000 lbs of cargo.

A DFS 230 glider.

A Gotha Go242
glider.

That was only a beginning. For the postponed invasion of Britain a specification was issued for a truly amazing aircraft, a Grossraumlastensegler –
Giant Transport Glider – which was to be capable of carrying a PzKW IV
tank, or a self-propelled assault gun, complete with crew, fuel and ammunition, or an 88-mm anti-aircraft piece plus its towing vehicle, or no less than
200 fully-armed men.

The specifications for the giant gliders were issued within days of the
official postponement of Sealion in mid-October 1940. The Messerschmitt
and Junkers Companies were the concerns chosen. Considering the nature of
the undertaking, it is doubtful whether any rival firms objected to being left

254

out: the programme, coded rather strangely Operation Warsaw, called for detailed design studies to be submitted by 1 November, which gave the design staff just fourteen days. Materials sufficient for 100 machines were to be acquired immediately by both factories.

Messerschmitt were instructed to build their gliders out of welded tubular steel, fabric-covered. Junkers, however, who had been pioneers in the construction of all-metal aircraft, were required to manufacture an entirely wooden glider. The Junkers directors vainly pointed out that they lacked any woodworking machinery, that they knew next to nothing about wooden aircraft, and that they had no skilled woodworking labour. The pleas fell on deaf ears and the Ju322 Mammut (Mammoth) began to take shape.

From the outset it was doomed: aircraft-quality timber and glues were practically unobtainable; bitter arguments developed between the design team and everyone else in the factory. Somehow a design was submitted on time to the Luftwaffe Technischen Amt. It resembled a huge bat and no doubt many at the Junkers concern fervently hoped that it would be turned down. No such luck: a telegram was immediately received demanding that production should commence at once – with double the initial quantity of 100 machines.

The prototype Mammut emerged with a 203' 5" wingspan. Generaloberst Ernst Udet inspected the incredible aircraft just before its flight trials and stated bleakly that, if it ever got into the air, it would be virtually unflyable, being, as he put it, 'as unstable as an autumn leaf'. He was to be proved absolutely correct.

The Mammut's maiden 'flight' in March 1941 was possibly one of the most expensive in the history of aviation. Three miles of forest had to be cleared from the end of the Junkers airfield at Mersburg. A four-engined Ju90, dragging the Mammut, staggered into the air using every inch of available runway. Almost as soon as they cleared the ground, the pilot of the Mammut was in trouble; so was the pilot of the tow plane. As Ernst Udet had predicted, severe stability problems made the huge glider all but uncontrollable. It reared above the straining Ju90, which was only just able to remain airborne by diving steeply; disaster seemed unavoidable when the pilot of the wayward behemoth dropped the tow and managed to pancake safely in a large meadow. There it lay for two weeks, before it was ignominiously towed back to the airfield by the two tanks which it was intended to carry. There were some rather half-hearted attempts to fly it again but, to the relief of the test pilots and all concerned, the Air Ministry cancelled the project. By that time there were ninety mammoths under construction; what could be done with them? The answer was simple; the carpenters recruited for the building of the gliders merely sawed them up into small blocks of firewood. The firewood had cost 45 million Reichsmarks.

Meanwhile, at the Messerschmitt factory at Leipheim near Ulm, the other half of Operation Warsaw was faring much better. It was true they had the advantage of working with construction methods they understood, and the head of the design team, Oberingenieur Josef Fröhlich was able to submit a much more conventional design. Willie Messerschmitt himself sketched the general outlines, and the proposals were submitted on 6 November 1940 and accepted with, as before, the instruction to double the order to 200 and start work at once.

An army of workers, including defaulters from Luftwaffe Penal Battalions, commenced work and in just fourteen weeks the prototype was rolled out for testing. It was an impressive sight with some novel features, including a clamshell cargo door – common enough now, but first used on the Messerschmitt

Professor Messerschmitt's drawing of the Gigant proposal which envisaged four Ju52 transports as the tow. The German words are R = Rolle (pulley), Landekufe (landing skid) and abwerfbarer Wagen (jettisonable dolly).

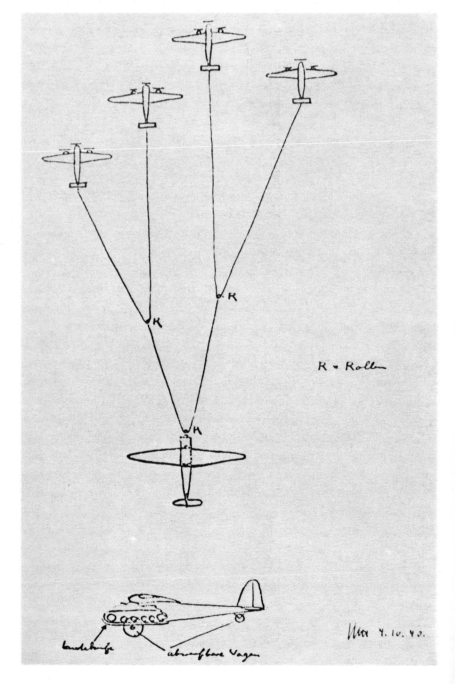

glider. The airframe, apart from its size, was conventional, the high wing braced by struts and the single cockpit – over sixty feet above the runway – located in the centre section. The glider – the word seems somehow inadequate – was designed to land on sprung skids, but for take-off purposes there was a jettisonable undercarriage of two very large Ju90 main wheels, with two smaller Me110 main wheels in front. These front wheels were free to castor to ease ground handling. The all-up weight of the undercarriage alone was over two tons.

The Me321 was named, appropriately enough, Gigant (Giant) and it was

The prototype Gigant is wheeled out. Its size can be seen from the figures round the undercarriage.

A Czech-built Pz IV tank about to climb the ramp into the 321 during tests.

The four tons of brick ballast being loaded into the Gigant. Note the clam-shell doors.

The single-seater cockpit of a Gigant. The vital trim wheel is on the pilot's left.

Opposite
For its initial test flights the Gigant was towed behind a Ju90. These pictures show a take-off sequence.

Top left: With the 'R-Geräte' rockets going full blast the huge aircraft roars along the Leipheim runway.

Top right: The pilot is now committed to flight.

Middle left: Although the main undercarriage is still firmly on the ground, the front wheels are just clear.

big: its wingspan of 180 feet was only slightly shorter than a present-day Boeing 747 Jumbo, and it weighed no less than forty tons: it was, in 1940, the second largest aircraft in the world (after the ANT–20, see page 265). As the prototype was wheeled out, eleven further Gigants were nearing completion and a further sixty-two were under construction. To achieve all that in just fourteen weeks was magnificent; but would it fly?

The man to whom the unenviable task fell to find out was Flugkapitän Bauer, an experienced glider pilot. For its maiden flight the Gigant carried a mere four tons of brick ballast inside its cargo hold, which had a capacity of 3800 cubic feet and a floor stressed to take a load of 44,000 lbs. It was 21 February 1941 when Bauer, in the prototype, was towed by a caterpillar tractor to the end of the mile-long concrete runway that was considered a minimum for take-off. That day the single-seat, narrow cockpit, high above

the runway, must have been just about the loneliest place on earth. The take-off would be marginal for, although the glider was as lightly loaded as possible, the only aircraft available with any hope of towing it into the air was the Ju90, one of the few four-engined aircraft the Luftwaffe possessed. This aircraft was considered to be underpowered when just flying itself, so the design staff had thoughtfully provided up to eight 'R-Geräte' (hydrogen peroxide rocket-assisted take-off units, which each delivered 1102 lbs thrust for thirty seconds), fitted beneath the Gigant's wings, and which could be parachuted to earth when the glider was airborne. The rockets would be lit as the Gigant got under way along the runway.

The Ju90 just managed to drag the glider into the air for its first flight. It was a most impressive sight – the Ju90 flat out and the rockets going full blast with smoke, flame and noise blinding and deafening the anxious observers on the

Middle right: The main wheels about to lift. To their left are the jettison cables.

Bottom left: The Ju90 claws for height. The Gigant has already jettisoned the main undercarriage, though the front wheels are still attached.

Bottom right: Made it! The Gigant glides over the airfield.

ground. After this Wagnerian departure and, with the glider airborne, the first hurdle cleared, the second now presented itself: dropping the two-ton main undercarriage. This called for fine judgment: if jettisoned too soon it could jam under the fuselage, or rebound and hit the glider, causing possible fatal damage; yet it needed to be jettisoned as early as possible to reduce drag. All went well and the first Gigant slowly climbed out at some 100 mph. The Ju90 dropped the tow at around 2000 feet and the 321 made a wide circuit of the Leipheim airfield at a majestic 87 mph.

That first flight lasted just twenty minutes; it may well have seemed longer to Bauer, who quickly discovered that the controls were practically immovable – scarcely surprising since they were all manual and the elevators alone had an area greater than the wings of a sizable light aircraft. By flying on the trimmers the Gigant was brought in for a successful landing, the pilot loyally reporting that the flight characteristics were surprisingly good, but adding that the controls were a little on the heavy side and suggesting that a wider cockpit, with a copilot to help with the pushing and pulling, would make things somewhat easier up front. This not unreasonable suggestion was adopted, though not until the 101st production aircraft.

Development flights continued and various pilots were invited to fly the prototypes. The captain of the fifth flight, the redoubtable woman test pilot Hanna Reitsch, struck a critical note in her report and remembers to this day that in her opinion the Gigant was

'impossible. It was so primitive because it in reality had to make only one flight – then it was finished. They couldn't be brought back. It was so

Hanna Reitsch, the only woman to fly the Gigant.

difficult to fly: you needed so much strength and what was too hard for me on a five-minute flight would be too much for a strong man on a one-hour flight.

'I tried using this argument to convince Udet that the project should be dropped, but he didn't believe me because Messerschmitt had said: "She is only a little girl, not a strong fighting man, so don't pay any attention to her".'[2]

They did not, but they ought to have done. It was obvious that the Ju90 was seriously underpowered and incapable of towing the Gigants operationally. The tow pilots were reporting that they could barely keep flying speed; on take-off the air-cooled BMW radial engines were seriously overheating.

Udet then made the radical suggestion of joining two Heinkel 111 twin-engined bombers together, and adding a fifth engine. This became the Zwilling or twin. It was calculated that the He111Z would be able to tow a fully-laden Gigant at over 130 mph. Construction of several Zwillings was put in hand but it would take some time before they could be operational; meanwhile the question of a suitable towing aircraft was assuming crisis proportions.

When Professor Willie Messerschmitt had first sketched his glider, he had proposed using four aircraft in formation to tow the Gigant. The possibility of such a system was examined and what emerged was the Troika-Schlepp – triple tow. Three Me110Cs, twin-engined fighters of a type that had been less than impressive during the Battle of Britain, were to be used, with three long 10-mm steel cables to enable the planes to tow in a V-formation.

One of the Me110 fighters used to tow the Gigant.

The Troika called for a great deal of skill on the part of the towing pilots. Early test flights were not encouraging and there were many accidents: on one training flight the three fighters were just towing the cables on their own in order to practise formation take-offs when one of the outer aircraft veered towards the centre machine, became entangled in its tow line, and both crashed.

Before towing off a Gigant, the Troika pilots trained by towing a three-engined Ju52 transport which had its outboard engines idling – just in case. As it happened it was a wise precaution, for hardly had the Troika got airborne when one of the three Me110s stalled and yawed to port. The Ju52 pilot immediately pulled the towline release and opened up the two engines; one of the towlines failed to jettison and the 300-ft steel cable thrashed about as the Junkers clawed for height on only two engines. It cut a wagon in half, scythed through farm buildings, hacked down several trees and finally wrapped itself round a telegraph pole which was uprooted from the ground. The sturdy Ju52 nearly stalled but somehow its pilot managed to keep airborne, landing safely still towing the heavy pole.

After that sort of rehearsal, the actual towing of the Gigant was clearly not a performance lightly to be undertaken. The take-off drill called for the Gigant to unstick first at about 55 mph; the two outer tow planes then left the ground, followed by the leader: the aim was to climb out at 80 mph. With forty tons behind them the two pilots had their hands full: the 110s were very close to stalling speed, and the slightest drop in power from the hard-pressed engines could lead to disaster – and disasters there were. On one

General Udet's suggestion of joining together two He111s, with the addition of a fifth engine, as an alternative to the Troika-Schlepp.

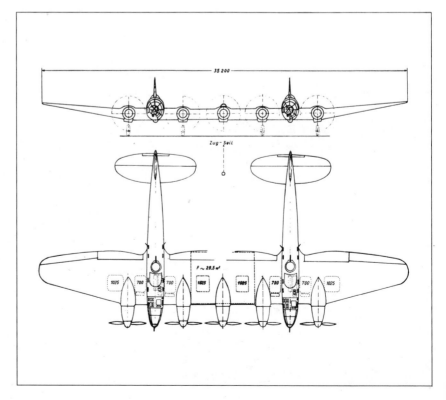

flight the Gigant pilot pulled his tow release and banked to starboard, a standard procedure for gliders; unfortunately one of the tow lines had not disconnected and an Me110 was snapped in half. Hanna Reitsch had a narrow escape on her second – and last – flight as a Gigant pilot. One of the tow planes lost power on take-off and dropped the tow; fortunately she still had the assisting take-off rockets firing, so she released the remaining tow planes and at a height of only 150 feet managed to make a heavy forced landing, on fortuitously downward-sloping ground.

Another test flight, made with a fully-loaded Gigant, established a grim record. As the glider was just airborne, the rockets on one side failed to ignite; the huge machine veered under asymmetric thrust, dragging the Troika together, and the three Me110s crashed into each other and dragged the Gigant down as well. The glider had been carrying troops and the death roll was 129 men, probably the world's worst aircraft disaster up to that time.

Undaunted by these events, production continued unabated with a second assembly line at Obertraubling. By the end of the summer of 1941 100 of the Me321A-1s had been delivered to the Luftwaffe and the B-1s with dual control were then nearing completion.

The Luftwaffe had formed units to fly the Gigant, but to where? The invasion of the British Isles, for which they had been conceived, was fast receding as the Russian campaign swallowed up more and more German forces. To help supply these huge armies, it was decided to use the Gigants as transports to the Eastern front, but almost at once this revealed serious shortcomings. Apart from the hair-raising problems it posed for the pilots, the

A Troika-Schlepp take-off sequence.

Below left: The take-off rockets were lit as soon as the Troika began to move.

Below right: Gathering speed down the Leipheim runway, passing further Gigants under construction.

Bottom left: Airborne. The Me110s would be very close to stalling: the R-Gerätes are expended but the take-off dolly has not yet been jettisoned.

Bottom right: A good illustration of the dangerously close formation of the Troika aircraft.

Troika-Schlepp had a maximum range of about 250 miles: more than adequate for Sealion but not for crossing the vast distances of Russia. The inevitable consequence was the need to stop to refuel: frequently.

The arrival of a number of 180-ft, 40-ton gliders on the overcrowded en route airfields caused chaos; they sat immobile on their skids, blocking the airfield runways until overworked and frozen ground crews could jack them up to fit wheeled undercarriages, enabling the aircraft to be moved. That of course was assuming that the undercarriages were available, to say nothing of stocks of R-Geräte units with their special and highly perishable fuels. All that every 250 miles. It was soon apparent that as an assault glider the Gigant might have been effective; as a transport it most certainly was not.

There were plans to use them on Operation Herkules, the invasion of Malta, towed by the Zwillings which were by then available; but Herkules was cancelled. Other plans included drops on Russian oilfields, ferrying troops to Sicily and, eventually, the relief of Stalingrad; but without fixed undercarriages they were simply impractical.

On a smaller scale, the Gotha 242 glider was facing the same problem. It, too, was being used as a cargo carrier and, in order to 'return the empties', there was a proposal simply to bolt two engines on the wing struts to enable it to fly back from the eastern front under its own power. The result was the Gotha Go244 – a powered version of the glider with a permanent under-

The shape of things to come. As the 321 unsticks it passes the first prototype of the powered version – the Me323C. The four engines were increased to six for the production version.

264

carriage and engines, capable of taking off and flying without difficulty when fully loaded.

If the scheme worked for Gotha, why not for Messerschmitt? The design staff at Leipheim were instructed to look into the possibilities of fitting the Me321 with a fixed undercarriage and four engines giving sufficient power to enable it to assist a take-off under tow, but to be able to sustain level flight at full load to its destination and then, when empty, to be able to take off under its own power to return to base. In the autumn of 1941 two Me321 gliders were converted into the first powered version: the Me323. The engines were Gnôme-Rhône 14-cylinder radials of the French Air Force, and an 8-wheeled undercarriage was designed to cope with rough airfields.

Although the two converted gliders came upto specification, it was soon decided to increase the number of engines to six, which would enable them to take off unaided at full weight, and thus avoid the hazards of the Troika-Schlepp and the need for specialised rocket fuels and trained men to service the R-Geräte. The Me323 was the second-largest powered aircraft in the world at that time. (Only the Russian Tupolev ANT–20 bis, with its incredible 260-ft wing span – 65 feet longer than a Boeing 747 – surpassed it.) With a twelve-man crew, including two flight engineers who sat in tiny compartments in the wings, it bristled with guns and was, at least on the Russian front, successful, lifting twelve tons of cargo for up to 500 miles. It was very slow,

Top: The Me323 on the ground and flying over the Eastern Front with its starboard inner engine feathered.

Bottom left: A Gotha Go244, the powered version of the earlier glider.

Bottom right: An ANT-20 bis, then the largest aircraft in the world.

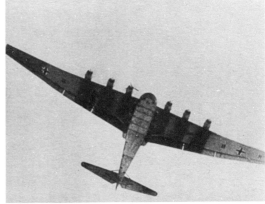

cruising at around 120 mph, and was plagued with engine overheating which, in view of the temperatures of the Russian winter, must have set up some kind of record. With redesigned engine cowls, however, it was used to supply not only the Eastern Front but also the Afrika Korps with guns, ammunition and petrol. The petrol was carried in 45-gallon steel drums which were appallingly vulnerable to fighter attack, many Gigants being shot down in flames over the Mediterranean.

The Luftwaffe then made a mistake that the USAAF 8th Air Force was to compound soon after. It was decided that if whole flights of 323s flew in formation their many guns – each machine carried up to twelve machine guns – could protect them from fighters. They could not. On 22 April 1943, sixteen Me323s took off from Trapani, Sicily, to fly fuel to Tunis. Near Cape Bon the formation was intercepted by RAF fighters and in the short battle that followed fourteen of the lumbering Gigants were ruthlessly shot down, mostly in flames. Of their 140 aircrew, only nineteen were rescued from the Mediterranean.

The 323 soldiered on. In all, 200 were built: useful transports when fighter opposition was slight, as in the early days over the Eastern Front. However, the German troops hated the so-called 'sticking plaster bomber'. They much preferred the corrugated-metal security of the Ju52s – Auntie Ju, as they called them.

The Gigants might seem today absurd anachronisms – particularly the glider. But if the timing of events had been only slightly different and if the gliders had been used in the assault role for which they had been designed, then 200 or so could have slipped silently out of some dawn sky at the time of Dunkirk to land 20,000 troops, 100 tanks and heavy artillery in the Weald of Kent, with little more than the rifles of the Home Guard to contain them.

The Great Panjandrum and Other Stories

Around the Devon town of Appledore, where the rivers Taw and Torridge converge to run into the Bristol Channel, there was stationed in 1943 the Combined Operations Experimental Establishment. COXE, as it was known, had been created to test and evaluate the various weapons and implements of war for the coming invasion of Europe.

The area was ideal: wide sandy beaches, which on occasion produced high surf; sheltered estuaries, some with steep shingle, others flat mud; there were rocks and sand dunes – everything that was required to test and develop the many strange devices that came to COXE.

The problems of mounting the biggest amphibious operation of all time were such that many were called and many were chosen; the market for the offerings of the smaller back rooms had never been so great. One of the most spectacular was the Great Panjandrum.

The Department of Miscellaneous Weapons Development, DMWD – known as the Wheezers and Dodgers, had been given the task of devising a method of breaching a concrete wall ten feet high and seven feet thick, which was said to be the first line of defence of the Atlantic Wall on the enemy coast. The beaches, it was pointed out, would certainly be mined and have obstacles and be covered by machine guns and artillery fire. One of the scientists working on this problem was Nevil Shute Norway, the well-known novelist, who was also an aerodynamicist; he had calculated that at least a ton of explosive would have to be placed at the foot of the wall to blow a hole wide enough for a tank to pass through. The question was how to get the explosive to the wall.

Various schemes were considered and turned down. Then one day an Air Force officer, a Group Captain Finch-Noyes, came from Combined Operations with a rough sketch of what was to become the Great Panjandrum. It was a bold concept: two 10-ft wheels with 1 ft-wide steel treads joined by a wide drum. The centre section would be packed with 4000 lbs of high explosive and round the circumference of each wheel there would be a number of cordite rockets which would propel the whole thing at 60 mph off a landing craft, through the surf and, indifferent to obstacles and mines, up the beach to the wall. There the wheels would collapse and the explosive would be detonated.

Within a month the prototype had been constructed in great secrecy at Leytonstone in north-east London. With equal secrecy it was transported under cover of darkness to Appledore. Strangely, in view of this secrecy, when it arrived at the Devon seaside resort it was simply rolled off its transporter on to the beach in full view of a large number of holidaymakers.

The beach chosen for the initial tests was Westward Ho and the trials which began on 7 September 1943 were to enliven many a drab wartime holiday for the watching crowds. For the maiden run the explosive drum was ballasted with 4000 lbs of sand and, since the behaviour of Panjandrum under power was, to say the least, speculative, a mere eighteen peripheral rockets were used. With some trepidation, Norway pressed the electrical firing button and with a roar the Great Panjandrum, all flame and smoke, thundered down the inclined ramp of the landing craft, forded the water in clouds of steam and rolled on to the beach. For a time it kept a straight course, then two rockets failed on one side and the machine swung away to the right, described a circle, and stopped in a dense cloud of smoke. It was underpowered.

The number of rockets was doubled and the next day the landing craft carried the Panjandrum to Instow beach on the Torridge estuary. Again it charged into the water, again rockets failed and, although it did travel about twice as far as on the first run, it was still considered to be underpowered. A third wheel was added to increase the number of rockets. The next test was pure farce: the three-wheeled Panjandrum was set up on a wooden ramp near the low-tide mark; unfortunately, when the firing button was pressed, nothing happened and, while the fault was being sought with ever-increasing urgency, the tide was inexorably coming in. The Panjandrum was slowly engulfed; when the tide ebbed and the machine was salvaged, the third wheel on which all hope rested had collapsed. The team went back to London and their drawing boards.

Three weeks later they returned with a new Panjandrum and more runs were made, now powered by more than seventy rockets. The display was sensational: down the ramp it roared, through the sea, hurling spray and steam high into the air. Then, just as it was about to run up the beach it suddenly turned back into the sea, overturning and detaching live rockets which zoomed over the sands, while the remaining rockets exploded underwater, sending up jets of high-pressure steam. Undaunted, the team once again salvaged the wreckage. They now reverted to a two-wheeled version with a rudimentary form of remote steering, consisting of long steel cables, with a breaking strain of a ton, rigged from either side of Panjandrum to winches on the beach. Norway was in charge of the winch brakes as the Panjandrum ran along the wet beach, working up to over 60 mph. Almost at once it began to veer off course; as Norway applied a touch of the port brake to correct the turn, the cable snapped like cotton and 2000 feet of steel wire came snaking over the heads of the onlookers.

The tests continued: with heavier cables, more rockets, fewer rockets, different treads to the wheels; but the results were depressingly consistent. Due to centrifugal force, at speeds over 50 mph some of the 20-lb rockets would become detached, usually taking two or three adjacent ones with them. As the rockets each gave 40 lbs of thrust for 40 seconds, they roared over the beach at very high speeds in quite unpredictable directions. The team spent several weeks trying various modifications to improve the rocket clamps and solve the steering problem when, to their great relief, DMWD were informed by Combined Operations that absolute accuracy was no longer essential; all Panjandrum had to achieve was to head in the general direction of the enemy.

It was in early January 1944 that the final trials took place. An impressive assembly of Whitehall Warriors and scientists had gathered at Westward Ho to decide on the fate of the Great Panjandrum which was waiting on board its landing craft, just offshore. The well-known prewar motor-racing photographer, Luis Klemantaski, was on hand to film the event; also present among the less distinguished observers was an Airedale dog named Ammonal, which was about to gain immortality.

At first all went well. Panjandrum rolled into the sea and began to head for the shore, the Brass Hats watching through binoculars from the top of a pebble ridge. Accelerating across the beach, the two gigantic catherine wheels were wreathed in bright jets of fire: to Klemantaski behind his ciné camera it seemed to be doing 100 mph. Then a clamp gave: first one, then two more rockets broke free; Panjandrum began to lurch ominously. It hit a line of small craters in the sand and began to turn to starboard, careering towards Klemantaski, who, viewing events through a telescopic lens, misjudged the distance and continued filming. Hearing the approaching roar he looked up from his viewfinder to see Panjandrum, shedding live rockets in all directions, heading straight for him. As he ran for his life, he glimpsed the assembled admirals and generals diving for cover behind the pebble ridge into barbed-wire entanglements.

Panjandrum was now heading back to the sea but crashed on to the sand where it disintegrated in violent explosions, rockets tearing across the beach at great speed – one pursued by the splendid Airedale, Ammonal – a scene which Klemantaski, returning to his still-running camera, was able to catch. It survives in the archives of the Imperial War Museum to this day. It seems somehow a very English end to Panjandrum.

'Panjandrum enlivened many a drab wartime holiday.'

It was the end, of course. Conversation between the Weezers and Dodgers and the Brass Hats was limited after they had been extricated from the barbed wire. The official reason for dropping the idea was the damage Panjandrum could do if one broke loose in transit on board its landing craft. But there remains a mystery surrounding the Great Panjandrum. Was it ever intended to be used or was it, as some writers have suggested, a hoax – part of the plans to delude the Germans into thinking that the invasion would be in the Pas de Calais, which was the strongest part of the Atlantic Wall where Panjandrum might just conceivably have been used, rather than the much less heavily fortified Normandy beaches where the actual landings were made? The lack of security at Appledore lends colour to the hoax idea. Sir Charles Goodeve, who was Head of DMWD (though he had left by the time of Panjandrum), simply says he does not know, though adding: 'We did test much more unlikely things than Panjandrum.'[3]

That is hard to believe.

To be fair, many of the weapons evaluated and developed by COXE were highly successful and played a vital role on D-Day and thereafter. There was, for instance, a series of highly unusual Armoured Fighting Vehicles (AFVs), known as Hobart's Funnies after their ingenious designer, Major General Percy Hobart of 79th Armoured Division. Hundreds of his 'DD' (Duplex Drive) Sherman tanks were used in the Normandy invasion. These tanks had been provided with high, collapsible canvas screens and water propellers; with the screens erected and the propellers engaged the tank could 'swim' ashore from the landing craft. The freeboard, however, was critical, being only two or three inches: in any sort of a seaway they could be swamped and sunk in seconds.

Hobart's Funnies included tanks that could lay bridges, cross soft patches of sand, and one type carried a mortar that could throw an explosive charge the size of a domestic dustbin against enemy strongpoints. But perhaps the best known of these specialised vehicles was the 'Crab' or Flail tank – a Churchill or Sherman with a revolving drum at the front which carried a number of steel chain flails to clear a path for infantry through minefields. These tanks alone saved hundreds of lives in Normandy and beyond.

Pluto – *Pipe Line Under The Ocean* – was a scheme to supply petrol directly from the south coast of England to the beach-heads. The planners had estimated that no fewer than 14,000 vehicles would be landed on D-Day itself, a figure that by D + 12 would have reached 95,000. To transport the fuel for that number would have required tankers to sail with the invasion fleets and few more vulnerable targets could be imagined. The solution was Pluto. Tested on a small scale between Swansea and Ilfracombe, it was duly laid under the Channel, the pumps being concealed in bombed buildings at various seaside towns in England. Though there were considerable difficulties initially, eventually Pluto was able to supply petrol direct from storage tanks in Liverpool to the Rhine.

Apart from petrol, the logistics of the invasion required a port facility to land 12,000 tons of supplies and 2500 vehicles a day. The capture of a port intact was out of the question, since it would either be destroyed in the fighting or by the retreating enemy and would take several weeks to clear. The answer was to transport two large ports with the invasion fleet: Operation Mulberry.

Churchill had foreseen the need for such ports in 1942; the man who actually came up with the solution was Commodore John Hughes-Hallet. It was a massive undertaking: 200 submersible cassions, made of reinforced concrete 60 feet high and displacing 6000 tons, were constructed along the Medway and Thames, using a million tons of poured concrete and 70,000 tons of steel. Two Mulberry ports were built: an American one for Utah beach and a British one for Gold beach at Arromanches. Capable of accommodating the 23-ft Normandy tides and berthing 26 ft-draught Liberty ships, they were towed across the Channel by a fleet of 150 tugs at $4\frac{1}{2}$ knots, and the first section was placed in position at Arromanches on D+1, 7 June.

Unfortunately on D+13 one of the worst gales in the Channel for many years wrecked the Utah Mulberry and left the British one, which was in a slightly more sheltered position, badly damaged but repairable. Until Cherbourg was captured on 27 June, the shortage of harbour facilities hindered operations, but without the use of the Mulberry the initial Normandy break-out would have been next to impossible.

The Phantom Fleet

Throughout all the planning for the invasion of Europe, one requirement was uppermost: to keep the enemy guessing the location of the main attack. For many reasons the Calais area was the most obvious and was the one the German staff considered the most probable. It was vital that this belief be continued, even after the landing in Normandy had been made. To achieve this, Operation Fortitude was mounted: a phantom invasion fleet sailing towards Calais.

Fortitude was a gigantic electronic hoax devised by Dr Robert Cockburn of TRE. In January 1944 he had been asked to simulate a major landing force heading for Boulogne and Dieppe. The easiest solution would have been simply to use ships, but the actual invasion was taking all the maritime resources available so it had been decided to try electronic methods.

Cockburn first found out from R. V. Jones's Scientific Intelligence files the location and type of every known German radar in Northern France. With this information, from March 1944 until D-Day the Second Tactical Air Force flew some two thousand sorties against the German coastal defence radar network; all the early warning sets in the Normandy area were put out of action, but in the Calais region a dozen or so were left operational – intentionally. These radars would be the ones that would plot the 'spoof' invasion: an Armada consisting of tens of thousands of strips of 'Window'

dropped from aircraft to simulate an invasion force covering 250 square miles of the Channel.

To achieve this called for extremely precise flying. Two experienced squadrons from RAF Bomber Command, No. 617 – the famous Dam Busters – flying Lancasters and No. 218 with Stirlings, had to fly, at night, elliptical orbits eight miles by two in exactly seven minutes, then advance a mile and fly another seven-minute orbit. The big bombers had to keep accurate formation and drop twelve bundles of Window each minute. As clouds of the aluminium foil floated down, the effect on the surviving German radar was exactly the same as a seaborne invasion fleet sailing towards them at eight knots.

Other aircraft flew around the 'phantom fleet' with powerful 'Mandrel' radar jammers, but these jammers were so disposed to leave just enough clear space on the enemy screens for them to detect the 'fleets'. Meanwhile the actual invasion area was completely blacked out by intense 'barrage' jamming, in case any operational radar had survived the pre-invasion air attacks.

To supplement Window fourteen RAF Air Sea Rescue launches sailed beneath the bombers, each flying a 30-ft naval barrage balloon with a large radar reflector inside the gas envelope. These balloons, nicknamed Filberts, returned echoes to German radars equivalent to 10,000-ton ships. In addition, four of the launches were fitted with a radar transponder, coded 'Moonshine', which, when interrogated by enemy radar pulses, returned a very large echo simulating a big ship.

To co-ordinate this complex spoof would have been difficult enough if there had been only one phantom fleet: there were in fact two. 218 Squadron plus three Moonshine boats and six Filberts formed the 'Glimmer' fleet, apparently heading for Boulogne, and 617 Squadron with the remainder headed for Cap d'Antifer: this 'fleet' was coded 'Taxable'.

Glimmer and Taxable were kept on course by radar navigation aids. 617's Lancasters used Gee and the Stirlings of 218 used a refinement of Gee called GH, in some respects similar to Oboe but with the advantage that several aircraft could use it simultaneously. The two spoof fleets 'sailed' on D-Day and for four hours kept up the deception. No German night fighters appeared, much to the relief of Cockburn, who not unnaturally had been worried that they might blow the whole operation.

As a final touch, other squadrons flew bombers on Operation Titanic, an apparent airborne assault on Cap d'Antifer and Caen. These Halifaxes and Stirlings also dropped Window to enhance the size of the force on the German radar screens. Over the fake dropping zones, pyrotechnics were dropped to give the sound effects of a small-arms battle on the ground, and parties of parachute troops from the Special Air Service also dropped with the sole object of creating the noise of battle.

Meanwhile, cloaked by an intense radar-jamming barrage – over 200 of the warships carried radar jammers – the real Armada was approaching Normandy. Postwar interrogation revealed that only one German radar station managed to plot the real invasion Armada, but by then the enemy was in confusion and, like the early radar warning of the approaching Japanese attack on Pearl Harbor, it too went unheeded.

No one can say how many lives were saved by Operation Fortitude on D-Day, but, for all its electronic brilliance, it would of course have been impossible – as would the actual invasion – without one essential requirement: total air superiority. The Window-dropping squadrons flew for four hours at 180 mph, as close as ten miles from the enemy coast, yet not one of the aircraft was intercepted, though they were plotted by German radar. Even in daylight the Luftwaffe was unable to inflict any significant losses on the great air Armada of slow transports and bombers.

It could have been a different story if the Germans had been able to capitalise on the undoubted lead they had over the Allied Air Forces in the design and development of a new form of air warfare.

The Jet Fighter

The jet-propelled Messerschmitt Me262 was at one time at least two years ahead of any possible rival, yet that lead, established in 1942, had been frittered away by the direct intervention of Hitler.

The story begins in the mid-1930s, when it was becoming apparent to a few far-sighted men that the theoretical limit of the piston engine/propeller form of aircraft propulsion would soon be attained at high altitudes. A young Royal Air Force officer, Flight Lieutenant Frank Whittle, was one of these men; another was Hans-Joachim Pabst von Ohain, then an obscure assistant to an aerodynamics professor at the University of Göttingen.

In the spring of 1936 von Ohain had interested Ernst Heinkel in the possibilities of a gas-turbine aircraft engine. Heinkel took the young engineer on to his staff and gave him the backing to build an engine – the HeS2A – which first ran on the test bed in September 1937. The purely experimental engine was, within its limits, successful although the output was only 176 lbs of thrust.

A practical flight engine was then built and developed as the HeS3A, offering just over 1000 lbs thrust. This engine was installed in a specially designed airframe, the Heinkel He178, which, piloted by Erich Warsitz, made the world's first jet-powered flight from the Heinkel Company's airfield at Marienehe on 27 August 1939.

Several flights were made and in November 1939 the small experimental aircraft was demonstrated to General Udet, but he was sceptical of the new-found propulsion as a practical power-plant for the Luftwaffe. In spite of this Heinkel continued development work on both engines and airframes, and the first practical jet fighter, the twin-engined He280, which was also the first ever to be fitted with an ejector seat, was designed by his company. It was first

The ill-fated Heinkel 280 which never went into production.

flown on 2 April 1941 and demonstrated to Udet and Dipl. Ing. Lucht, Chief Engineer of the Luftwaffe, three days later, when the prototype attained a maximum speed of 485 mph at nearly 20,000 feet.

The average speed of contemporary piston-engined fighters was around 350 mph, but Udet again questioned the Luftwaffe's need for jet aircraft and, although nine prototype He280s were flown, it was never put into quantity production. This lack of interest might partly have stemmed from Heinkel's personal unpopularity with Udet and his successor, General Milch. In the event the rival Messerschmitt Company received contracts, under the title of 'Projekt 1065', to construct a jet fighter, the Me262.

By that time Messerschmitt was already involved with an earlier project – the rocket-powered fighter, the Me163, which was the result of a somewhat unwilling ménage à trois between Alexander Lippisch, a brilliant designer of small, tail-less delta-wing gliders, Hellmuth Walter, who had produced a very efficient, small, lightweight, liquid-fuelled rocket engine, and the Messerschmitt Company. The team had built an unpowered, small delta airframe to investigate, on the lowest priority, the possibility of a rocket-powered interceptor fighter. Designated Me163, it was first tested as a glider; after some initial trouble with flutter of the rudder and ailerons, it performed extremely well with a gliding angle of 1 : 20, which was practically in the pure sports sailplane class.

The flights were made by a Messerschmitt test pilot, Heini Dittmar. One day in the summer of 1940, having been towed to an altitude of 16,000 feet, he was gliding back to the factory airfield at Augsburg, which General Udet was by chance visiting. He dived the small delta steeply towards the airfield and zoomed past the General at some 400 mph, pulling the glider into a near-vertical climb before coming down to a perfect landing. On this occasion Udet *was* impressed. 'What engine has that plane got?' he enquired; told it was unpowered and learning of the proposal to fit a rocket engine when a higher order of priority could be obtained, he immediately ordered that it should be done – in spite of a 1940 order of Hitler's that all research which would take longer than eighteen months to complete was to be shelved.

The powered flights of the Me163A could not, on security grounds, be made from Augsburg, so the aircraft was taken to Peenemunde West (Karlshagen) for the rocket-powered trials, which took place in the summer of 1941. The engine used for the early flights was the Walter HWK R11 203, which gave a thrust of 1653 lbs, enabling Dittmar easily to exceed the then world speed record of 469.22 mph. That record was broken on the fourth flight, when he achieved 571.78 mph. (Naturally wartime security prevented the new record being claimed.)

The flying characteristics of the aircraft were considered excellent, though the take-off was from a two-wheeled dolly which had to be jettisoned and the landing was made on a sprung skid. The biggest shortcoming, however, was the very limited duration of the rocket motor, which was just long enough for a climb to 13,000 feet and a short level flight; when the fuel was exhausted, the 163 had to glide back to base. Since high-speed runs at altitude had been terminated by the fuel running out while the 163 was still accelerating, Dittmar suggested that, if the aircraft was towed to altitude, there would be enough fuel to discover the true maximum speed. Lippisch had calculated it would be in excess of 1000 km/hr, which in those days had the same, almost mystical unattainability as the four-minute mile. Accordingly, on 2 October 1941 Dittmar was towed off the Peenemunde airfield by a Messerschmitt Bf110 and cast off at 13,000 feet; he lit the rocket engine and the 163A accelerated to an unbelievable 623.85 mph – 1002 km/hr or Mach .84.

During that flight, by far the fastest level speed ever attained, Dittmar experienced the effects of 'compressibility', later to be popularly known as the 'sound barrier'. He reported:

'My airspeed indicator was soon reading 910 km/hr and kept on increasing, soon topping the 1000 km/hr mark. Then the needle began to waver, there was a sudden vibration in the elevons and the next moment the aircraft went into an uncontrollable dive, causing high negative "G".

'I immediately cut the rocket and for a few moments thought that I had really had it at last!

'Then, just as suddenly, the controls reacted normally again and I eased the aircraft out of its dive.'[4]

Below left: Heini Dittmar immediately after his world speed record flight.

Below right: Dittmar's aircraft, the Me163A, takes off from Peenemunde in 1941 and (*bottom left*) climbs away at nearly 500 mph.

Bottom right: The prototype Me163A (left) compared with an early production 163B Komet.

Opposite
Top left: The
Walter HWK
109–509A rocket
engine.

Top right: A
somewhat anxious
Luftwaffe
serviceman,
protected to some
extent by special
clothing, fuels a 163
with T Stoff.

Middle left: The
entire rocket motor
had to be flushed
with clean water
before any engine
runs could be made.

Middle right: The
163 was not a
'throw-away'
fighter, as its
well-equipped
instrument panel
shows.

Bottom: Protected
by his special flying
suit, complete with
goggles and gloves,
a 163 pilot climbs
into his cockpit.

Dittmar was not the first pilot to experience the effects of compressibility. Fighter pilots on both sides had found that, when in high-speed power dives, strange buffetings and even the apparent reversal of controls took place. Dittmar was, however, the first pilot to experience it during level flight.

The German Air Ministry Technical Branch (*Technischen Amt*) were sceptical. Not without reason: their most advanced research wind tunnel could only achieve Mach .80. General Udet overruled the sceptics and on 22 October, less than a month before he inexplicably committed suicide, he approved an order for no less than seventy of the rocket planes, the Me163B, as preproduction prototypes for an armed fighter version for the Luftwaffe. It was planned that with these aircraft the Luftwaffe would have a rocket-fighter unit operational by the spring of 1943.

When Udet shot himself in November 1941 there was a danger that the project would die with him. Although his successor, Field Marshal Erhard Milch, confirmed the order, he reduced the priority, and it was not until February 1943 that the first powered flight of a 163B, or Beta, took place at Peenemunde, piloted by Rudolf Opitz. The development of the rocket fighter was slow and subject to disagreements between Lippisch and Willy Messerschmitt, which culminated in April 1943 with Lippisch leaving the Company and taking no further part in the project.

By then it was obvious that the war was far from over, and the small fighter offered a possible solution to the increasing problem of USAAF daylight bombing raids. Albert Speer, Hitler's minister for armaments, ordered that enough rocket fighters, now named Komet, should be produced to maintain 1000 aircraft in operational squadrons, for although its range was very short, it was cheap to make and could protect vital local targets, such as the synthetic oil refineries near Leipzig.

The first operational group, Erprobungskommando 16 (test detachment 16), was formed under an experienced fighter pilot, Hauptmann Wolfgang Späte, at Bad Zwischenahn, where their tactics against the USAAF bombers were worked out. When enemy bombers approached, a formation of Komets would take off, climbing nearly vertically at 440 mph, taking only 5 minutes 45 seconds to reach 37,000 feet; they would then level out and accelerate up to 560 mph, at which point they only had enough fuel remaining for about two minutes of powered flight. Directed by ground radar to a position 3000 feet above the American bombers, the formation would then dive into an attacking position, making simultaneous approaches from all points of the compass.

That, at any rate, was the theory: in practice the tactics fell considerably short of this ideal. For a start, there were many fatal accidents in training, mainly due to the highly temperamental fuel. The Komets were powered by a Walter HWK 109–509A rocket motor which gave an unbelievable 3307 lbs of thrust for a weight of only 366 lbs. The fuel was a mixture of C Stoff (57% Methyl alcohol, 30% Hydrazine Hydrate and 13% water) and T Stoff (an 80% concentration of Hydrogen Peroxide). Unfortunately, these two fuels were highly incompatible and, when mixed together, they decomposed in-

stantly into high-temperature gases with explosive force. Even fuelling a
Komet was a very dangerous operation. The two fuels were pumped into the
aircraft's separate tanks from road tankers, each clearly marked with large
Ts or Cs; they never came within half a mile of each other. First one would
drive up, deliver its Stoff, then everything including the airmen handling the
fuel was washed down with water (the one virtue these deadly liquids had
was that they were soluble in water). The tanker would then drive away and
the second tanker arrive. T Stoff was the more dangerous since it was capable

of spontaneous combustion when in contact with any organic substance. That ranged from a passing bee to the airmen.

The storage and handling of these fuels alone weighed heavily against the Komets ever becoming practical weapons of war. T Stoff could only be stored in tanks made of aluminium, anything else corroding away or bursting into flames; C Stoff could only be stored in glass containers, since it corroded practically everything else, especially aluminium. Training films were made for the guidance of Luftwaffe ground crews unfortunate enough to be attached to a Komet unit. One scene shows a single drop of T Stoff falling into a saucer of C; the result is a crack like a rifle shot. In another sequence, a rag has a small quantity of C Stoff poured on to it: within seconds it is blazing spontaneously. The slightest carelessness could and did have fatal results: one mechanic lost his life when pouring C Stoff into a container that had previously been used for T Stoff.

Starting engines fuelled with these murderous fluids must have been a tense moment: first, the entire rocket motor and jet pipe were flushed out with water from a high-pressure hose; then the pilot ran up a small electric pump which introduced a precise quantity of a catalyst, calcium permanganate and potassium chromate, to the T Stoff. This decomposed into high-pressure steam, driving the main pumps which delivered the two fuels in the correct ratio into the rocket's combustion chamber. Satisfied that the pressures were correct, the pilot gingerly opened the throttle, which had only five pre-set positions: off, idle, and three positions of thrust.

Take-off had to be from a smooth, paved runway and exactly into wind. It was, by all accounts, a wild ride. If the Komet did not explode as the throttle was opened wide for take-off (several did), the pilot would hold the aircraft on the runway until he rotated at 174 mph. Acceleration was tremendous, and the undercarriage had to be jettisoned before the speed rose too high, since the large wheels would cause severe turbulence. (On the other hand, if the undercarriage was released too soon, it could bounce up and hit the Komet.)

By the airfield boundary the Komet would be flying at nearly 500 mph; the pilot then pulled up into a near vertical climb at 440 mph. At this point the rocket often cut out; too low to bale out, all the pilot could do was to lower the landing skid and try to put down in the first field he saw. His chances of survival were almost nil: with its short length the Komet would usually overturn in a forced landing, and with full tanks the unstable fuel would explode immediately. Mano Ziegler, one of the few Komet pilots still alive, wrote of the result of a 163 engine failure he observed on take-off:[5]

'Anxiously we watched the Komet touch down far outside the airfield perimeter, rebound into the air, drop back again like a brick and then skid into some rough ground and turn over on its back. A split second later a blinding white flame shot up, followed by a mushroom of smoke.'

Not all crash landings resulted in an explosion, though the end was often, in some ways, even more horrifying. Again Ziegler was a witness:

'. . . Joschi's aircraft dropped like a stone, hit the airfield at an angle and skidded along the ground for some fifty metres before coming to a standstill. All this had taken place at least two kilometres from our flight line where we had been standing, and we ran as fast as our legs could carry us.

'. . . Surely it could not be too bad. At least there was no fire and no explosion. The fire engine and ambulance reached Joschi's machine within a minute of the crash, but our Joschi was no more. The T Stoff from fractured fuel lines had seeped into the cockpit and poor Joschi, probably unconscious as a result of hitting his head on the instrument panel, had been dissolved alive. . . .'

Even if all went well, the cockpit was liable to fill with steam, forcing the pilot into an instrument take-off. Nevertheless, the pilots found the Komet very exhilarating. Ziegler: 'Away I climbed like an express lift and I was reclining on my back with nothing around me but the infinite blue of the sky.' Hanna Reitsch too found the 163 'fascinating: it was like sitting on a cannon ball intoxicated by speed, climbing in one and a half minutes to 30,000 feet'.[6]

Once at 30,000 feet the rocket's fuel was soon exhausted, and the world's fastest fighter became the world's fastest glider – with an engineless landing in prospect. Tracked by radar, the pilots were guided home by radio, but even such brilliant glider pilots as Hanna Reitsch found the landing 'difficult'. The problems were many. In the first place, the approach speed, at nearly 140 mph, was very high for its day. Simple flaps were fitted but due to the exceptionally clean aerodynamic design the 163 seemed to float for ever, defying the pilot's efforts to get the speed down to 100 mph for touchdown. With a dead engine there was no 'going round again', no possibility of a burst of throttle to extend a badly judged approach: once committed to a landing, that was it. Even a perfectly executed touchdown could end in disaster; the spring skid had to be lowered, or the resultant shock on making contact with the grass airfields could result in crushed vertebrae. In addition, the tanks often contained unburnt fuel and several aircraft blew up following a heavy landing.

When all went well, the Komet finally came to a standstill leaning on one wingtip; it was then helplessly marooned in the middle of the airfield until a special tractor (the Scheuschlepper) came to recover it – a prime target for any Allied aircraft. In July 1944 and again in August the Komet base at Bad Zwischenann was bombed. On 16 August the Komets were formed into an operational unit, I/JG400, at Brandis, near Leipzig: their task was the protection of the Leuna synthetic oil plants, thirty miles from the base.

When tested in actual combat against the American bombers and their long-range fighter escorts, the shortcomings of the Me163 Komet as an interceptor fighter were starkly revealed. Their prime objective was the bombers, the 'Dicke Auto' ('fat bus') in Luftwaffe slang, but to get at the B17 Fortresses and B24 Liberators they had to avoid being themselves intercepted by the escorting Mustangs and Thunderbolts. To achieve this the Komets had to approach at around 580 mph, which meant they were overtaking the slow-flying American bombers by some 340 mph. Because of the high closing speeds the attack had to be broken off not less than 200 yards from the target, and since the maximum range of their 30-mm cannon was 650 yards, the fighters had only $2\frac{1}{2}$ seconds for the actual shooting for tail or beam attacks and one second for the head-on pass so much favoured by German piston-engined fighters. Only the most exceptional pilots could hope to make a hit and in fact very few actually did. JG400's best day was 24 August, when a section led by Oberfeldwebel (Staff Sergeant) Schubert claimed three B17s shot down. (Schubert brought back a gun-camera reel to prove his claim – the only Me163 victory known to exist on film.) He did not score another, for his Komet blew up on take-off shortly afterwards. A week later the only factory in Germany (at Kiel) producing C Stoff was bombed to the ground. Fuel from dumps was transported by rail but, with the dislocation caused by Allied bombing, it either did not arrive or took so long that it had deteriorated and was unusable.

Oberfeldwebel Schubert beside his Komet. The small propeller drove a generator for the radio.

The B17 which Schubert shot down. This is a frame from his gun-camera film, the only known pictorial evidence of a successful Komet attack.

In the last days of the war the surviving pilots of JG400 used what little fuel they had but only succeeded in damaging a single Mosquito. By March 1945 2000 Allied bombers were attacking the Reich in daylight and there was little any Luftwaffe unit could do. On 8 May JG400 surrendered to British forces. The forty-eight remaining Komets were divided between the Allies; of the 350 built, ten still survive in museums.

While the captured Komets were being examined at Farnborough and elsewhere, the Japanese were building a copy. Drawings and a pattern aircraft had been sent from Germany by U-boat in the spring of 1944 and the Mitsubishi concern produced the Japanese version, the J8M1 'Shusui' – or 'Rigorous Sword'. Its first powered flight was made on 7 July 1945. A faithful copy of the Me163, right down to its flying characteristics, it crashed on take-off due to engine failure.

The True Jet

The existence of the German experimental jet and rocket aircraft, which had been reported by Allied Intelligence, was confirmed by Photographic Reconnaissance. On 23 June 1943, a set of very clear prints of Karlshagen, the Luftwaffe airfield at Peenemunde, revealed four small tail-less delta-wing aircraft. Constance Babington Smith measured the wing span as 30 feet and, following the usual practice with unknown types, identified the aircraft simply as 'Peenemunde 30'. They were in fact Me163Bs.

More significant than the actual aircraft was the inclusion in her report of 'Evidence of Activity' at the airfield: [7]

'The airfield shows signs of considerable wear, and most of the track marks are of the kind normally made by the wheels of aircraft. There are, however, a few tracks of an unusual kind, leading from points near the hangar and the small buildings where the tail-less aircraft are seen towards the centre of the airfield. Each of these tracks is a fairly well defined dark streak, originating in most cases from a discoloured patch, and gradually fading out.

'These tracks appear to be of various lengths between 100 and 200 yards. . . .

'It may be of interest to note that photographs of Augsburg taken on 20 June showed several pairs of discoloured patches on the airfield, rather similar to those at Peenemunde.'

These streaks were correctly interpreted as being made by jet aircraft taking off or running up their engines on a grass airfield. The first reaction was an immediate photo-reconnaissance of *British* airfields where jet prototypes were being tested, and similar marks were found, particularly clear examples being photographed at Boscombe Down.

The twin marks discovered at the Messerschmitt factory airfield at Augsburg were almost certainly made by the Me262, shortly to become the world's first operational jet fighter. Work on this advanced aircraft began

Above: The tell-tale evidence of jet test-flying, burnt into the grass runways, shows up clearly at Boscombe Down airfield, photographed during 1944.

Right: The Me262, possibly the best jet *airframe* of the war.

in the autumn of 1938, when the German Air Ministry had invited Messerschmitt to begin design studies for a fighter airframe to be powered by revolutionary and highly secret power plants. This was the 'Projekt 1065' (see p. 276) which eventually caused the rival Heinkel 280 to be dropped.

Messerschmitt completed the preliminary design by June 1939 and had a mock-up by March 1940 when contracts for three prototype airframes were awarded. The airframe emerged as a very clean low-wing monoplane with excellent proportions and incorporating swept-back wings, with underslung nacelles for the twin jets. The new fighter epitomised that maxim of aircraft designers: 'What looks right is right.'

However, both the airframe and the power plants were untested. The BMW jet engines selected for the three prototypes were of the axial-flow type – probably not the easiest configuration to pioneer, since they present certain design problems even today. They were expected to deliver 1000 lbs thrust but on the test bed produced only 570 lbs – not nearly enough for flight trials.

The only alternative possible was the Junkers Jumo 004 – another axial-flow jet – but that engine was nowhere near ready and did not even commence bench-running until November 1940, and then immediately ran into serious difficulties. Meanwhile the three airframes were completed – and engineless. It was now April 1941 and interest in jet propulsion was fast waning at the German Air Ministry, General Udet even stating that the Luftwaffe had no foreseeable requirements for jet fighters and that the existing piston-engined aircraft could fulfil all future commitments. His successor, Field Marshal Milch, concurred and nearly stopped all further experimental work on jet propulsion.

In spite of low priority and what amounted to hostility in official circles, the Messerschmitt team continued to work enthusiastically. Lacking gas turbines, they fitted a single Junkers Jumo 210G piston engine to the first prototype, to evaluate the flight characteristics of their design. The first flight was made in April 1941 and, although seriously underpowered – the Junkers 210 only offered 600 hp – several successful flights were made.

In mid-November the first two examples of BMW 003 turbojets arrived for installation. Prudently Messerschmitt had retained the piston engine in the 262's nose – a justified precaution, for as soon as the throttles were opened for take-off, the turbine blades broke away from both jet engines and the pilot, Flugkapitän Fritz Wendel, only just managed to land safely. The engines were removed and considerable redesign work was found to be necessary – they did not reappear until late 1943.

Eight months were to pass before the alternative Junkers Jumo 004 engines arrived. These had been flight-tested under an Me 110 and were giving 1850 lbs thrust. They were fitted to the third airframe (PC+UC) and the flight-testing was transferred to Leipheim where a very long paved runway had been laid down for the Gigants.

Early on 18 July 1942 Wendel began high-speed taxi trials. He discovered that the 262, which then had a conventional tail wheel, showed a marked reluctance to raise the tail: the elevators, lacking the slipstream from a propeller, were ineffective. He decided that the only solution was to jab the wheel brakes to lift the tail clear of the blanketing effect of the wings. On his first attempt at take-off, roaring down the runway at 112 mph, he slammed on the brakes for a second; up came the tail and the Me262V3 was smoothly airborne for the first time on turbojet power alone. After twelve minutes he landed, reporting that:

> 'Immediately I touched the brakes, the tail lifted and the elevators began to bite. My turbojets ran like clockwork and it was a sheer pleasure to fly this new machine. Indeed, seldom have I been so enthusiastic during a first flight with a new aircraft as with the Me262.'[8]

Soon afterwards the Chief Test Pilot from Rechlin arrived at Leipheim to fly the jet. Although carefully briefed by Wendel, he got the braking all wrong and ran out of runway, ending up in a cornfield with a very bent aircraft. This resulted in an even cooler attitude towards the 262 in Berlin, though fifteen machines were ordered, and in December 1942 it was decided that limited production could commence at a rate of twenty a month, this being considered by the Air Ministry, despite protests from Messerschmitt, a sufficient number for experimental purposes.

The initial turning-point for the potentially unbeatable fighter came in April 1942 when General Galland flew the fourth prototype (PC+UD) at Lechfeld. He was very impressed with the aircraft and, a day or so later, told Goering that he was convinced that the Me262 could give the Luftwaffe a very marked advantage over Allied piston-engined fighters. He suggested further that all single-engined fighter production should now be confined to the FW190 and the production lines so released be used to build the 262s. At a conference on 2 June 1943, it was at last agreed that the jet-powered Me262 should go into series production. The fourth prototype was demonstrated to Goering who reported on it enthusiastically to Hitler, but he would not agree to mass production.

The tail-wheel undercarriage was not considered satisfactory for average service pilots and a fully retractable tricycle undercarriage was tested on the fifth prototype. Tricycle landing gear is, of course, universal today; in 1943 it was still something of a novelty. The tests were satisfactory, however, and the type was now ready for production, waiting for the order to start.

More demonstrations were given before Goering, Milch and Galland at Regensburg in November 1943. Significantly Goering asked Professor Messerschmitt if the Me262 fighter could be modified to carry a bomb; he was told that this would present no difficulty. A fortnight later, on 26 November, a 262 was flown to Hitler's Headquarters, then at Insterburg in East Prussia, for inspection by the Führer. Impressed, he demanded immediate mass production of the jet *as a bomber*.

It was a disastrous and inexplicable decision. Another twin-engined jet prototype, the Arado 234, designed for high-speed reconnaissance, had already been tested and was far more suitable for conversion to a bomber; indeed, a bomber version was eventually built. Meanwhile Hitler's directive inevitably delayed the Me262's production, for in spite of Professor Messerschmitt's assurance that it had been designed to carry bombs, in fact it had not. Not even the most rudimentary bomb shackles had been fitted, and even after Hitler's order the first production batch, starting in May 1944, were fighters, the 262A–1 Schwalbe (Swallow).

As a fighter the Me262 was revolutionary, attaining 540 mph at nearly 20,000 feet. The fastest contemporary Allied fighter, the North American P51D Rolls-Royce-powered Mustang, could only manage 437 mph. Yet when Hitler discovered that his orders were being disobeyed, he demanded that all Me262 fighters built be at once converted into bombers. The bomber version, Sturmvogel (Stormbird), had to carry its two 1100-lb or single 2200-lb bomb externally, which cut its speed down to that of Allied piston-engined fighters.

Several schemes were proposed to enable the Me262 to fulfil its bombing role without fundamental reconstruction. One of the wildest was to *tow* a 2000-lb bomb, fitted with wooden wings and attached behind the jet with a rigid tow-bar, the inevitable two-wheeled jettisonable dolly being used to support the bomb on take-off. The tactics envisaged were for the Sturmvogel pilot to attack his target in a shallow dive and then release the bomb, explosive bolts jettisoning the tow-bar and the bomb's wings. The flight trials proved difficult: the bomb's wings had been designed with too much lift, causing it to oscillate wildly and making the towing jet so uncontrollable that one test pilot had to bale out. On a later flight, a bomb refused to part company with its 262 and the pilot had to land still towing it; on yet another flight, a tow-bar parted during a turn, releasing the bomb which glided away. After that episode, the idea of the towed bomb was abandoned.

In November 1944, in the face of ever-increasing and damaging USAAF daylight bombing raids, Hitler rescinded his order and demanded thousands of Me262 *fighters* – though adding, to save face, that they must be capable of carrying at least one small 550-lb bomb. The production version of the fighter, Me262B, proved easy to fly, provided the pilot had considerable experience on piston engines. In fact, the pilots of the world's first operational jet fighter unit were mainly Messerschmitt test pilots. In April 1944 they were formed into Erprobungskommando 262 (Ekdo 262) at Lechfeld, with the dual function of training Luftwaffe pilots and intercepting high-flying Mosquito and Lockheed Lightning photo-reconnaissance aircraft, which were largely immune from attack by German piston-engined fighters.

Later, the main use of the jet fighter was to be against the 8th USAAF bomber formations, and surviving American pilots still vividly recall seeing them in action. Colonel Johnson was the captain of a B17 flying on a daylight raid to Nürnberg in early 1945 when three Me262s attacked his formation:

'My tail gunner called them out at 6 o'clock high and he said "way high"; I remember that like it was yesterday; the next thing we knew the gunners had all started firing, then the tail gunner called them out one more time:

"Here they come!", and three of them came through the formation, and they shot down three of our airplanes and then they were gone. They were quite good.'[9]

The original Ekdo262 had become an interceptor unit under one of the Luftwaffe fighter aces, Major Nowotny, with some thirty aircraft. Within a month of starting operations against the USAAF in October 1944 these were reduced to three. Most of the losses were caused not by enemy action but by crashes, many due to engine failure and inexperienced pilots. Nowotny himself was killed in action on 8 November, and the surviving pilots then formed the nucleus of JG7, under Colonel Steinhoff, claiming thirty 'kills' against the Americans.

The 262s, though very much faster than the P51 Mustangs and P47 Thunderbolts could be and were shot down. Lieutenant Ben Drew of 361st Fighter Group destroyed two by diving on to them in his P51D as they took off from their airfield at Achmer. In level flight a Mustang had little chance, since

Lieutenant (later Major) Ben Drew after shooting down two 262s.

A P51D North American Mustang of the type flown by Lt Drew.

the German pilot could break off the attack simply by opening the throttles; the only hope of success was by 'jumping' them from a higher altitude.

As the war drew to its close, the Germans desperately tried to increase the output of 262s. Allied bombing of supplies and aircraft factories made this difficult even though, by extensive dispersal, the jets were produced in woods and heavily camouflaged, makeshift factories. In all 1433 were built, although probably only a hundred or so actually flew operationally.

General Galland himself formed the last 262 unit – Jagdverband 44 – an élite group of hand-picked pilots including no fewer than ten holders of the coveted Ritterkreuz (Knights Cross). Operating mainly from the Munich-Augsburg Autobahn, JV44 flew until their base was overrun by US infantry on 3 May 1945; it had existed for only a month but claimed fifty US bombers. The three 262s that Colonel Johnson saw were almost certainly from JV44. When it ceased operations, the world's first jet fighter ended its short career, but it had set the seal on basic jet-fighter design for the next thirty years.

With hindsight it is obvious that, had the Me262 been available in substantial numbers even a year earlier, it would have had a considerable influence on Allied air operations. General Galland has stated many times that if it had been available operationally in the spring of 1943, the Luftwaffe could have stopped the daylight bombing offensive which was to have crippling consequences. It is also possible that a large number of jet fighters, with developed engines and trained crews, could have gone a long way to restore the air supremacy that the Luftwaffe never really regained in the west after the Battle of Britain. Had this been so, and it is not too fanciful since the Allies had no answer to the 262 – certainly not in mid-1944, then the D-Day landings might well have been, at the very least, much more costly than they were.

Hitler is blamed for the delays, but in fact the greatest setback in the development of the German jet fighter was the engine problem. The BMW was not ready; the Junkers Jumo 004 was under-developed and caused many of the crashes that the type suffered: with a life of about fifteen hours, it was never a reliable power-plant.

If the Germans had been really intent on a jet fighter force from 1939 – and had put as much scientific effort and resource into that programme as into the V2 rockets – then they could conceivably have had a formidable jet-fighter force by early 1943.

Had the German jet fighters appeared in large numbers in 1943 it would have proved difficult to counter them. The only Allied jet fighter to see active service was the Gloster Meteor, and that did not make its first flight until March 1943. Sixteen Mk Is became operational with 616 Squadron in July 1944, just in time to chase the V1s. The Mk III, with Rolls-Royce Derwent engines and a maximum speed of just under 500 mph, did not enter service until January 1945.

The first British jet engine (which was, incidentally, the first gas turbine designed as an aircraft power-plant to run anywhere) was started up by its designer, Flight Lieutenant Frank Whittle, on 12 April 1937. Dogged by a chronic shortage of practically everything – especially money – the whole project was run on a shoestring. The attitude of the Air Ministry was one of almost total indifference. Working in a disused foundry at Lutterworth, Whittle and his staff of six built and rebuilt the jet engine, and on 12 April 1941, four years to the day from the original engine test-run, his first engine was cleared for flight trials.

Unlike the German axial-flow design, this engine was of the much more predictable centrifugal type. A small airframe – the Gloster E28/39 – was built round it and made its maiden flight, the first jet-powered flight in Britain, on 15 May 1941. The pilot, Jerry Sayers, reached about 370 mph at 20,000 feet, a somewhat better performance than the contemporary Spitfire. Afterwards he commented that the Gloster jet was the easiest aircraft he had ever flown. That historic aircraft, W4041, survives in the Science Museum, London.

Following the successful flight of the E28/39, which was designed as a purely experimental and research aircraft, not as a prototype, the Government decided to sanction the manufacture of jet engines to power a twin-engined fighter to be constructed by the Gloster Company and named Thunderbolt. (To avoid confusion with the American P47 which had been allocated that name, the British jet was changed to Meteor.) The firm who got the contract for the engines was the Rover Car Company, who had little or no experience of any form of aircraft engine. Whittle remembers that

> '. . . they [Rovers] struggled on for quite a long time and weren't getting anywhere. Fortunately the decision was taken that Rolls-Royce would take over from them. . . .'

Rolls-Royce, now arguably the finest designers and constructors of aircraft jet and turbo-jet engines, became involved in the business almost casually.

The diminutive Gloster E28/39 takes off on a test flight from Farnborough.

Stanley Hooker, a Rolls-Royce engineer, had seen a Whittle engine in February 1940 and had been impressed. He visited Lutterworth several times and became friendly with Whittle and, realising the potential of the jet engine, he asked the Director of Rolls-Royce, Mr (later Lord) Hives to see the gas turbine for himself. Hives asked Hooker what power the new engine was giving; Hooker replied about 1000 lbs of thrust. Hives was not in the least impressed: 'That wouldn't pull the skin off a rice pudding,' he said.

Hives was, of course, used to thinking of the output of aero engines in terms of horsepower. Hooker did some simple calculations and went back to Hives: 'Do you know what thrust the Merlin engine gives in the Spitfire?' he asked.

'No', Hives replied.

'Well, it gives 1000 lbs of thrust.'

Hives looked at him, then pressed a button; a secretary came in. 'I'm going down with Hooker to see this jet engine on Sunday,' Hives told her.

It was August 1940 and the Battle of Britain was being fought over Southern England. After seeing Whittle's engine, Hives made up his mind to take Rolls-Royce into jets. The difficulty was Rovers. Hives sent for Hooker and told him:

'Tonight we're going out to Clitheroe and we're going to have dinner with S. B. Wilkes [Managing Director of Rovers].'

Hooker remembers:

'We had a pleasant dinner, five bob in those days and pretty good. At the end of the meal old Hives turned to Wilkes and said: "What are you doing with this jet engine? You don't know anything about aircraft engines; that's our job." I remember he added, "You grub about on the ground". He then said: "I'll tell you what I'll do. I'll give you our tank engine factory at Nottingham; you give me this jet job".

'Wilkes said: "Done".'

So for an initial cash outlay of fifteen shillings Rolls-Royce entered the jet age.[9]

Hooker, who was highly experienced with superchargers, which employed a common technology, was put in charge of the jet-engine development. The company produced the Rolls version of Whittle's design, named the Welland; it proved a very reliable engine, passing its 100-hour test and powering the production Meteors.

If the Messerschmitt 262 was a far better airframe than the Meteor, and it was, then the Rolls-Royce engine was superior in almost every respect to the Junkers Jumo 004. Sir Frank Whittle is convinced today that, had he had adequate Government backing and the development resources of Rolls-Royce, the RAF could have had Meteors in 1942, two years earlier than they did.[9]

Although the Meteor was the only Allied jet to enter service during the war, the Germans also had a remarkable jet bomber, the Arado 234. This aircraft, as has been mentioned, was originally designed as a high-speed recon-naissance aircraft, small numbers of which photographed over Southern England, Hull and the Normandy area in late 1944. Flying at 30,000 feet at

An early Gloster Meteor I on a test flight. Unlike the Me262, the Meteor's Rolls-Royce engines were better than its airframe.

Opposite

Top: An Arado 234 A series takes off from its jettisonable dolly with rocket assistance and, with its clean airframe, climbs quickly to 32,000 feet.

Middle left: A later version, the AR234B–2 with a conventional retracting tricycle undercarriage, is prepared for flight.

Middle right: An Arado 234C, the only four-engined jet aircraft in production during the war.

Bottom: The Arado's extensively glazed cockpit was well laid out and had excellent visibility – downwards as well – essential in its original design function as a reconnaissance aircraft.

nearly 450 mph, these twin-engined jets had little difficulty in eluding Allied fighters, although one of them, returning from a reconnaissance flight over the Humber, was shot down by a Hawker Tempest of 274 Squadron over Rheine Airfield on 11 February 1945.

The Arados used operationally were mainly prototypes. These early versions took off from a tricycle trolley which was jettisoned on take-off. They had to land on a simple sprung skid so beloved by German designers, and braked by parachute. This was satisfactory on a large grass airfield, but the problem, as with the Me163, was the immobility of the Arado once it had landed – a perfect target until it could be towed to a camouflaged dispersal point.

Apart from the prototypes there was a bomber version of the 234, named Blitz (Lightning), which had four BMW 003A jet engines and a normal retractable tricycle undercarriage. Arados of various marks took part in the Ardennes offensive in December 1944. They had been formed into a jet unit, KG76, composed of experienced bomber pilots who flew support and reconnaissance sorties during the closing months of the war, but in spite of a top speed of 540 mph, several were shot down and only a small quantity of the 200 or so produced were actually used operationally.

The Arado 234 was another German first, indeed a double first: the first jet bomber and the first four-engined jet aircraft. As soon as hostilities were over, all the surviving Blitzes were collected for evaluation by the Allies; several came to Farnborough and were extensively flown. Only one is known to exist today: it is part of the American Smithsonian Institution's National Air Museum reserve collection and is being restored for eventual exhibition.

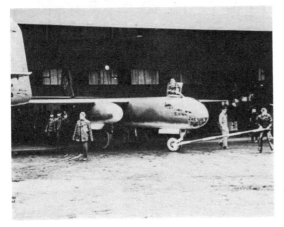

The Helicopter

That universal work-horse of all the minor, and major, wars since 1945 played
little or no part in World War II. Helicopters did exist before the war – Hanna
Reitsch flew one of the first practical helicopters in February 1938. This was
the Focke-Achgelis Fa61; it was not by any means the first helicopter, nor was
Hanna Reitsch its first pilot, but the series of remarkable flights she made
gained worldwide publicity for the very simple reason that they took place
indoors.

The Fa61 had, during 1937, established several international helicopter records, including the altitude record of 8002 feet and a speed record of 76.15 mph. The record-breaking pilot was Edwald Rohlfs, but in the atmosphere of growing distrust of Nazi propaganda, the reports of the records had been muted and, to gain the international notice which the Germans desperately wanted, a more sensational demonstration was required. According to Hanna Reitsch, who has survived more flying adventures than almost any other pilot, it was General Udet himself who thought up the brilliant propaganda coup that was to force the world to notice the achievements of the German helicopter. He persuaded her, at that time not only an attractive young woman, but also a noted international glider champion, to learn to fly the Fa61 and to demonstrate it for fourteen successive evenings *inside* the huge Deutschlandhalle in Berlin during the 1938 German Motor Show. Each evening she flew the small helicopter under perfect control before audiences of 20,000, including no doubt the military attachés. It was a sensational début, for at that time most rotary-wing aircraft were autogyros, which are incapable of vertical flight.

The Fa61 was a true helicopter, though by modern standards crude. It was basically the fuselage of a Focke-Wulf FW44 Stieglitz (Goldfinch) trainer biplane, complete with its original 160-hp Siemens radial engine, which drove

Wartime helicopters.

Below left: The Flettner F1282 Kolibri.

Below right: The Fa61, flown by Hanna Reitsch. This was the earliest helicopter to go into production.

Bottom left: The Fa223 Drache, the largest helicopter of the war.

two 3-bladed rotors carried on outriggers. The small propeller in the conventional position was fitted simply to cool the engine, but it flew well enough. After the Deutschlandhalle flights, a second Fa61 ascended to 11,243 feet, a record that was to stand for some time.

German wartime helicopters included the Flettner F1282 Kolibri (Hummingbird). This was the first military helicopter and it was the only one to be used operationally during the war years. About twenty were delivered to the German Navy, being used principally on board ships for anti-submarine patrols and communication flights, mainly in the Aegean and the Mediterranean.

The F1282 first flew in 1940 and used the intermeshing 'eggbeater' technique of two rotors to eliminate torque effects. It was powered by a single 140-hp Siemens-Halske radial engine and had a top speed of 90 mph. It could easily operate from ships and was entirely successful, though like many early helicopters it was limited by the very small offensive load it could carry. Nevertheless, 1000 were ordered for the German Navy in 1944, but by then Allied bombing made the production impossible.

The most advanced wartime helicopter was the Fa223 Drache (Kite). This was a very large machine which could carry at least six people and lift a heavy load. Designed primarily for communications, it pioneered the role of the helicopter as an airborne crane: a short reel of German wartime film in the Imperial War Museum Archives shows an Fa223 lifting the fuselage of a crashed Me109. 400 Draches were ordered, but again Allied bombing prevented production, only a dozen or so being completed. In 1945 a surviving Fa223, flown by a German crew, was tested at the Airborne Forces Experimental Establishment at Beaulieu airfield in Hampshire, where it was subsequently destroyed in a crash.

At Beaulieu yet another remarkable German rotary-wing aircraft was test-flown after the war: the Fa330 Bachstelze (Wagtail). This small machine was not, strictly speaking, a helicopter but a rotary-wing kite. It was carried in dismantled form in two watertight compartments on the deck of Type IX ocean-going U-boats; its function was to provide a high vantage point for spotting targets in the Indian Ocean and the South Atlantic, where isolated 'independents' – single merchant ships – sailed these little frequented waters without escorts for protection. The low height of a surfaced U-boat's conning tower strictly limited the range of search, but, towed by the U-boat, the Bachstelze could climb to some 500 feet, enabling its pilot/observer greatly to extend the submarine's field of vision. A telephone cable connected the pilot to the U-boat's commander and, on sighting a ship, he was in theory winched down to the deck. However, if the vessel reported was thought to be a warship, or if an aircraft appeared, the submarine would crash-dive and the unfortunate pilot had then to jettison the rotors, which flew upwards, deploying a parachute as they departed which enabled him to descend into the sea still seated in the simple tubular fuselage. He then released his seat straps

Opposite Bottom right: An American Pitcairn autogyro, with British markings. Unlike helicopters, the autogyro's rotors were not powered but rotated like the sails of a windmill. Although they could be clutched to the engine to spin them up for a jump take-off, the autogyro could not hover or descend vertically. This picture shows tests conducted on HMS *Massey*. The Pitcairn was able to land and take off from the small landing deck, but autogyros could not carry a worthwhile offensive load. The RAF used a similar autogyro, the Avro Rota, to calibrate the early CH Radars.

and, in the cynical words of a wartime report, 'drowned in the normal way'. Two Fa330s survive in England: one in the Science Museum, the other in store for the RAF Museum.

A little-known British rotary-wing development was the Rotajeep, one of a number of proposals tested by the Airborne Forces Experimental Establishment from 1942, for utilising rotating wings to enable military loads, ranging from a single soldier to a tank, to be towed into battle with the Airborne Forces. The Rotajeep was a standard US Army Jeep with the addition of a simple fuselage and tail unit and a pylon which carried a folding 2-bladed rotor. Test flights were made in 1942, when the Rotajeep was towed behind a Whitley at speeds up to about 150 mph; although the tests were reasonably successful, serious problems of stability arose and no free flights were attempted. Had the problems been overcome and the trials continued, the towing aircraft would have released the Rotajeep which would have drifted down like a sycamore leaf to land at a mere 36 mph. Safely arrived, the crew could then fold the rotors, start the jeep's engine and drive into action. The Rotajeep idea was not developed. Nor was a similar proposal – the addition of no less than 155-ft rotors on to tanks; one was actually built but, perhaps wisely, not flown.

Opposite: A sequence of stills from a German wartime film showing the flight of a Bachstelze from a U-boat. It was carried in a knock-down form in a pressure-tight compartment on the U-boat's deck, and was quickly assembled and flown, towed by the submarine.

The Rotajeep

The only Allied helicopter to appear in any numbers during the war was the Sikorsky R4, known to the RAF as the Hoverfly, which first flew in June 1942. This helicopter was the first to achieve series production and was to set the seal on helicopter design with its classic single 3-bladed rotor and small torque-stabilising tail rotor. Production began in early 1944; most examples were used for training and evaluation, though a small number did operate in the Far East and thus it was technically operational during the war and continued to be used post-war. There is a beautifully restored R4B Hoverfly in the RAF Museum, Hendon .

It is not possible to examine all the many weapons that scientists on both sides were designing and developing during the six years of war. A sizable book could be written on German rocket weapons alone: over ninety were proposed by 1945. But one further German Secret Weapon does deserve mention: a very early guided missile. It was the Henschel 293 – what would now be called a 'stand off' or 'smart' bomb. This small, rocket-boosted, glider bomb was briefly mentioned earlier when it came to the notice of Allied Intelligence; it was years ahead of its time and could have been devastatingly effective during the Normandy landings.

The Henschel 293 was one of a number of guided missiles that the Germans developed, principally as anti-shipping weapons. Work had begun in 1939 on the Hs293 and another device – the SD1400 Fritz X guided bomb, which was a 1400-kg armour-piercing, free-falling bomb, capable of being steered by radio control. It was a simple device but nevertheless sank an Italian battleship, the *Roma*, off Sardinia in September 1943.

The Henschel 293 was a much more sophisticated weapon – in effect a small aircraft, with monoplane wings and a tail attached to a slender fuselage, consisting mainly of a 550-kg bomb with an additional compartment for the stabilising gyroscopes and radio-guidance equipment. The missile was carried externally by a parent aircraft, usually an He111 or He177. When dropped from its aircraft, it fell free for about one second and then a Walter 109–507 liquid-fuel rocket engine, running on peroxide of hydrogen, which gave a thrust of 600 kgs for ten seconds, accelerated the bomb up to 250 metres a second. When the first rocket engine burnt out, a second, externally-mounted auxiliary BMW 109–511 rocket motor gave an additional fifteen seconds of thrust. Special drag bodies on the wingtips limited the maximum speed of the missile to about 600 mph, but this could only be achieved in a steep dive.

Once the 293 was clear of the launching aircraft, its controller could control its flight with a control stick, left/right, up/down. To enable him to sight the small machine, red smokeless flares were carried in the tail, allowing a trained operator to hit a target 20 km from the release point.

Testing of the Hs293 commenced in December 1940 in the Baltic, off Peenemunde. On the second flight a test missile hit the target, a small barn, plumb in the centre. Later test flights were made against a derelict 5000-ton

The Henschel 293.
In a later version
the speed-limiting
drag bodies behind
the wingtips
contained control
wires, thus
countering Allied
jamming of the
radio command
signals.

Below left:
A 293 under its
parent aircraft, an
He111. The
torpedo-like object
beneath the
Henschel is the
second-stage BMW
rocket motor.

Bottom left:
The 293 was
launched when
5–10 kms from the
target. The bomb
aimer was then able
to guide the missile
from the Heinkel by
radio, using the
control stick. The
pilot (*below*) had to
fly a precise course
so that the bomb
aimer was not
unsighted.

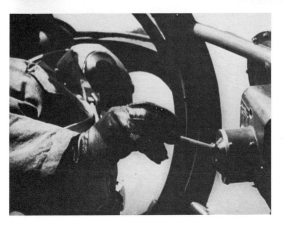

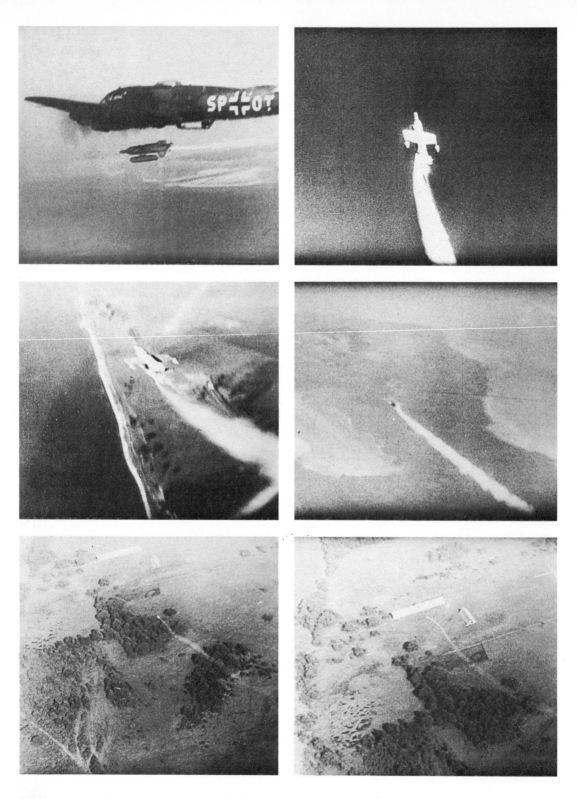

At the moment of release a Henschel under its rocket power accelerates away from its Heinkel. The following sequence of stills is from the second test flight at Peenemunde in early 1941. The target is a long structure which represents a ship. The smoke trail shows a height correction being made by the controller as the 293 approaches its target, hitting it squarely in the centre.

ship which was soon riddled. To achieve accuracy, the controllers were trained on an ingenious simulator and then allowed three actual air launches, the third firing usually proving right on target.

The shortcoming of the Hs293 was the radio link. The frequencies used at the outset were 27 or 60 mHz – frequencies actually set aside for the purpose by prewar international agreement. Eighteen different spot frequencies were available, nine in each band, which could be preset in the field. The aerodynamic control of the missile was via the ailerons and elevators; no rudder was fitted. The radio command technique was very simple, utilising variable width-pulses of audio-modulation. Only the ailerons were proportionally controlled; the elevators used a rather crude method known as Bang Bang – that is, they were either fully up or down. In practice the Germans refined this to some extent by utilising a speed-related limit to the up and down movement, which was governed by a pressure plate sensing the airspeed.

Film surviving in the Imperial War Museum archives and shown in the BBC Television *Secret War* series shows that the control system was perfectly adequate to control the missile-firing training runs. In action the picture was very different. After some initial success in the Bay of Biscay and the Mediterranean, the Royal Navy was able quickly to jam the simple radio channels and the missile was countered so successfully that its use was discontinued by 1944.

German scientists concerned with the development of the Henschel 293 were well aware of the jamming problems; indeed, before it went operational, aircraft with suitable radio receivers flew over all the likely target areas to map the existing radio occupancy of the channels likely to be used. Most of them were already full of Allied navigation aids or radar, leaving only two clear channels.

Conscious of the vulnerability of the radio channels to jamming, the Germans had under development a refinement – the 'fly by wire' system, much used to this day for short-range missiles. The Hs293 had its drag bodies removed from the wing tips and two bobbins of 0.2-mm steel piano wire substituted. Two wires were used with a bobbin on each wing which held 18 km of wire. Similar bobbins in the launching aircraft contained a further 12 km – a total of 30 km of wire. The wires were unwound as the missile flew towards the target, the audio-command signals passing through them completely immune from interference and jamming.

For various reasons it took too long to develop the 'fly by wire' system and it did not achieve combat status with the Hs293. Other proposals for countering jamming included the use of highly directional UHF links, but this too was not developed before the war's end. But perhaps the most advanced development was the Hs293D. This was a remarkable achievement, being no less than control by television. The Fernseh Company, in collaboration with the research laboratories of the German Post Office, designed and produced a miniature TV system of 224 lines with vertical scanning. The camera, named Tonne A, used a super Iconoscope and was fitted behind a glass, electrically-

heated window in the nose of the 293. The entire airborne video chain, pulse
and sweep generators, video amplifier and the camera tube, were contained
in a single chassis, approximately $17 \times 17 \times 40$ cms. This was long before the
days of transistors and integrated circuits and no fewer than 29 valves were
employed: a remarkable example of miniaturisation.

The camera's output was fed into a 20-watt transmitter operating on
73 cms, with a directional Yagi antenna to minimise interference, the entire
missile TV channel only increasing the weight by 130 kg. The parent aircraft
had a television receiver for the bomb aimer who was now, so to speak, able to
'fly' the missile as if he were a pilot on board. The advantages of the TV
control are obvious: once the missile was launched, 20 km from the target, the
mother plane could immediately turn for home, climbing for cloud cover, if
any existed, while the bomb aimer could continue to 'fly' the Henschel at the
target, monitoring its progress on his TV screen, and the nearer the missile got
to its victim, the more accurately the controller could aim; he could even 'jink'
the weapon to upset the aim of the target ship's anti-aircraft gunners.

As it was, this ingenious television development, which today forms an
important element of modern weapons, was, like so much else that Germany
produced, too late to see operational service.[9] Even if it had been available in
quantity, by 1944 Allied air superiority was such that the mother planes
would invariably have been shot down before any significant number of
missiles could be launched.

One final German anti-shipping weapon deserves mention, because it is
very little known: the Kurt bouncing bomb. This was undoubtedly copied
from the famous Barnes Wallis dam-busting weapon, though in fact it was
nearer to another bouncing bomb designed by Wallis – the much smaller
Highball, two of which could be dropped from a Mosquito. Kurt was rocket-
assisted, the rocket breaking off on contact with the water, leaving the 850-lb
bomb to bounce over the sea for up to 500 yards before sinking alongside its
target, then exploded at a given depth by a hydrostatic fuse. Kurt was
extensively tested, initially using a twin-engined Me410, though later experimental drops were made by a single-engined FW190 which was able
to carry two of the bouncing bombs. But Kurt, like Highball, never bounced
in anger; the project was cancelled in 1944.

In view of the number and undoubted quality of many of the wartime German secret weapons, it is natural to ask, if their scientists were able to develop such advanced technology as that, for example, required by the A4 rocket, how near were they to the atomic bomb? The answer is that they were nowhere near; one reason was the consequence of the Nazi party's racial policies, as Albert Speer recounted in 1977:

> 'It is one of the ironies of history . . . that the possibility of Germany having an atomic bomb was spoiled by Hitler considering that Einstein's theories and all atomic research were 'Jewish Physics' . . . and this was one of the reasons that we had no cyclotron or anything else; the lead we had in atomic research before the war was neglected and not used. . . .'[9]

The lead to which Speer referred was of course mainly the work of those many brilliant Jewish scientists who left Germany in the mid 1930s to escape the anti-semitism of the Nazis. Many went to the United States to work on the Manhattan Project – the atomic bomb.

The only known pictures of the Kurt bouncing bomb. An FW 190 drops *two* bombs, which bounce over the sea for a considerable distance before sinking to explode hydrostatically.

Bletchley Park, the
Victorian mansion
which was the
headquarters of the
Government Code
and Cipher School
throughout the war.

6. ENIGMA

All the weapons, devices and countermeasures described in the preceding chapters were closely guarded state secrets during World War Two; most were released soon after; a few remained classified until the expiration of the thirty-year rule. But there is one wartime secret which has not been released; indeed it is probable that it never will be. It is the wartime work of the British Code and Cipher School; in particular the method of penetration by them of the German machine codes now known generally as Enigma: the 'Ultra Secret', which remains – still secret.

During the six years of the war, 10,000 men and women worked on breaking the German military ciphers. The cover name for the department was 'Room 47, The Foreign Office'. In reality the location was just outside the small Buckinghamshire town of Bletchley, where a collection of wooden huts surrounded a large Victorian mansion of unsurpassed ugliness, known as 'BP': Bletchley Park.

The wartime activity at Bletchley and its outstations was the most closely guarded secret of the war – a secret which has been well kept, for it was not until thirty-one years after the war had ended that a retired RAF Intelligence officer, F. W. Winterbotham, wrote *The Ultra Secret* – a book which revealed for the first time the nature of British wartime codebreaking and some of the far-reaching consequences it had on the course of the war. The first *official* disclosures were not made until October 1977, when the Public Record Office, London, released the texts of thousands of deciphered 'Ultra' messages. Prior to that release of texts (which will take years to sift and evaluate), one would have searched the archives in vain for even a reference to either '*Ultra*' or '*Enigma*'.

'Enigma', the generic term for the German ciphers, is an oversimplification: it was a house of many mansions, though it was the name of the first device that the Germans used for the enciphering of their messages. 'Ultra' was the British code-name for the intelligence which was derived from Enigma and other machine ciphers during World War Two.

Cryptography has a long pedigree: secret writing is mentioned by Homer in the *Iliad* and Herodotus described how the Greeks received secret information of the intentions of Xerxes which led to their victory at Salamis – the first decisive battle of the Western World. The Arabs, during the Middle Ages, developed cryptography; indeed the very word 'cipher' is Arabic.† The

---

†'Sifr' is Arabic for 'zero'.

Venetians used codes and ciphers extensively; but the real coming of age for cryptology occurred with two related inventions: the telegraphic code invented by Samuel Morse in 1844 and the establishing of reliable long-distance wireless telegraphy around the turn of the present century.

The telegraph enabled military commanders to keep in touch with their forward units and required special signal corps to be formed for the purpose. Enemy agents quickly discovered that the wire telegraph could be tapped, so codes were devised to prevent the messages being read. The telegraph had other obvious limitations, being suitable only for a relatively static war and clearly could not be used to communicate with ships at sea.

The invention of Wireless Telegraphy (W/T) reduced these limitations; a military or naval unit could be contacted at almost any distance and two-way instantaneous traffic be instituted, though at the cost of such traffic being available to an enemy who simply required a suitable receiving set in the safety of his own territory. If this was a disadvantage for the user, the advantages of mobility and simplicity offered by W/T outweighed it overwhelmingly. Military and diplomatic messages multiplied and by the early months of the First World War had become a torrent of dots and dashes; traffic on a scale that was unprecedented jammed the available narrow wavelengths from end to end.

The senders had to assume that the enemy would be 'listening in', so to secure the messages, all of them to a greater or lesser extent secret, codes and ciphers were required on a massive scale, and, to penetrate the codes of the signals so freely available, code-breakers – cryptanalysts – perfected their skills.

One of the first overt acts of war perpetrated by the British was the cutting of the German transatlantic cable on 5 August 1914 by the cableship *Telconia*. Deprived of their cable circuits, the Germans were forced to send much of their diplomatic traffic to the Americas by wireless, to which the British tuned. The intercepted messages were decoded by a brilliant team working in Room 40 of the Old Admiralty building. This section – by far the most efficient codebreakers of the 1914/18 war – began their work with the aid of a German naval codebook salvaged from the light cruiser *Magdeburg*, which had sunk in the Baltic in 1914.

As the war progressed 'Room 40', under the legendary Captain Hall, RN, solved over 15,000 German intercepts, culminating in the greatest coup of cryptanalysis: the penetration, by Nigel de Grey, of the German diplomatic codes 0075 and 13040, which resulted in the solution of the 'Zimmerman' telegram, the publication of which was to be largely instrumental in bringing the United States into the war in 1917.[1]

After the First World War, the activities of Room 40 were made public in Britain and were doubtless noted elsewhere. It was realised that the type of codes used extensively during the war, which relied on the substitution of words or phrases by code-groups of letters or figures, could, however large – and some ran up to 70,000 code elements – eventually be compromised. The reason was simply repetition; given sufficient messages in a given code, the cryptanalysts could reconstruct the code and recover the plain text from known phrases; forms of address, or another identical message sent in a simpler and already broken code, would provide a key. There was also the danger that the actual codebooks would fall into enemy hands, as had happened with the *Magdeburg* (codes had also been recovered by divers from sunken U-boats).

Apart from the vulnerability of large codes, their use had other, more fundamental, limitations; the sheer volume of military traffic posed an almost insuperable problem of logistics in the drawing up, printing and distribution of thousands of different codebooks. There was also the time-consuming and tedious process of encoding and decoding the messages; a forward field signals outpost under fire was not the ideal place for such work.

In 1915 an American, Edward Hebern, who had become fascinated by cryptology, devised a simple machine-generated code based on the then very new electric typewriter. The letter keys were, in reality, switches. When, for example, 'A' was pressed, an electrical circuit was completed, current flowed to an electromagnetic actuator, and a mechanical-type hammer printed the letter 'A'. Each key was permanently connected to its appropriate letter. Hebern simply rearranged the wiring so that the 'A' key printed, say, 'K', 'E' was 'R', and so on; thus 'RETREAT TONIGHT' would possibly print as 'EGSEGKS SUJMBZS'. The important point of this early electromagnetic enciphering was its simplicity of operation, for, with the addition of suitable switching circuits, 'EGSEGKS SUJMBZS' could be typed on the machine keys to print out as the original plaintext 'RETREAT TONIGHT'. The machine was reversible and very quick, encoding and decoding took no longer than the time required to type the message, and the operator had a permanent printout of both the code and the recovered plaintext. The messages encoded by Hebern machines could be transmitted by Morse code to a ship at sea and typed on to an identically-wired typewriter, which would unfailingly decode them and if required encode a reply.

The codes generated by Hebern typewriters are those known as 'mono-alphabetic substitution' and, although secure from casual readers – a similar system was offered to businessmen recently – would not cause a half-way competent cryptanalyst any difficulty in their breaking. The codebreaker, given such a message of reasonable length, would make a frequency analysis of the letters or figures of the encoded text. All western languages have a characteristic repetition rate of letters whatever the content of the text. (In 1843 Edgar Alan Poe wrote a short story, 'The Gold Bug', in which he solved a mono-alphabetic substitution cipher by frequency analysis, and established the order of letter repetition of English as: e, a, o, i, d, h, n, r, s, t, u, y, c, f, g, l, m, w, b, k, p, j, v, q, x, z.)[2]

Letter-frequency analysis is the cornerstone of cryptanalysis. It would not take the codebreaker long to penetrate a simple substitution cipher, for 'e' is by far the most common letter in English and any three-letter word ending in 'e' is as likely as not to be 'the': 't' and 'h' often appear together. Vowels would soon be recovered, as would key consonants and before long enough of the plaintext would be deciphered to enable the gaps to be filled from the sense of the message.

To avoid the characteristic 'give away' of the letter frequency, it would be necessary to change the encoding so often that frequency analysis would be impossible, or at least very difficult. Hebern was aware of this and in 1917 began to experiment with a second encoding machine using rotors which switched the connections of his electric typewriter each time a key was pressed, thus changing the entire code alphabet. After a great deal of work he produced his 'Electric Code Machine' – US Patent 1,683,072 – and succeeded in selling some of them to the US Navy in 1928.

The machine looked at first glance like a typewriter but it was not; it did not type anything but it had a keyboard with just twenty-six upper case letters arranged in the same order as a commercial typewriter keyboard. Above the keys on a sloping panel there were twenty-six letters printed on small glass windows, each with an illuminating bulb behind it, again arranged in precisely the same order as the keyboard. On the top of the machine, in the position that the typehead and platten would occupy on a standard typewriter, there were five rotors arranged parallel to the keyboard. Each rotor had the twenty-six letters of the alphabet engraved on its circumference and each could be preset against an engraved datum.

Each rotor was made of insulated material – probably the early plastic, Vulcanite – and had twenty-six contacts on either face, one for each letter. The contacts were wired together in pairs in a definite pattern, each of the five rotors having a different wiring. It was this internal wiring which performed the actual enciphering. Let us consider for a moment the operation of a single rotor: if the 'A' key was pressed an electric current flowed via a spring contact brush to the 'A' contact on the first rotor, through the rotor's internal wiring, to emerge on the other side as, say, 'F', lighting up the 'F' window on

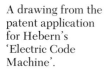

A drawing from the patent application for Hebern's 'Electric Code Machine'.

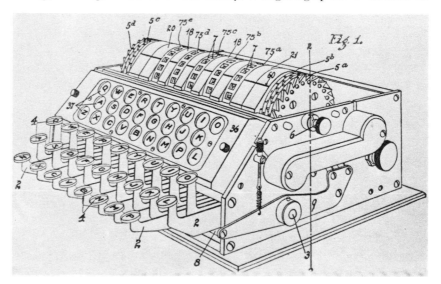

the front of the machine. If 'A' were pressed again, the rotor would advance one letter and the contact would pass the current via its wiring to, say, the 'Y'. 'Y' would light up on the front panel. Thus even a single rotor would provide twenty-six completely different cipher alphabets.

Hebern's machine had five such rotors wired in series; when rotor one had made a complete revolution, rotor two moved forward one letter; when it had made a complete revolution, three advanced one letter; and so on. Thus the Hebern five-rotor machine could generate 11,881,376 different cipher alphabets (26^5).

To use the Hebern machine the operator would set up a 'headcode' – that is, a definite starting order for the five rotors, say 'BKZFJ', which would determine which of the ciphers was used first. As the plaintext was tapped out on the keys the code-letter equivalents would appear in the windows, to be copied down by a second cipher clerk. Deciphering was effected by setting up the same headcode: BKZFJ. The cipher text would then be typed on the keys, the plaintext appearing letter by letter in the windows.

The enormous number of cipher alphabets produced by the rotors gave Hebern's machine a considerable degree of security; there was no question of frequency counts revealing anything. Only the most complex and time-consuming mathematics involving group theory could be used to penetrate the ciphers. The time taken to break a Hebern code would have been so long as to render the intercept useless, certainly during wartime.

Though Hebern's rotary machine was the first to be manufactured, it was not the only one in the field. In 1919 a patent was taken out by Jugo Koch of Delft for a cipher machine which he called 'Geheimschrijfmachine': secret-writing machine. Koch does not appear to have constructed his invention; at all events a German engineer, Arthur Scherbius, bought the patent rights and made the machine, renaming it 'Enigma': a puzzle. Scherbius's machine was essentially similar to Hebern's, though they seem to have been independently arrived at; it had only three rotors, but the third drum 'reflected' the circuit back through the other two, giving the equivalent of six rotors. This, however, was achieved at the cost of never being able to encipher a letter as itself: that is, an 'A' in the original text would never appear as 'A' in the encoded message – a seemingly trifling defect, but one which was to prove a serious weakness.

By 1923 Scherbius had his Enigma in production in his Berlin workshops and it was placed on public exhibition at the International Postal Union Congress and the Leipzig Trade Fair, where it was offered as an inexpensive, reliable means of safeguarding commercial cables and telegrams. The German Post Office actually demonstrated Enigma by sending a coded greetings wire to the Congress, which the machine publicly decoded. Arthur Scherbius was doubtless congratulating himself on what must have appeared an auspicious start to his venture; his Enigma, however, was attracting other than purely commercial interest. Discreet enquiries were made and the machine was withdrawn from the exhibition to reappear in the Berlin

'Chiffrierabteilung' – the Cipher Department of the Reichswehr, the small army permitted to the Germans under the provisions of the Treaty of Versailles. The head of the 'Chi' was Colonel Erich Fellgiebel, an experienced signals officer who was to rise to Major General and the command of all the German Armed Forces signals.

The result of Fellgiebel's examination was the total withdrawal of Enigma from the commercial market. It continued in production – with significant improvements – for the nascent Wehrmacht. Its appearance had been timely, for Germany was in political turmoil: the first stirrings of the Nazi party under Adolf Hitler were apparent – the celebrated 'Beerhall Putsch' had occurred in November 1923, and scarcely a year later Hitler had published *Mein Kampf*. By the time Hitler had assumed power in Germany in 1933, Staff studies had begun to sketch their ideas for a new form of warfare: *Blitzkrieg* – a war of total mobility. (It owed much to the writings of two British military thinkers, Major General Fuller and Captain Liddell-Hart, whose revolutionary proposals had largely been ignored in their own country.) This radical concept integrated massive motorised columns and armour, supported by a tactical air force; its successful deployment required fast, reliable communications that could only be furnished by radio. Enigmas – lightweight, battery-powered and rugged enough to be operated in the back of army signals trucks on the move – were ideal.

The Enigma that was issued to the German armed forces had initially three rotors and a plugboard that could make a final superenciperment. An assessment of the machine, made presumably by the 'Chi', was that to an enemy

'its messages would be completely indecipherable without an Enigma machine; and even with a [captured] Enigma, though theoretically it would then be possible to break the code, it would require an ability that few cryptographers possess'.

The assessment was optimistic, for the secrets of Enigma had already been penetrated.

The Poles, surrounded as they were by powerful potential enemies, had, between the wars, developed one of the most efficient Intelligence Services in the world. Their code and cipher bureau, BS4,† based in Warsaw and headed by Colonel Givido Langer, had achieved some remarkable successes, including the Battle of Warsaw in 1920 when Polish forces under Pilsudski halted the Bolsheviks at the gates of the city, due in no small measure to the solving of the Russian codes by Polish intelligence.

After this early success, the Poles broke the German Reichswehr ciphers, which they read without difficulty until a certain date in 1928, when a new cipher began to be used which the BS4 cryptanalysts suspected was mechanically generated and which they could not break. The account of what followed is the result of interviews and fragments of evidence from various sources in Poland, France and England. It is believed to be accurate, but until

†Biuro Szyfrow (Cipher Bureau). No. 4 was the German Section.

the British archives on the subject are made public, some of the details must remain speculative.

What is not in question is that the Germans were using the Enigma machines for their military radio traffic: this was the source of the cipher that the Poles could not read. BS4 were fairly certain that the encoding machine would be a development of Scherbius's commercial Enigma which Polish intelligence officers had seen when it was on public exhibition. It was therefore vital that an example of the military Enigma be procured, and on an unknown date in 1928 the opportunity arose. According to Colonel Tadeusz Lisicki, a Polish ex-Signals officer now living in Britain, late on a Friday afternoon an official from

Colonel Lisicki (*right*) examines the French copy of Enigma, which had just been restored to working order by BBC Communications Department for the 1976 television programme.

the German legation in Warsaw began to make urgent enquiries at the Railway Parcels Customs Office regarding a packing case consigned to the Legation from the Foreign Office in Berlin. He demanded that it be cleared through Customs immediately, and such was his anxiety that the Poles became suspicious, thinking – correctly – that a mistake might have been made in Berlin and that something had been sent by ordinary freight that should have been consigned to the Diplomatic Bag. The persistent German official was informed with regret that the parcel had not yet arrived and that, in any event, the Customs Office was about to close for the weekend.

The Excise men then contacted Polish Military Intelligence, who lost no time in opening the case. At once the reason for the German's anxiety was revealed: in the box, carefully packed in straw, was a brand-new military Enigma. Over that weekend, experts from BS4 examined the machine thoroughly before it was skilfully repacked, to await collection on Monday morning.

The examination of the Enigma gave the Poles valuable information – in particular, the internal wiring of the three rotors, and also the addition of the plugboard (Stecker), which provided a final superencipherment. It was clear that the military Enigma was an advance on the civil version and it was obvious that to keep pace with its developments exceptional cryptanalysts would be required, involving advanced techniques in higher mathematics. BS4 therefore recruited three brilliant young mathematicians from Poznan University. (Poznan had been under a long period of German occupation until 1918 and was still a German-speaking region of Poland and a thorough knowledge of that language was obviously essential.)

One of the trio, Marian Rejewski, had a remarkable analytical talent; ironically enough, he was sent to Göttingen University in Saxony for postgraduate training in most recondite higher mathematics pertaining to group and permutation theory and statistics – essential skills for cryptanalysts. The second member, Jerzy Rozycki, was very different and would be able to offer brilliantly imaginative solutions to problems. The third, Henryk Zygalski, complemented the other two: a diligent, steady plodder, capable of exploring every possible avenue tirelessly. In 1932, after four years of training, they began work with BS4 on the Enigma intercepts. They were to break the codes in just four and a half months – a very remarkable achievement, even though they did have help.

According to evidence given by Rejewski himself in 1976 in Warsaw,[3] the Poles had managed to acquire, via a Swedish contact, a commercial Enigma which they adapted to military standards. But there was far more valuable assistance from another source. Sometime early in 1931 a low-grade clerk in the German Ministry of Defence approached the French Service Renseignements (Intelligence Service) with an offer to sell them certain information on ciphers, including documents relating to one of the most closely guarded secrets of the Chiffrierabteilung – the Enigma machine. The clerk's name was given as Schmidt, which may or may not have been genuine; in any event the man gave himself the prophetically gloomy code-name 'Asche'

Members of Unit 300 at Cadix. Marian Rejewski is on the extreme right and Captain and Mme Bertrand are at the centre of the group.

Below left: Jerzy Rozicki.

Above: Henryk Zygalski.

The superencipherment plugboard or *Stecker* which increased the difficulties of the codebreakers.

(ashes). The French not unnaturally were very much inclined to regard Asche as at best an opportunist, at worst a double agent; the offer seemed too good to be true. But one man, Captain Gustave Bertrand, then Head of the French Intelligence Service Cryptography Bureau, was disposed to believe Asche's story; he had interrogated the poorly-paid young man with a life-style beyond his means who, although he was not himself in a position to gain access to highly-classified documents, had a brother, well placed in the higher reaches of the German Army Command, who apparently was willing – doubtless for a consideration – to supply secret information.

Asche remains a shadowy figure – no known photographs of him exist, but Bertrand, together with another French agent 'Rex', who acted as an interpreter (Asche spoke only German), and other members of the Service Renseignements, met him nineteen times between 1931 and 1939 in a dozen European cities, and received photographs of hundreds of highly-classified German documents. An early exchange (in 1932) was priceless: the German Army instruction manual for the Enigma machine; a codebook giving the keys; and a sample enciphered message with its plaintext equivalent. Copies of these Bertrand passed over to BS4, who were working with French Intelligence.

It is difficult to overestimate the value of Asche. His stolen documents certainly helped the Poles in the breaking of Enigma, and although it is possible that the three mathematicians could have solved the problem without him, it would probably not have been before the Germans had developed the machine and made it very much more difficult to break. The consequences, had that happened, could well have been profound.

When the Poles broke Enigma in 1934, the German code clerks were simply setting the three drums according to a prearranged schedule, the Tageschlüssel or day key, as set out in the Army cipherbook, copies of which Asche was able to produce. However, from the moment that Enigma became general in the German forces, the machine was constantly developed. To continue to read the ciphers, more than purely mathematical techniques were required; BS4 came to the conclusion that several copies of the current Enigma were essential if they were to be able to continue to crack the German messages.

The Polish copies were based on the known commercial model, with the additions which the examination of the Enigma in Warsaw Customs had revealed, aided by mathematical analysis. The actual machines were built under conditions of great secrecy at the AVA telecommunication factory in Warsaw and were used by BS4 from 1934. They worked well for a time, but in October 1936 the Germans began making changes. The superencipherment plugboard was enlarged. In 1937 the 'reflecting' rotor wiring was altered and the keys, that is the initial setting of the three operational rotors, were no longer simply copied from a book; instead, a 'repeated indicator' technique was used: the codebook gave the operators the plugboard connections and the Ringstellung (or rotor setting), which was achieved by

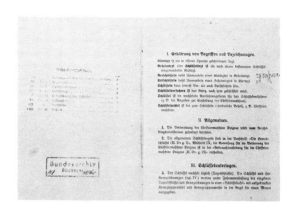

German Signal Corps manuals for Enigma, like those passed to Captain Bertrand's Service Renseignements by Asche.

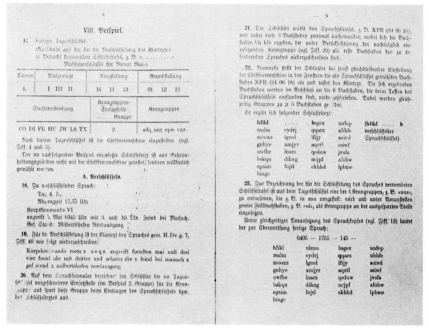

twisting the outer ring of the rotors, on which the twenty-six letters of the alphabet were engraved, against a datum mark, effecting a transposition (A to F, say) of the cipher alphabet. Each of the three rotors would be differently set. Having done this, the operator would place the rotors in the machine and set up the Grundstellung (literally, ground setting), that is the key or starting position of the three rotors as they appeared in the rotor windows on the top of the machine. The Grundstellung key would be dependent on the Kenngruppe or radio 'net' of the sender; these would be different for each net and would be changed every month prewar, or three times a day during the war.

Let us suppose that the Grundstellung key was 'AAA', an obvious and unlikely combination, but one that we will use for clarity. The operator, having set the key, would then choose at random three letters, and repeat them: LOXLOX. This might be encoded by the Enigma as AOBRMV. The operator made a note of this, then set the three rotors to LOX and encoded the message by tapping out the plaintext (Spruchschlüssel) on the Enigma's keys.

The Grundstellung or key setting set up on an Enigma machine: in this case 'E L K'.

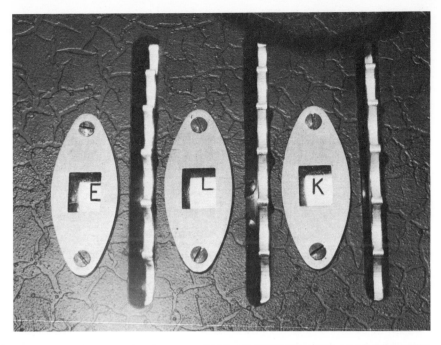

A copy of an original sketch of a Polish 'bomba', drawn from memory by Marian Rejewski in Warsaw in 1976. 'Silnik' is Polish for motor.

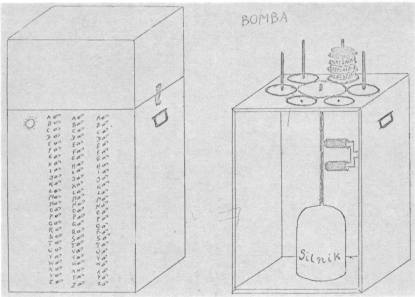

As he did so, a second cipher clerk noted down the cipher text in five-letter groups. When the encoding was complete, the message would be sent by radio in morse. The radio signal would begin by identifying the sender and the recipient by their radio call-signs; the message would start with AOBRMV and then continue with the five-letter groups of the enciphered text. When the entire message was received, it would be passed to the code clerk for decipherment. He would obtain the plugboard connections, the Ringstellung and key of the net – AAA – from his codebook; he would then tap out 'AOBRMV' on his Enigma; this would decode as LOXLOX – the three random letters that the encoding clerk had used. LOX would then be set up on the three rotors and the enciphered text tapped out on the keyboard, the German plaintext emerging letter by letter in the illuminated windows to be taken down by a second clerk.[4]

The point of this random selection of the Enigma rotor setting was to ensure secrecy: no spy or agent could know which three letters a given code clerk would use and the clerks were ordered never to use the same three letters twice (although they often did). There was also a rule that the cipher text in any one key was not to exceed eighty groups of five letters.

To enable the cryptanalysts of BS4 to recover the Enigma ciphers, the Poles built an electro-mechanical device which Rozycki named a 'bomba' (after the ice-cream). This machine ran through all the possible settings of the three drums until settings were found which deciphered the message on the Polish-built copies of Enigma. No Polish bombas have survived, but in 1976 Rejewski made a sketch of one from memory for 'The Secret War' television programme. Precisely how they worked is not altogether clear, but they produced results, though they had certain drawbacks. In the first place, they were expensive to construct, and one bomba was required for each rotor setting; because of the reflection through the rotors, six bombas were needed for a given Enigma key. Secondly, they did not perform the entire operation: there was a complementary aid known as 'the light table'. This was, as the name implies, an illuminated table on which large perforated sheets of card were placed, one on top of another; they were then manipulated in a certain way until holes appeared where registration occurred, which represented possible drum settings.

Aided by a highly efficient radio interception service, the German Army and Air Force Enigma ciphers were being 'read' on a day-to-day basis. One intercept – from the Air Ministry in Berlin – was classic:

'To all airfields; bring in Ernst Röhm:

Dead or Alive.'

It was 30 June 1934, now known as 'The Night of the Long Knives', when Hitler ruthlessly disposed of former colleagues who might challenge him.

The Polish cryptanalysts of BS4 were able to improve their techniques, reaching a peak in the first six months of 1938 as German military traffic increased almost daily. However, their remarkable achievements came to an end on 15 December 1938: that was the day on which the Germans issued each Enigma machine with two additional rotors, so that the three operational rotors were now selected from five. Since each rotor setting required a bomba, the additional rotors increased the number of bombas needed by a factor of ten – from 6 to 60 – and of course the highly-trained staff to operate them. The Poles of BS4 simply did not have the time or the resources available from their peacetime budget. The Enigma traffic was once more secure.

Fortunately, in France Captain Bertrand had foreseen, at least in part, that the Poles would be in need of help. Just before the appearance of the two extra rotors he had approached the British with a proposal that they should

The French copy of the five-rotor Enigma. The cover has been removed and the two spare rotors can be seen on the right. The three operational wheels show the ELK key setting. The small electric bulbs illuminated the letter windows in the cover – which corresponded to the layout of the keys. (German-'issue' Enigmas appear to have had the standard commercial keyboard layout.)

co-operate with the French. The British Secret Service, that most withdrawn of all organisations, was to say the least diffident; but in the atmosphere following the Munich crisis and the inevitability of a new war with Germany in the not too distant future, the suggestion was not summarily dismissed. Encouraged, Bertrand sent, as a bride price, samples of Asche's intelligence documents and also hinted at the Polish success in penetrating certain German ciphers, by the use of advanced cryptanalytic techniques.

The official reaction of the British remains under lock and key in the London archives, but just before his death in 1976 Bertrand gave certain information to the BBC, and additional evidence was also gathered in Poland. From these sources it would appear that the British were persuaded to attend a tripartite meeting on 9/10 January 1939 in Paris, between representatives of Polish, French and British Intelligence. The presence of the Poles caused difficulties, since the British were not at that time on officially friendly terms (this being prior to the Anglo-Polish pact). More pertinently, the British doubted if the Poles of BS4 could show them anything about cryptanalysis which they did not already know.

What took place at the meeting is unknown; it probably simply served to establish the credentials of the participants. The British representative must have conveyed a favourable report back to his London masters, for a second and, as it turned out, decisive meeting was arranged for 24 July – this time not in France but Poland. The rendezvous was appropriate to the secrecy of the occasion: the headquarters for the Enigma operation, code-named by the Poles as 'Wicher' (gale); the building, Lasy Kabackie, was deep in a pine forest near Pyry, twenty kilometres south-east of Warsaw.

The hosts included at least two senior Polish Secret Service officers, Mayer and 'Luc' (Colonel Langer), and one or two BS4 cryptanalysts, including the mathematician Rejewski. The French delegation consisted of Captain Bertrand and a cryptanalyst, Captain Braquenié. There remains some doubt as to the British representation. It certainly included Commander A. Denniston, then Head of the Government Code and Cipher School (GC & CS), and Dilwyn Knox, at that time Chief Cryptanalyst. There was a third man, 'Professor Sandwich', whose real identity has never been satisfactorily established. All accounts agree that he was present; all agree that he was not what he purported to be – he had been introduced as a Cambridge mathematician. Who was he? One of the Poles present (Mayer) has said he was Menzies, the deputy, and later Head of MI5 (and later still to be immortalised by Ian Fleming as 'M' of the James Bond stories); Mayer claimed to know Menzies personally, which lends weight to his identification. On the other hand, Captain Bertrand, who also knew Menzies, was emphatic as recently as 1976 that whoever 'Professor Sandwich' was, he was most certainly not Menzies.

General Colin Gubbins, of the Special Operations Executive (SOE), has also been suggested as a candidate for 'Sandwich'. Colonel Lisicki has said that Gubbins was in Poland at the time, though not at the meeting:[5] he was elsewhere discussing the question of supplying arms to partisans in the event of Poland being overrun by the Germans. Alan Turing, the mathematician who was to prove a key member of British wartime codebreaking, has also been suggested; his candidature is gravely weakened since the Poles were surprised at the 'Professor's' obvious ignorance of mathematics. Rejewski has recently stated that 'Professor Sandwich looked peculiar, as though disguised'. Since the true identity of the bogus professor is still regarded in Britain as a state secret, there the matter must rest; suffice it to say that there was a third man as part of the British delegation.

The meeting began with 'Luc' revealing the extent of the Polish penetration of Enigma and the problem posed by the Germans' introduction of the additional rotors. A long discussion followed and two possible courses of action emerged. The first, put forward by Bertrand, was that a 'deception gambit' should be played: that the Germans would be supplied with information, through his contacts, that the five-rotor Enigma ciphers were 'blown'. This would have been relatively easy to authenticate; all that Bertrand would have to do would be to leak the plaintexts of Enigma traffic from Asche's activities to convince the Germans that the French had deciphered them. They would then, Bertrand argued, drop the system as insecure. However, even if this succeeded, the Germans would hardly drop *all* ciphers and a new improved form of Enigma would inevitably appear.

Colonel Langer took the position that a better course would be a new tripartite effort to break the five-rotor cipher. This alternative was adopted by the meeting and the three intelligence services agreed that:

1. The Poles would continue their mathematical work on the Enigma ciphers.
2. The French would maintain their intelligence contacts with their agents in Germany.
3. The British would use their greater resources to design and construct at least sixty bombas to break the five-rotor Enigma.

The Poles offered to help the British all they could; their mathematicians revealed all they knew and plans of the bombas were also supplied. But perhaps the most valuable gift was two examples of the 'AVA' copies of the German Enigmas, which arrived in Paris immediately after the meeting.

Bertrand travelled to London on 16 August 1939, accompanied from Paris by Tom Greene, the British Embassy's diplomatic courier, carrying a Polish AVA Enigma in the Diplomatic Bag. According to Bertrand, Menzies met them off the boat train at Victoria Station. Sixteen days later Germany invaded Poland and the Second World War began.

Ironically the Poles, who had done more than any other nation to break the Enigma cipher, were to be the first to suffer from 'Blitzkrieg', the highly mobile war that Enigma made possible. Within days it was obvious to the Polish General Staff that the country was bound to be overrun; the Intelligence Section, including BS4, was evacuated from Warsaw and, by the final collapse at the end of September, had reached Romania – then neutral. The journey was not without incident: the train in which they travelled was attacked constantly from the air, and the Poles reluctantly decided to destroy their bomba, since there was a distinct possibility of it falling into German hands and compromising the entire team. In the event, Luc's team, the whole of the prewar BS4, which included the vital three mathematicians, Rejewski, Rozycki and Zygalski, arrived safely at the French Embassy in Bucharest.

From Bucharest the cryptanalysts immediately went on to Paris; some, if not all, of the Enigma engineers from the AVA factory also travelled by the same route. By 20 October 1939, Bertrand had collected them together and established them at the Château de Vignolles (code-named 'Bruno'), in Gretl-Armainvillers, some forty kilometres north of Paris. Here, as team 'Z', they worked as a specialised decoding unit within Bertrand's Service Renseignements. A British Intelligence representative, Captain McFarlane, nicknamed 'Pinky', was attached.

Several copies of the AVA Enigma were constructed. To preserve secrecy, the work was farmed out to light engineering works around Paris, no one concern being given enough of the machine to have any idea of its purpose. The final assembly was supervised by an engineer from AVA named Palluth (code-named Lenoir). The example shown in the BBC television programme 'The Secret War', and which is illustrated on page 318, is probably one of these.

The possession of the Enigma machine was of little value without the bomba, though team Z continued the work of the mathematical analysis of intercepted Enigma radio traffic, which was now very heavy. The team were helped when in January 1940 Alan Turing visited Bruno, bringing with him sixty complete sets of the 'perforated sheets'. Each set consisted of twenty-six sheets with 1000 holes punched through: according to a Polish source, these were improved versions of the Polish originals, which Turing had made to cope with the five-rotor Enigmas. No information has ever been released as to how they were used, but once again the ciphers were broken and the decodes

The Château de Vignolles, code-named Bruno. Captain Bertrand is on the extreme left.

The Officers' Mess at Bruno. Luc, Colonel Langer, is on the left.

Bruno. Left to right: Colonel Langer (Luc), Captain Bertrand and the British Intelligence representative Captain McFarlane (Pinky).

were passed – according to Bertrand via a teleprinter link – to Allied Intelligence until 14 June 1940. By that date the Germans had broken through the Allied lines and were within a few kilometres of Bruno. The Château de Vignolles was hastily evacuated with the most important files, the perforated sheets and, of course, the Enigma machines.

To Bertrand – and practically everyone else – it seemed probable that the German forces would overrun the whole of France in the course of the next few weeks, so the team, having arrived with thousands of other refugees at Toulouse, were flown in military aircraft to Algiers, then a French colony, to await the political outcome of the Armistice. Bertrand himself remained in France and went underground to help set up the resistance movement. With the partition of France and the establishment of the Vichy Government, Bertrand, now calling himself 'Monsieur Barsac', managed, with help from General Weygand, to buy the small Château Fouzes on the outskirts of Uzes, a county town near Avignon. The members of team Z now set out from Algiers in ones and twos, using false names and papers, to join Bertrand and the handful of officers from the Service Renseignements who had managed to slip into unoccupied France. The team, renamed 'Unit 300', moved into the Château (code-named 'Cadix'), and once again began work.

Unit 300 was protected from German agents, French collaborators and Vichy police by a counterintelligence bureau of the French Army, operating from premises on the Promenade de la Plage, Marseilles, and posing as 'Entreprise de Travaux Rurals' (in the event, a fairly accurate description of their activities). The 'firm' was directed by Captain Paillole who had been in the prewar 'German' section of the Service Renseignements. Unit 300 returned the patronage by giving Paillole intercepts of relevant German radio traffic.

Bertrand has said that during their period of operation the cryptanalysts at Cadix broke 673 German signals, mainly those sent to the Afrika Korps;

A snapshot of Château Fouzes (Cadix) taken by Captain Bertrand in 1941.

lacking a teleprinter circuit, these intercepts were sent to London via a radio transmitter which the British had delivered to Lisbon, where Bertrand collected it. The British end of the radio net was operated by Poles from a large requisitioned house in the North London suburb of Stanmore.

The protection of 'Entreprise de Travaux Rurals' must have been effective, for Unit 300 continued its work until 8 November 1942, when the Germans occupied the whole of France. Four days later a motorised column entered Uzes and troops smashed down the doors of the Château Fouzes; it was empty, though the last member of Unit 300 had barely left through the back door as the Germans arrived at the front.

The Unit dispersed south; some – Rejewski and Zygalski among them (Rozycki had gone down with the SS *Lamoricière* when she was sunk in the Mediterranean earlier in 1942) – managed to escape over the Pyrénées into Spain, where clandestine organisations conveyed them, via Gibraltar, to Britain. Some were caught en route, to be interrogated by the Gestapo, including the Chief Engineer of Unit 300, Palluth, who was to die in a German concentration camp. Colonel Langer was also imprisoned, but survived the war. Not one of the captured Poles, though subjected to the most rigorous interrogation by the Gestapo, gave away so much as a hint that Enigma had been penetrated. Many took their secrets to their unmarked graves in German concentration camps.

Captain Bertrand, alias Monsieur Barsac, was arrested by the Gestapo and questioned, fortunately by a man who was a double agent and whom Bertrand had once employed. In exchange for his silence Bertrand was released, though not before he had been told that Asche had been betrayed by another French agent – Rex – and shot. With his wife he eventually reached England and a reunion with the surviving members of Unit 300 at the White Horse Inn, Boxmoor, in Hampshire, near the Headquarters of the Polish Army Signal Corps.

An informal group at Cadix. Zygalski is on the right.

With the dispersal of Unit 300, the Franco-Polish attack on Enigma came to an end; they had done a great service to the Allied cause, though in fact the major work on the German ciphers had passed from France to England.

Soon after the tripartite meeting in Poland in the summer of 1939, the British cryptanalysts of the Government Code and Cipher School had been evacuated to Bletchley Park where work began to solve the Enigma cipher. The man eventually appointed to head the establishment was a naval officer, Commander Edward Travis, and a discreet recruiting campaign was implemented, largely among the mathematicians of Cambridge University. Early recruits were Gordon Welchman and Alan Turing.

Turing was by common consent brilliant; in 1936 he had published a classic paper on 'computable numbers', now recognised as the theoretical basis of the modern computer. He was certainly a member of the British delegation to Poland in July 1939, when he was given complete details of the BS4 bomba. By the outbreak of war he was at Bletchley Park working on a British version – the 'bombe'. It is not known how much it owed to its Polish prototype, but it seems to have been a big step forward, and Turing's contribution was considerable, for he had the two essential qualifications – mathematics and mechanical engineering – at both of which he excelled.

Gordon Welchman, another Cambridge mathematician recruited, received a courteous letter at the time of the Munich crisis in 1938, asking him if, in the event of a war, he would be willing 'to serve King and Country'.[6] He replied that he would and subsequently was requested to attend the Code and Cipher School in London for what he has described as 'indoctrination'. The head of the school at that time, Alastair Denniston, then asked Welchman to report on the first day of war, should it come, to Bletchley Park.

Welchman duly presented himself at Bletchley, and Denniston sent him to join 'Dilly' (Dilwyn) Knox, then chief British cryptanalyst, Turing and others in a building known as 'the cottage', which was part of the stables behind the hideous mansion. By then, aided by the possession of the AVA machine, the group were beginning their work on the Enigma cipher. It is possible, indeed probable, that further copies had been manufactured in Britain by that time. This would have presented few problems: due to the priceless gift of the Polish machine, the vital internal wiring of the five rotors was known, and was to remain virtually unchanged throughout the war. The technique of the plugboard (Stecker) and the settings of the keys were known in principle, but apart from some decodes – supplied by either Bertrand or the Poles – no Enigma message seems to have been broken at Bletchley before Welchman joined. There does not appear to have been any sense of urgency to achieve this, for when Denniston sent Welchman to work with Knox and Turing in the cottage, as he recently recalled:

'... Dilly didn't feel that he needed other cryptographers and he sent me along to work by myself on [radio] call signs and "discriminates".'

As things turned out this apparent snub was to prove fortuitous; Welchman

quickly realised that the radio call signs were in effect the addresses of the sender and recipient and the 'discriminates', as Denniston called them, were the codes that the Germans used to indicate the vital keys in which that particular message or messages had been enciphered. It was while engaged on analysing these call signs and keys that Welchman became aware of the magnitude of the task they were all embarking on:

'I think that the thing that really made me get a feel for the overall problem was when I was given a precious collection of decodes; where they came from I do not know, very probably the Poles gave them to us, and my German was good enough to get the hang of what was going on and it suddenly dawned on me we weren't really dealing with a cryptographic problem; we were dealing with the entire command communications system that the Germans had developed for their Blitzkrieg: here were the commanders talking to each other; reporting, getting their instructions from High Command and so on . . .'

'The call signs came alive in my thinking as representing actual units, not a radio station, and the study of 'discriminates' made me begin to distinguish between the different kinds of traffic that was being sent.'

Although the British had yet to break Enigma, a simple analysis of the traffic which Welchman undertook with the help of the Navy 'Y' intercept stations revealed the scope and complexity of the German armed forces' signals organisation, which was in 1939 by far the most comprehensive system of military communication in the world. Without a quick, easy-to-operate and secure encoding system, there could be no radio; without radio there could be no Blitzkrieg. It was as simple as that. (The only alternative to Enigma that could offer total security would have been the 'one-time pad'; apart from the much longer time required for encoding and decoding, it has been calculated

The entrance to the stables at Bletchley Park. The house seen through the archway is 'the cottage'.

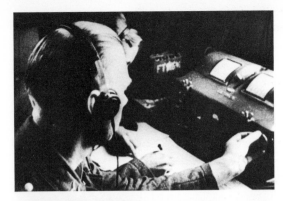

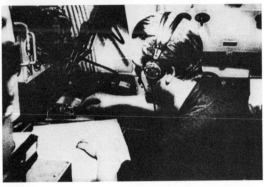

Above: Radio was essential for the Luftwaffe and U-boats. Encoded Enigma signals would be sent by morse code.

Right: A four-rotor Enigma which the German Navy used for the Triton cipher. It defied the best efforts of Bletchley Park until 1943.

that all the printing presses of Germany doing nothing else night and day would have been unable to supply the needs of the German forces, such was the volume of the enciphered radio traffic.)

Enigma was the solution. Welchman, as he plotted the movements of units from their call signs, realised that once the unyielding secrets of the five-letter groups that formed the texts of the intercepted messages were broken, a huge organisation, equivalent in numbers to a major part of the Wehrmacht Signals Corps, would be needed to deal with the avalanche of Enigma intercepts. It was cryptanalysis on a scale hitherto undreamt of.

As Welchman considered the problem, he suddenly thought of a possible approach that could lead to the solving of the ciphers:

'I dashed over to the cottage where my boss, Knox, was working and reported to him only to discover that it had already been thought of by other people and in point of fact they were developing the equipment that would enable us to break Enigma.'

Far from being disappointed that his ideas had been pre-empted, Welchman was now 'in the know'. Without his approach to Knox it could have been months before he was told about the possibility of an imminent breakthrough, due to the strict application of the 'need to know' rule;† as it was, he was then in the position, due to his traffic analysis, of realising the size of the task that Bletchley Park was about to undertake:

†A person engaged in classified work was told only enough to enable him to carry out his duties.

'I thought a lot about it, and came up with an organisation plan, took it to Travis, got it approved . . . and we got permission to recruit straight away. . . .'[6]

They took on many skills: radio operators to man the intercept station; girls from the WRNS† to act as decoding clerks; engineers, statisticians, mathematicians, intelligence experts: a complete organisation that would eventually number 10,000 men and women, sworn to utter secrecy.

Within a few weeks the basic organisation was ready and waiting for the moment when the cryptanalysts had broken the five-rotor Enigma ciphers. This was an intimidating prospect. The military Enigma, as used by the Army and Luftwaffe, had 10^{21} possible initial settings of the machine; for the Navy Enigma, which would use four operational rotors out of eight, the figure would be 10^{23}. Thus even possession of an Enigma machine was of little help. The Germans must have considered the possibility of one or more being captured: to try all the possible settings of the machine, even with the aid of a modern computer, could take up to fifty years. No wonder the Germans had confidence in the security of the codes.

Yet the codes were broken. The principal aid was the bombe – a dangerous cover name, since had the Germans discovered it they could have concluded that the atom bomb was being developed at Bletchley, which was well within their bomber range. Apart from the name, the affinity that this British bombe had with the Polish prototypes is not known in any detail. Dr I. J. Good, another mathematician who worked at Bletchley, stated in the course of his lecture 'Pioneering work on computers at Bletchley', which he delivered to an invited audience at the National Physical Laboratory in 1976:

'. . . so there had to be some further ingenuity in the Bombe [compared with the Polish Bomba]. This I cannot describe but I can only say that Gordon Welchman had one of the basic ideas and Turing another one. My impression is that Turing's idea was one that might not have been thought of by anyone else for a long time and it greatly increased the power of the Bombe. . . .'

Precisely what those two crucial ideas were we do not know: Turing is dead and Welchman is still constrained by the Official Secrets Act which he signed all those years ago. It is, however, reasonable to assume that the British bombe worked very much more quickly than the Polish original and that the British machines were large objects. Dr Good has said that they were 'about ten feet high' and they were certainly the 'bronze goddesses' to which Winterbotham refers in *The Ultra Secret.* From conversations with people who made and serviced them it was possible to build a model of a bombe for the BBC television programme and to form a general impression of the way in which they worked. They were not electronic, but rather electro-mechanical. In a sense they were Enigma machines in reverse, but far more complex, simulating the three operational rotors many times. They also had a plug-board on which a 'menu' was selected; this menu was really a set of electro-

† Women's Royal Naval Service.

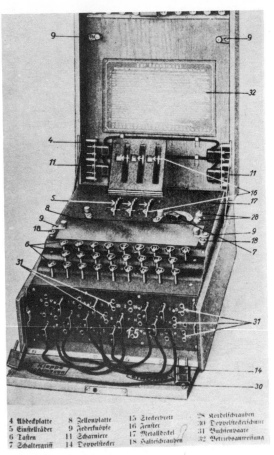

1 Halteverrichtung	8 Zellenplatte	25 Stirnwand
2 Federknöpfe	9 Federknöpfe	34 Doppelsteckerschnur
3 Haltehebel	10 Transparent	37 Meßbereglühlampen
4 Abdeckplatte	16 Fenster	42 Blatthalter

4 Abdeckplatte	8 Zellenplatte	15 Steckerbrett	28 Kordelschrauben
5 Einstellräder	9 Federknöpfe	16 Fenster	30 Doppelsteckerschnur
6 Tasten	11 Scharniere	17 Metalldeckel	31 Buchsenpaare
7 Schalterariff	14 Doppelfeder	18 Halteschrauben	32 Betriebsanweisung

The Enigma machine from a German army manual. This particular machine uses 26 figures on the rotors instead of letters.

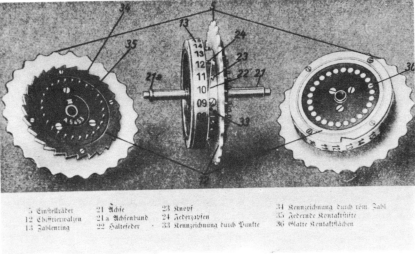

5 Einstellräder	21 Achse	23 Knopf	34 Kennzeichnung durch röm. Zahl
12 Chiffrierwalzen	21a Achsenbund	24 Federzapfen	35 Federnde Kontaktstifte
13 Zahlenring	22 Haltefeder	33 Kennzeichnung durch Punkte	36 Glatte Kontaktflächen

magnetic instructions to the bombe which reduced the number of possible initial states of the Enigma machine from 10^{21} to a much lower, more attainable figure. The menu was drawn up in Hut 6 for the Army and Air Force, in Hut 8 for the Navy, the cryptanalysts culling the information from the intercepted radio traffic. They were aided greatly in their work by the Germans themselves; indeed, without that aid the task could have been impossible.

Key

1	locking mechanism	23	button
2	spring knob	24	spring pegs
3	holding catches	25	front of case
4	cover plate	26	catch for front panel
5	indent for setting rotors	27	battery compartment
6	letter keys	28	screws
7	control handle	29	letter keys
8	battery cover plate	30	double-ended plug cord
9	spring catches	31	pairs of sockets
10	letter windows	32	instructions for use
11	hinges	33	datum for Ringstellung
12	cipher rotors	34	plug cord/rotor number
13	rotor figures	35	spring-loaded contacts
14	double plug	36	fixed contacts
15	plugboard	37	spare bulbs
16	rotor-setting windows	38	bulbs for letters
17	metal cover	39	bulb tester
18	holding screws	40	plug and cable test
19	stay for lid	41	jacks for cable testing
20	reversing cylinder	42	message holder
21	rotor spindle		
21a	spindle-locating collar		
22	spring for holding setting or rotor		

12 Chiffrierwalzen   20 Umkehrwalze   29 Tastenbolzen
13 Zahlenringe   25 Stirnwand   38 Glühlampenfeld
17 Metalldeckel   26 Haken   39 Lampenprüfung
19 Haltehebel   27 Batteriekasten   40 Kabelprüfung
41 Unverw. Buchsen zur Kabelprüfung

A graphic of the British bombe, based on the recollections of men who worked on the original. From the size of the electric typewriter it would have stood nearly six feet high.

It must be realised that there were very large numbers of Enigma machines issued to the German forces – a figure of 200,000 has been suggested – and they were in daily use encoding a tremendous volume of traffic, which meant that the messages contained the same phrases time after time: 'with reference to', 'To Officer Commanding', 'By order of the Führer', possibly even 'Heil Hitler'. Such repetition is meat and drink to cryptanalysts since, once decoded in one cipher, they provide 'keys' to others. Weather reports helped, too: European weather systems tend to move from west to east, thus the British knew in advance the sort of meteorological forecasts the Germans would send, particularly to the Luftwaffe.

German cipher clerks unwittingly helped in several ways. Often a head-quarters signals officer would have to send an order to several units, each on a different 'net' (Kenngruppe), each with its individual Enigma keys. The army used many of these nets. Incredibly, the men operating the machines would send an identical message enciphered in different keys; when Bletchley broke one of these they had a plaintext equivalent for all the other settings, not only for that particular message but for all subsequent ones, until the keys were changed again.

The method of setting up the keys invited carelessness which offered valuable help to the codebreakers. It will be remembered that the operators had to think up three random letters to be tapped out twice on the machine; many used 'XYZ' or even 'ABC' or, contrary to orders, the same three letters – perhaps their initials or those of a girl friend – over and over again. The units of these men would become known from their radio call signs and Bletchley's Hut 6 would soon have the key for the day. There were other common practices which helped: for example, 'Q' is a letter little used in German; 'CH' on the other hand is very common and many units used 'Q' for 'CH'. Again, there were no punctuation marks on the Enigma keyboard, so 'YY' was often used for stop.

The cryptanalysts also relied heavily on 'females' which were often present in the keys. Suppose XYZXYZ were the 'random' letters an operator had used and that they had encoded as POQPAB: 'P' appears twice. When a letter appeared twice in the key cipher it was known as a female; if thirty or so of these females were received in the same key, the bombe's menu could be plugged up with a fair chance of decoding the messages. The Poles seem to have discovered the technique – though not the term; that was coined at Bletchley and originally meant an alignment of the holes in the perforated sheet which was used on the light tables. Turing, as has been noted, improved on the original light-table technique and adapted it to the bombe.

The Enigma machine itself helped. Because it 'reflected' the pulses through its three rotors, it could never encipher a letter as itself (if it had, rotor 1 would have short-circuited the other two). This defect, too, was exploited by the British, who would send out an aircraft to destroy a known lightbuoy – one marking a dredged channel for 'E' boats off Calais perhaps. Radio interception stations would be alerted to listen particularly for traffic from the relevant command; soon a radio message would be sent warning the boats, and the cryptanalysts would be fairly certain that the phrase 'Erloschen ist Leuchtonne' ('the lightbuoy has gone') would appear in the text. Then, by comparing the plaintext German phrase with the cipher groups, they would look for a point in the message where none of the plaintext letters appeared in the cipher. Because of Enigma's inability to encode a letter as itself, that section would, with luck, be the cipher equivalent of the phrase.

F Q Z P A   M S L O K   code group
L EUC H   T O N N E   plaintext

When that sort of information was available it would be set up on the plugboard behind the bombe as part of the 'menu'.

The bombes consisted of twenty-five to thirty sets of three rotors, which were wired in exactly the same way as the Enigma machines and also had the twenty-six letters of the alphabet engraved on their circumference. Each set of three rotors was arranged vertically, one above the other, the top one representing the first rotor of the Enigma, the middle the second and the bottom the third. They were colour-coded and were changed by the WRNS operators on instruction from Hut 6 or 8. The cryptanalysts could ascertain which three of the five rotors were in use, probably by mathematical analysis of the key cipher or the presence of 'females' in the key.

The plugboard had many rows of jacks like a telephone exchange, except that the jacks were arranged in lines of twenty-six and each was labelled with a letter of the alphabet. The plugs – again standard telephone exchange equipment – enabled the 'menu' to be set up. In the example above they would be arranged to instruct the bombe to indicate when the first set of rotors turned an L into F, the second E to Q, and so on. The menu having been plugged up and the correct rotors put in position, the machine would be switched on to commence its search.

The rotors were electrically driven and clicked round interminably, mimicking the Enigmas. When the first wheel had completed one revolution of twenty-six letters, the second one below it moved forward one letter; when this had completed its twenty-six letters, then the third wheel started its slow

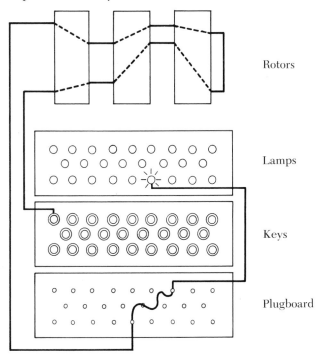

Rotors

Lamps

Keys

Plugboard

A simplified diagram showing the internal wiring of a 3-rotor Enigma.

rotation. On completion of the third twenty-six letters, that trio of rotors would have tested no fewer than 17,576 (26^3) possible combinations. At the same time, the other thirty or so sets of rotors would be doing the same thing. However, when a set of rotors found the letter substitution that the 'menu' had programmed it to, say L into F, it would throw a switch; when all the rotors had completed their programme and FQZPA MSLOK had become LEUCH TONNE, the machine would switch off and the WRNS who operated it would report a 'stop'. It could have taken ten hours or ten minutes.

It should be emphasised that the bombes were not, in themselves, decrypting machines; their function was to recreate the state of the enciphering Enigma, its rotor selection and the setting of the keys. Once a stop was achieved, this information was available and the settings would be tried on an Enigma. If it was a 'good stop' – and not all were – then the message would appear as plaintext and the shout of 'reds up' or 'greens up' would be heard in the huts – the colours being messages in a common key and usually coded relative to their anticipated importance.

The Enigmas which were used at Bletchley were British-built and had the advantage over the German originals in that they printed out the decodes on strips of gummed paper which, exactly like a telegram, were stuck to a sheet of paper and sent to the intelligence huts for analysis.

It is impossible to say how many bombes there were; some were at Bletchley, others were in the 'outstations' scattered around the countryside, usually in large country houses that had been requisitioned, surrounded by landscaped grounds behind high stone walls. Such houses have always been withdrawn, glimpsed distantly through ornamental iron gates at the end of long gravel drives; during the war they were guarded with absolute secrecy, though the only sign of their change of status would be barbed wire and a sentry. Such a house was Gayhurst Court – an elegant Elizabethan manor, with later additions *circa* 1940, in the grounds. It was here that at least some of the bombes are known to have operated. The machine rooms there were staffed by WRNS who had volunteered for service with the Royal Navy and had been posted to HMS *Pembroke*, then sent to Bletchley or one of the outstations, where they were required to operate the bombes on an eight-hour shift, for the duration of the war. There were three shifts each twenty-four hours. Helen Rance, an ex-WRNS operator who worked at Gayhurst Court, remembers 'there were fifty girls to each shift',[6] so there must have been a fairly large number of bombes at that station alone.

The real work of cryptanalysis was conducted in Huts 6 and 8 at Bletchley; it was here that the menu was prepared and also where the 'Stecker' or plugboard of the Enigma was solved. This board was responsible for a very large percentage of the 10^{21} figure of combinations but was apparently solved by another of Turing's machines which has been described as 'an ingenious set of rods'.

The first decodes at Bletchley were made, according to Welchman, in April 1940 during the Norwegian campaign. From that time the quality and number of intercepts rose steeply until, by the Battle of France in early May, the codebreakers in Hut 6 were reading a significant proportion of the Enigma traffic. It should, however, be emphasised that by no means all the signals were broken: some were only partially solved, others not at all. Certain keys took longer to recover, so a system of priority was used: the traffic which, from its origin as revealed by direction-finding and the call signs used, was considered to be the most important was dealt with first, and usually colour-coded red.

By the second week of May it was obvious from the intercepts that a major offensive was being launched. German armour, led by a brilliant apostle of Blitzkrieg, General Heinz Guderian, in two days smashed through the old battle lines that had been fought over inconclusively for the four blood-soaked years of the First World War. By 13 May, German tanks had crossed

The classic use of Enigma. General Heinz Guderian watches his signal staff decoding Enigma signals in the back of a truck during the German breakthrough at Sedan in 1940.

A Stuka dive-bomber, the spearhead of Blitzkrieg.

the Meuse and continued their advance, driving at top speed along the straight, empty, poplar-lined roads of France. Guderian was driving with them in his signals truck, complete with an Enigma, keeping in touch by radio with his forward elements, co-ordinating demoralising close-support attacks on the French troops with Stuka dive-bombers. It was a classic example of the use of Enigma.

These enciphered radio messages were intercepted and many broken, but to the men in Hut 6 there was little jubilation in their accomplishment, for the picture revealed was grim. The Allied armies were clearly unable to stem the headlong advance of the German armour. The British War Cabinet met and, largely in the light of intelligence derived from the Enigma decodes, decided to evacuate the British Expeditionary Force.

Gordon Welchman, then working in Hut 6, has said:

'I think the most important contribution in the Battle of France was simply making it quite clear, from the German reports of their progress, that the situation was hopeless and this gave time for the organisation of that extraordinary fleet of small ships that brought the troops from Dunkirk. I don't think that would have been possible if we had not had the early warning.'[6]

The Dunkirk evacuation began on 27 May; when it ended on 4 June 340,000

Two of the surviving huts at Bletchley, photographed in 1977. The one on the right was Air Intelligence Hut 3.

men had been brought to England. In the military sense Dunkirk was a defeat. For the cryptanalysts in the wooden huts at Bletchley Park, it was a victory; for the first time since the days of Room 40, twenty-five years earlier, codebreakers had been able to influence the tactical conduct of a battle.

The intelligence aspect of Enigma was the province of other huts at Bletchley – principally Hut 3, where skilled interpreters pieced the information together. Nothing was too small; everything, however trivial, was collated and filed in a huge card index containing hundreds of thousands of names, units, postings, supply requisitions, details of promotions, courts martial and leave of absence. A transfer of a single Air Force lieutenant could reveal an impending attack. The card index grew until it was virtually the archive of the entire German Command structure.

As the intelligence mounted, a special organisation was needed to handle it. It was distributed under the name 'Ultra' and Special Liaison Units (SLUs) were formed by an RAF Intelligence officer, Group Captain Winterbotham, who recalls how the men, mostly sergeants, were recruited:

'I interviewed each of these sergeants personally to see that he was the sort of man who I thought would do the job; some I turned down, but the majority went on. Only then were they taken to a school to learn the [en]-ciphering and the job. As they came to the school – and by that time I knew their names – I would tell them, "You understand that what you are going to learn is one of the greatest secrets of the war. You must swear here and now that you will never divulge it."

'At that moment the officer commanding would draw a revolver from his holster and point it at the man, saying, "If you ever do, I personally shall shoot you."

'The fellows got really frightened.'

As the war progressed, the organisation centred at Bletchley grew, and more and more German radio signals were intercepted for the codebreakers. The actual radio interception was made at several stations as far apart as northern Scotland, Dorset, the Midlands and on the east coast. Many of the stations were in requisitioned country houses like Beaumanor Park, near Loughborough, with its array of directional rhombic aerials hidden in a spinney. Here during the war 600 girls of the Auxiliary Territorial Service (ATS) worked in shifts round the clock taking down the faint morse signals from Germany and Occupied Europe. The sets used were mainly American RCA AR88 communication receivers with highly selective crystal 'gates' to enable the operators to cut out interfering signals. It was a tedious job, for the signals that were copied, day after day, night after night, with the greatest possible accuracy, were to the operators a meaningless series of letter groups.

Very important signals would be received on several sites as far apart as possible, in the hope that if one radio signal was fading or jammed by interference, it might be clear at another location. The intercepted messages were sent by dispatch rider or teleprinted over secure land-lines to Bletchley.

What were the most significant decodes? Until all the material in the Public Records Office has been released, it will be impossible to say. However, F. W. Winterbotham, the guardian of 'Ultra' intelligence, has revealed some of the important messages that undoubtedly affected the conduct of the war. The Battle of France, as we have seen, was one; the Battle of Britain, according to him, was another:

'I remember talking to Dowding personally after the Battle of Britain and he said that it was the greatest help to him to know what Goering's policy was, because as Goering got more and more desperate, he gave the order to his fighter squadrons, "You must bring the RAF [fighters] up to battle".

'The Luftwaffe then sent greater and greater formations of fighters over here to draw the RAF but Dowding only used a squadron or so to meet these attacks.'

That coat-trailing by the Luftwaffe failed, but by the beginning of September 1940 the strain on the RAF was becoming intolerable,

'then came the amazing signal for the Luftwaffe bombers to change from attacking the fighter airfields to London. That was a change of policy by Goering which saved us . . .'

Air Marshal Dowding was glad to avail himself of the Ultra intelligence. Much later in the war, the fire-eating American General Patton was a great user of Ultra; he, like Guderian, had his signals truck travelling with his tanks, the difference being that this one was receiving the decodes via Bletchley. His arch-rival, Field Marshal Montgomery, on the other hand, did not care for Ultra and, again according to Winterbotham, at times ignored it – Arnhem being one of those times:

'[Ultra] did warn Montgomery that he had got a couple of German panzer regiments against him there. . . . It was a rest centre for German troops from the Falaise battle; the place was alive with Germans. Montgomery would take no notice at all.

'A special messenger was sent over to him at Brussels the day before [the Arnhem landings] to say, "Look, you are going to jump into a hornet's nest". He did not bother to open the message: he turned the messenger aside . . . .'[6]

Some of the most brilliant successes of Ultra were during the North African campaign, particularly with the decoding of messages giving details of the routes of Rommel's Afrika Korps supply ships which were as a consequence sunk by the Royal Navy in large numbers. It has been said that the conditions were so favourable for the codebreakers during the North African campaign that at times 8th Army HQ in Cairo had the Enigma telegrams before Rommel himself.

If Ultra intelligence was flowing from the Enigmas of the Army and Air Force, it was a different story with the German Navy. Possibly as a result of the activity of Room 40 during the First World War, the German Navy were much more security-conscious than the other services, being aware that radio was the only possible link with their fleets at sea. So from the outset they had their own version of Enigma ciphers, known generally as 'Schlüssel M' (Key M). There were in fact some thirteen different ciphers in use, of which the most important from the Allied point of view was Hydra – the cipher used by the operational U-boats in the North Atlantic.

The Enigma machines used by the U-boats had, as has been noted, four rotors to be chosen from eight, giving the cryptanalysts a figure of 10^{23} to cope with.[7] German Naval cipher clerks were far better disciplined and made fewer mistakes. For a year between 1940 and the summer of 1941, Bletchley failed to break Hydra. Patrick Beesley, who served in Naval Intelligence in the U-boat tracking room at the Admiralty in London during the war, has recounted in his recent book, *Very Special Intelligence*, how cipher materials and spare rotors were captured in 1941 from three German armed trawlers. The material was described as 'of inestimable value', but the men in Naval Hut 8 had still not solved Hydra when, on 8 May 1941, U110 was captured following an action off Greenland with the Royal Navy corvette *Aubretia* and the destroyers HMS *Bulldog* and *Broadway*. A boarding party led by Sub Lieutenant David Balme managed to recover the Enigma machine, its rotors and the current cipher books intact from the U-boat – a prize which must have consoled the Admiralty when U110 sank while under tow to Iceland. The capture of U110 was not officially admitted until 1958, and the fact that Enigma was also captured has yet to be officially admitted. Beesley, however, who was in a position to know, states that its possession enabled Bletchley to penetrate Hydra at last.

Hydra was eventually replaced by another U-boat cipher, 'Triton', which, with the aid of improved bombes and the experience gained with Hydra, was also broken by April 1943. The result was that the vital convoys could be rerouted clear of the 'wolf packs' of U-boats. One further consequence was the hunting down of the 'milch cows' – the tanker U-boats – to such good effect that every single one of them was sunk.

Of Ultra in general, Peter Calvocoressi, who was Head of the Air Force section of Intelligence Hut 3 at Bletchley, has said:

'There is no doubt that [Ultra] was not only astonishing but extremely important and that it had some triumphant successes. But people ought not to get away with the idea that this meant that nothing else mattered. Ultra had its successes when it was working but it did not tell us everything.

'There were always things it did not tell us, things we wanted to know, and there were many, many occasions when it only told a bit of the story – half the story; even less, and you were left to a certain extent guessing.'[8]

Enigma was not the only cipher machine used by the Germans; there was another. Known to the British by the whispered code-name 'Fish', it was known in Germany as the Geheimschreiber – secret-writing machine. It was used only for the highest grades of traffic: the German Foreign Office to keep in touch with embassies in still neutral countries; Hitler's directives and broad strategic plans to distant commands. The Enigma ciphers were not regarded as secure enough for this purpose: the essence of Enigma was its use tactically where speed was essential. The Germans had considered that the problems of solving the ciphers, though not totally impossible, would take so long that by the time they had been broken the information recovered would be historical and militarily useless. Foreign Office dispatches and strategic

The Geheimschreiber was a self-contained enciphering machine, producing the cipher text on telegraph tape or directly to cable or radio transmitter.

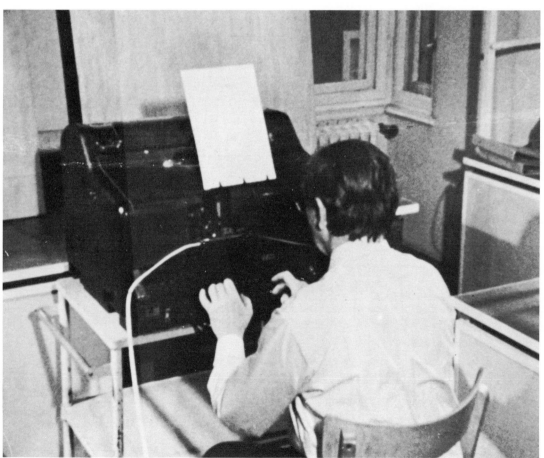

plans, on the other hand, tend to be of far longer currency; such traffic needed a totally secure cipher.

Siemens und Halske Aktiengesellschaft, the German Telephone and Telegraph Company, designed and built a machine with which they claimed to offer that chimera of cryptography, the unbreakable cipher. It certainly had attractive features, one of them being what is known as 'on line encipherment': a machine on which the plaintext is automatically transmitted in cipher directly to a telegraph line or radio transmitter without involving that weakest of weak links – the cipher clerk. Decipherment was simply the reverse process; the machine accepted the ciphertext and printed out the plaintext.

The Geheimschreiber was fundamentally a teleprinter in that its operation depended on the Baudot or Murray telegraph code – a code that was by no means secret – which was and is in widespread international use for telegrams and cables. The Murray code consists of thirty-two separate elements, providing twenty-six letters, ten figures, punctuation and teleprinter functions – line feed, carriage return, letters space and letter and figure shift. To provide all this from thirty-two elements, the code is used twice: in a lower case for letters; upper for figures and punctuation.

Each of the code elements consists of five units of equal length† (typically 20 milliseconds), which can only be in one of two possible states: Mark or Space – in the simplest terms, on or off. The letter A in the Murray Code would be: Mark, Mark, Space, Space, Space.[9]

The essential thing about the Murray Code is that it is a binary system and thus capable of digital manipulation. The Siemens Company were by no means the first to realise this. In 1917 Gilbert Vernam, a research engineer of the American Telephone and Telegraph Company, devised a machine cipher based on the telegraph code. It combined the code elements from the teleprinter with an enciphering key consisting of a tape with random five-unit code elements punched into it; the cipher text was achieved by adding the code element from machine and tape. He devised a simple rule for the addition:

$$Mark + Mark = Space$$
$$Mark + Space = Mark$$
$$Space + Mark = Mark$$
$$Space + Space = Space$$

By considering the Marks as '1' and the Spaces as '0', the following example illustrates the principle:

Plaintext	1,	1,	0,	0,	0.	(A)
Key tape	0,	1,	1,	0,	1.	(P)
Ciphertext	1,	0,	1,	0,	1.	(Y)

Thus $A + P = Y$

†To be strictly accurate, the code consisted of $7\frac{1}{2}$ units, there being a start pulse and $1\frac{1}{2}$ stop pulses for the teleprinter. Since these were the same for all 32 elements, they did not affect the coding.

The cipher was secure enough, but unfortunately it required a key tape as long as the enciphered text for both sending and receiving, so it was not considered a practical proposition at that time (though it was revived in a modified form as SIGTOT, a US Army World War II cipher).

The Geheimschreiber machine did not require a key tape and thus did not suffer the disadvantages of the Vernam system. It was, in fact, not dissimilar to the Enigma in that it used rotor wheels to encipher the code elements. There were five rotors for this purpose, each of which could be preset to a given key by the operator. Unlike Enigma, the five drums did not transpose letters but the five basic units of the Murray code which constituted a single character. The rotors had preset pins to achieve this; the number of pins on the five rotors varied but were from forty-seven – the lowest – to eighty-nine – the highest; all were prime numbers.

The Geheimschreiber did not always transpose; at some settings of the key rotors certain elements would not be changed at all. A second row of five rotors effected a transposition by binary addition of the Murray code elements, achieving the same result as Vernam's key tapes and producing a very convenient and secure system. All the operator had to do was to sit at the machine, which had a conventional teleprinter keyboard, and type out the plaintext; the machine enciphered it, transmitting the message instantaneously by land-line or radio at sixty-six words a minute. If the signal was intercepted and fed to a teleprinter, it would simply print as 'garble', with incorrect letter and figure shift, random letters, figures and punctuation – in short, a meaningless jumble of telegraph signals. At the legitimate receiver a similar Geheimschreiber, with its ten drums correctly set, would accept the cipher signals, subtract the encipherment addition and print out the original German plaintext.[10]

The ten rotor wheels of the Geheimschreiber.

The Germans considered the Geheimschreiber to be in the same security class as the 'one-time pad' – the system much used since the war by Russian agents which is *totally* unbreakable. (Several 'one-time pads' were discovered in the Krugers' house in the London suburb of Ruislip by the Special Branch.) The one-time pad consists of a string of five-figure groups which are completely random. Only two copies of each list exist: one for the sender, the other for the recipient of the message. The text is encoded in a fairly simple numerical code, often based on a page, line and word or letter in a certain book, of which both sender and recipient possess identical editions. The numbers from the one-time pad are added as a key, the product being the cipher text. After a message has been enciphered, it can be transmitted with impunity; the figures which form the key are never used again: the pad is destroyed. It is strictly 'one time'. Since the numbers are random and there can be no question of a cryptanalyst discovering a pattern – at least not with one short message to work on – the system is unbreakable; but for military use it would be next to useless, simply because of the number of 'one-time pads' required. Also it calls for tedious encoding and decoding. The Geheimschreiber, by adding to the Murray telegraph code elements, essentially did the same thing, with one important difference: the key figures on the one-time pads, being random, were infinite; the wheels of the Geheimschreiber generated an enormous number of key figures but they were finite and sooner or later would repeat and reveal the pattern of the original text.

It is not known just when Bletchley began to decipher the Geheimschreiber code. It seems probable that there was little of it during the early years of the war; most of the very high-level traffic it enciphered would have been sent by land-line and therefore immune to interception, at least in Britain. However,

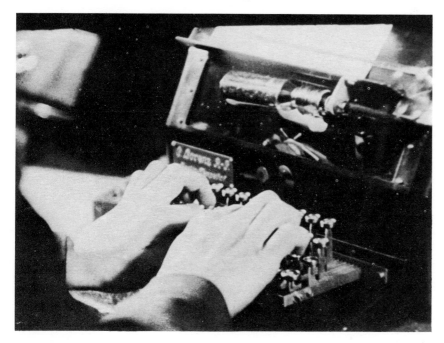

German Army cipher traffic sent by teleprinter over land-lines was considered immune to interception. However, a telegraph line passing through Sweden was tapped and the Geheimschreiber code broken.

one of the telegraph circuits, that from Germany to occupied Norway, passed through neutral Sweden. Swedish Intelligence tapped the cable and a crypt-analyst Arne Beurling succeeded in solving the cipher on paper during May 1940.[11] A Swedish teleprinter mechanic working to a specification drawn up by Beurling managed to construct a machine which printed out the German plaintext. That Beurling's feat was a considerable one is obvious, but it should be pointed out that the early form of Geheimschreiber was much easier to crack than later versions.

A mathematician, W. T. Tutte, who was working in a research section known at Bletchley as the Testery – its Head was Major Tester, also managed to solve some of the Fish traffic by similar laborious paper and pencil methods. The date is unknown, but it could have been the summer of 1942, for in September of that year yet another Cambridge mathematician, M. H. A. Newman, joined the Testery. In a 1976 interview, Professor Max Newman recalled that:

'They had got out some of the [Geheimschreiber] messages by a very slow hand process by comparing certain runs . . . with others by a process which it seemed to me was an imitation of what the machine that enciphered it was doing on the other side.

'It occurred to me that we should be able perhaps to make a machine which would imitate theirs and do the work for us.'

Newman persuaded Commander Travis to authorise the setting up of a group, which was to become known as the 'Newmanry', in Hut F at Bletchley. The early staff were largely mathematicians: Newman chaired the discussions and Turing and Welchman acted as consultants. The main designer of the eventual machine was Wynn-Williams of TRE, with assistance from several engineers from the British Post Office Research Station at Dollis Hill, a London suburb. The machine was built there and soon installed at Bletchley. It was electronic and, according to the recollection of Good, had 'between 30 and 80 valves'; it was constructed on two standard Post Office 19-inch equipment racks, about eight feet high. It featured a photo-electric reader which could scan 2000 telegraph characters a second; the machine had two such inputs.

The intercepted German telegraph cipher was fed into one of the readers in the form of paper tape, with the five-unit Murray Code elements punched into it. The tape was joined to form a large loop which ran continuously over a system of pulleys past the photo-electric cells. The 'Key' tape, which contained deciphering telegraph units, was also glued into a loop, but usually a smaller one than the message; the tapes were then set in motion, rotating at high speed through the two readers. Telegraphic tape, like modern eight-unit computer tape, has small transport holes which engage a driving sprocket; the sprockets kept the two tapes in synchronisation, but since the key tape was either a larger or a smaller loop, with each revolution a different key unit would pass through the reader against the message units. For example, if the message loop was 2000 characters long and the key tape contained one less, there would be 3,998,000 different combinations before the sequence repeated itself. The electronics subtracted the key elements from the message by binary arithmetic; the results were printed on what Good has described as 'a primitive printer' – probably an adapted teleprinter.

Because of the whirling tapes and pulleys, the WRNS operating the machine nicknamed it 'Heath Robinson'. It lived up to its name; its success rate was very low and tape breakages were common. This was, of course, before the days of synthetic adhesives, and joining the tapes into loops posed real problems, as one of the WRNS operators, Odette Wylie, remembers:

'It was a long time before we found some sufficiently gluey material that would stand up under the strain of going round and round at great speed. The fact that we had to get the two tapes to run exactly synchronised was also a very difficult operation. When they did break it was not just a question of breaking and lying on the floor, they flew into the air and got entangled in the machine, in little corners, very difficult to get out again.

'We hadn't the remotest idea what the machine was doing. We were just given two tapes and told to put them on the machine, starting at the right place and finishing at the right place, but we really did not know what we were doing at all: they were just tapes. . . .'[12]

Apart from the problems of tape breakages, Heath Robinson was difficult in other ways. The binary counting was inaccurate, due to unreliable relays, and the single loop of tape which provided the key was inadequate. Certain improvements were incorporated, mainly at the suggestion of the cryptanalyst Donald Michie and the mathematician I. J. Good, which improved the performance sufficiently to justify Newman's faith in a machine to attack the Fish cipher.

What was required was a 'Super Robinson', which would have a separate key tape for each of the ten† enciphering rotors of the German machine, to be read against the message tape simultaneously. In January 1943 two Post Office research engineers, T. H. Flowers and S. W. Broadhurst, who were specialists in high-speed switching, had been called in to suggest improvements. Flowers suggested a new concept entirely, and he and Newman immediately collaborated in the design of what was to become the world's first electronic computer – Colossus; Newman drew up the main specification and Flowers became responsible for the engineering design.

Flowers, whose Post Office work was the design of automatic telephone exchanges, was able to bring a radical new approach to the problems at Bletchley:

'It occurred to me that electronic equipment, including valves, could be made to do the same function as mechanical switches very much faster and more reliably, and that this would solve our problems.'[13]

†How did Bletchley know that the Geheimschreiber had ten rotors? Two German Army Geheimschreibers had been captured by the Eighth Army in North Africa. There is also evidence from a member of Siemens' staff in Munich that 'during the war naturally we lost several machines'.[12]

There was some opposition to the proposal. Valves had a reputation for unreliability, but Flowers pointed out that from Post Office and BBC experience valves that were never switched off were very reliable. It was decided to go ahead with Colossus, with no fewer than 1500 valves – far more than any single electronic device built up to that time.

The machine was assembled in the AC Bridge Laboratory on the ground floor of the GPO Research Station at Dollis Hill; work began in February and Colossus Mk I was installed at Bletchley in December 1943. Like Heath Robinson, it mirrored the German Geheimschreiber, but the flimsy and inadequate key tapes were now replaced by electronically-generated keys. The ten Geheimschreiber rotors were simulated by ten rings of thyratron triode valves. These valves, which contained argon gas, acted as very high-speed switches and were capable of passing high current. (The ten rings of thyratrons were rings only in the electrical circuit sense: they were physically in rows.) One valve only in a particular 'ring' was conducting at any given moment, then its neighbour took over, thus simulating the rotation of the

Photographs of Colossus taken at Bletchley in 1943 and only released – without explanation of its use – 33 years later. The captions on the photographs are as released.

The electric line typewriter which provided the printout is clearly visible, as is the Murray Code tape loop threaded over pulley wheels.

The rear of the Colossus rack: the thyratron 'rings' are revealed.

344

Geheimschreiber rotor wheels. As each thyratron conducted, pulses were passed to other circuits which performed counting in binary arithmetic and Boolean logical operations; all of which means that keys were generated by the Colossus and subtracted from the original message which was fed into the machine from the familiar punched Murray code five-unit tape.

The speed at which the tapes were read was staggering: five thousand characters per second. This was attained partly because the tape no longer needed to be synchronised with a key tape, and therefore the driving of the message tape was independent of the paper sprocket holes and was transported solely by pulleys. The sprocket holes were used, however, to generate timing pulses by photo-electric cells in the main tape-reader; these timing pulses synchronised the electronics with the mechanical movement of the input tape. The method of operation was the now familiar 'on line' programming; it took the form of a synergy: a dialogue between man and machine, which has only become general with modern computers relatively recently.

The punched tape which contained the German cipher text was in the form

A close-up of the Colossus operating position. The WRNS operator altered the plug connections on instructions from the cryptanalyst.

PHOTO ELECTRIC CELL
AMPLIFIER UNIT

FRICTION
DRIVE WHEEL

MOTOR

LAMP HOUSE

PHOTO ELECTRIC
CELLS AND
AMPLIFIERS
BEHIND
THIS PANEL

ADJUSTABLE
PULLEY

PULLEY WHEEL
FRAME

PHOTO ELECTRIC
CELL AND
AMPLIFIER RACK

BOLTED
TO

PULLEY WHEEL
FRAME

of a loop passing continuously through the photo-electric readers. With each revolution of the loop, the cryptanalyst would ask the machine – via the WRNS who controlled the programme with switches – to make certain adjustments to the cipher keys. The cryptanalyst, who sat in front of an electric typewriter on which the output of the machine was printed, would be looking for the tell-tale letter recurrence which would indicate a gradual solving of the cipher text. The dialogue would continue until decipherment was possible.

The point about Colossus was that, being almost wholly electronic, any result it obtained was precisely reproduceable; it did not – unlike the electro-mechanical Robinson – make errors.† Once the correct key had been found, it would decipher all further traffic in that key. Colossus began work at Bletchley in December 1943 and produced results almost immediately. The Geheimschreiber, like Enigma, was developed during the war years.

According to a representative of the Siemens Company, five different versions of the Geheimschreiber were developed during the war. The 1939 model, probably the one known to the Germans as 'the enciphering teleprinter 52AB', was not considered by them as totally secure, though a later model, the 52C, was. '52C' may have been the designation of the example that exists in Germany today. This machine, in addition to the ten rotor wheels, has a further complication: some of the rotors were driven by a system of pawles, so that their rotation was not constant; they paused in an irregular pattern. To deal with these irregular-moving rotors and to effect other improvements in the light of experience gained in the first Colossus, Mark II, an improved model, was designed and built.

The function built into the Mk II Colossus to solve the 'eccentric' rotors was Conditional (branching) IF Logic; in other words, Colossus could make decisions. This ability is of course fundamental to modern computers, but Colossus was by far the first to use the function. The Mk II machine was larger and faster than Mk I; 2500 valves were used and an input reader that would scan at the rate of 5000 characters a second. It was possible to parallel up to five readers, giving a reading speed of 25,000 characters per second – a speed that would not be exceeded by postwar commercial computers for a decade. The output was printed out at fifteen letters per second on an electric line typewriter.

Ten Mk II Colossi had been ordered from the GPO Research Station in March 1944. The first was required to be ready, installed and working at Bletchley by 1 June (in time for D-Day). It seemed an impossible target but, by dropping practically all other work and diverting most of its skilled forces to the task, the first Mk II Colossus was operational on exactly 1 June, the remainder of the order following shortly afterwards.

As the Allied armies invaded Europe, the work of the Colossi staff grew in

†Jack Good, in his 1976 lecture at the National Physical Laboratory, Teddington, stated that 'Colossus was capable of carrying out more than 10^{11} consecutive elementary Boolean [and/or] operations without error'.

volume and importance. The small band that had battled with Heath Robinson had grown to twenty cryptanalysts, twenty engineers and over 250 WRNS operators.

As to the nature of the traffic the Colossi deciphered, that has never been divulged. It would in any case be part of the Ultra intelligence, but it would be of the highest grade – Colossus was never used on Enigma messages. Recently the Public Records Office released photographs of Colossus, here reproduced, but without giving any information as to how it was used. There is some direct evidence that Hitler's directions to Von Kluge, which led to the German disaster of the Battle of Falaise – a battle of decisive importance to the land war in France – were deciphered by it.

With the official release of Ultra intelligence, the extent of the Allied penetration of the German command structure is now becoming clear. The influence of the cryptanalysts at Bletchley on the conduct of the war was profound – even decisive; at the very least it must have saved the lives of many Allied soldiers, sailors and airmen. It had to be used with great caution however; during the war the users of 'Ultra' were ordered never to take action based on the intelligence that could not be attributed to other sources: reconnaissance, prisoner of war interrogation, etc.

The Germans, even today, are reluctant to believe the extent to which their most secret ciphers were compromised. The sinking of U-boat tankers, the sudden alteration in the course of convoys away from an assembled 'wolf pack', and other fortuitous moves which foiled their tactics were put down to treachery. They were, it should be remembered, often based in occupied countries, surrounded by hostile populations. Agents there were; but no agents, not even those of what many Germans considered the omnipotent 'British Secret Service', could have furnished the flood of high-grade in-

An aerial
photograph of
Bletchley Park.
This is a recent
photograph and
some of the original
huts have been
replaced, but the
general layout is
much as it was in
wartime. The
house, with the
stableyard and
cottage, remains
unaltered, though
the housing estate
on the left is
postwar.

telligence that constituted the output from Bletchley. It came from one source and one source only: the Germans themselves. Yet the Chistelle, the German cipher bureau, constantly reassured doubting commanders that the ciphers were secure; they continuously improved their machines; indeed, a new Enigma was due to enter service in 1945 which, had it done so, Bletchley would have been unable to break. But like so much German scientific wartime effort, it came too late.

Thus the bombes and Colossi continued to hum and clatter away on the German secrets to the last day of the European war, when they fell silent for the first time in over four years. The cryptanalysts and mathematicians went back to their universities: some into the new science of computers; others became chess Grand Masters – one, Harry Golombek, became Chess Correspondent of the London *Times*. Another Bletchley man, Roy Jenkins, was to become a Cabinet Minister and Chancellor of the Exchequer. The servicewomen – the ATS and WRNS, who had held their nation's secrets in their hands – became wives and mothers, their suburban neighbours learning nothing of their wartime work. The 'Huts' of Bletchley Park were to become, first a teachers' training college, then later – rather appropriately – a Post Office Engineering School. Some, though not all, of the country houses reverted to their former owners, though many, in the changed circumstances of the postwar world, remained empty until bought as management training summer schools or were divided up into luxury homes.

What became of the Colossi – the world's first electronic computers? When the war ended some of the mathematicians pressed them beyond the parameters on which they had been built. It was found they could do more, much more, than decipher German codes and, although the new technology of the computer that they had pioneered was to be developed openly elsewhere, the originals disappeared – without trace. Were they simply dismantled, to be sold in unidentifiable lots in the surplus stores, along with the other electronic bric-à-brac of war?

The bombes, it seems, were quickly disposed of. Helen Rance, one of hundreds of ex-WRNS of HMS *Pembroke*, remembers the 'eerie silence' in the rooms of that stone frigate when the bombes were finally switched off. Several of the girls could not resist rolling the heavy drums across the floor – something they had never been allowed to do before; then:

'. . . we sat down and took all the drums to pieces with screwdrivers; everything was dismantled. I do not know what happened to it all after that . . .'

If the official history of Ultra is ever published, then a true assessment can be made. For the moment, let F. W. Winterbotham, the man who wrote the first words on the subject, have the last:

'I don't think that any General or army before or since or in the future is ever likely to be in a position of knowing exactly what his enemy is going to do. I think history will have to decide what role Ultra really played.

'I am a little prejudiced myself. I think it did a great deal.'[13]

NOTES

Chapter 1

1 Air Scientific Intelligence (ASI) Report No. 6, 'The Crooked Leg', by R. V. Jones. Public Record Office (PRO) File Air 20 1623 8850. For a technical description of X- and Y-Geräte airborne equipment, see 'German Radio Communication Equipment', War Department Technical Manual, TME 11.227 (US Printing Office, Washington, DC, 1944).

2 'Indications of new German weapons to be used against England.' PRO File Air 20 1622 8917.

3 Transcript of BBC interview with Professor Jones, 1976.

4 Cherwell Archive.

5 All Allied POW interrogation files are closed for 100 years. This evidence is quoted from ASI No. 6, 'Evidence of A231'. PRO File Air 20 1623 8850.

6 C. F. Rawnsley and Robert Wright, *Night Fighter* (London, 1975), p.20.

7 Transcript of BBC interview.

8 See Appendix A2 of '80 Wing Progress Report No. 14'. PRO File Air 20 6037 8792.

9 RCM/12 PRO File Air 20 6020 8792.

10 Transcript of BBC interview, 1976.

11 'Radio Countermeasures', 80 Wing Report No. 12. PRO File Air 20 6019 8792.

12 Transcript of BBC interview with German pilot, who now lives in England and wishes his name to be withheld.

13 Transcript of BBC interview (in German), 1976.

14 'Enemy Activity', 80 Wing Report. PRO File Air 20 6037 8792. This report, dated 8.12.40, reviews several accounts of enemy aircraft which were forced down due to RCM.

15 Transcript of BBC interview, 1976.

16 For accounts of 'Meaconing' see PRO File Air 20 6019 8792 and other 80 Wing reports.

17 ASI Interim Report, 'The X Geräte', by R. V. Jones. PRO File Air 20 1669 8850.

18 *Ibid.* (part 2).

19 'Summary of Conclusions' at meeting held at Thames House, 27.9.40. PRO File Air 20 6020 8792.

20 Transcript of BBC interview (in German), 1976.

21 Norman Longmate, *Air Raid* (London, 1976), p.182.

22 PRO File Air 20 6037 8792. See also Appendix to 80 Wing Progress Report 13, 'The X Geräte Examined'. PRO File Air 20 6037 8792.

23 Transcript of BBC interview, 1976.

24 PRO File Air 20 6019 8792.

25 Transcript of BBC interview (in German), 1976.

26 PRO File Air 20 6019 8792.

Chapter 2

1 Transcript of BBC interview, 1976.

2 Transcript of BBC interview with Arnold Wilkins, 1976.

3 BBC transcript.

4 BBC transcript, translated from German.

5 Transcript of BBC interview, 1976.

6 Lecture, reprinted in *Journal of Navigation*, Vol. 28 (January 1975).

7 TRE Paper, 'Basis of Radar' (5th ed., 1945).

8 Quoted in Guy Hartcup, *The Challenge of War* (Newton Abbot, 1970), p.137. Also paraphrased by R. V. Jones in BBC transcript.

9 BBC transcript, 1976. For a technical explanation of the Cavity Magnetron see also Willshaw and Megaw, 'The Magnetron', *Engineering* (1946), and Willshaw, Stainsby and others, 'High Powered Pulse Magnetron Development and Design for Radar Applications', *The Proceedings of the Institution of Electrical Engineers*, Vol. 93, part IIIa, no. 5 (1946).

10 Quoted by Sir Bernard Lovell in BBC interview, 1976.

11 Lovell, 'Historical Notes on H2S' (TRE paper, 1944).

12 Transcript of BBC interview, 1976.

13 Quoted by Lovell, 'Historical Notes on H2S'.

14 ASI No. 7. PRO File Air 20 1624 9434.

15 TRE File No. D1100 part 1, February 1941.

16 TRE Enemy Investigation Group Report No. 5/38.

17 For an account of this flight see TRE Report 5/16A, 14.8.41.

18 See PRO File Air 20 1631 9491 for an account of the raid.

19 *Ibid.* For a complete technical description of the Bruneval equipment see TRE Report No. 6/R/25, 'Final Technical Report on the German RDF Equipment Captured at Bruneval on 28 February 1942', 8.5.42. See also PRO File AVIA 26 291 T1289 (1942).

20 For a description of the equipment in this aircraft see TRE Report 3/M/12, 'German AI System in Ju88', 20.5.43.

21 BBC transcript, 1976.

22 BBC transcript, 1976.

Chapter 3

1 BBC transcript, 1976.

2 BBC transcript, 1976.

3 Sir Arthur Harris, *Bomber Offensive* (London, 1947).

4 Transcript of BBC interview, 1976.

5 PRO File Prem. 3/110, COS 43, 27.8.43.

6 PRO File Prem. 3/110, COS 43/202 (0).

7 PRO File CAB 69 8563 D.O.(43) 24, 29.9.43.

8 David Irving, *The Mare's Nest* (London, 1964), p.56.

9 PRO File CAB 69.

10 For a full description of the Lubbock rocket see PRO File CAB 69 8563: Annexe C, 'Tentative Design of Peenemunde Rocket', I. Lubbock, 19.10.43.

11 Irving, *op. cit.*, p.154.

12 For the minutes of this meeting see PRO File CAB 69 5 856/3 D.O. (43), 10th Meeting, 25.10.43.

13 PRO File CAB 69 5 8563 D.O.(43) 31, 16.11.43.

14 PRO File Prem. 3/110, COS (0) No. 5, 2.11.43.

15 Transcript of BBC interview, 1976.

16 Transcript of BBC interview, 1976.

17 *Svenska Dagbladgt*, 14 June 1944.

18 PRO File CAB 98 37 9141, Annexe CBC(44) 24.

19 PRO File AERO 1983 EA228/1.

20 See PRO File CAB 98 37 9141.

21 RAE Report 1695, 4.12.44.

Chapter 4

1 J. G. Crowther, *British Scientists of the Twentieth Century* (London, 1952).

2 Donald Macintyre, *U-Boat Killer* (London, 1956).

3 All figures for Allied and German losses in this chapter are from official British records and differ in certain instances from other published sources.

4 BBC transcript, 1976.

5 Quoted in Lovell, 'Historical Notes on H2S'.

6 Popham, *Into Wind* (London, 1969).

Chapter 5

1 The account of events at Shoeburyness is based on a transcript of BBC interviews recorded in 1976 with Commander Ouvry and Lt. Commander Lewis.

2 Transcript of BBC interview with Hanna Reisch (in English), 1976.

3 Author's conversation with Sir Charles Goodeve, 1977.

4 Quoted in James Gilbert, *The World's Worst Aircraft* (London, 1975).

5 Mano Ziegler, *Rocket Fighter* (London, 1953).

6 Transcript of BBC interview with Hanna Reisch, 1976.

7 PRU Interpretation Report LS74, 2.7.43, 'Photographs taken on sorties N/860 on 23.6.43 – Tailless Aircraft at Peenemunde'.

8 Quoted in William Green, *Warplanes of the Third Reich*, 3rd ed. (London, 1976).

9 Transcript of BBC interview, 1976.

Chapter 6

1 For the story of the decipherment of the Zimmerman telegram, see David Kahn, *The Codebreakers* (London, 1973).

2 In most published versions of 'The Goldbug' J and V are omitted. They were placed in the sequence by the author after a simple letter count of a page of English text.

3 Interview with BBC researcher Susan Bennett.

4 Enciphering technique based on a German Army instruction book in the Bundesarchiv.

5 In conversation with the author, September 1977.

6 Transcript of BBC interview, 1976.

7 The sequence of the German Navy's development of their Enigma machines was: 1934 – 3 operational rotas chosen from 5; 1938 – 3 from 7; 1939 – 3 from 8; March 1943 – a new Enigma machine was issued to U-boats with 4 operational rotas chosen from 8.

8 BBC transcript, 1976.

9 For a clear and simple explanation of telegraph codes and the mechanics of teleprinters, see *The Teleprinter Handbook* (Radio Society of Great Britain, 1973).

10 Information on the Geheimschreiber is based on a BBC interview (in German) at Siemens AG, Munich.

11 Beurling went to America after the war to become Professor of Mathematics at the Institute for Advanced Studies, Princeton.

12 BBC transcript, 1976.

13 BBC transcript, 1976.

PICTURE CREDITS

Acknowledgement is due to the following for permission to reproduce pictures:

A & AEE, Boscombe Down, page 284 top; Admiralty Surface Weapons Establishment, 96 top left; Aerofilms, 348; *Aeroplane*, 51; Associated Press, 15 middle; BBC, 59 bottom, 69, 71 right, 329 bottom, 338, 340, 347; BICC, 247 top; BZ Stuttgart, 326 right, 328, 329 top; Constance Babington Smith, 148; Stewart Bale Ltd, 188; General Bertrand, 313 top, 321, 322, 323; Bundesarchiv, 135, 178, 260, 333; Crown Copyright, 42, 110, 115 top, 124, 129, 132, 134, 136, 138, 146, 153, 170, 183 top, 216, 228 top; B. Drew, 288 top; *Flight*, 53 top, 66, 71 top left, 83 top left, 224 middle left & bottom right; Galinski, 166, 171, 313 middle; Gloster Aircraft Ltd, 65 bottom right; HMSO, 74 right, 76 (from J. G. Crowther and R. Whiddington, *Science at War* (1947)); Hawker Aircraft Ltd, 65 top, middle & bottom left, 162; Imperial War Museum, 10 top, 53 bottom, 69 inset, 78, 79, 80 bottom, 83 right, 99 bottom, 104 bottom, 114, 117 top, 120, 122, 128, 151, 158, 163, 185, 193, 199, 206, 211 top, 215, 223, 224 top left & right, 226, 228 bottom, 231, 234, 238, 241, 243, 245, 249, 254 top, 256, 262, 265 bottom left, 273, 292, 293 middle right, 334; Imperial War Museum film stills, 1, 2, 10 bottom, 13, 17 top & middle, 26, 33, 35, 38, 40, 45 inset, 49, 60, 67, 80 top left & right, 84 right, 88, 99 top, 104 top right, 111 top right & bottom, 113, 115 bottom, 117 bottom, 121 top right & bottom, 150, 179, 183 bottom, 187, 196 top right, middle & bottom, 200, 207, 208, 209, 210, 213, 220 bottom left, 224 middle right & bottom left, 235 top, 236, 240, 246, 247 bottom, 248, 251, 254 bottom, 257, 258, 259, 261, 263, 264, 265 top, 269, 271, 275, 277, 279, 282, 284 bottom, 290, 293 top, middle left & bottom, 294, 296, 299, 300, 303, 326 left, 341; Brian Johnson, 12, 15 left, 17 bottom, 25, 28, 93, 95 top, 145, 211 top inset & bottom, 273 top, 288 bottom, 304, 311, 313 bottom, 316 top, 318, 325, 335; Keystone Press Agency, 41, 62, 101 bottom; Colonel Lisicki, 315; Ministry of Defence, 297; National Film Board of Canada, 194, 220 top & bottom right; Novosti Press Agency, 265 bottom right; NRK Fjernsynet, Oslo, 8; Torbjörn Olansson, 167; Alfred Price, 85; Public Record Office (Crown Copyright), 106, 140, 344, 345; Radio Research Station (National Physical Laboratory), Slough, 71 bottom left, 74 left; Radio Times Hulton Picture Library, 164, 181; Marian Rejewski, 316 bottom; Rolls-Royce, 27; Royal Aircraft Establishment, Farnborough, 121 top left (via Alfred Price), 169, 173, 175; Royal Radar Establishment, 83 bottom left, 96 top right & bottom, 101 top; Science Museum, London, 95 bottom left; John Tarlow, 15 right; Fritz Trenkle, 22, 59 top, 104 top left, 111 top left, 219, 230, 233, 302; US Navy National Archives film still, 196 top left, 203, 235 middle & bottom; Günther Unger, 32; Vickers, 84 left.

The diagrams on pages 18, 22, 38, 45, 59, 71, 90, 154, 155, 156, 157, 192, 243 and 331 were drawn by David Ashby.